© 2021 Matthias Schwenteck
ISBN 978-1-7370335-2-3

First Edition

All rights reserved. No part of this publication may be reproduced, distributed, or transmitted in any form or by any means, including photocopying, recording, or other methods, without the prior written permission of the author, except in the case of brief quotations. For permission requests, contact the author, Matthias Schwenteck www.somaticconsent.com

Permission was granted by all the people mentioned whose personal stories I related.

ORGASMIC BLUEPRINT

Tools for Mastering Pleasure, Desire & Consent
For Singles, Couples & Intimacy Professionals

by Matthias Schwenteck

DEDICATION

This book is dedicated to the innocent being in all of us who started to explore the world with our hands before we could walk and talk. And to the ones who wish to transform wholeheartedly, contributing to everybody's evolution, by gifting their power from a place of love and care.

"Grandma how do you deal with pain?"
"With your hands, dear. When you do it with your mind, the pain hardens even more."
"With your hands, grandma?"
"Yes, yes. Our hands are the antennas of our Soul. When you move them by sewing, cooking, painting, touching the earth or sinking them into the earth, they send signals of caring to the deepest part of you and your Soul calms down. This way she doesn't have to send pain anymore to show it."
"Are hands really that important?"
"Yes my girl. Think of babies: they get to know the world thanks to their touch. When you look at the hands of older people, they tell more about their lives than any other part of the body.
Everything that is made by hand, so it is said, is made with the heart because it really is like this: hands and heart are connected.
Think of lovers: When their hands touch, they love each other in the most sublime way."
"My hands grandma... how long since I used them like that!"
"Move them my love, start creating with them and everything in you will move. The pain will not pass away. But it will be the best masterpiece. And it won't hurt as much anymore, because you managed to embroider your Essence."
~Elena Barnabé

MISSION STATEMENT

Somatic Consent represents all humans without borders. Its teachings transcend nationality, culture, colour, age, gender and belief systems—guiding us towards interpersonal connection through conscious engagement.

Based on the neurological blueprint of our very existence as human beings, Somatic Consent merges scientific research with spiritual self-realisation—providing a collective and transformative system of human engagement.

WHAT PEOPLE SAY

"I highly recommend Somatic Consent and believe we all would have benefited from learning its methods as children. The teachings are a road map to an empowered life and healthy, conscious relationships. If we all practiced them, the world would be a more peaceful and harmonious place. Meeting Matt in 2011 changed my life. I went from being a shy, insecure young woman without boundaries or knowing my worth, to an international facilitator, inspiring thousands of men and women to be the best version of themselves. The methods of Somatic Consent are at the foundation of what I teach as a relationship and sex coach. They are an invitation to come in contact with and share something much deeper than most imagine possible, which, for me, is the most precious experience a human can have."
Susanna Beatrice

"What drew me is a combination of the following things: simplicity via the hands, focus on sexual/life force pleasure energy, and the neuroscience with it. That combination is just so much me, it felt like finding a soulmate in approach. It is a unique combination of theoretical and practical that nourishes both the academic in me and the practical energy body worker."
Jonathan Beger

"What drew me to this specific teaching is that I am working a lot on feeling myself and the full range of my emotions, a combination of releasing the pattern of needing others to feel Self. It all resonates and I would love to teach it. I think it is so important for children to learn this form early on, can you imagine a society where this is part of the basic schooling?!?"
Bas van der Tang

"Somatic Consent has helped me accept all that I am, in particular the messed up, fearful, not enough parts of me. Knowing that these parts are my survival strategies, they are not wrong and they are welcome. My journey is also helping me see my true light and what I am here to offer to the world. I am learning to embody and feel my way through life and in particular interactions with other people. I have learnt to feel my limits which was previously unknown to me being a people pleaser. I have learnt to feel my

desires which were also repressed. I am learning to be able to say no and can see why that was and still is difficult for me. Opening the sensory inflow has transformed the way I experience everything, combining this with sexual energy opens my body to new states of receptivity and bliss."
Lisa Cleminson Grezo

"I really appreciate the lens Matt uses and how he connects tantra and his own experiences/training with The Polyvagal Theory. I love how he reframes the idea of being selfish and how it is good and important to do that through having boundaries and agreements in place to maintain safety. Everything he says about embodiment resonates with me as well, and it feels really good to be able to trust a lot of things that I had been feeling in my body for some time and didn't fully understand. I also love his humour and authenticity."
Karina Perez

"What drew me specifically to this teaching was the direct link between experienced sensations and deep relational patterns. It is like a fun, pleasurable Sherlock Holmes path. So much vital information for life-expanding options. Personally, the combination of theory, bodywork, the nervous system and attachment makes this knowledge especially liberating."
Janne Mattson

"I actually discovered Somatic Consent serendipitously. I took an online class about Touch, Shadow and Relationships because I was interested in the Shadow aspect. Matt's explanation of the Somatic Consent Engagement System and how it relates to our patterns of behaviour when we don't get what we want or we don't say no to what we don't want really resonated with me. It helped me to understand certain passive aggressive tendencies I employ as a defence mechanism. Through Somatic Consent I feel as though I can rewire certain behaviours and reactions, I feel more connected to my true 'yes' and I feel more empowered to say no and enforce my boundaries."
Heather Broussard

"So much has emerged within me from a daily practice of this. Noticing how safe I feel (during the practice) has made my body begin realizing how deeply unsafe I usually feel. I have awoken to the reality of a mind full of thoughts, in a body that doesn't feel safe. After noticing how desperately my body is screaming for security, I have begun holding hot bread at every meal. I finally understand now why I, as a Jew, was taught to say the Blessing, to acknowledge the meditation in food, while holding it in my hand. This slowing down to experience allows us to notice so much. It demands my Truth.

It strips me of my stories, like my need to give to be worthy of friends. It is bringing me Home, back to my foundation. It's been a really painful and honest 8 days. It has awoken in its embodied aspect, parts of me that were only skimmed with other teachings. And even so, all of that other work was dependent on groups or partners or whatever. This work is Freedom. Taking back myself, and finally experiencing in an embodied manner exactly when I am selling myself short and not in my integrity."
Shmuel Schuck

"To slow down, to feel, experiencing activation causing a change in thoughts and behaviour in normal life circumstances. Allowing to take a few minutes to go back to the basic practice of what it feels like to me. Liberation! Freedom!"
Luna Hilda

"This practical, no-nonsense work really speaks to me. It provides a flawless framework, encompassing much more than touch, consent and intimacy. It takes you from the restraints of intellect to an embodied experience of life. From the roots of human nature and 'shoulds 'of culture, to the science and spirit of human evolution—at all levels of being."
Nina Edmondson

"Whatever difficulties we may have encountered in the past, that we are experiencing in the present, or that will appear in the future, whatever they are, Matthias addresses in simple, practical ways. Most of us can relate to body shame, setting boundaries, experiencing numbness, activating some past trauma, and the actual fear of finding bliss. Matthias leads us on and upward toward the experience of sexual healing, becoming orgasmic and transformation. His holistic system is our guide in this exciting experiment. The Somatic Consent Engagement System provides maps of the human condition and a means to help us awaken. One day if it is possible, I hope you have the powerful experience of studying with others in a group led by Matthias."
Harry Faddis

CONTENTS

13.....Foreword
16.....About the author
17.....A note from the author
20.....How it all began
21.....Introduction

Chapter 1: Foundations of Somatic Consent
24.....Tuning into your authentic self

Maps: *Pleasure in your hands, Direct/Indirect Pleasure, 3 Components of Pleasure, Learning Giving and Receiving, The 3 Minute Game*

25.....The Importance of Touch
28.....Why Waking Up your Hands Works
30.....How we're Programmed to Give while in Action
31.....How we Compromise our Experience to Fit in
33.....How Perception is Formed
35.....How Tuning into your Sense of Touch Trains your Brain
38.....Waking Up Your Hands: Tuning into Pleasure
45.....The Practice of Waking Up Your Hands
55.....The Direct and Indirect Routes of Pleasure
58.....Activating the Noticing Part of your Brain
62.....Rewiring your Brain for Pleasure and Connection
65.....The 3 Components of Pleasure
71.....The Pull and the Push of Pleasure
75.....Receiving what you Really Want and Giving what you are Willing to Give
82.....The 3 Minute Game
92.....The 3 Minute Game and the Direct Route of Pleasure
95.....Spiritual Connection through Surrender

Chapter 2: The Somatic Consent Engagement System
102.....Tools for mastering pleasure, desire and consent

Maps: *The Somatic Consent Engagement System 1, Engagement System 2, 3D Multi-dimensional, SCES, Base, Mixed Emotions, Spectrum of Limits, Engagement Zones, Shadows, Apex*

105.....Exploring your Personal Reality
113.....The Foundational Base of Self-Love,
       Self-Care and Self-Pleasure
118.....Exploring Boundaries and Limits
       Map of Mixed Emotions:
121.....Recognising Feelings and Emotions
129.....The Spectrum of Limits
135.....Expressing your Boundaries and Limits
137.....The Engagement Zones: Who is it for?
       Permission and Agreements: The Four Doors to
       Desire, Pleasure and Consent
153.....The Basement of Shadows
172.....The Apex of Love, Care,
       Integrity, Generosity, Gratitude and Surrender

Chapter 3: Embodied Empowerment & Spiritual Development
182.....The Grounded and Spiritual Self in Union

Maps: The *Polyvagal Theory, Noticing and Meaning, Mind Map, Window of Tolerance, Numbness Bar, Empowerment and Choice, Spiritual Development, Spiritual Bypassing*

183.....The Polyvagal Theory: Surviving and Thriving
198.....Shifting states: Dysregulation,
       Self-regulation and Co-regulation
201.....The Hybrid State
203.....The Bliss State of Immobilisation and Surrender
205.....Noticing and Meaning: Connecting the Dots
217.....The Window of Tolerance: Personal Growth
224.....Self-Regulation and Trauma Release
226.....Co-Regulation and Trauma Release

228.....The Numbness Bar: Repression and Expression of Feelings and Emotions
238.....Empowerment and Choice
243.....OM and Spiritual Connection at the Apex
247.....Spiritual Bypassing: Seeing Beyond Self-Trickery

Chapter 4: Intimate Relating
255.....**The Real You Sees the Real Me**

Maps: *Four Pillars of Relating, Relationship Map, Low and High Drama, Radical Responsibility, Communication 1, Communication 2, Who is talking and who is it for?, Six Levels to Bliss, Relating: Brother, Sister, Lover, Procreation, Being on the Edge/Becoming Orgasmic*

256.....The Four Pillars of Relating
259.....Relationship: The Zone In-Between
270.....Languages of Love:
           Shadows, Base, Engagement Zones and Apex
280.....Low and High Drama:
           Lifting the Unconscious Vei
288.....The Three Powers of Radical Responsibility
298.....Communication: Bridging the Gap
309.....Who is Talking and Who is it for?
           Listening and Communicating
321.....The Six Levels to Bliss
           Relating Dynamics:
330.....Brother, Sister, Lover and Polyamory
336.....Procreation: Goal-driven Sexual Agenda
           Relaxed and Transformative Sexuality:
342.....Being on the Edge and Becoming Orgasmic
348.....Cerebrospinal Fluid and the Appearance of "I Am

Chapter 5: Transformational Leadership and Facilitation
358.....**Being the gift**

Maps: *Zone in the Zone, Treatment and Co-Creation, De-armouring, The Session Tree*

359.....Transformational Hands-on Work
361.....Giving and Receiving for Hands-onPractitioners

365.....The 3 Components of Pleasure for Practitioners
369.....The Zone in The Zone:
   The Direct and Indirect Routes for Practitioners
377.....Treatment and Co-Creation: Healing and
   Co-Regulation Offering the Best for your Clients
382.....Empowerment Massage: Co-creation Coaching
   De-Armouring:
387.....Trauma Release and Re-traumatisation
398.....The Session Tree:
   Clarifying your Unique Offerings

401.....Conclusion
402.....Acknowledgments
403.....Resources
409.....Reference List
417.....All Maps Links
418.....Community

FOREWORD

Some time ago I received an email from a man asking about The 3 Minute Game. It came as a surprise because 25 years had passed since I'd invented it in 1994, while developing a workshop called, *Power, Surrender & Intimacy*, for The Body Electric School.

I'd wanted to create a tool to help people learn and practice asking for what they want.

The game arose from my reflection on the 12-Step Program, specifically that we can decide to surrender our life and will to a power greater than ourselves in order to remove our insanity. In the context of relationship, the dynamics of power/surrender work together to create the energy of intimacy. I was also aware of the Rumi poem:

> *"The breeze at dawn has secrets to tell you. Don't go back to sleep.*
>
> *You must ask for what you really want. Don't go back to sleep.*
>
> *People are going back and forth across the door sill*
>
> *Where the two worlds touch.*
>
> *The door is round and open. Don't go back to sleep."*

Asking for what we want is one thing; waking up is another; and learning to hear a "No" to our requests, a mature part of this exchange.

The man who emailed me was Matthias Schwenteck. He was curious about the spiritual, metaphysical and somatic aspects of the game. In contrast to a Cosmopolitan UK article which had billed the game as a 'way to improve your sex life', Matthias had looked much more deeply into the dynamics that unfold as we play it.

He'd discovered many points of growth, conflict and development that went far and beyond any considerations I'd had. In fact, he explained to me just *what* I'd created in a new language and model of relating with one another. This is the *Somatic Consent Engagement System* (SCES), through which he utilises the game for a higher level of presence and personal growth.

I was very happy to discuss this work with Matthias and to offer him my permission to use The 3 Minute Game as part of the SCES. As we continued to talk over the next six months, Matthias continued to develop and clarify all of the aspects of this new system which is based on the fundamental principle of *being*—that is—our experience of life in-the-moment.

The system he describes in this book deepens our understanding of somatic experience, is informative in certain aspects of neuroscience and guides through a simple process that we can all relate to. Just like skiing, relating is difficult when done incorrectly, and can be easy and elegant when we know how. Then, there is no effort involved, just a letting go, being in-the-moment, one turn at a time.

Whatever difficulties we may have encountered in the past, that we are experiencing in the present, or that will appear in the future, whatever they are, Matthias addresses in simple, practical ways. Most of us can relate to body shame, setting boundaries, experiencing numbness, activating some past trauma, and the actual fear of finding bliss. Matthias leads us on and upward toward the experience of sexual healing, becoming orgasmic and transformation. His holistic system is our guide in this exciting experiment. The SCES provides maps of the human condition and a means to help us awaken.

There are differences in our desires: What we've always wanted (and have never gotten); and what we want in this moment (here and now). The first is our usual preference or our default need, somewhat easily requested and fulfillable. The second is a deeper need. The expression of our yearning; its end is not a request for pleasure in receiving or giving; but is, rather, a cry to the gods for fulfilment.

This is the field in which Matthias works and in which his maps excel. Simply and practically, we learn something new each step of the way as we're led to more expanded states of pleasure, awareness and intimacy... towards the state of being outlined in the Kamasutra;

*"...but when the wheel of sexual ecstasy is in full motion,
there is no textbook at all, and no order."*

The paradox is that the suggestions, maps and system in this book support us in our practice... by guiding us to experience a state where guidelines are transcended.

Please look to yourself and at yourself and determine if you are highly satisfied with your erotic, sensual and spiritual life, whether alone or with others. Be honest, for therein lies your path to learning. Whoever and wherever you are, I'm sure that the Somatic Consent Engagement System can enrich your experience of life. In these teachings, I believe, you will encounter the experience of finding a wise elder, who has only your best interests at heart.

Harry Faddis, D.D., C.P.C.C.
The Easton Mountain Retreat Center
https://www.eastonmountain.org/
November 23, 2020

ABOUT THE AUTHOR

Born in Germany, Matt has three children, was married for eight years and lives a nomadic lifestyle, travelling around the world speaking, teaching and sharing his wisdom.

Since his tantric awakening in 1997, he's been fascinated by the human condition, especially in regard to empowerment through expanded awareness. Like others interested in this topic he later experimented with medicines which open the doors to perception—including LSD, mushrooms, kambo, ayahuasca, san pedro, peyote, marijuana and bufo.

Matt finds himself inspired by everything which resonates with the key values of connection, transformation and love. In his continuous search for authentic experience, he has researched, studied and facilitated many pathways to psychological, physical, sexual, emotional and spiritual liberation.

These pathways include Autogenes training, Meditation, Yoga, Tao Yoga, Advaita Vedanta, The Path of Love, Holotropic Breathwork and Rebirthing, Reiki, Kashmiri Massage, The Polyvagal Theory, TRE, the Somatic Nervous System, Trauma, Quodoushka, Neo Tantra, Human Design System, Family and Systemic Constellation, NLP, Landmark Forum, Radical Honesty, Circling, Authentic Relating, Biodanza, Sexual Shamanism, ISTA, The New Tantra, The Wheel of Consent, Cuddle Party and Ritual Play.

Matt has been a facilitator in the fields of Sacred Sexuality and Tantra with teachings grounded in trauma research and neurophysiology for over 20 years.

In 2011, he found his calling within the dynamics of somatic embodiment and consent and developed the Somatic Consent Engagement System in 2019. He's guided thousands of people through their own evolutionary process—via festival events, workshops, retreats, trainings, online courses, summits and private sessions as well as educating hundreds of practitioners and facilitators to empower their own professional practices.

A NOTE FROM THE AUTHOR

My intention with this book is to be inclusive. That anyone, no matter who they are can take something of value from it. I don't identify with society's concepts of masculine and feminine. Although I identify as a heterosexual male, I often feel multi-sexual and at times female in a male body. Please forgive me if my language appears divisive. Whenever I differentiate between gender I refer to how a person's nervous system was initially developed and is still wired—not to gender identity.

You'll find *my personal truth* within these pages—so please question everything. Some passages might resonate with you more than others. My invitation is that you *find what rings true to you and make it yours*. To find your truth through your own experiences so as to deepen your personal reality of love, intimacy, connection and relationship.

My native language is German, my second English. My main language, however, is Touch. I love engaging and expressing myself in the most authentic ways possible and believe the two are inseparable. Touch goes hand in hand with honest relating to ourselves and others, based on feelings experienced in the moment, 'right here, right now'.

> *"Of all the paths you take in life, make sure a few of them are dirt."*
> *- John Muir*

This quote struck me as an apt way to begin this book—because within its pages we're going to get raw and real about what makes us tick. In order to live more connected, intimate and empowered lives, we have to be willing to do things differently. To take unfamiliar pathways. To be brave about getting our hands a little dirty when we encounter parts of our inner selves hidden until now. Only then can we find a way back to our authentic, connected nature.

Are you ready to embark on a road less travelled?

We all want to feel our best. We all want meaningful connection with those dear to us. But many of us settle for a meagre amount. How many of us feel an emptiness in our lives? How many of us are actually keeping ourselves from experiencing deeper levels of intimacy due to patterns of interaction we've been conditioned to accept as normal? And how can we expect to be fulfilled if we don't know or tell the truth about what we want and feel?

Throughout life, we all develop unconscious survival strategies in order to be accepted. Most of us have the neurological patterning that; "If I do something to make you feel happy, you will love me—and I will belong". We've been conditioned to believe that we're better people if our actions focus on *giving* for the sake of others—and that *receiving* through our own action is connected to selfishness, violation, abuse or other shadow behaviour. I used to believe that if I was a caring person, my action towards another should primarily benefit them.

But what if we're also allowed to go into action for our own benefit—to *receive* pleasure—and that this isn't at all selfish but *greatly adds* to the benefit of all involved?

What if tuning into your sense of touch was a key to upgrading your whole experience of life? This is where Somatic Consent comes in, a rational, radical guide to transformative empowerment and intimate relating.

Empowerment lies at the heart of our journey of learning to express ourselves through our voice, body, feelings, emotions and sexuality. It's about knowing you have choices and about choosing what's best for you. When we become empowered, we are sovereign beings with no one having power or authority over us and where our voice and desires matter. When we're empowered, we treat ourselves, others and the earth with love, respect and dignity. This is the world that I choose to live in.

This book introduces you to a change in the way you experience your sense of touch—and *everything* is based on that change. It's not going to teach you a new technique, but rather wake up your ability to notice the physical, sensory inflow from your skin. When this sense awakens, it opens the door to a gold mine of awareness and pleasure.

This practice neurologically upgrades your ability to physically feel. It leads to an increase in emotional intelligence, self-knowledge and relaxed inner trust. This establishes self-confidence, grounding, the ability to own your desires and limits and express them freely. It creates ease, intimacy, excitement, fun, freshness and flow in relationship with others.

You see, when your brain focuses only on the *outer world*—on what you're *giving to it*, instead of noticing what your *inner world is receiving from it*—your experience of life is significantly reduced.

My intention is that every human being has the strength and confidence to speak and live their truth, to feel more alive in their body, to feel joy, pleasure and connection.

By combining your awareness of *inner sensory inflow* while IN ACTION *to the outer world*, you can learn to deprogram yourself by dropping old patterns —and creating an awakened state that encompasses profoundly present, joyous and expansive experiences of touch, connection and intimacy. This practice is both personal and collective, both scientific and spiritual.

The Somatic Consent Engagement System is a personal development system inspired by verbal dynamics of consent, The Polyvagal Theory and somatic practices of embodiment. Here we activate conscious engagement and loving connection to self, others and the world we live in.

HOW IT ALL BEGAN

I think in pictures. Whenever I learn something new, ponder a concept or communicate my feelings and thoughts, I experience them clearly in my mind's eye as a three-dimensional reality. Because of this, I love drawing maps and making videos to help explain concepts. Maybe you're a highly visual person too, someone who can learn and relate easily through visual context. One of the people who inspired my map making was Clinton Callahan, a master of the art and one of my mentors.

The first 'concept map' I drew was the Procreation Map, which explained my experience of what happens during and after climax. The Window of Tolerance Map relating to our comfort zones followed. This map visually explains the spaces where we feel safe or unsafe and includes the space between the two, where we have the potential to grow.

When a diagram of the *Wheel of Consent* was handed to me in 2011, I was fascinated by its concepts and complexity. In an effort to fully comprehend its depth, I began to draw it out in different ways.

I later realised the learnings within it couldn't be fully grasped with my intellect alone. They had to be experienced and understood by my body. That shift happened due to my own physical practice. I was then inspired to draw more visual images, in order to help others bridge this learning process.

The maps in this book are visual guides that clearly relay the concepts of sensory inflow and consensual touch. They help bridge a gap—they give a logical overview which guides and connects analytical understanding to the actual neurologically embodied and emotional experience. Together they create a storyline of physical, psychological, emotional and spiritual transformation.

INTRODUCTION

*"Connection, the ability to feel connected, is
neurobiologically wired, that's why we're here!"*
-Brené Brown

I first encountered the deeper dynamics of *giving and receiving* through The Wheel of Consent which asks us to define who the action is for when we do something. At the time I didn't foresee where it would take me in terms of my personal and professional development, though I found the subject deeply intriguing.

Over the next few years, while practising somatic work both personally and professionally, I began to thoroughly explore these dynamics in terms of touch and relating. I was so used to going into action *to give*. Was it really possible to *receive* for my own pleasure while touching another person?

Because giving and receiving can be interpreted in more than one way, the more I practised, the more confused I became—falling into the misconception that the pleasure I was causing *through* my action was what I was aiming for, rather than the pleasure *experienced* by feeling my own skin. This confusion deepened over the years until, in 2014, I attended a training where I was finally made aware of the Direct Route of pleasure from the sensations I was receiving through the sensory inflow of my somatic nervous system.

Everything fell into place.

This is when I realised that to fully grasp the concept of *receiving* pleasure while doing (through touch), cognitive understanding is never enough. You need to imprint and embody the learning within your nervous system—through personal experience and practice.

When you do this, your body makes a neurological 'switch' from focusing on the active role of giving, to the active role of receiving (being).

This realisation showed me the clearly infinite possibilities of deepening somatic embodiment for the purpose of personal and spiritual development.

I began to experiment and experience the magic. This fuelled my motivation to facilitate training courses and workshops on the subject—providing guidance and support for others to craft their own personal path of awakening.

For the following six years, I mentored and co-taught over seventy consent based international training courses including *Like A Pro*. This led to creating the curriculum for educating consent facilitators and practitioners and co-founding the School of Consent. In 2019 I developed the Somatic Consent Engagement System.

Somatic Consent offers a series of maps which help to explain the underpinning theories for personal and spiritual development in a visual manner. These maps will enable you to grasp the concepts with your analytical working mind. However, as you're heading on a *somatic* journey, your body needs *practical experience* to understand in an embodied way.

Many words can paint a picture and many pictures can create a movie but nothing can substitute the depth of your understanding through personal experience. Just like imagining what food tastes like by looking at the menu in a restaurant, it pales in comparison with the actual experience of tasting it.

The name *Somatic Consent Engagement System* comes from a combination of:

- Somatic - relating to the neural pathways of action(efferent) and inflow of sensation (afferent).
- Consent - relating to permission and agreement.
- Engagement System - relating to The Polyvagal Theory, the ventral vagal complex and the ability to establish safety and connection.

Let's embark together on a clear, fun, authentically playful and practical path to experiencing profound connection—to yourself, others and your world like never before.

Are you ready to start living more fully?

CHAPTER 1

FOUNDATIONS OF SOMATIC CONSENT

Tuning Into Your Authentic Self

"Touch is the first language we speak."
- Stephen Gaskin

What are your fondest, earliest memories of touch?

One of mine is sitting on my father's lap and feeling his whiskers tickling my face. It felt so nice and a little scratchy. Another is the feeling of a fresh duvet cover after a bath. Another the cosy sensation of my big toe rubbing against my second toe. That felt amazing. I remember it so well because when we three kids were small, we slept in my parent's bed with our heads at the foot end. I'd rub my toes together to create a self-calming sensation if I was still awake and the others were sleeping. All these memories are from the ages of 3 or 4 years old.

We've all, however, been touched against our will by being washed, fed, dressed and held before we could speak and choose. We've all therefore learned very deep patterns of belief that the action coming towards us is more important than how we feel about it.

For most of us, this results in trying to *change how we feel* about what's happening—rather than changing, with confidence, *what* is happening.

One fundamental truth we all share is a deep desire to touch and be touched, in a way that is intimate and profound—exactly how we want to. The core of this book helps you to unveil the authentic desire of your true self and shows you how to express what you really want, while allowing others to do the same. What you'll realise is that we all, in fact, have a choice.

THE IMPORTANCE OF TOUCH

To be human is to feel and experience emotion. If we look at common daily verbal expressions, it's clear that our sense of touch is intrinsically emotional.

"Please keep in touch."
"That person rubs me up the wrong way!"
"I didn't mean to hurt your feelings."
"I can't stand that slippery politician."
"I'm touched by what you said."

When we encounter someone who's emotionally clumsy, we call them tactless, which literally means they lack the ability to be 'in touch 'with the other.

So how does this connection between emotion and the sense of touch form?

It begins very early in life. Your nervous system's ability to perceive sensory touch was developed and activated before birth, so that by the time you were born, your sense of touch was already established. The inflow of sensations from contact with your primary caregivers caused the first adaptive neurological mechanism to take place, activating the ventral vagus nerve, responsible for social engagement through expression of emotion.[1]

The inflow of sensation is a preverbal, primordial system and therefore functions as your default scheme of communication and relation to the world around you. It forms the very base of your feelings of safety—human connection.

People born without the sense of sight or with a hearing disability can develop great bodies and minds and experience a great life. But those born either without the biological components for a sense of touch or don't receive touch during their infancy and first years of life, experience disastrous consequences. That's what happened in orphanages in Romania during the

Ceausescu regime in the 1970s and what followed in the 1980s in grossly understaffed orphanages.[2] With no-one having the time to hug, hold, caress or be loving in a tactile way towards these children, terrible results began to unfold. The children developed compulsive, self-soothing, rocking motions, attachment disorders and cognitive delays which weren't just neuropsychiatric problems. Due to touch deprivation, their general growth was stunted and their gastrointestinal and immune systems underdeveloped and compromised.

Studies conclude that just 30 minutes of loving touch a day has tremendously positive effects on development.[3] This minimal amount of hugging and limb manipulation was enough to completely reverse all of the harmful effects of previous touch deprivation in orphanages and incubated babies.[4,5]

The critical role of touch within childhood development wasn't always understood. In the 1920s, John B. Watson, the founder of the psychological movement 'behaviourism', advised parents to never touch or hug their children unless they were being rewarded for an extraordinarily good job or difficult task—advising in this case to pat them on the head and give them a handshake at the end of the day.[6]

Thankfully, these days, most parents don't raise their children this way. However, it can be a very different situation outside of the home where no-touch policies exist for supervisory adults such as teachers and coaches. While these laws are well-meaning, they are not always truly helpful. If a young child reaches to get a reassuring hug from their teacher, it is what they *need* somatically at that moment.

Touch is a social good, an opportunity to create bonds of trust, cooperation and empathy. Touch is social glue. It's key to our survival. It's what binds sexual partners into lasting couples. It's what bonds parents to their children. It connects people in community together within the workplace to produce effective teams.

In his book, *Touch: The Science of Hand, Heart and Mind*,[4] neurobiologist, David J. Linden states that doctors who appropriately touch their patients during an examination are rated as more caring, and more importantly—their patients produce lower stress hormone levels and higher healing results.

In 2010, The National Basketball Association completed a wonderful study on teamwork.[7] They watched videos of all teams in the NBA games in the first half of the season and had people note down all of the instances of celebratory touch. This included all pats on the chest or buttocks, high fives and any other touch that team members made to celebrate a basket.

They came up with an index of celebratory touch for each team and hypothesised whether the index for the first half of the basketball season would predict what would happen in the second half. Their results found that teams engaging in more celebratory touch won more games in the second half of the season. More importantly, these teams played in a more co-operative fashion, for example, the star being more likely to pass the ball to another player who had a better chance of a shot.

According to the Touch Test study of almost 40,000 people in more than 110 countries, more than half of us say we are not getting enough touch in our lives. This leads to 'touch hunger' when our feelings of connection, empathy and trust slowly degrade.[8,9]

There's been much research into and recognition of the importance of touch[10]. However, there's been very little research into the specifics of this incredible sense. Let's begin to explore why the majority of us are numb to the infinite possibilities our sense of touch can offer and how to wake up these hidden wonders—which affect not only our capacity to feel more pleasure but heighten every single aspect of our lives.

You're literally holding the key that unlocks this new world within your hands.

WHY WAKING UP YOUR HANDS WORKS

"Where attention goes energy flows."
- James Redfield

If I were to ask which part of your body directs your perspective, your opinions, reasoning and the judgment of what is right or wrong for you—would you point to your head?

Some may be driven by their hearts, but the truth seems, most of us identify so much with our intellect, that we use our bodies as convenient vehicles to transport our minds from A to B. What your hands can do is form the bridge between rational and conditioned thinking—to grounded knowledge of who you are at your core in totality. Beginning with your hands, you are able to shine a light on the truth of your very being by discovering yourself in a completely embodied way.

From this embodied perspective you are able to function in a fully informed and authentic way from within, in balance and harmony with what is right *for you*.

Your hands are tools you use to make sense of the world around you. They have an incredible amount of nerve cells which relay the information they encounter directly to your brain. Each nerve cell or *neuron* has a long cable that snakes away from it. This cable, several times thinner than a human hair, is called an *axon* or nerve fibre. A nerve is an enclosed bundle of axons and is where electrochemical impulses from the neurons in your hands travel to the spinal cord, where they synapse (make contact with) other nerve cells—which in turn send the information to the thalamus and sensory cortex in your brain.[11,12]

We experience touch as a unified sensation, but it's actually created by different specialised sensors working in parallel. We have many different kinds of nerve endings in our skin—each one a micro machine, specialised in transferring a certain kind of information.

Different objects feel different when you touch them, right? One kind of nerve detects heat and another cold. One registers pain and others register sexual sensations, vibration, pressure and texture. The density of different kinds of nerve endings vary depending on where they are on the body, which is why you experience different sensations from the same object on different parts of your body.

One type of nerve ending, the C tactile afferent, is specifically linked to pleasant touch and is most responsive during slow gentle stroking. We're hardwired to like this kind of touch. In babies it stabilizes heart rate, can improve weight gain and forms the first part of social bonding.[13]

Sensory neurons are the brain's portal to the external world.

Your fingertips have a high density of nerves with 'Merkel endings 'which are the best at detecting fine tactile form.[14] You'll have noticed that your lips, tongue, genitals and cornea are very sensitive too—but you wouldn't be able to read Braille with them. This is because these parts of the body aren't discriminative, as they have less Merkle endings.[15] I'm sure you've experienced getting something in your eye. Although it can really hurt, it's actually very hard to tell precisely where in the eye it is.

I'm sure you'll agree that anything we bring our attention to in-the-moment jumps to the forefront of our experience. When we focus on a problem it's called worrying. When we focus on a new lover it's called obsession. When we focus on a new subject it's called learning. Focus makes our experience more profound. This also happens with the messages being relayed by your nerves. By bringing your awareness to the sensations being picked up by your nerve endings, you amplify your experience of them. This is, of course, easier said than done. It's hard to focus when we're distracted by constant environmental stimuli.

However, that's not the only reason we have trouble noticing the sensations. There's another cog in the works. We all accept many beliefs without question. Beliefs which *limit our ability to receive.*

HOW WE COMPROMISE OUR EXPERIENCE TO FIT IN

"You have to do your own growing, it doesn't matter how tall your grandfather was."
-Abraham Lincoln

In any society the world over, our sense of belonging and connection with others and our 'tribe', is perfectly programmed.[16] Most of us have a social engagement system that is so conditioned to fit in—that in order to belong and be loved, we believe we have to fulfil others' needs and give preference to their wishes—rather than listening to what it is *we* really want.

Although cultures differ, each one has their own social engagement system that its citizens tend to adhere to. From my own observation and generally speaking, examples of this are; The UK, where it's common to compromise your boundaries in order to avoid seeming pushy or rude. Germany, where it's socially acceptable to be direct—here rules are taken very seriously and it's not uncommon for a stranger to shout at you if they observe you parking your car in the wrong direction or riding your bicycle without a light. The US, where people seem to be pushed to achieve personal wealth in order to be accepted. And Bali where the opposite is true—without contributing to community duties, you'd have no social support network and find it very hard to survive.

Can you relate to any of the above?

Due to these cultural systems, we find it hard to go into action towards a sensory felt pleasure that is just for ourselves. Instead, we are often dependent on another person's response to feel something positive. When we go into action to please others in order to be accepted, we tend to base our actions primarily on making the other person happy. This can lead to self-neglect and co-dependency. This way of interacting not only invites a world of misunderstandings within relationship, but by continuously giving without nourishing ourselves, it increases the chance of burn out.

This is the reason why most of us are no longer aware of our sensory inflow when we touch. We've long forgotten to be acutely present to the sensations pouring into our bodies through tactile contact. This socialisation of dependency on others for our own pleasure began in infancy at the pre-verbal stage, so that as an adult it is well and truly programmed. Subsequently, we drift away from our own desires and lose motivation to produce action towards sensory felt pleasure for ourselves. We tend to do or give to others, in order to provoke a response from them—trying to *indirectly* receive the pleasure we seek, rather than use the natural capacity of our skin and nervous system to receive the pleasure *directly*. *It's important to note here that when you're holding an object with one hand and moving it over the other,* **one hand is in action, while the other is being done to**. After observing that many people had a hard time noticing the inflow via their afferent neurons, I realised that this ability was the fundamental BASE to everything else. Without it, it's difficult to access a deep state of relaxed pleasure.

We assume that the person doing the action is giving and the person being done to is receiving, but actually who is receiving and who is giving is determined by who the action is for and the agreement made between the two people.

If the action is for you, you are receiving.
If it's for the other, they are receiving.

HOW PERCEPTION IS FORMED

"Each one sees what he carries in his heart."
- Johann Wolfgang von Goethe

If you presume you can take in reliable, rational information about the outside world through your sense of touch and make non-emotional decisions about it—you're about to enter the rabbit hole. While your brain serves up your experience as 'real', actually, the raw data coming in through your sense of touch is blended with your own personal reality as well as the genetic data of your DNA. Your senses are not designed to give you the most accurate representation of the outside world. Instead, your brain 'messes' with the data—putting it through filters based on your personal experiences, memories and belief system. Depending on your personal conditioning, your brain either emphasises the data coming in through your sense of touch or diminishes it.[17,18]

When it comes to general perception, there are three main filters:

Deletion occurs when we overlook, tune out or omit details of our experience because we either fail to notice them or we discount them as unimportant.

Distortion is a personal prejudice that twists our perceptions. We amplify or diminish our experience, seeing it differently than someone else may, who has different conditioning and therefore different beliefs and emotional triggers.

Generalisation occurs when we reach a global conclusion based on one or two experiences, understanding these limited experiences as a general truth while paying no attention to exceptions.

Have you and another person ever remembered completely different details of an experience you had together?

Biohacking the Cerebellum

The cerebellum is the part of the brain which coordinates and regulates muscular activity.[19] Due to the conditioning we all experience in regard to touch, this part of the brain is programmed to focus on reaching out to the world. In doing so we focus on *giving* while doing rather than *receiving* while doing.

The transformational work of Somatic Consent takes you back to your default setting of *receiving* through touch before social conditioning overwrote your body's natural understanding of 'how to belong'.

The inflow of sensation is a natural function of the human experience and the foundation of what we tap into in order to biohack previous programming. When we re-learn how to *receive*, we re-establish an authentic connection to our experience of life and are able to reset, reboot and engage with more pleasure and connection with the world around us.

HOW TUNING INTO YOUR SENSE OF TOUCH TRAINS YOUR BRAIN

"To touch is to experience, but to feel is to live."
- Loren Klein

1. Your sense of touch is connected to your emotions

This may come as a surprise to some, but there is no touch sensation without emotion. The two go hand-in-hand. All streams of information come in via nerves and the spinal cord to the brain and distribute into two different systems.

- The **discriminative system** within the somatosensory cortex is all about the facts. It tells you where on your body you are being touched, in what way and how intensely.

- The **emotional touch system** within the insula is completely separate. This part gives different kinds of touch their particular emotional tone.

We're used to thinking that certain sensations produce a certain emotion but this is a trick the brain plays on us. For example, we experience a pain sensation along with the negative emotional reaction because these two different brain systems are active simultaneously.[20]

When you touch something, your brain also compares your past experiences with your present one, so that it can decide whether you are safe or not. This is one reason why the information coming in through your sense of touch is either emphasised or diminished.

By tuning into your sense of touch you develop *interoception*—a deep awareness of inner sensations and emotion. With increased interoception you become much more aware of emotions connected to and triggered by prior experience which (usually unconsciously) affect your present one. With this deeper awareness you gain greater clarity in knowing what you want, what you don't want, can more easily communicate your desires and limits and are more able to self-regulate in times of stress.[21]

We'll come back to this theme later when we talk about creating safety in relation to consent.

2. It wakes you up to your internal experience and whole-body awareness

We're hard-wired to pay attention to sensations that originate in the outside world and to discount ones that originate from our own motion. As you walk down the street moving your limbs and torso, your clothes move against your body but you don't usually notice these sensations at all right? The sensations that result from our own movement don't enter our consciousness because they're strongly suppressed. Our awareness is focused on making connection to the outside world. In terms of evolution, this is important for survival. It's where the things are that we might want to eat, that we might want to mate with, that we might want to run away from.

In the same way, when you attempt to pleasure yourself, electrical signals flow from the *motor cortex* in your brain, down to the muscles of your arm and hand so that you can produce pleasure through movement. A copy of those signals also goes to a part of the brain called the cerebellum. The cerebellum transforms these signals into inhibitory signals and feeds them into the *somatosensory cortex*, (the fact-based touch centre) which suppresses the sensations.[22] This is the very reason it feels so different when pleasuring yourself than when another person is touching you.

However, when you slow down enough to tune in, you include the *posterior insula* (the emotional touch system).[23] Then, when you're in movement, motor impulses combine with the somatosensory cortex and you experience an inflow of feelings that may seem alienating or strange. This is neurological biohacking taking place. This somatic experience comes with the benefit of deeper connection to feeling, thereby enriching and intensifying your sense of touch. Somatic Consent is based on awareness of this sensory inflow, which is specifically related to pleasure and connection.

3. It helps identify whether an action is for you or for them

Your body's natural somatic function related to action and touch is always either;

- For *your* benefit or pleasure
- For *their* benefit or pleasure (the other person).

This means that in order to do one, you have to fully stop doing the other. In order to be in pleasure for yourself, you have to stop being in action for the pleasure of others. Of course, they can exist simultaneously, but we have to *stop focusing* on one in order to *find* the other. Once you stop being in action *for others,* you can find the deepest layers of your own pleasure.

The moment you're able to bridge the motor part of your brain (which instructs the muscles to move) and the sensory part (what you're feeling in the moment), you access your preconditioned brain and connect with your subconscious mind. Here you access the potential to reset and reboot your system of engagement with self and others—and rewire it back to wholeness.

WAKING UP YOUR HANDS

Tuning Into Pleasure

"There is a bigger universe at hand."
- Marc Webb

I had my first orgasm at around 11 years old and was, of course, immediately hooked. I masturbated more often than I brushed my teeth and at the age of 15 experienced ejaculation for the first time. This, as I'm sure you can relate, increased my fascination. At 16 I began to have intercourse with a girl of the same age. We explored a lot. As a teenager and young man, I continued to be very sexually active and thoroughly enjoyed sensual play. I was always very potent and would orgasm as much as possible.

At some point I picked up the term 'multi-orgasmic 'and presumed it meant that a multi-orgasmic man could orgasm and ejaculate as much as he wanted to. By then, my highest score was twelve orgasms during one night in three different encounters. At 27 I fell deeply in love. We locked ourselves in a room for a week like junkies with a high-quality drug. We didn't eat or sleep. We had constant sex. I was still counting orgasms at that point and I remember the tally was twenty-five. And then something different happened.

I crashed, emotionally, physically and psychologically. I felt sick for three months. I couldn't eat or sleep well. I had constant headaches and nausea. On top of that and the most disconcerting was I found any thought about sex—disgusting. I became depressed and suicidal, ending up one night on a balcony. My hands were holding the railing. The impulse to jump was in my legs. Game over. Well, very nearly. Instead, I got a terrible pain in my chest, collapsed and cried for hours. Then it happened. Two words came out of nowhere: LOVE & TANTRA. This was a few years before the internet was established and I had no idea where that word 'Tantra 'came from.

The message was remarkably clear within all the confusion and pain—and I knew I had to follow it up, no matter what. The next morning, I went to the biggest bookstore in town to look the word up. They had two books on Tantra and I started reading, slowly and curiously. Every word resonated. I found myself thinking, "That's me, that's me and that's me too". The books described spiritual transformation through regulating sexual energy, and how to be multi-orgasmic without the orgasm of procreation. Love and tantra and how to get there. I was sold and dedicated from that day on.

One part of those books is the cornerstone of everything I'm offering today—the presence that occurs when noticing the sensation you feel in your hands when you touch—and the sensation you feel in your body when touched. After 25 years of research, I've given up trying to exactly define what love or tantra is. Living it and sharing it with the world is much more exciting!

Joy is in your fingertips

Joy is at the tips of our fingers. All we have to do is simply feel it. However, due to all the factors influencing our sense of touch, the seemingly trivial task of experiencing pure sensation when in action becomes challenging.

Trying to grasp the dynamics of sensory inflow with your intellect won't get you very far. To become fluently aware of your sensory inflow, you have to retrain your physiological experience of it so that your body remembers on a cellular level. We can get around the brain's hard wiring with the simple practice of 'Waking Up the Hands'. This practice is so incredibly simple that many dismiss it, thinking it can't be that easy.

> **I'd like to underline just how very important this practice is.**
> **It's the only doorway to all the treasure in this book.**

The two types of neurons associated with touch

Neurons are brain and nervous system cells responsible for:

1) receiving sensory input from the external world, and
2) sending motor commands to your muscles.

They both relay information via electrical signals.

There are two types of neurons within the somatic nervous system, known as *afferent* and *efferent*.[24]

- **Afferent neurons** support sensory inflow coming from the skin. When you feel your heartbeat, notice you're hungry, need to go to the toilet or when you touch somebody or something, they carry the sensory data from your internal body and external skin to your brain.

- **Efferent neurons** carry motor impulses from your brain to your muscles so that you can move parts of your body towards something in action. They are responsible for everything movement based.

After observing that many people had a hard time noticing the inflow via their afferent neurons, I realised that this ability was the fundamental BASE to everything else. Without it, it's difficult to access a deep state of relaxed pleasure.

The potential to physiologically engage a relaxed state of pleasure is crucial to maintaining balance, empowerment and deep intimacy within relationship.

This is why, when working with clients and students, I always begin with the fundamental step of waking up awareness of **afferent inflow**.

How does waking up the hands work?

Your brain isn't a static entity. It is constantly being shaped by everything around you. Most of the time we are unaware of this process and therefore don't have much control over it.

Within your brain, neurons communicate at dedicated sites called synapses through the use of neurotransmitters. When neurons communicate regularly with each other, long term memories and habits form. This process is called *long-term potentiation (LTP)* or *neuroplasticity*. When you practise waking up your hands, you nourish and nurture a new way of experiencing your world. This increases the efficiency of communication between the neurons responsible for the new embodied memory. It creates a new habit of being naturally aware of sensory input as well as increasing your ability to self-regulate in times of emotional upheaval and stress.[25]

All you have to do is slowly feel an object with your hands for just five minutes per day

It sounds very simple doesn't it? And it is, though this simple process has tremendous results.

After only three minutes of practice, oxytocin is released which begins to regulate the nervous system. Oxytocin is the love and connection neurotransmitter and hormone directly linked to human bonding and increased trust and loyalty.[26]

Feeling an object for five minutes allows oxytocin to flood your system. Much like breathing, sleeping and drinking, feeling and connecting through oxytocin is a necessary need for human survival. The release of oxytocin allows the nervous system to stay regulated. In this way, touch-related connection is vital to our existence. The practice activates the safe part of the parasympathetic system, which induces a calm, relaxed state. This pleasurable state of relaxation is vital for our well-being. It not only aids physical and mental balance and healing but recalibrates the entire manner in which we relate with others.

When we're deprived of oxytocin we tend to ignore, avoid and suppress any uncomfortable feelings and emotions that come up. I call this the Numbness Bar. We'll explore this in depth later in the book. What's important to be aware of now is that emotions go hand in hand with pleasant sensations. Repressing one inherently affects your ability to experience the other.

Feeling an object is not about love or relationship, it's about whether sensory neurons in your hands can connect with the pleasure centre in your brain.

PLEASURE IN YOUR HANDS

SOMATIC

SENSORY
AFFERENT, NOTICING, FEELING, DIRECT ROUTE
PLEASURE & PAIN

MOTORY
EFFERENT, SENDING SIGNALS TO MOVE, DOING, ACTION, REFLEXES

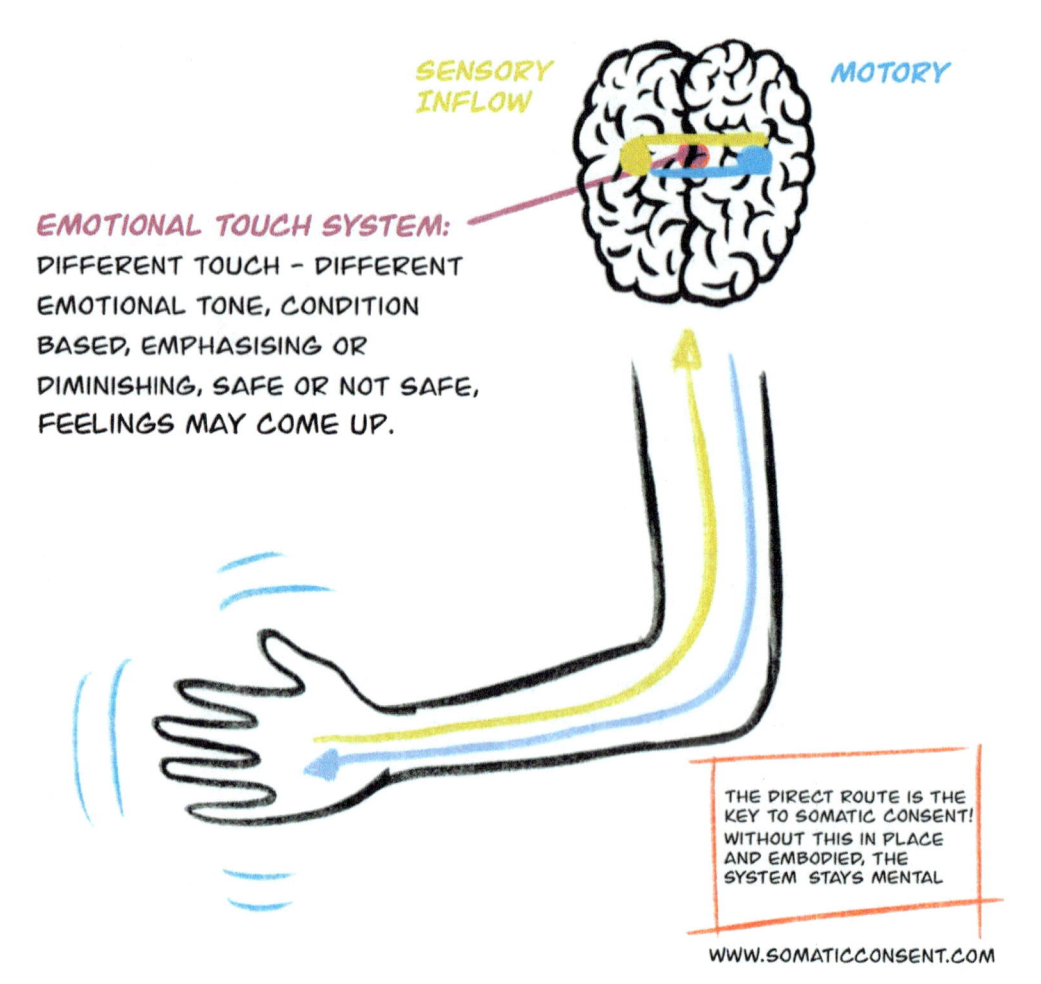

SENSORY INFLOW

MOTORY

EMOTIONAL TOUCH SYSTEM:
DIFFERENT TOUCH - DIFFERENT EMOTIONAL TONE, CONDITION BASED, EMPHASISING OR DIMINISHING, SAFE OR NOT SAFE, FEELINGS MAY COME UP.

THE DIRECT ROUTE IS THE KEY TO SOMATIC CONSENT! WITHOUT THIS IN PLACE AND EMBODIED, THE SYSTEM STAYS MENTAL

WWW.SOMATICCONSENT.COM

You notice a whole new world of sensory experience

Waking up the hands heightens your awareness of sensory inflow as you go into action. It is essentially a practice of pure, mindful presence to your sense of touch. You're probably already aware that mindfulness positively changes the emotional environment of your brain and brings about deeper connection and insight to your experience of self, others and the world.[27]

As you touch and direct your attention solely to the information being relayed by the afferent neurons in your hands to your brain—*you notice that you're experiencing pleasant sensations.*

It's important to note here that when you're holding an object with one hand and moving it over the other, **one hand is in action, while the other is being done to**.

It's different from an experience of touch with another person, where **one gives and one receives**.

This practice wakes up your ability to notice the sensory inflow, so that when you touch another, you are **able to receive in your full capacity**.

When you drop into this sensory experience, you may also notice other sensations or emotions. Each person is different so it's difficult to predict exactly what you will notice. When I practise, I notice a tingling sensation leading from my hand to my arm, which sometimes includes other parts of my body. I feel my muscles softening and my body relaxing. My breathing slows. I release a sigh as I drop in deeper. The practice is a 'keener' experience of enjoyment in the moment. Being here in the simplicity of just being me—with no agenda and where no 'shoulds' exist.

Others have described it as;

"A rush of joy when I realise how simple it is to connect to myself."
"I was so tuned in, I felt pleasure, even from the breeze on my hands."
"There was an experience of oneness with everything around me."
"Relaxation and connection to the energy inside myself and outside myself."
"Sensual tingling and a sense of joy."
"Pulsating, like noticing the rhythm of my heartbeat throughout my body."

"It bubbles up, gets really intense and feels a little overwhelming, but I can go a little further each time so that my ability to accept that amount of pleasure increases."

"I felt I'd entered a new dimensional space where only what really matters exists."

Our hands naturally reach out to feel so we're going to allow them to do just that. It's time to embody *direct pleasure*, through action by yourself, for yourself. Are you ready?

Explore and experiment now as you tune into what's *coming in* via your hands. Focus on and notice *the inflow* of sensations. Bringing all your attention to the information, insight, emotions and feelings as you experience.

THE PRACTICE OF WAKING UP YOUR HANDS

"It's in your hands to make the world a better place."
- Nelson Mandela

Step 1.
Lean back

If you learn forward, your abdominal muscles and spine will engage and activate your sympathetic nervous system. Leaning back will help ease your body into the parasympathetic state of relaxation. It also helps you to relax if you place a cushion on your lap for your arms/hands to rest on. The cushion is just like using stabilisers when you're learning to ride a bike. It'll support your arms and then your nervous system will be more likely to relax. When you become more adept, you'll no longer need the cushion prop.

Step 2.
Choose an object, any object and bring it to the cushion

It doesn't matter which object you choose, feel free to use a different object each time. It could be any one of the many objects lying around your house. Maybe you could have a walk around and make a list of all the possible things to experiment with. Your keys, a stone, cork or piece of wood, a shell, watch, feather, cloth, your phone charger, a plant, the pepper pot or even the family pet (if it'll keep still for a few minutes)! Allow yourself to relax into the experience while your hands begin to notice how the object feels.

You'll probably notice your brain labelling the 'object', for example, "It's a book", "a pencil" or whatever you're holding. You may think about what you can do with it. All that is unimportant. You have to consciously choose where you direct your attention, so just bring your focus to the sensations coming in through your skin as you allow your hands to experience pleasure.

Step 3.
Stay where you are and use your hands to notice everything about the object

Discover the object with your hands. Notice its size, shape, texture, temperature and weight. Whether it's sturdy or delicate, soft or rough. Just allow yourself to explore and feel the details. If you want to, close your eyes, though you may find it easier to look at your hands while touching the object. Notice how fast you're moving your hands. Move your hands as slowly as you can so that you can soak up all the fine details of sensation.

Can you notice any change when you slow down? The slower you go, the more your sensory nerves can detect and enjoy pleasure.[23]

If your mind wanders

If you find yourself thinking about the email you haven't sent or what you're going to have for dinner—no problem! It's great you noticed you were distracted. Now bring your relaxed focus back to the sensations in your hands again... and again.

If you're used to observing your thoughts, you'll probably notice some unusual ones come up. Maybe judgement, irritation, boredom, attachment or aversion to the object, doubt or even guilt or shame for trying to feel pleasure from a mere thing. If this happens, simply bring your attention to the sensations you *feel*. This is the most important thing. Everything else is unimportant.

Continue for a while

When you notice the inflow, just like with most meditation, allow yourself to open up to noticing. Relaxing, breathing, feeling, surrendering to the sensations. Letting everything else go. You just are. There's no need to think of or do anything else. Feeling the sensations. Relaxing. Surrendering to the experience.

Step 4.
Noticing the inflow of pleasure

At some point you'll notice how nice it feels. This may seem strange to you, that you can feel pleasure simply by touching an object without anyone else being present with you. It's just you and your skin. Again, don't worry about what your thoughts say—just allow yourself to tune into as much sensation as possible.

Step 5.
You'll notice a 'physiological shift'

When you stay tuned in, you'll notice a difference in how your body feels as your physiology changes. Your breath will slow down and become regular. Your muscles will release any tension they were holding onto. This is because your nervous system has shifted into deeper relaxation in the parasympathetic state. With this your brainwaves slow down to Alpha or Theta and your blood chemistry changes as oxytocin is released and cortisol and adrenaline are inhibited. When this shift happens, you'll feel a very pleasurable state of calmness and balance. Both grounded and deeply connected to self. This fundamental somatic, neurological shift needs to be physiologically accessed before consent can be experienced in any depth during The 3 Minute Game (which you'll learn to play soon).

Interestingly, when your brainwaves change to Alpha, your brain also releases Acetylcholine, a neurotransmitter responsible for increased levels of attention, motivation, creativity and long-term memory. Alpha brain waves also open the filter (known as 'the conscious critical faculty') between your conscious and subconscious mind. This allows access to more intuitive insight and creative inspiration. With deeper relaxation your brainwaves slow further to Theta, the trance/hypnagogic state where you are able to re-program learned habits through visualisation of sensory experience.[28]

> *For the roles of empowered receiving and giving to open up fully to you, your hands need to be capable of experiencing pleasure fluently. Your emotional fluency is connected to this capacity.*
>
> *Only then will you know with clarity and certainty (beyond learned patterns of touch) what is truly pleasurable to you and what isn't. Through this you are able to access deeper sensual awakening.*

After practising for a few minutes, reflect on the experience you just had.

What came up for you?

What did you feel?

What did you notice about yourself while feeling the object?

Was anything difficult for you?

Was it difficult to stay connected to the experience?

Could you allow yourself to feel the sensations fully?

Did anything prevent you from fully experiencing the sensations?

How did that feel in your body?

What can prevent you from tuning into the inflow of sensation?

1. **If your body feels like it's making an effort.** If your spine, abdominal or arm muscles are engaged, your nervous system will be in a more alert 'working 'state and it'll be harder to relax. So, make sure you're leaning back and your arms aren't held up high but are resting on the cushion in your lap.

2. **If you're moving your hands too fast.** Remember the part of your brain that *controls your hand muscle movement* is different from the noticing part which *takes in the information from your hands*. Your brain isn't used to doing both of those at once—yet. That's why it makes a difference when you slow down. You may even have to stop and use your other hand for a while. Slowing down is the 'magic formula'. If you have an agenda you tend to speed up. When you speed up, your nervous system automatically switches on the sympathetic response, which isn't bad or wrong in itself, it's just that at these times, neurologically, you feel less. This is due to the cerebellum, located in the back of your brain which controls action, switching your insula—the feeling centre—off. If you were able to feel a lot, your nervous system would get overloaded. In moments of slow touch you feel more and in these moments, the working mind is silent. Within this state, one has an experience of restful, embodied *being*.

3. **If your mind became distracted** and you didn't notice that your attention had been directed elsewhere. This just takes a bit of practice. It's our mind's job to flip from one thing to another, constantly assessing our environment so that we stay safe. Keeping your attention on the sensations being picked up from your skin is the same as keeping your mind focused on an 'object 'of

meditation such as your breath—and the same guidelines apply. Notice you're distracted—then simply bring your attention back to your object of focus (in this case, the sensations in your hands when coming into contact with whatever they're touching). It's important not to worry about being distracted. This just puts more unnecessary thoughts in your mind. Be kind to yourself. Dismiss those thoughts as unimportant and just go back to the sensations, again and again.

4. **If you attach meaning to your experience** (meaning making). This is when we project a certain expectation or story onto what we're experiencing. It easily distracts us from our actual experience in-the-moment and can result in bias and disappointment. When you tune into the inflow you'll notice that the usual 'mind chatter 'quietens and slows. By activating the noticing part of your brain, you bypass the automatic function of the 'meaning making 'part of your brain which is usually busy being logical, judging your environment and attaching stories to your experience. If you notice any story, meaning or expectation coming up, remind yourself that you're simply engaging in self-care, going into action *for you*, experiencing your personal relationship to pleasure. No-one is here to give to—you're just being you, noticing the sensations coming in during the process of *experiencing* pleasure, without any specific goal, touching however you spontaneously want to touch the object, for as long as you choose to.

We'll explore 'meaning making 'more deeply in the section on The 3 Components of Pleasure.

5. **If unexpected or confusing emotions come up.** You could be really surprised at how much pleasure suddenly flows in and feel tearful, suddenly uplifted, a sense of relief or even embarrassment, guilt or shame at feeling pleasure in this way.

Emotions are complex and connected to your lifetime of memories and conditioning. As you bring all your attention to the experience, nerve cells relaying the pleasure you feel also trigger memories connected to pleasure—to beliefs, emotions, patterns of behaviour and assumptions associated with it.

Just know that whatever comes up for you is part of the process and absolutely fine! Don't be discouraged, stay curious and set aside a few minutes each day to continue experimenting. Whether it's easy or it takes time, bring all of your attention to your skin—until your awareness of the inflow is natural and you don't have to remind yourself anymore to put your focus there.

I encourage you to allow yourself to see where it takes you. If you notice unpleasant or challenging feelings that last for more than two minutes, it's probably an indicator that they are worth looking into. It may be overwhelming at times because you aren't used to experiencing these feelings, even the pleasurable ones. When a situation is unknown, it alerts the nervous system and we may interpret them as 'dangerous'. We'll go much deeper into this later when discussing the Numbness Bar Map and The Polyvagal Theory, but for now, just observe, notice what you notice and never force, stopping whenever you need to. Your experiences will change and develop as your body begins to trust—and feeling the direct inflow finally drops in, becoming second nature.

6. If you are used to going into action for others and focusing on *giving,* you may experience a numbness/lack of sensation. Just like not having used and trained a muscle, not only will the concept sound foreign, but the habitual neurological pathway of your action for your own sensual pleasure (feeling *for yourself*) simply won't be trained. It will feel confusing because your brain won't yet know what to do with the incoming sensations, so it adapts by shutting off and avoiding feeling this new experience until it has been repeated often and a new neurological pathway has been formed.

What others have shared about their initial difficulties:

"I felt a sense of shame come up".
"My mind was so full of stories, I couldn't focus on my experience".
"I was doing it too fast so couldn't feel much".
"I think my expectations got in the way".
"I judged myself for doing the exercise".
"I kept getting distracted".
"I feared losing control".
"I aimed for pleasure, so my action was goal oriented and distracted me away from my present experience".

As you practise, explore with curiosity, staying in tune with impulses of the moment—without any specific goal. This will ground you more deeply in yourself and influence how you engage with life in general. Allow any feeling to arise. The ability to simply stay with the stimuli without the need to do anything specific takes you back to the innocent state used to explore objects and the world around you in the early years of life.

As infants we intuitively practised touch in its purest form, picking up random objects, putting them in our mouth, feeling them, playing, improvising, discovering and above all—enjoying. If you have kids, I'm sure you've observed this innocent, curious, exploration and absorption of information from the world around them. Over time we were told by our caretakers not to touch in this way and subsequently, even though it was sometimes necessary to be protected, we grew up associating touch in its pure form with guilt and shame instead of a playful space void of doubts.

Do you remember times in your childhood when you were forbidden to touch something or someone?

Which feelings arise when you recall this memory?

Waking up your hands not only re-establishes your ability to feel more; it increases your quality of touch—allowing you to redefine your relationship with touch and sensation. You'll become very aware of feelings or challenging emotions that arise and learn how to respond in-the-moment, in a calm and rational way. Actively noticing the inflow helps your nervous system to remember what habit has made it forget. You re-learn *how to experience pleasure and nourishment through your own action.*

When you keep your attention focused on the sensations, the experience of inflow increases in intensity. I'm sure you've heard the phrases; 'Neurons that fire together wire together 'and 'Use it or lose it'. This refers to neuroplasticity—the rewiring of your neural synapses to form new habits.

Being able to notice and enhance your feelings of pleasure develops a deeper physical and spiritual capability for connection with your partner and the world you live in. It offers a new way to communicate through touch where you're genuinely present to what is happening in the moment, without the mind adding *meaning* to it. The more you practise, the more you will feel, tune into your genuine self and develop high sensitivity and attunement.

After about three weeks of continuous practice, you'll notice an exceptional increase in awareness of feeling and pleasure as your neural pathways regenerate. You'll also experience a profound increase in the release of oxytocin (responsible for the feeling of safety, connection and ease in your body).

After three months, your *experience of* increased pleasure (without any effort to consciously direct your attention *while in action)* will be natural and organic. This will build the foundation of *receiving* when you touch somebody for your own pleasure.

It's been interesting to observe the different ways in which people respond, as well as the difficulties some have. It can take time and practice to access the moment when the inflow of sensation drops in—and your whole physiology changes. Some find it second nature, others may need a few weeks. The speed at which it happens usually relates to how self-aware the person initially is. If you've spent time practicing mindfulness and inner reflection in the past, you'll usually find the process much easier and quicker.

However long it takes, I promise it will be well worth the investment. Be assured that everyone with an intact nervous system can do it. When your body realises at a physiological level that your hands are a source of your own pleasure—*for you*—and not just instruments to achieve tasks with or to **do** to and **give** to others—everything will change.

This is how you re-establish the full capacity of your sensory nervous system, re-learning what it means to truly experience pleasure from your skin.

Witnessing this vital element of self-activation has been such a joy to observe in others. The fundamental shift in awareness triggers deep insight, empowerment and awakening on many levels. One example is the ability to self-regulate your nervous system's trauma response into a balanced state whenever you need to. In challenging times when fear, anger and frustration arise, your amygdala engages the sympathetic nervous system which prepares your body for fight or flight. Here rational decision-making is impossible. When you learn to notice the inflow, you not only re-learn how to experience pleasure, but are able to activate a relaxed state of being—on demand.

This practice is by no means limited to adults. It's a wonderful way to teach children how to self-regulate in times of stress. Here are two anecdotes from people trained in Somatic Consent.

"I am a primary school teacher, at a tiny private school with 13 pupils. Most kids come to us having had negative educational experiences because, basically they were 'being themselves 'too much for the regular state schools. For a couple of weeks now I've had a new girl in my group. She'd been at home for months. Although she's very willing to go to school, her past experiences have made her put up such a barrier that it was almost physically impossible. Her little body was all cramped up with stress and glued to her father in the mornings. I decided to show her and her father the exercise of waking up their hands, so that every morning before coming to school, they could practise for five minutes. She holds onto the object while traveling to school after doing the exercise. It's helped to calm her somewhat and I'm very curious to see how this exercise of self-regulation will deepen for her in the coming weeks." - Bas van der Tang

"I would like to share an experience I had with my 11-year-old daughter last night. She woke up screaming and crying at two in the morning. She was absolutely terrified and could not talk about what had scared her. So, I brought her to my room and put an object in her hands while talking her through the process. After five minutes she was calm and could clearly articulate what had frightened her so much (she'd felt like someone was choking her). She was able to go back to sleep peacefully for the rest of the night. It was so beautiful to be able to ease her out of a dorsal vagal shutdown response and into a ventral state of relaxation." - Heather Broussard

This practice is a way of life. Waking up your hands connects you to many aspects of your being. It heightens awareness, grounds you in self and creates a sense of safety within your nervous system, which leads to *all further transformations*—personally, interpersonally and spiritually.

The biggest obstacle is the idea that feeling pleasure in the hands is similar to the feeling of sexual climax (which is all about the goal of satisfaction and gratification). Rather, the pleasure we tune into increases prolonged, orgasmic capacity during relaxed arousal as well as deeply intimate, sensual connection with a lover. We'll talk about this in much more depth in the section, Being on the Edge.

To experiment with the inflow of sensations in your hands, I welcome you to practice alone or with a partner, with the help of this online starter course and app.

Self-Love course   Android App   IPHONE App

Instructions:

- Scan the QR code with your phone camera.
- For Android you may have to use a QR Code Reader app like 'Google Lens'.
- Choose your browser.
- You'll be directed to the webpage.

THE DIRECT AND INDIRECT ROUTES OF PLEASURE

"I want you to know that it is pleasure not pain that is your birthright."
- Christiane Northrup

Now we'll take a deeper look at the Direct and Indirect Routes of pleasure. The Direct Route of pleasure is a revolutionary way of biohacking your ability to feel more deeply—and what you practise when you wake up the ability to feel the inflow of sensations in your hands. This practice not only challenges your established belief system of what is possible through touch, it also challenges any limitations you may have accepted, opening up infinite possibility to explore who you authentically are beyond any learned patterns of touch.

Within the Somatic Consent Engagement System, the Direct Route is the default, foundational key to intimate connection because it awakens the nervous system's ability to *receive* while in action. When you're clearly aware of your own internal experience (what you are receiving in the moment), you become grounded and balanced in self. You tend to know what you want and don't want and can more easily communicate your desires in a calm and authentic way. This begins to open up the possibility for deep, intimate relationship.

How you go into action and feel stimuli from the outer world

The motor cortex

When you want to go into action, impulses are sent from the motor cortex (working brain) via *efferent neurons* in an outflow—to motivate your muscles into an action. Examples could be picking up a glass, scratching your back or putting a key in a lock.

The sensory cortex

The sensory cortex is the headquarters of the discriminative system. It receives information via *afferent neurons* in your skin and transfers this data to your brain. This part is all about the facts—telling you where on your body you are being touched, in what way and how intensely. It registers pleasure, pain, vibration, pressure, temperature, texture and fine tactile form.

DIRECT/INDIRECT PLEASURE MAP

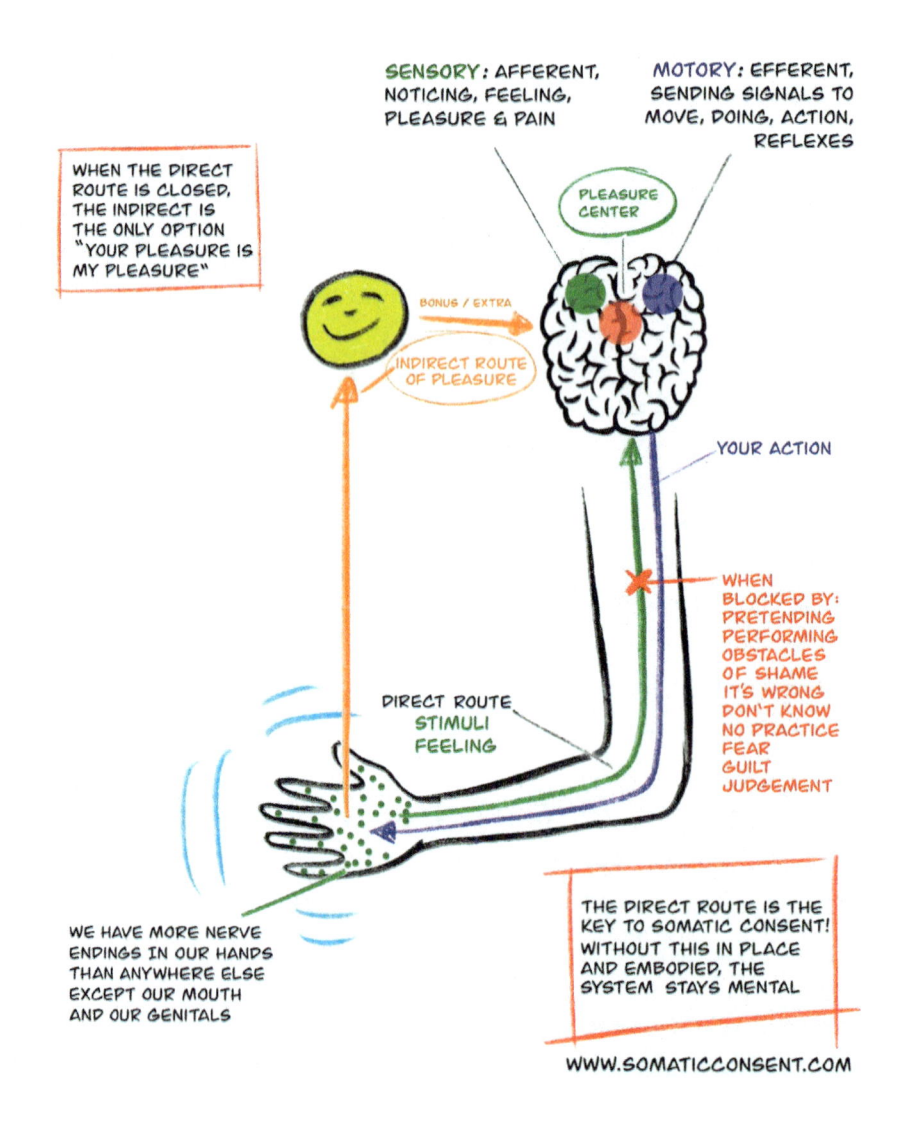

SENSORY: AFFERENT, NOTICING, FEELING, PLEASURE & PAIN

MOTORY: EFFERENT, SENDING SIGNALS TO MOVE, DOING, ACTION, REFLEXES

PLEASURE CENTER

WHEN THE DIRECT ROUTE IS CLOSED, THE INDIRECT IS THE ONLY OPTION "YOUR PLEASURE IS MY PLEASURE"

BONUS / EXTRA

INDIRECT ROUTE OF PLEASURE

YOUR ACTION

DIRECT ROUTE STIMULI FEELING

WHEN BLOCKED BY:
PRETENDING
PERFORMING
OBSTACLES
OF SHAME
IT'S WRONG
DON'T KNOW
NO PRACTICE
FEAR
GUILT
JUDGEMENT

WE HAVE MORE NERVE ENDINGS IN OUR HANDS THAN ANYWHERE ELSE EXCEPT OUR MOUTH AND OUR GENITALS

THE DIRECT ROUTE IS THE KEY TO SOMATIC CONSENT! WITHOUT THIS IN PLACE AND EMBODIED, THE SYSTEM STAYS MENTAL

WWW.SOMATICCONSENT.COM

The direct route of pleasure

When you touch something that feels pleasant it's because the sensory route is experiencing an inflow of sensory information and sending signals to your brain which light up the pleasure centre in the limbic system. This is the *Direct Route of Pleasure*. Sounds obvious right? The problem is that the working brain, responsible for action, *isn't directly connected* to the limbic system which is where sensory 'inflow' is felt. This means that the motor dynamic *does not go into action with the 'intention' of sensory based pleasure*. This is one reason why most people lapse into depending on the other person's response to discover pleasure themselves, which lessens the awareness of their own sensory sensations even more.

The indirect route of pleasure

Let's imagine that someone hasn't activated their Direct Route and therefore isn't able to deeply feel their own experience of touch and the pleasure possible through this route. When they go into an action towards another, they tend to do it to get a response. When the other person looks happy—the one in action feels a reward. When the Direct Route is numbed or blocked we tend to *do*, in order to get something back. We hope that our partner experiences pleasure and expresses it in response—so we can get rewarded. The dynamic of experiencing pleasure through someone else's reaction to your touch is called the *Indirect Route of Pleasure*. You are going into action so that you get a response.

Have you ever been touched this way, sensing that the person touching you is waiting for your reaction or confirmation that it feels good?

Have you ever pretended and performed to please your partner?

Have you ever relied on getting a response from a partner in order to feel good about yourself?

Experiencing pleasure through someone else's reaction to our touch and the *Indirect Route of Pleasure* is what most people learn in order to survive or to feel they belong in our conditioned society. When we acknowledge that we all do or have done that and can feel empathy towards this limiting dynamic, we are finally able to see that there's a way out of this loop, by going into action through the *Direct Route*.

ACTIVATING THE NOTICING PART OF YOUR BRAIN

"I hope you find, as I did, that happiness comes from noticing and enjoying the little things in life."
- Barbara Ann Kipfer

Luckily, the logical and rational working brain isn't alone in the neocortex. There's also a *noticing* part that is responsible for deeper internal awareness. The aim of this work is to switch this part of the neocortex back on. When you bring awareness to the inflow, you bring emphasis to it—developing and enriching it. You *tap into* the somatic sensory system, shifting your focus from the mind into the body. This is the process of embodiment. In doing so, you also *tap away from* your working brain's lifelong conditioning (engaging in action towards others to find pleasure). With this more embodied experience, you can more easily access authentic, personal truth instead of clinging to moral and cultural structures which often dictate what is right and wrong, what you should, shouldn't or have to do.

The more you practise waking up your hands, the more your motor dynamic can go into action towards sensory inflow for your own pleasure. This enables you to embody the experience of *doing and receiving in the same moment, as you touch.*

When your body re-learns how to **do and receive simultaneously**, conditioning within your personality structure related to shame, guilt and fear stored within your limbic system's emotional databank gets challenged. This is the beginning of rewiring your brain back to its natural function of human engagement—before any social conditioning took place.

Relationship to self and others through the indirect route

We are social beings. Our nervous systems thrive when we're in harmony with those around us. This is how our social engagement system works. (We'll take a deeper look at this vital aspect of the human experience later in *The Polyvagal Theory*). Through communication of facial expression, gestures, words and touch we engage in a feedback loop of cues that enable us to stay safe and co-regulate with others in difficult times. It is through the social engagement system that we access the Indirect Route of pleasure—and we most definitely need it. However, if we rely solely on the Indirect Route by reading cues from others, we only utilise half of our built-in 'social survival compass'.

If you connect primarily to the Indirect Route, it provides one-sided input. This input may be more or less accurate depending on the other's capacity to share their truth/be authentic with you, as well as your personal perception and capacity for empathy. This indirect information becomes easier to decypher when some degree of connection, bonding and intimacy is present (which are all, interestingly, consequences of tuning into the Direct Route).

If we lean heavily on the Indirect Route, the person in action responds solely on feedback from the other, getting dependent on their reaction—which isn't necessarily authentic. And if we look at the other dynamic, when we think someone is doing something for us, we become used to responding in specific ways in order to make them feel appreciated, acknowledged or entertained by performing, pretending and acting. And so, a joyful response can be inauthentic, based on the pleasing dynamic of obligation.

As a consequence of this shadow-dance of guesswork and half-truths, deep connection doesn't have much chance of forming. We never really show ourselves enough for the other to truly see us. This results in two people engaging with each other, where no-one is actually receiving much value at all. I'm sure you can see how this could lead to immature and conditioned behaviour which often results in the breakdown of relationship.

Relationship to self and others through the direct route

The spiritual master, Osho said that love is nourishment, and you have to fill your own bowl with conscious love before being able to function well in relationship. So if two people come together hungry and thirsty, with begging bowls wishing to be filled by the other's love, they end up exploiting each other in some way to get their needs met and bowls filled.

> *The Direct Route of Pleasure helps you to fill your bowl. By activating your sensory inflow, you wake up a chain of events that help you nourish the awareness, self-care and self-love essential to converse and connect with others in the most optimal way.*

When you access the Direct Route, the oxytocin released rewires neural circuits related to safety and connection. Oxytocin enhances your capacity for compassion and empathy (ability to feel the other on an emotional level). This connection enables your whole nervous system to relax. Your needs become more transparent to you. You're more able to ask for what you want and say what you don't—which opens up a much deeper level of honesty and intimacy. With this, your experience of intimate touch becomes one of organic flow, rather than pre-learned or premeditated routine full of expectation or sense of duty. You feel more genuinely loving, because there are no hidden agendas, unspoken desires or resentments. You come from a place of fullness and abundance, instead of a place of lack, grasping, expectation, or exploitation of the other to get your needs met.

Being alone *without* a partner can be beneficial when initially activating the Direct Route. I invite you to go out into nature and experience yourself—with all you choose to come into tactile contact with. The magic of presence can be accessed any time we choose to connect to our own sensory pleasure. Tune into the warmth of the sun and the sensation of the breeze on your skin, the water when you go for a swim. Revel in the experience of these timeless moments. In this way you'll soon notice that the inflow, being open, gives your experiences in life a completely different, deeper quality and value. The inflow becomes your natural expression of interaction with your environment in the here and now—without plan or agenda—a divine dance in present moment engagement of what is. So that when it does come to touching another person:

A: the usual goal or agenda of touch will no longer be relevant and is taken out of the equation.

B: When you feel yourself through your sensory inflow, it leads to a space of relaxed arousal. This develops your capacity to feel deeper. You'll become a master observer of whatever feelings come up in the moment. You become more finely tuned to your physical, emotional and psychological desires and limits.

And, just like having a taste of gourmet food, you won't want to go back to eating junk. Uninspiring touch won't be enough for you anymore. You'll recognise immediately when someone touching you isn't tuned into their Direct Route of sensory inflow—and has instead, a goal or agenda. You'll become less willing to pretend and perform for the other person's need to get a response out of you. You'll be more able to express your limits and no longer go along with something you feel uncomfortable with. No evolution takes place if we come with a begging bowl. We automatically spiral into survival mechanisms to get our needs met, where we try to get something out of others because our own capacity to feel total is blocked.

This is why loving yourself by filling your own 'bowl', enhances physical, emotional and psychological fullness so that you're able to relax, feel grounded and fully be yourself. Only then can we give genuinely from a place of love and care for the other—free of ulterior motives.

When both people have activated the Direct Route, they have established the groundwork for relaxation, authentic communication and authentic touch. Through this they have the possibility of expanding into interpersonal consciousness—an awakened state—where a sense of merging connection with each other takes place.

This is the basis of human existence and *evolution*—and why Waking Up The Hands is so vital.

We'll go deeper into the function and necessity of the Indirect Route and how it is utilised in hands-on professional practice in Chapter 5. First we need to put the Indirect Route aside so that we can establish the Direct Route of inflow as our human base for individual development.

REWIRING YOUR BRAIN FOR PLEASURE AND CONNECTION

"You must unlearn what you have learned."
- Yoda

The Direct Route is a key to infinite possibilities, to layers of personal and spiritual awakening that we never outgrow. The importance of practising the Direct Route's inflow of sensations with others, over and over again, can't be emphasised enough. Through your practice you'll discover deeper layers of yourself which are activated through conditioned shame responses, but there's no need to be afraid of what comes up. It's all part of growth and I'll show you how to integrate it in fun ways using other tools throughout this book.

If you've learned that pleasure is shameful in some way, if you have any self-judgment about it connected to guilt or fear, or a part of you believes that pleasure isn't good, allowed or is even dangerous—you may experience some confusing emotions as you practise. This may be because your limbic system has learned that it is somehow wrong to touch and feel another person *for yourself*. Your nervous system may not have any reference points for going into action to receive for your own pleasure. And the more you are aware of the Direct Route, the more likely it is you'll be confronted with vulnerability and hidden desire. This may activate the 'unsafe' side of your nervous system, which is a normal response when engaging in something that isn't familiar. We'll go into this response in depth with The Polyvagal Theory Map.

---

*We can also get confused when we focus on the action itself, rather than **who the action is for**. If the action is for you, you are receiving. If it's for the other, they are receiving.*

The key is to re-learn that focusing on your own pleasure as you touch is a positive and healthy way to authentically engage with yourself and others. By practising going into action for yourself, you'll tap outside your established and limiting comfort zones and enter a 'learning field' where you can explore any limiting aspects of yourself—while learning to playfully accept and embrace them.

Can the rest of the body feel the somatic inflow?

Absolutely! Your hands are like tentacles creating a new reality of what you see and feel. Once you open up this door, your perception changes. Once you activate your hands, you begin to notice the somatic inflow with the rest of your skin.

> *The sensory inflow is both too simple and too profound for the intellectual mind to grasp. When your hands get it - your body and mind will get it at a holistic level.*

While studying architecture in my 20s, I was fortunate to have a professor who also happened to be a Zen master. During our first semester he instructed us to go out once a week, whatever the weather. While outside we learned to feel the world with our bodies while moving our hands in the shape of landscapes, the contours of buildings and other forms around us. It was a very beautiful and effective exercise that gave me insight into the world I'm a part of by perceiving my experience differently than I usually did. Activating the sensory inflow in your hands is similar. It isn't just about your hands. Through them, you learn to perceive pleasure with your whole body in a totally different way. We utilise the hands as a starting point (due to the high amount of nerve endings) to begin noticing and embodying somatic inflow to the brain. When you embody this understanding via your hands, you will ultimately feel the inflow of sensations all over your body and experience yourself in totality—as you are.

What can I do if confronting emotions come up while practising?

If emotions surface it's possible to self-regulate. If you're with another person it's possible to co-regulate.

Self-regulate by focusing on self-care. Spend time alone being kind and loving to yourself. Give yourself time and space to ground back into a loving relationship with self by going for a walk in nature, having a bath, getting a professional massage, breathing regularly, doing yoga, dancing, sport, art, cooking or whatever it is that you're naturally drawn to doing.

What do you do to care for and connect to yourself?
What are you naturally drawn to doing alone?

Co-regulate through encounter, engagement and connection to others. Re-establish safety within your nervous system by taking turns to listen to each other. Ask for a hug. Ask if the other can tell you that you're still loved when you feel this way.

What makes you feel connected to another person?

THE THREE COMPONENTS OF PLEASURE

"We live in a fantasy world, a world of illusion. The great task in life is to find reality."
- Iris Murdoch

The three components of pleasure, *attention, meaning* and *stimuli,* are all about bringing your attention to what is physically happening in your skin—and to know the difference between sensation and the stories we all attach to our experience of touch. Noticing stimuli through focused attention is a necessary factor for somatic awakening.

3 COMPONENTS OF PLEASURE

ALL 3 COMPONENTS ARE CONNECTED SIMULTANEOUSLY

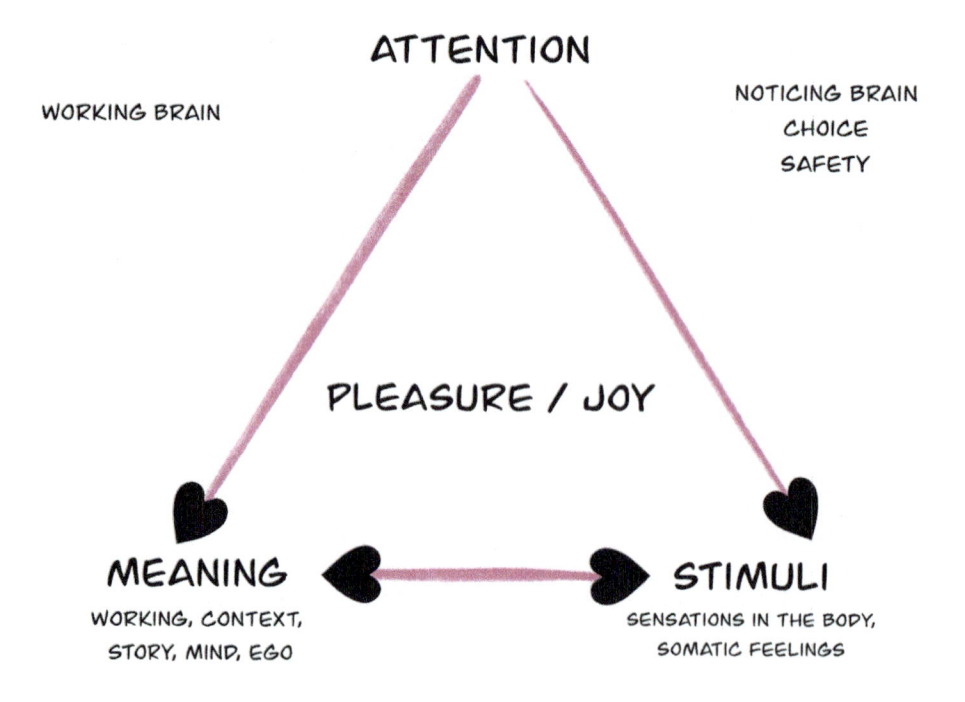

ATTENTION

WORKING BRAIN

NOTICING BRAIN
CHOICE
SAFETY

PLEASURE / JOY

MEANING
WORKING, CONTEXT,
STORY, MIND, EGO

STIMULI
SENSATIONS IN THE BODY,
SOMATIC FEELINGS

WHEN WE SLOW DOWN, WE CAN CHOOSE WHERE OUR ATTENTION GOES

WWW.SOMATICCONSENT.COM

This map contains aspects of the Noticing and Meaning Map and the Direct and Indirect Route of Pleasure Map.

When you practise waking up your hands you are engaging the *noticing* part of your brain. This is the part of the brain we wake up through mindfulness of any sort.

When your *noticing brain* is activated, you can *choose* to bring your moment-to-moment attention *internally*—i.e. to what's going on inside your body regarding thoughts, feelings and sensations—or *externally* to what is going on outside your body.

When you direct your attention to your internal world, there are two different things you could focus on:

- Attention to **stimuli** (the sensations coming in via the *Direct Route of pleasure*) or;

- Attention to **meaning** (the story your mind links to whatever is happening) and the *Indirect Route of pleasure,* such as thoughts, fantasies, agenda/goal towards climax or your partner's positive response to what is happening.

Attention to stimuli vs attention to meaning

Stimuli refers to the *Direct Route of pleasure* and your **somatic experience**. You notice what is happening on your skin, because of the *inflow* of sensations from physical stimuli.

Because of the incredible amount of nerve endings in your hands, when you bring all your attention to them and slow down enough—you notice sensations in the form of pleasure being relayed via the nerves which connect to nerve cells in your brain. When you do this, you *intensify* the experience.

If, however, while touching someone with one hand, you're holding something such as your mobile phone in the other and focusing on that, you won't feel much at all from your contact to the person because your attention is zoomed in instead, like the lens of a camera, onto the phone. Maybe you've noticed how it feels, when your partner is distracted—and their attention isn't present to their own experience when they touch you. Would you agree that being touched with full presence is a much more intensive, intimate and exquisite experience?

Meaning is related to the context your working brain gives to your experience and the *Indirect Route of pleasure*. It is the story your working brain comes up with during action, the meaning your mind gives to what is happening. This alters how you feel about your experience.

We all have a tendency to get lost in the story and meaning, which can be triggered by touch. Instead of focusing on the present moment, connecting to ourselves and to our partners, we often drift into making future plans, indulge in past memories or create sexual fantasy.

If, while touching your partner, your attention jumps from being aware of the stimuli in your hands—to how your partner may be feeling, or you begin to wonder what your partner may be thinking about what you're doing—the *meaning* takes the attention away from the *stimuli* and your *direct experience*. When your thoughts about the other's experience become more present than your own sensations, their response becomes more important than embodying your own experience of touch. You lose your ability to fully sense the stimuli coming in from your hands, as the *meaning* (story) gains prime attention and the stimuli takes second place.

The Direct Route of stimuli and Indirect Route of meaning exist simultaneously. The barrier to growth is that most people have a dependency on the other person's response through the *Indirect Route* (meaning) and neglect the connection possible by tuning into their own sensations, independent of any story (stimuli).

When something comes into contact with your skin, you recognise input that travels to your sensory cortex as raw data. The *working mind* gives meaning to your experience, creating *context* which amplifies the stimuli, or suppresses it, either consciously or unconsciously. This affects how you emotionally feel about that touch—whether it's connected to a story of love, foreplay, eroticism or something else.

A common meaning (story) many get caught up in is; "When I touch someone it is foreplay to sensual pleasure—which is foreplay to sexual arousal—which is foreplay to sex. When the sensation of the stimuli is *attached to the meaning*—that sensual pleasure must lead to sexual encounter—and sexual encounter must lead to sex—and sex must lead to orgasm, we create a *meaning* atop of the stimuli. This has a negative effect on the stimuli. It gives the stimuli we feel an added *agenda*. So that whenever we feel stimuli, we go through this protocol.

The stimuli and meaning are usually and naturally inter-related. They are always present together. We have to be able to differentiate between them, however, so that the stimuli isn't 'over-written' by the meaning (stories) we attach to them.

All lines linking the three points in the Three Components of Pleasure Map are equally important.

Awareness of where you direct your attention (to 1. meaning or 2. stimuli)

Awareness of the relative focus you give to either component.

The main learning here is the possibility to differentiate and choose.

Visualisation Experiment

Imagine that right now, your lover (or someone you'd like to be your lover) is wrapping their arms around you...

Feels good, right? Now imagine the same thing happening while you're standing on a bus. Now, turn around and see it's not your lover embracing you—but a stranger.

Not so nice right? The same situation with a different *meaning* can create a different experience and possibly be a complete turn off.

Now imagine you turn around and see a great friend you've been missing. They've been away for a year and wanted to surprise you. How would that feel? Is that a more pleasant scenario?

To become fully embodied in somatic experience we have to be capable of understanding the difference between *meaning* and *sensory stimuli*. Otherwise, the meaning will always interfere, speaking loudly over your experience, dictating its 'story' so that the sensations can't be sensed in their purity and depth.

---

*Focusing your full attention on the sensory stimuli in the present moment without any story whatsoever is the Direct Route and the **primary dynamic**.*

> *Focusing attention on any meaning you give to your experience is a 'bonus or éxtra' formulated by the working brain, the indirect Route and **secondary dynamic**.*

> *When the difference is clear, we are fully capable of using and intensifying the meaning through conscious choice. We are aware of any meaning without losing connection to our own direct experience.*

To break out of any mind loop dictated by the working brain, ask yourself where your attention is being directed. This way, when you touch someone or something you can choose to bring your attention to the action itself—and in doing so, you can more easily tune into the sensations being experienced by your skin.

Have you ever been touched by someone who is fully engaged in the experience with you, while having their attention in the experience of their own skin instead of creating a story about what their touch means to you? This is, in many cases, the most exquisite touch we can experience. It feels full, flowingly authentic, present and alive.

Differentiating between the direct and indirect route and using them together

When you activate your hands to become aware of the Direct Route of pleasure, you bring your full attention to the stimuli. As the meaning making (story or context) is going on at the same time, it can be difficult to differentiate between the two routes; however, when you consciously choose to focus on the *stimuli* you experience the full depth of your tactile sensory capacity. This tremendously increases the possibility for pleasure and opens up a deeper connection to self and your partner as you explore touch in a more genuine manner—because while doing so you become less dependent on fantasy, story or meaning.

When you've significantly raised your awareness of the stimuli *and* are able to focus on it without getting lost in the meaning, you're able to differentiate between the two routes. Then, specifically when it comes to touching others, it's easy to *add* the Indirect Route of 'meaning 'as a sort of 'bonus 'on top of what you already feel—like the icing on the cake. The increased amount of pleasure and connection that ensues is only possible when you're aware of *the difference between the two routes* of pleasure in the first place.

THE PULL AND THE PUSH OF PLEASURE

"Pushing will get a person almost anywhere - except through a door marked pull."
- Unknown

We all have the capacity to feel pleasure and it's vital for our physical and mental well-being. This is a well-researched fact in the fields of physiology and neurology. Inability to feel pleasure, or *anhedonia*, is one of the most important factors influencing many psychological problems, including depression.[29] Feeling pleasure releases the neurotransmitter dopamine, which lights up the reward centre in your brain.

We all know and want more pleasure—so why is it sometimes elusive? One less researched or understood element of pleasure is that you cannot push or force it. Do you generally feel relaxed if you force yourself to do something? Pushing or forcing doesn't calm the nervous system at all. It's more likely to make you feel unsafe and trigger the fight or flight response. Do you feel pleasure when you're on high alert? Not usually!

We gain pleasure from many sources and they are all connected to our senses. What kind of food and drink do you get pleasure from? How about the things you like to listen to? Music, the sounds of nature, someone giving you a compliment or saying, "I love you"? Which scents do you prefer? What kind of visuals light you up? Maybe a view of the ocean, scenery during a road trip, a loved one's face, art, a friend laughing with you, your favourite team playing a game? We tend to be pretty clear about the rest of our senses. We know what we love to see, hear, smell and taste.

When it comes to touch, many of us are a little mixed up. We tend to think that we 'should 'want or do things that we don't actually *want* at all. This, of course, is due to social conditioning—generalisations about what's 'normal' imprinted in our subconscious from films, novels, articles, peers, advertisements and other stories. We are programmed into accepting these expectations—and push ourselves and others to adhere to them. We often do what we 'think 'we ought to because we've generally accepted it as the norm (and fear being rejected if we want something different). When this happens, we get distracted away from the actual pleasurable sensations we may feel, as we try pushing through with our habitual processes.

> *The nervous system needs to be in a state of relaxation for you to be able to notice the inflow of sensations from touch.*
>
> *This means you can't focus on sensations and push yourself to perform at the same time. As soon as you start pushing you lose the ability to go deeper.*

What can we do? The answer is to be aware of what *feels like a push* and what *feels like a pull*.

A push feels something like this: "I really don't like that but I should feel comfortable with it by now."

When we think this, we tend to force ourselves to go through or along with whatever it is—and may think there is something wrong with us for not being comfortable with the situation. Or we go into habitual action to seek pleasure that finally leads to a 'pleasure goal 'such as orgasm.

Pushing is in total contrast to everything this book is about.

A pull feels something like this: "That sounds exciting! I'd love to do or try it".

Maybe it's something you already like or would really like to experiment with. You may feel a little nervous about it if it's a new experience, but nevertheless, you feel *drawn* to get pleasure from that experience. By following the *pull* to your own pleasure without any notion of a pre-planned route to a goal, you explore the moment and see where it takes you.

Following the pull rather than the push is relevant for many experiences in life of course. I remember times in the past when I eagerly tried to push myself through an experience everyone else was doing. One example was a breathwork session that promised transformative spiritual experiences.

There was quite a bit of peer pressure in the group and I wanted to belong—so I allowed myself to be coaxed and pushed by the facilitator to go deeper, 'to fake it till you make it 'and to push through any resistance I felt. It didn't work for me and back then I didn't understand why. A few years later I had a very different experience. The facilitator wasn't pushy at all, instead he invited me to find the intuitive flow of my breath, to allow it to go wherever it wanted to take me, even if the breath was suspended for some moments. I followed the joy of my breath rather than pushing myself to breathe in a way that didn't feel good to me. This was a much deeper and liberating experience.

Can you think of times you've followed the pull? How did that feel?
Can you think of times you gave in to the push? How did that feel?

When you follow the pull to your own pleasure, you bring your awareness to where you *already feel pleasure.* Imagine you're already experiencing some kind of pleasurable touch, maybe feeling someone's hand on your back, holding someone's hand or sharing a hug. This already feels good right?

When you bring your full attention to the pleasure you are already feeling what happens? That's right—the pleasure increases! This is because, by bringing your attention to the inflow of sensations, you activate the Direct Route of pleasure. In doing so, much more information is relayed from your skin to the pleasure sensors in your brain. This starts a chain reaction. Your nervous system relaxes, your brain waves slow down, your breathing regulates, your blood pressure normalises and your muscles soften. With these changes, you experience a general state of pleasurable well-being.

Next time you feel like you're pushing yourself, I invite you to stop, take a breath and notice any inner dialog. Do you notice yourself thinking you should be feeling something different? An urge to speed up or to follow a well-versed pattern of touch? Do you feel any pressure to perform? Now, instead, feel into the pull. Wait for the impulse towards what *already* feels good —and slowly follow the impulses of that *pull*. When you feel pleasure it's like a warm light in the dark beckoning you to come towards it. Rather than trying to control it or to change its location, notice that warm light and follow its lead. Allow yourself to relax into the pleasure you're *already experiencing* —whatever or wherever that pleasure is.

When you're aware of your 'pulls', you'll be aware of what you want and have the insight to ask for it.

When you're aware of the 'pushes' you'll know where your boundaries are, be able to set limits in agreements with others or/and, consciously explore expanding your comfort zones.

RECEIVING WHAT YOU REALLY WANT AND GIVING WHAT YOU ARE WILLING TO GIVE

"Every gift requires two freedoms: the giver's and the receiver's."
- Peter Kreeft

Receiving and giving are major themes within Somatic Consent. Many common quotes state something along the lines of, "You can only truly receive if you can give". However, as you've most definitely noticed while reading, all my research points to the opposite. Without learning how to fully receive, you never learn how to truly give without an agenda.

But what does that actually mean? Being able to fully receive means we acknowledge our needs—accepting, respecting and caring for ourselves. It's what self-love is about.

Receiving is one of the most natural things we do, it's how the somatic nervous system functions. We receive information from the environment that we come into contact with. The inflow of information perceived by sensory nerves in your skin enables you to *feel and experience the world*.

When we receive the nourishment we need, we feel grounded in self, whole and able to simply and authentically be *who we are*. This is the true essence of experiencing yourself as a gift. Rather than being selfish, it is the vital step in being able to *give unconditionally*. This means being able to give and let the gift go, allowing the other to do with the gift as they please, while being free of any attachment or sense of 'you owe me'.

We often say; "I want to give you...." and mostly assume that the person we're with also wants to have that. We presume the giving is for them, when in reality, we are the one who wants something.

> *The hands are connected to the heart, they are symbolic for giving and receiving. Waking up your hands is the easiest and most profound way of developing your ability to receive so that you can truly give from a place of love and care.*

Want to and willing to

Before we look at receiving and giving in more detail, let's look at *want* and *willing to*. These are very important to differentiate between.

Want to is something *you* want for *your* own reasons because it brings *you* a benefit. It might or might not have something to do with another person (*them*). The 'pleasers' and 'helpers' amongst us might say, "I want to do nice things for other people". But truthfully ask yourself what it is that you're receiving in return. Maybe it's seeing the other's face light up, or feeling the excitement build before giving them a surprise present and feeling appreciated in return. Maybe whatever you want to do for the other will also make your life easier in some way. In most cases, whenever we want something, we want to *receive* something.

If you want to, it's about **receiving** *for you.*

Willing to is something you wouldn't choose for *yourself.* Nevertheless, you're *willing to* do something or allow something to be done to you because you care about *them* (the other). It's something *they* want, that brings *them* some kind of benefit.

If you are willing to, it's about **giving** (a gift) and it's *for them.*

There's a whole spectrum between *want to* and *willing to*, a whole array of subtle differences between feeling a, "Hell yes, I want that" and what you may be ok about doing (willing to do). We'll explore how to tune into your boundaries and Spectrum of Limits soon.

For now, let's look at the difference between what we **want to receive** and what we are **willing to give**. When the difference is fuzzy, it gets much harder to ask for and receive what you want—as well as maintain your boundaries. We often end up going along with things we only feel lukewarm about or would really prefer not to do. This then, of course, leads to misunderstanding and resentment. A much better solution is to:

1. Discern what you want (and don't want)—which you learned by tuning into your sensory inflow and becoming more embodied and centred in self.
2. Be able to ask for what you want and be able to receive it/ say what you don't want and set limits.

With practice, it becomes easy to know the difference between want to and willing to. With this knowledge clearly in place we really understand what our desires actually are—and can ask for them. When we receive what we ask for, *we focus on just that*. Not on doing or giving back but *receiving in the moment*.

Receiving is inherently vulnerable. When you receive fully you come into connection with feelings of deep gratitude totally unconnected to any sense of duty, guilt, payback or reciprocity. When we believe we owe somebody something for their gifts, we tend to focus on perpetually giving back—without relaxing into the pure form of receiving.

It is in **fully receiving** that we learn how to **fully be.** When we can fully be, we know how to **fully give**. We fully give when we don't need anything back in return. This happens when we come from an unconditional, altruistic place of love and care which we'll talk about in much more depth very soon.

Learning Giving and Receiving

In order to give without wanting something, we have to stop giving for a while to find out how receiving feels.

When we embody receiving we can put our desire aside. Without knowing our desire, we can't put it aside.

When we know what we need to put aside, giving becomes clear and authentic, because receiving will be authentic.

Receiving
- Put your desire first / what do you want
- Take care of their limits / what are they willing to

Giving
- Take care of your limits / what are you willing to
- Put your desire aside / what do they want

www.somaticconsent.com

Receiving and giving can be confusing if we focus on the action

Can I ask you to reflect for a few moments on the words receiving and giving?

What comes to mind?

Did you find yourself thinking of *receiving* as something that happens *to you*? Did you find yourself connecting *giving* to being *in action*?

Now experiment by leaving aside who is doing the action. Imagine yourself in a scenario where receiving is *for you*—and giving is *for them*.

Does that feel different?

Let's break down each word to see why it gets confusing if we focus on **the action** *instead of* **who it is for.**

How we usually perceive receiving

When you **receive** it can be something that comes your way and happens to you. Can you think of all the things you've received in your life? Presents, appreciation, an electricity bill, an insult, an email, a smile, a dinner invite, a telephone call, a hug, a suggestion, a slap, your salary, an award, a report, good news, bad news. All these things come towards you or happen to you. They are *for you* but aren't all necessarily what you **want**. Does that sound right? They are happening to you whether you want them or not.

The other type of receiving

When you ask another person for permission to go into action toward them, *for yourself,* you create a whole new dynamic. Let's say you want to stroke someone's hair, you ask, they say yes and you go into action. So, you're the one in action. It isn't happening to you, nothing is coming towards you. But you are **receiving** what you want, which means it is *for you.*

How we usually perceive giving

When you **give** it can mean you are going into action, doing something to/for another or presenting something to someone (whether the other person wants it or not). Have you ever done something to someone as a gift that they didn't seem too excited about? Sometimes we give because it feels good. In this case, ask yourself who the gift is actually for.

The other type of giving

You can also give a gift by allowing someone to do something to you (you are willing to allow them to go into action towards you—to do something they want to do). An example could be if you give someone permission to feel your arm (if that's what they expressed they wanted to do). You give a gift by giving permission, which allows the other access to your body.

In this case, you are *not* the one in action. They are. It is *for them*. But you are the one giving the gift of access.

No matter which direction the action is in, the gift is either *for you* (they're giving it to you and you're receiving it) or it's a gift *for them* (you're giving it to them and they're receiving it).

Don't worry if those concepts sound confusing or complicated right now. Giving and receiving in relation to touch are not clear for most people who haven't neurologically embodied the two separately. Through playing The 3 Minute Game in the next section, they'll become very clear and second nature—especially once you learn how to truly receive for yourself through awareness of the somatic inflow.

For now, just note that when I use the words *receive* and *give* it's **not about who's doing the action**, it's about **who the action is for.**

In the following chapters we're going to look very closely at **who the gift is for**. By doing this you'll experience both *receiving* and *giving* fully and have a lot of fun in the process.

When you play with the dynamics of 'who the gift is for' your old ways of relating will be challenged while new ways of experiencing pleasure will nourish and bring exciting change to your relationships. The practice will uncover different elements of yourself as you voice your needs and desires. By expressing what you want, you make yourself vulnerable—and in doing just that, deeper understanding, intimacy and connection are free to flow.

A student of the SCES shared her experience of a touch exchange exercise:

"When it was my turn to receive (his action for me) I sat and closed my eyes. The guy in action began touching me so gently on my arm and hand that I began to cry. He continued to stroke my face slowly, gently wiping the tears away. It was the first time I'd been touched with presence without feeling the pressure of an agenda. It was quite a realisation for me. I remember feeling a lot of grief for past wasted opportunities when I could have been experiencing this kind of touch and instead settled for less".

Let's take a closer look at understanding *who the gift in an agreement is for.* This will enable you to expertly clarify your pulls and pushes—and give you the tools to make conscious choices towards or away from them.

THE 3 MINUTE GAME

"You can discover more about a person in an hour of play than in a year of conversation."
- Plato

The 3 Minute Game is the perfect tool to help us become fluent in practising consent. It's an extremely fun practice involving touch. Touch, as you know, comes in all forms and isn't always sexual. Therefore, you really don't have to be lovers to play. You can play with family members, friends or as a practitioner with your clients. I'm sure you'll be astounded at what becomes possible through playing. It's much more than just a fun or superficial game. Although very simple to play, it takes you to the very roots of who you authentically are.

The 3 Minute Game isn't about performing a specific kind of touch—or doing anything that doesn't feel right or comfortable. Instead, it encourages you to *feel into* what's true, right and genuinely pleasurable for you and allow that to guide you. To follow the *pull* rather than the *push*. Not only does the quality of your touch and the amount of pleasure you receive through being touched dramatically increase; it helps clarify exactly what you're drawn towards and want—and how to put your trust in and value these aspects of yourself.

This game highlights your boundaries, enables you to express your limits and allows you to navigate the nature of consent. Much of this insight becomes apparent when you notice the embodied difference in feeling when you **receive** and **give**. By playing it'll become crystal clear that giving and receiving has nothing to do with who is in action—but is determined by **who the action is for**.

Playing The 3 Minute Game doesn't replace other interaction with your partner—but brings clarity to where it's difficult to ask for what you want, where it's difficult to say no, when self-care is necessary and where shadow strategies emerge.

When you wake up your dormant ability to tune into the information your nerves are relaying to your brain, not only do you wake up the potential to feel more pleasure in your hands—but the rest of your body too. When you combine this sensory awakening, tuning into your pleasure in-the-moment without a goal—with the empowerment The 3 Minute Game brings—you and your lover can experience ecstatic heights like never before. You can call this Tantra, sacred sexuality or whatever you like. The fact is, there is no limitation in the amount of pleasure we can feel and this simple practice expands our capacity for love and transformation.

It works best when you set aside the time to indulge in it, taking in turns and playing for at least 30 minutes and up to as long as you like. I suggest playing in a room or place where the atmosphere feels comfortable and right for all players. I recommend avoiding the bedroom or lying down the first few times to avoid any sexual association, until you become more adept at playing. Be curious and allow yourselves to explore. Then notice how your learnings influence and enrich your daily life as you progress over time, as you uncover elements of your being and tune into new depths.

The 3 Minute Game originates from professional life coach and spiritual director, Harry Faddis who worked as an instructor at the *Body Electric School* in Oakland, USA,
working mostly with gay men. In one of his workshops *Power, Surrender and Intimacy*, he noticed that most people found it very difficult to ask for what they really wanted.

Faddis was also inspired by the 13th century Sufi poet, Rumi's quote; "You must ask for what you really want. Don't go back to sleep."

What was this spiritual master getting at? How do we awaken when we ask for what we want? Faddis began exploring this question by inventing The 3 Minute Game.

He realised that, although asking for what we want sounded simple, it was a difficult thing for most to do. This game gave participants an equal share of time to receive what they wanted/ desired.

Through playing and observing others play he soon realised the depths we can go to through equal exchange, and the level of transformation and awakening possible when we perceive power dynamics in a different way. This happens when we *gift our power* from a place of *love and care* and feel gratitude when this is reciprocated. The game guides us from embodied and grounded well-being to the most evolved state any human can experience—

that of spiritual connection.

The original questions of The 3 Minute Game are:

1. What do you want to do *to me* for 3 minutes?
2. What do you want me to do *to you* for 3 minutes?

As you can imagine, 'doing' is a very broad field. There are so many things we can do. For this reason, Betty Martin, creator of the *Wheel of Consent* adapted Faddis 'game to a purely somatic version by narrowing all action down to touch.

Before playing the 3 minute game

Before you begin to play, take a few minutes to 'land' in your body. This simply means bringing your awareness away from the outer world of distraction—to your inner world. In doing so, you guide the working mind's focus away from making meaning, derived from your environment to calmly noticing your body and 'what is' in-the-moment. You can practice this by feeling an object in your hand for a few minutes while noticing the sensory inflow of the Direct Route.

Do you feel more grounded now? More centred? Do you feel that you've landed? If so, you're ready to play!

The feeling of landing, being grounded and steady in self is why we put so much emphasis in the beginning on the sensory inflow and how it all works. Now you can harvest the nectar of waking up pleasure in your hands!

How to play the 3 minute game in relation to touch

Take turns asking each other two questions.
With each question, you make an offer to the other person.

These two questions are both *offers* by one person, for the other to make a *request*. When requests are made by one person ("Can you…" / "Can I…") they need a, "I can…" or a, "You can…" from the other before consent is established and anything happens.

The four dynamics of the 3 minute game

The 3 Minute Game is a very simple tool to help you tune into and playfully express your authentic desires and limits in a safe container. By playing you explore the four different dynamics found within The Engagement Zones of the Somatic Consent Engagement System (SCES).

Each of the four Engagement Zones provide a different angle of insight into yourself and others as you play and relate. You'll find that each of them bring different qualities to your experience of touch and connection. They open up the possibility for much more transparency and ease, confidence and empowerment, consent, playfulness and intimacy.

You'll notice they also bring unconscious survival shadow strategies to the surface. This may include falling into the role of people-pleasing, being a martyr, feeling entitled, being greedy, pushing for or stealing what is not yours to take or other behaviour you may have habitually lapsed into and may not have been aware of before. They give us the opportunity to acknowledge these parts of ourselves and integrate them into personal growth. All four Engagement Zones guide to an interpersonal space that people can share. One of spiritual surrender—together.

These are the 4 dynamics you'll explore within the Engagement Zones

'You' refers to the reader. 'They' refers to the other person.

You do what you want - (You're in action for yourself)
You do what they want - (You're in action for them)
They do what they want - (They're in action for themself)
They do what you want - (They're in action for you)

- Each person takes turns to make the two *offers* to the other.
- Each person states their desire when it's their turn to make a *request*.
- Each person takes time to reflect on whether they feel within their limits towards what they are being asked to give—before answering authentically and giving permission/ coming to an agreement.

"How do you want me to touch you for 3 minutes?"

Person A: Makes the **offer**: "How do you want me to touch you for 3 minutes?"
Person B: Makes a **request**: "*Can you* give me a foot massage?"
Person A: (Reflects: "Is that within my limits?" Am I willing to give that kind of touch?") and answers accordingly, either agreeing to the request **(I can)**,

expressing their limits, such as, "Only if you wash your feet" or saying "no" if it isn't what they are willing to do (is beyond their limits).

Person B: Respects person A's limits and an **agreement** is made by both for person A to go into action for person B (for them).

"How do you want to touch me for 3 minutes?"

Person A: Makes the **offer**: "How do you want to touch me for 3 minutes?
Person B: Makes a **request**: "*Can I* feel your back?"
Person A: (Reflects: "Is that within my limits?" Am I willing to allow that kind of touch?") and answers accordingly, either giving **permission** to the request **(you can)**, expressing their limits, such as, "Yes, but don't scratch, pinch or poke me" or saying "no" if it isn't what they are willing to allow (it's beyond their limits).
Person B: Respects person A's limits and has permission to go into action for themself.

It's important to keep your attention on what is actually agreed upon. Sometimes we may have an urge to change the dynamics and follow the impulses, thinking "Oh I'm sure they'd like me to… (touch them in another way or in another place)".

Is this actually something you have agreed on?

The game teaches us to take turns. It shows you when to put your own desires first and when to put your desires aside, so that you or the other can relax into the action when it's for you and enjoy *exactly what is being asked for*.

3 MINUTE GAME

ORIGINAL BY HARRY FADDIS
POWER, SURRENDER AND INTIMACY

ADAPTATION, RELATED TO TOUCH

- WHAT DO YOU WANT TO DO TO ME?
  - ↕ OFFER
- HOW DO YOU WANT TO TOUCH ME?

⟩ GIVE, LIMITS, WILLING TO, DONE TO, THEIR ACTION

WHEN YOU MAKE AN OFFER
1) PUT YOUR DESIRE ASIDE
2) RESPECT YOUR LIMITS

- WHAT DO YOU WANT ME TO DO TO YOU?
  - ↕ OFFER
- HOW DO YOU WANT ME TO TOUCH YOU?

⟩ GIVE, LIMITS, WILLING TO, DOING, YOUR ACTION

START FROM RECEIVING WITHOUT THE OFFER

- CAN I...?, MAY I...? = RECEIVE, DESIRE, DOING, YOUR ACTION
  - ↕ REQUEST
- CAN YOU...?, WILL YOU...? = RECEIVE, DESIRE, WANT, THEIR ACTION

WHEN YOU MAKE A REQUEST
1) PUT YOUR DESIRE FIRST
2) RESPECT THEIR LIMITS

JUST ASK THESE TWO QUESTIONS TO PLAY THE GAME AND TO EMBODY SOMATIC CONSENT.

PLAY THIS GAME A FEW HUNDRED TIMES
3, 5, 10, 30, X MINUTES.

WWW.SOMATICCONSENT.COM

I prefer to be intuitive when I touch; Will this disrupt the natural flow?

Some people are sceptical when first introduced to the dynamics of The 3 Minute Game. Many of us believe we know ourselves and our preferences pretty well by now, and may dig our heels in when an alternative is offered. This is all normal and natural. We all want to do things our way. **The 3 Minute Game will help you to do this more.**

I'm often asked; "Doesn't it make touching more awkward?", "How can I relax and be embodied when I have to think about what I'm allowed to do or not?" or I'm told, "I prefer to be in the flow when touching," or "I can already intuitively feel if something is right or wrong."

The 3 Minute Game isn't meant to replace the natural flow of touch within your relationships. It's a *training tool* to help you expand your present habits of touch. Think of it more as a doorway to deep relaxation, insight, increased pleasure and greater empowerment.

Firstly, it provides the safety necessary for both people to fully relax. You create a space where you can truly let go. What happens when you feel safe? You no doubt allow yourself to be, authentically—as you are. In other words, you are in the most optimal place to really flow with what feels true and right for you.

Desires ever change and we only ever live in the here and now.
If you don't feel safe you most likely know what you don't want.
You can only know what you really want in-the-moment, when you feel safe.

Secondly during the game, we learn the dynamics of interaction and differentiate between *who is doing the action* and *who it is actually for* as well as clarifying any problems separating the Direct Route from the Indirect Route of pleasure.

Playing The 3 Minute Game also gives you real insight into what is happening with the person you're in contact with. Naturally, touching someone is by no means only about one person. Both people have to want to play. If we only fixated on what one person wants and doesn't it'd be a pretty one-sided interaction, void of any real connection or possibility for intimate exploration.

One SCES practitioner shared that playing with different people helped her explain it using different terminology. And that each time she plays, she becomes more and more confident in an embodied way, adding to her ability to flow with what she desires. Her partner was a little unsure about playing at first, wondering whether she was trying to trick him into something or worried that he'd feel judged. After playing he discovered for himself what her enthusiasm was all about, felt the benefits for himself, enjoys owning and voicing his truth and is now as excited to play as she is.

Being 'intuitive 'when touching helps, but this would be relying purely on the Indirect Route and your own perception of 'how things are'. Doesn't it make much more sense to understand how it is for your partner by listening to their own direct experience? Here there is no room for presumption.

It is deeply illuminating to share your truth with another person. When we feel heard and seen we can more easily relate to the other. Connection, bonding and intimacy result from this. Once your skin and nervous system has embodied a new understanding of touch, you and your partner will be able to expand together so much more naturally and authentically than before.

As you can see, although The 3 Minute Game may question certain presumptions and habits, rather than complicate your experience of touch, it reteaches you to deeply let go so that you can expand your present experiences of touch—by learning how to *receive* and *give* phenomenal pleasure.

Before beginning The 3 Minute Game it's fundamental to know the following:

Asking for *permission*, expressing *limits* and making *agreements* **together** are an integral part of the SCES. The whole system won't function without this basic framework. These conditions are not about teaching other people about their boundaries or about pushing others in any way whatsoever.

We aren't able to go into conscious action without permission, agreements and the acknowledgement of boundaries.

- Permission and agreements define consent
- Our spoken limits protect our boundaries

These fundamental aspects of consent are not about 'what one person wants'. Your preferences, personality, perception or personal philosophy have nothing to do with this framework.

These are not pedantic rules or unnecessary structure that restrict you from following your 'flow'. On the contrary, it's about tuning into *what is real* and creating a container where *both are safe* to *follow their flow* because **both know what will happen**.

Soon we'll explore exactly how the two questions in The 3 Minute Game enable you to maintain the natural flow of a touch. This is the experience I later refer to as the 'Apex'.

Is the 3 minute game about sex?

The 3 Minute Game isn't about learning sexual techniques or specific things to spice up your established routine. It's an exploration of self, of touch and the connection and intimacy possible with another person. Knowing and expressing what you want and don't want makes such a difference to who you are on every level. It's an entirely new way of experiencing yourself and relating. This means that your sexual experience will naturally be infused with a richness you've never encountered before.

The need for touch and the need for sex

The need for touch and in particular touch that isn't sexual, is fundamental to our well-being. It nourishes a different part of us than sexual activity does. There are many different ways to experience touch that aren't about sex, such as hugging your kids and friends, holding hands, having a massage or cuddling.

Touch is a human need that helps us experience other people and connect with them emotionally. Your nervous system also needs stimulus on your skin to function properly. If you don't get enough touch, the nervous system's capacity for co-regulation (by coming into contact with others) into a state of relaxation is diminished.

The amygdala is responsible for your fight or flight response. It monitors your environment so that you can avoid potential danger. When it perceives a potential threat, stress hormones are released. Through sensual and importantly *consensual* touch (either alone or with another) oxytocin is released in the limbic system. Oxytocin not only increases connection to others but inhibits the release of stress hormones cortisol and adrenaline. This balances the nervous system—enabling you to self or co-regulate and restore a sense of ease and well-being.

This is the reason why, in challenging moments, the practice of waking up the hands by feeling an object gives you the self-soothing capacity to calm your ner-

vous system whenever you need to!

The 'need 'for sex is more accurately, a need to express ourselves as sexual beings, which we do through how we express our gender, who we find attractive and our sexual preferences. It's *not the need* for a specific sexual activity.

Your need for touch can't be met through sex, and your need to express yourself as a sexual being can't be met through touch—because they're different human needs like breathing and drinking. You can't quench your need for water by breathing air, and vice versa.

Sex and touch are related to two different parts of the brain. One is the emotional touch centre, the other, the reward centre. Sex can work without emotion when it's locked in the internal fantasy world—and feeling can work without any sex at all. Sure, both combined together give a completely different meaning and that's why many stories are based on the conflation. When you know how to distinguish between these different needs, as you experiment, you'll discover deeper layers of your sensual self and bring much more awareness and flow to sexual play.

THE 3 MINUTE GAME AND THE DIRECT ROUTE OF PLEASURE

"Play is the highest form of research."
- Albert Einstein

After awakening my own sensual inflow, I began implementing The 3 Minute Game in empowerment sessions with students and clients in my professional practice and came up with the same results over and over again.

When I asked, "What do you find pleasurable and how do you want me to touch you?" I soon realised that almost nobody could relate to this question and most looked confused, responding with; "Just do something", or "You're the expert, don't you know what to do?" or "Nobody's ever asked me that before, I don't know".

With the second offer, "How do you want to touch me?", most people would go completely blank. If they did respond, they mostly did so to get a reaction, saying something such as, "I want to tickle you", or "I want to slap you", or "I'm afraid of what I'd do if I could". They often wanted to pinch, hair pull and dominate. Most would stare at my face while doing so, to see how and if I'd respond. Sometimes people tried to turn me on, in order to allow themself to be turned on, using my turn on as justification to allow themself to feel. Others would be too ashamed to feel themselves when touching me or be afraid of getting turned on—and so avoided it altogether.

While playing within these dynamics with clients, they sometimes did something to knowingly cause me pain. I purposefully tried not to react (within my limits) to make their response agenda obvious to them. And all these interactions rang a bell. It was extremely interesting to recognise my own previous habits of reaction in other people. I realised I'd responded in similar ways when I'd started to experiment with the dynamic of *my action for my pleasure*—often going into action to get a reaction. This was before I'd embodied the Direct Route and was still functioning purely from my working mind and its meaning making dynamic with an agenda.

It became clear that most people had difficulties with the two offers of The 3 Minute Game and the four different dynamics they open up when both take turns. And it became obvious why. The Direct Route is *dormant* for almost all of us. This means that most of us are unaware that we can receive through *our own action for our own pleasure*—and so, most of us engage and relate within the Indirect Route as our default.

The direct route
The vital element to spiritual growth
via embodied empowerment

The Direct Route of sensory inflow must be embodied before playing The 3 Minute Game, otherwise we easily fall into our usual automatic habits of *doing* or *giving* something (due to the urge for recognition, appreciation, to be loved and to 'belong'). When we do this we simultaneously bypass what we actually want, desire and rings true to us. Whether our go-to habit is one of doing or one of giving will depend on where exactly we are 'stuck'.

In order to be able to fully *receive* through your own action, you first need to pause and stop *giving*. This concept is comparable to finding your true yes:

> *When we stop automatically saying 'yes', it enables us to find our true 'no'. Only when we're fully aware of what feels like a 'no', can we know our true 'yes'.*

When you stop giving, your focus can be directed to the inflow and you will feel the difference between the two routes. If you don't know how it feels to receive while you're in action (doing an action for yourself) it is difficult or near impossible to put yourself second while in action and giving for someone else. If we can't differentiate, the two dynamics get hopelessly mixed up.

The *Wheel of Consent* by Betty Martin was also inspired by Faddis '3 Minute Game. It helps clarify the difference between giving and receiving, as well as defining who is doing an action and who it's for. As already mentioned, when we're aware of who an action is for, the *do-er isn't always the giver*, but can be the *receiver* too. While very effective as a teaching aid for consent, I realised that the formula offered by the Wheel needed a substantial expansion. I saw the potential to guide spiritual growth related to power and surrender from an intimate place of love and care.

After six years of mentorship with Betty Martin, six months of background interviews and sessions with Harry Faddis and this realisation in mind, I developed the Somatic Consent Engagement System to *include this vital element*.

The SCES enables you to take all the fragmented parts of self and realise your wholeness. It guides you to become both grounded in self—and spiritually expansive. When the Direct Route is activated, the two questions in The 3 Minute Game guide both players to personal empowerment and an experience of spiritual connection.

The SCES provides logical and transparent bridges to;

- Your ability to perceive the sensory inflow of the Direct Route.
- Your capacity to recognise and integrate your personal shadows relating to the Indirect Route. Understanding when you're not asking for what you really want or acknowledging that you in fact have limits when you give.
- Absolute empowerment of self.
- Surrender to all you are—and through this become a vessel of receiving.
- Gift your power, from a genuine place of love and care to support others in surrendering to all they are.

All my research points to this combination providing the perfect balance of personal and spiritual growth, accessible to anyone.

*This version of The 3 Minute Game is meant for two-way touch within personal relationships. It plays out quite differently in a professional setting. We'll talk about these different dynamics later in Chapter 5.

SPIRITUAL CONNECTION THROUGH SURRENDER

"No matter where you are, you feel at home, because that feeling of home is the Divine within you."
- Panache Desai

We'll go into the deeper aspect of the human condition that practising The 3 Minute Game can reveal in much more depth in further chapters. For now, let's take our first look at the concept of surrender.

Faddis, the inventor of The 3 Minute Game has been a recovering alcoholic for over 30 years and is therefore very familiar with the second step of the AA's 12 step recovery program. This step states that your sanity can be restored by surrendering to a power greater than yourself.

By expressing authentic desire and relaxing into the 'being state of surrender '(the state of fully receiving), participants had the chance of experiencing this step while playing the game.

So how is your sanity restored by giving up your power/control? What is the power you are surrendering to and how can one truly surrender to it?

How is your sanity restored by giving up your power?

Your sanity is restored by giving up your power/control because you allow yourself in these moments to just be—as you are. There is a timeless peace experienced in the state of *just being.* Here there is no need to act or fulfil any role. The state of being is *total relaxation of the mind and nervous system* which enables a feeling of being complete. There is no pressure to go anywhere or do anything. Being is enough. You are enough. The other person is enough. In this state of bliss, we recognise the divine within each other. We can't usually dwell in this state at all times, however, whenever we're not in this state, there's an underlying sense of yearning or longing to be there, to connect in the most profound way to ourselves, others and the world around us.

What is meant by a power greater than yourself?

If we believe that someone has power over us and can therefore abuse us in some way, we will be intent on protecting ourselves and unwilling to surrender. Likewise, if we believe someone has no power, why would we surrender to them? Usually, the word 'power' is understood in the context of *abusive power over others*. We all have power or energy within ourselves.

When you play The 3 Minute Game you enter equal ground.

In the question: "Tell me what you want…", the 'wanting' person has a desire, something they want to receive—which the other has power over (they decide if they will give it or not).

Beyond this dynamic, due to his deep spiritual background, Faddis understood that the gift of power was not just limited to the giving side. Not only does the person in action give a gift of power/energy (that of altruistic love and care) so that the other can surrender—when the other can fully *experience themselves in their natural state of being within the state of surrender*, they also gift their own power/energy (by releasing their grasp on control). In this situation, *both are winning*. There is a shared *interpersonal* experience of *giving and receiving* where the separate 'giver' and 'receiver' dissolve, merging into the experiential gift of shared oneness. *This is the power which is greater than one individual self.*

When two people engage in power and surrender and the giver gives with a whole-hearted "yes", it is a gift for the other person. If the gift isn't given from a place of love and care *altruistically,* then the dynamic of interpersonal transcendence will not be possible. Love and care have to be the motivation behind the gift giving for the receiver to thrive in the connection of deep truth and trust. When love and care are present, the receiver *is able to* fully surrender.

The state of surrender (which enables the merging of oneness with others, the natural world and ultimately with Source/God/Super-Consciousness) is at the root of not only Tantra and Sufism, but all occult (*hidden*) mystic traditions, including those of Christianity and Judaism. The Kabbalah of mystic Judaism literally means **receptivity**. Its teachings outline the art of learning to receive Divinity. Rabbi David Aaron speaks exactly of this in his insightful teachings.[30] *"When you are offered a gift, do not take it; instead, make of yourself a space that can receive it."*

I understand this in the context of fully 'being 'in a state of surrender. To receive by allowing things to be—as they are. Also, in a very practical sense, it's a useful way to understand how to tune into the Direct Route. It's not about taking, *as an act* of grabbing or forcing. It's about relaxing into the being state, and while there in that presence, noticing what you are experiencing.

Ultimately, surrendering to a power greater than yourself is much different than giving away your power to another person. It's about giving up your power of control over a restricted sense of yourself as a separate unconnected individual. When you 'give this up 'by relaxing into *beingness/is-ness*—you surrender your limited concept of self. What results is a more expansive connection to your partner and infinite consciousness. This is a greater power than the separate individual sense of self/the limited ego of 'me', 'myself 'or the identification of 'I'.

How can we truly surrender?

Evolutionary speaking, most of us are still quite immature emotionally, sensually, sexually and spiritually. This is because we tend to repeat patterns of behaviour (shadow strategies) in order to get our needs met and to protect ourselves. We're so programmed to do this, believing that our actions should follow a certain pattern—that we tend not to question these old patterns, experiment with different approaches and find new territory. To have the courage to explore outside the box means engaging deeply with ourselves and others, which isn't always easy or without suffering. The more we practise, the easier it becomes. The more we share deeply, the more we are vulnerable, and, as long as both come from a place of love and care, within this vulnerability deep intimacy forms. This is a space where we can exchange the truth and trust necessary to enable surrender and expansive connection.

- *The key to spiritual connection is to be able to surrender into your natural state of being—without any need to do anything.*

- *To be able to surrender into your natural state of being, you have to know how to fully receive and be—just as you are.*

- *To be able to fully receive, the Direct Route must be embodied **without simultaneously** 'trying 'to give anything back in return.*

Are you ready to make the decision that changes everything?

The key to unlocking great personal growth and interpersonal experience is activating the noticing part of your brain in relation to touch by fully switching on your Direct Route of pleasure. Everything else emerges from this foundation. With this change, personal and interpersonal spiritual growth is very accessible.

- **If you want to embody the Direct Route**—by practising noticing and feeling—your experience has a great chance of flowing in the direction of increased pleasure, connection to self and intimacy in relationship.

- **If you don't want to embody the Direct Route**—your experience has a greater chance of sliding into the shadow of survival strategies that cause endless loops of repetitive misunderstanding and the breakdown of relationship.

If you decide just to play the game for fun, you can of course. But, if you want to awaken depth, freedom and flow within yourself and relationships, follow the outline above to experience the four dynamics in all the depth they can take you. Presence is what's required for the insightful 'lightbulb moments 'to happen, that will change *everything in your life*. It won't always be easy, but I promise it'll be very worth your while.

When you find the deeper layer of receiving through your own action, via the Direct Route, you recognise that as a human being (not a human doing) your most natural state is that of pure 'is-ness', which isn't at all dependent on any action you do. Playing The 3 Minute Game provides natural, personal and spiritual development, as you allow yourself to be—without a goal.

Are you ready for that kind of change? Are you ready for your standards to rise?

When you wake up your hands, your own experience of touch will be here in-the-now, evolving as you practise being sensually inspiring, intuitive and relaxed. This will make tactile experience much more enjoyable for yourself and the person you're touching. This naturally also means you'll get less and less tolerant of habitual, unremarkable touch from others. You'll notice immediately when someone you're engaging with isn't present to their experience in the way you are.

Start from where you are

You don't need any prior preparation or training. Your previous experience doesn't matter. What matters is that you're willing to explore beyond what you already know—that you're curious about expanding your experience of what's possible.

Much of how the process unfolds is dependent on the amount of awareness you've already developed about yourself, as well as your ability to notice and communicate what you want. There may be times you find it a little harder to tune in and times that feel vulnerable or embarrassing. You may also experience a limit in the amount of pleasure you can allow yourself to experience at first. (We'll talk about this more in the section entitled, The Pleasure Ceiling). Your old shadows may also show up from time to time and present challenges. However, this, I truly believe, is *part of the fun* of progress and evolution. There is definitely room for playfulness as we grow.

This process happens over time. I also still encounter new enriching discoveries while playing. We never stop learning and growing. Accepting that fact as a fundamental truth, provides the right space you need for your journey, allowing you to settle into 'just being', enjoying and allowing the experience of your pleasure to unfold.

- *It's very important that people you play the game with know that they are being initiated into a game that involves touch. Otherwise, obvious complications and misunderstandings will occur. A mutual desire to play this game is the first step of the consensual agreement.*

Check out the **Self-Love** online starter course which supports you in building a foundation of self-care and empowerment. The **Touch, Consent & Play App** guides and assists you in establishing the Direct Route of pleasure and playing The 3 Minute Game.

Self-Love course   Android App   IPHONE App

- Scan the QR code with your phone camera.
- For Android you may have to use a QR Code Reader app like 'Google Lens'.
- Choose your browser.
- You'll be directed to the webpage.

CHAPTER 2

THE SOMATIC CONSENT ENGAGEMENT SYSTEM

Tools For Mastering Pleasure, Desire And Consent

"Nobody can make you feel inferior without your consent."
- Eleanor Roosevelt

How do you usually engage with others?

Which ways of interacting with others are deemed correct by your culture?

Are there differences in the way you engage with your lover, friends, family, colleagues or strangers?

Do you feel more relaxed when you trust the person you're engaging with?

You already know that sensory neurons receive the inflow of information from your skin and relay it to your brain, producing the experience of sensation, pleasure and connection—while motor neurons send information to muscles to generate body movement.

You also know that it isn't enough to try grasping the concept of sensory inflow using only your analytical working mind. You have to have a real physical experience of it. Only then can your nervous system embody these new learnings, and open up a world of opportunity for growth and expansion.

Every human being has had the preverbal experience of being touched against their will and learned to undermine their feelings about it. We all learned at an early age to adapt ourselves to liking what we don't like, by trying to change *how we feel about it*—rather than changing *what is happening*.

We have all also been brainwashed into an ideology of what touch and relationship means. Most people have assumption-based relationships where second guessing is the norm. Because each of us has a unique experience of life, how we perceive can be very different. Due to this, what usually happens is that one person has one understanding and the other an entirely different one. This is usually never communicated so that friendships dissolve, family members become alienated from one another and misery occurs, based on the failure of the 'romantic dream 'which fell apart.

> *When you engage with another person, it is consent that creates the safety needed for the nervous system to work effectively and for sensations to be experienced fully.*

Assumption-based relationships don't usually last very long. Many couples stay together for the sake of their children and when the kids leave home, they're finally faced with one another. They then often find they not only have no idea who their partner is in any great depth—they have no idea who they are as individuals without them.

SOMATIC CONSENT ENGAGEMENT SYSTEM

-AFFERENT
INFLOW
SENSORY DATA
DIRECT ROUTE
OF PLEASURE

-PERMISSION CAN I...?
-AGREEMENTS CAN YOU...?
REQUEST OR OFFER

POLYVAGAL THEORY
-SOCIAL ENGAGEMENT SYSTEM
SAFTEY, CONNECTION INTIMACY

-EFFERENT
ACTION
MOTOR IMPULSES
MOVEMENTS

SOMATIC CONSENT

WWW.SOMATICCONSENT.COM

EXPLORING YOUR PERSONAL REALITY

"Your personality creates your personal reality."
- Dr. Joe Dispenza

This book relies on your ability to notice. So, let's begin with these questions;

Do you notice what you want?

Maybe you've never asked yourself this question seriously before. Maybe you're usually moving so quickly through life that you've never slowed down enough to feel what it is you really want.

I invite you to slow down right now and notice.

Take a few deep breaths in and breathe out with a sigh in order to quieten the chatterbox mind.

Let your body speak to you right here, right now. And if nothing comes up, take a little more time. Take all the time you need, because the answers are there—and are important.

Do you trust and value what you notice?

Did something arise?

Maybe a longing or desire?

Did you push it down?

Did you judge it to be wrong or bad?

The truth is, what you want matters. It doesn't matter what it is; it matters that you trust what comes up and value it as important to you. We often shut down our desires before they see the sunshine because we judge them. Maybe they're too embarrassing, maybe you're afraid of being too needy or too greedy. Maybe you're afraid of rejection.

Maybe you need to hear it again. What you want matters, and the more you trust that, the more you step towards empowering yourself.

Do you communicate what you want?

How often have you seen yourself chewing on something you want, too scared to speak it out?

How often have you minimised your desires, cutting them down to a size you think someone can deliver?

How often does your fear of rejection keep you from speaking your impulses?

How often have you not known how to express what you want?

You're not alone. It's inherently vulnerable to ask for what you want—but so freeing to take the leap and raise your voice by making a request. I recommend starting small.

Ask for something that doesn't feel too vulnerable.
It's like training a muscle.
It takes time, practice, determination and patience.
Try to ask others a few times a day: "Can I…?" or "Can you…?"

It doesn't have to be to do with touch. Can you please make me a cup of coffee? Can you help me with this? Can I come over later? Can I tell you how I feel?

Do you allow yourself to receive?

If you have the courage to ask and you receive a YES, feel for a moment and let this gift sink in. Know that you're worthy of receiving.

And when the response is a NO, notice whether you can still be in connection with what you want. Being able to own and express your desire is a gift. Notice also whether you can celebrate the limits of the other, because owning and honestly expressing our limits is a crucial part of authentic relating, consent and the development of intimacy.

Do you allow yourself to feel grateful?

Being grateful feels vulnerable, though the more you allow yourself to receive and acknowledge the gifts that come towards you, the more you'll expand your capacity to receive. What might at first feel scary and uncomfortable will begin to feel delicious and deeply nourishing.

As you expand your capacity to receive, you learn to fill yourself up. From this place of fullness, you then become capable of giving from a place of generosity—to yourself, to your loved ones and to the world you live in.

First and foremost, the Somatic Consent Engagement System shows just how important it is to find and function from a grounded place within yourself. This is your Base. The foundation of knowing and caring for yourself. Having a sturdy Base means you're aware of your needs, desires, boundaries and are able to set limits. It's also here where you learn to recognise the shadows of self which arise when your needs aren't met.

From here we'll explore the Engagement Zone—where you interact with another person and consent is asked for and granted through permissions and agreements. The Engagement Zones open up the *four empowering dynamics of relating.*

The Somatic Consent Engagement System was developed over many years of personal and professional practice and my own spiritual journey. It's presented as a three-dimensional pyramid structure, a map leading you to experience embodiment of trust, safety and connection through self-knowledge and consent. It includes the shadow world as well as higher spiritual dimensions of human connection.

ENGAGEMENT SYSTEM

INTIMATE RELATING, PERSONAL AND SPIRITUAL DEVELOPMENT BASED ON THE DYNAMICS OF CONSENT AND THE POLYVAGAL THEORY.

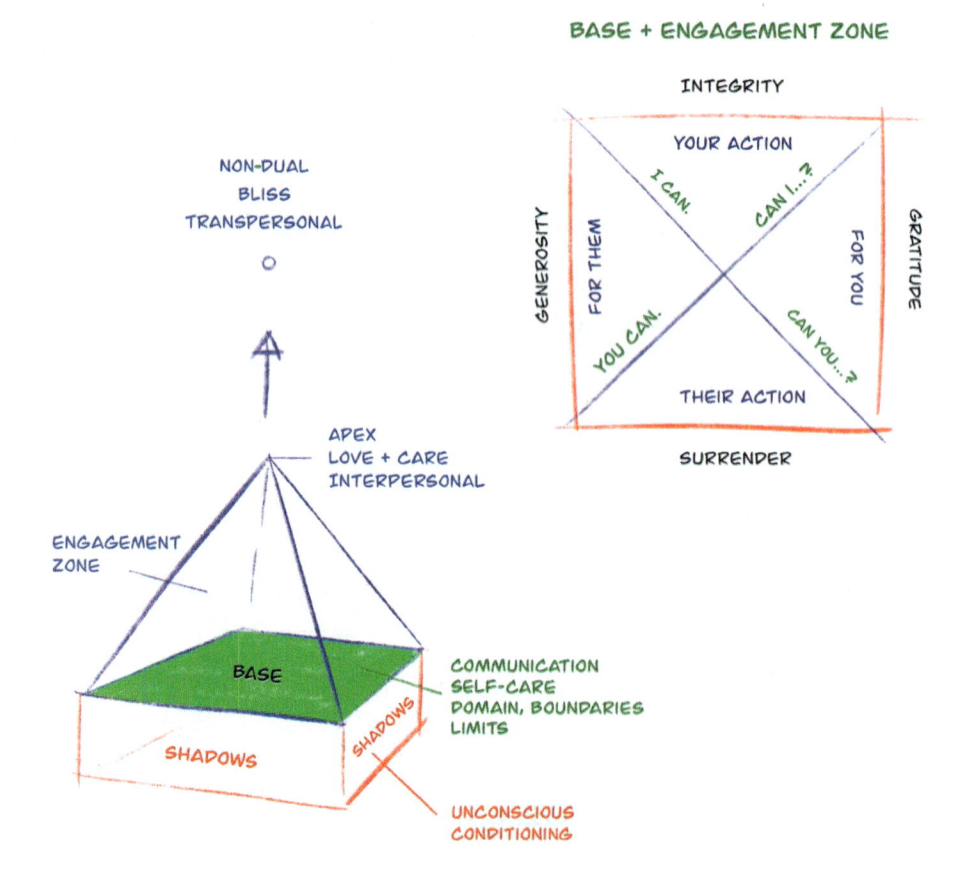

BASE + ENGAGEMENT ZONE

- INTEGRITY
- YOUR ACTION
- I CAN.
- CAN I...?
- GENEROSITY
- FOR THEM
- FOR YOU
- GRATITUDE
- YOU CAN.
- CAN YOU...?
- THEIR ACTION
- SURRENDER

- NON-DUAL BLISS TRANSPERSONAL
- APEX: LOVE + CARE, INTERPERSONAL
- ENGAGEMENT ZONE
- BASE
- COMMUNICATION, SELF-CARE, DOMAIN, BOUNDARIES, LIMITS
- SHADOWS
- UNCONSCIOUS CONDITIONING

WWW.SOMATICCONSENT.COM

- The 3D four-sided pyramid is built on a sturdy **Base**. The Base is you. It represents your solid foundation of self-care. It represents what you have a *right to* and *responsibility for* as an individual.
- Below the Base is the **Basement** which represents your subconscious. The subconscious houses all of your internal programming, all of your memories including those you use for creative inspiration. The Basement is the realm of shadow behaviour.
- Above the Base are the **Engagement Zones**, created by the four dynamics of The 3 Minute Game. This is a place of honest communication between yourself and other people, whether a lover, friend, family member, colleague or stranger. This is the place of experimentation where you and whoever you're engaging with get clear about who an action is for, ask for permission, communicate limits and come to agreements.
- At the top is the **Apex**, the interpersonal space of love and care where relationship is harmonious. Here we experience a win-win situation of relaxed being, fun, play and spiritual transformation.

On the right side is a 2D diagram of the same pyramid viewed from above. Here you can clearly see the four Engagement Zones.

ENGAGEMENT SYSTEM 3D
MULTI-DIMENSIONAL

TRANSPERSONAL

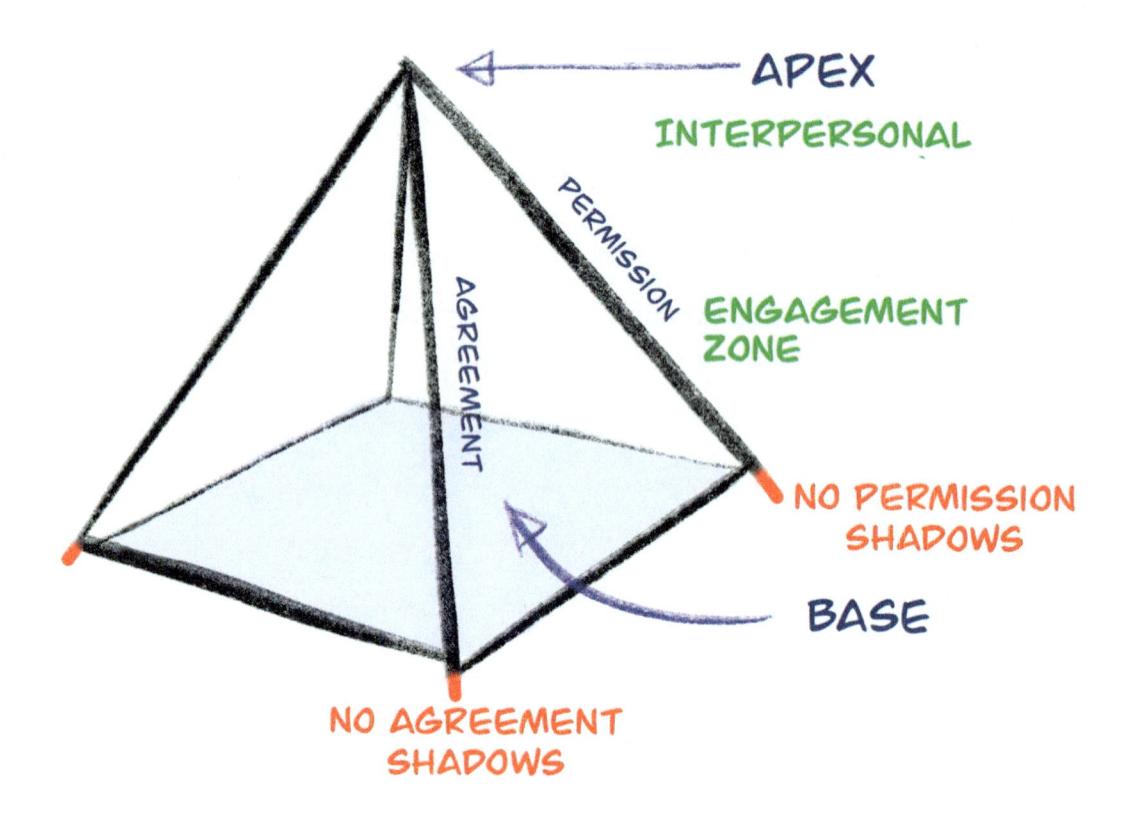

- APEX
- INTERPERSONAL
- PERMISSION
- AGREEMENT
- ENGAGEMENT ZONE
- NO PERMISSION SHADOWS
- BASE
- NO AGREEMENT SHADOWS

WWW.SOMATICCONSENT.COM

In the next map you can see the types of shadow behaviour that arise when we try to get our needs met without communicating what it is we want, asking for permission or coming to agreements.

SOMATIC CONSENT ENGAGEMENT SYSTEM MAP

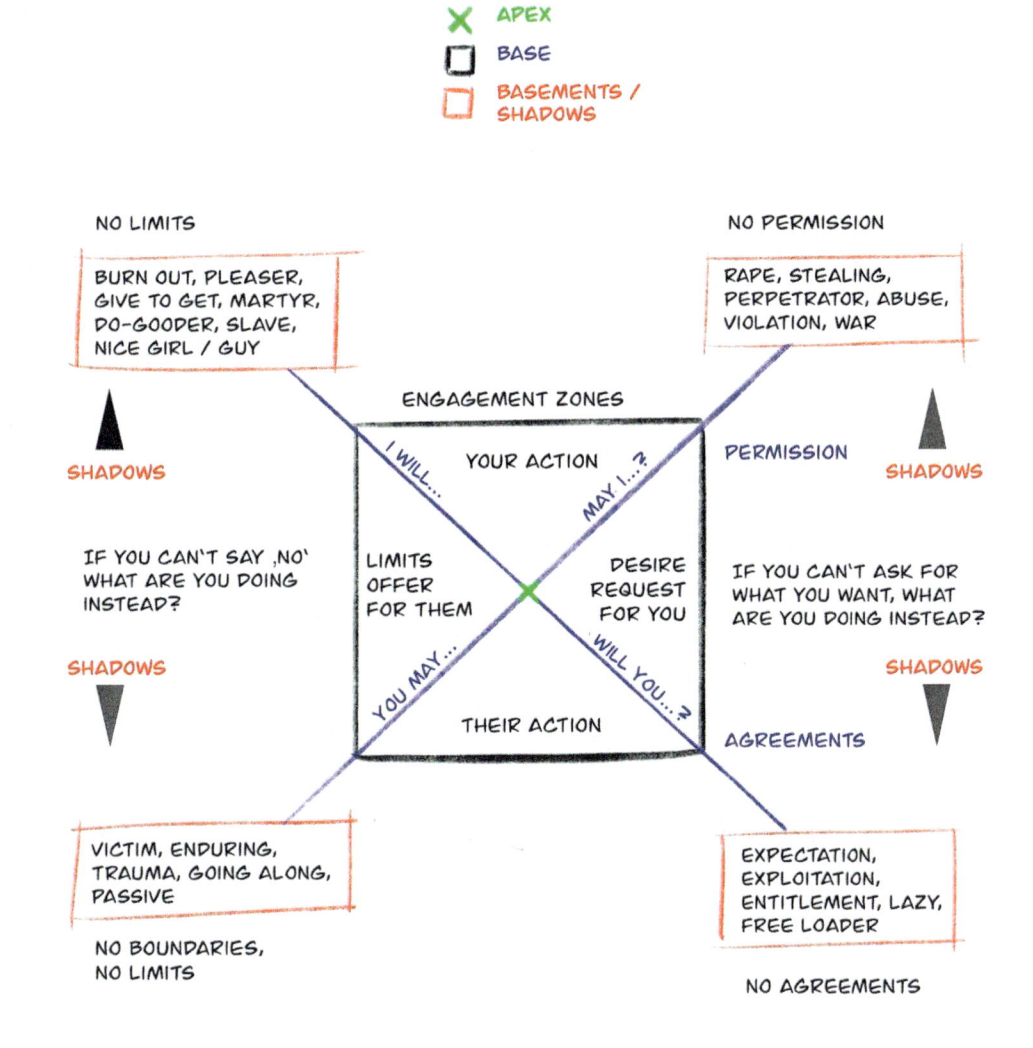

X APEX
☐ BASE
☐ BASEMENTS / SHADOWS

NO LIMITS

BURN OUT, PLEASER, GIVE TO GET, MARTYR, DO-GOODER, SLAVE, NICE GIRL / GUY

NO PERMISSION

RAPE, STEALING, PERPETRATOR, ABUSE, VIOLATION, WAR

SHADOWS

ENGAGEMENT ZONES

YOUR ACTION
I WILL... / MAY I...?
PERMISSION

SHADOWS

IF YOU CAN'T SAY 'NO' WHAT ARE YOU DOING INSTEAD?

LIMITS OFFER FOR THEM

DESIRE REQUEST FOR YOU

IF YOU CAN'T ASK FOR WHAT YOU WANT, WHAT ARE YOU DOING INSTEAD?

SHADOWS

YOU MAY... / WILL YOU...?
THEIR ACTION
AGREEMENTS

SHADOWS

VICTIM, ENDURING, TRAUMA, GOING ALONG, PASSIVE

NO BOUNDARIES, NO LIMITS

EXPECTATION, EXPLOITATION, ENTITLEMENT, LAZY, FREE LOADER

NO AGREEMENTS

WWW.SOMATICCONSENT.COM

Each part of the Engagement System is explained clearly, step by step in the sections below. Let's begin by exploring the very foundation of self. Your Base.

THE FOUNDATIONAL BASE OF SELF-LOVE, SELF-CARE AND SELF-PLEASURE

"Being attuned to oneself is the foundation of harmony in all other relationships."
- Dr. Paul TP Wong

Within relationship dynamics between people, the Base of the pyramid structure stands for the foundation of personal rights and self-responsibility.

You take responsibility for your personal Base through self-care. You care for your own body, thoughts and beliefs, feelings and emotions, wants, desires, boundaries and limits. You understand clearly that this is your job alone, and nobody else's—and that you gain autonomy, sovereignty and empowerment through it. If you rely on someone else to take care of your rights and responsibilities, you give away your personal power to them. To some it may seem daunting to have to take care of themselves the whole time, but this isn't about going it alone, secluding yourself from others, being stoically independent or totally self-sufficient.

BASE MAP

INFLOW, SELF-LOVE AND SELF-CARE

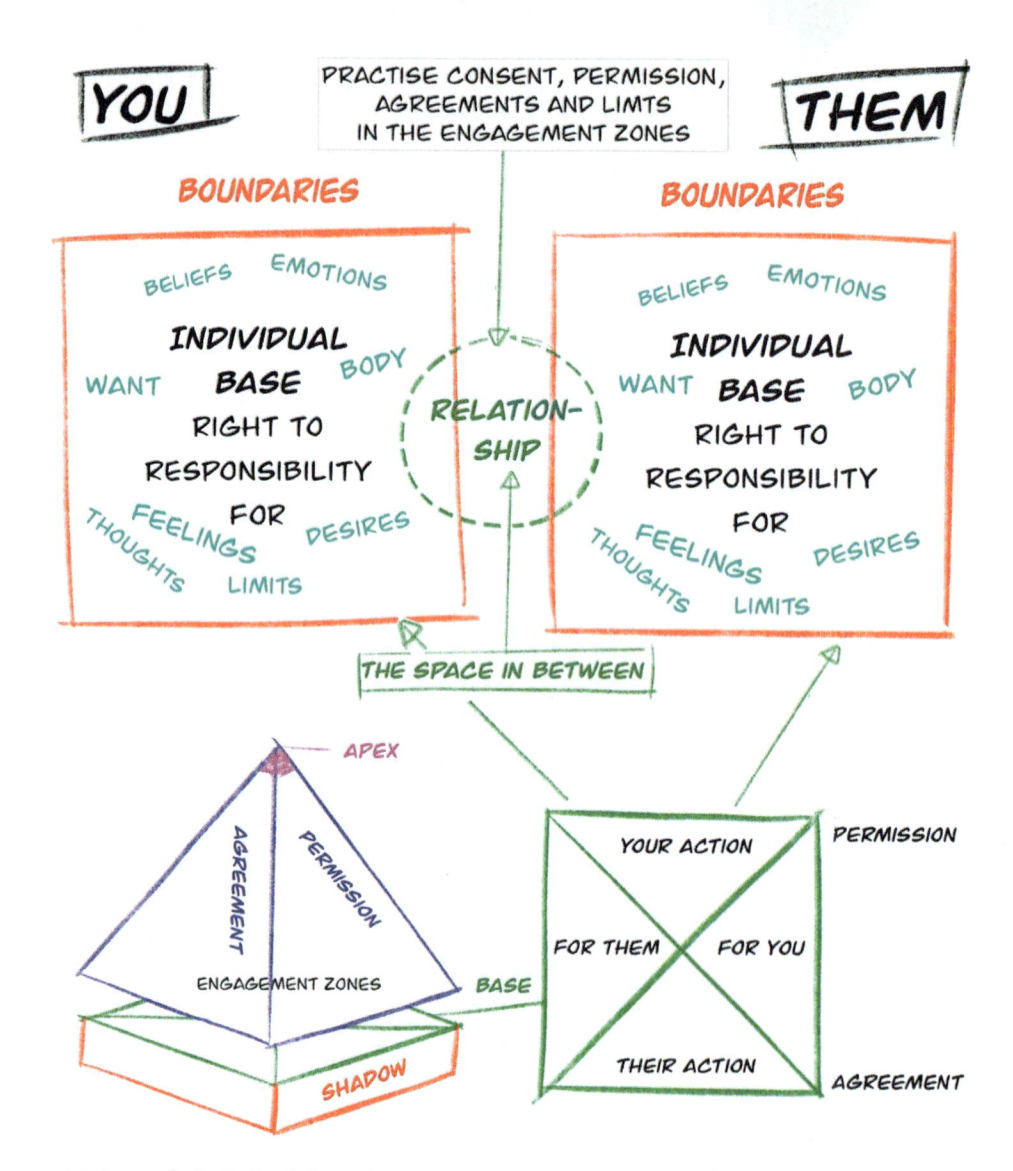

YOU — PRACTISE CONSENT, PERMISSION, AGREEMENTS AND LIMITS IN THE ENGAGEMENT ZONES — **THEM**

BOUNDARIES

INDIVIDUAL BASE
RIGHT TO RESPONSIBILITY FOR

BELIEFS, EMOTIONS, BODY, DESIRES, LIMITS, FEELINGS, THOUGHTS, WANT

BOUNDARIES

INDIVIDUAL BASE
RIGHT TO RESPONSIBILITY FOR

BELIEFS, EMOTIONS, BODY, DESIRES, LIMITS, FEELINGS, THOUGHTS, WANT

RELATIONSHIP

THE SPACE IN BETWEEN

APEX — AGREEMENT — PERMISSION — ENGAGEMENT ZONES — BASE — SHADOW

	YOUR ACTION	PERMISSION
FOR THEM		FOR YOU
	THEIR ACTION	AGREEMENT

NO AGREEMENTS, NO LIMITS, NO RELATIONSHIP

WWW.SOMATICCONSENT.COM

- **When you look at the map, imagine you are viewing it in the first person.**
  You = first person. Them = means the person you are engaging with.

The Base Map demonstrates how to relate healthily with yourself. It's about knowing yourself and your rights and taking adult responsibility. This gives you the safe and sturdy foundation, on which to build and enrich your relationships with others. If your Base is intact, you function from a centred, grounded, empathic and empowered place.

"There is no 'we' in responsibility."
- Clinton Callahan

```
                    WELL-BEING
                       ↑
                              SELF-CARE
    YOUR BASE
    A RIGHT TO
       AND
    A RESPONSIBILITY
       FOR            NO SELF-CARE

                       ↓
            NEGATIVE OUTCOMES
```

You have to be connected to your inner world to have a solid Base. This begins with tuning into your somatic inflow (activating sensory awareness). Then, you always know the difference between the **Direct** and **Indirect** route when engaging with other people, touching and being touched.

Recap:

The Direct Route of receiving pleasure happens when you are tuned into and fully aware of the sensory information coming into your own body when you touch another person or are being touched. It orientates you to how you feel in-the-moment, greatly raising your awareness and your ability to speak up about your needs, desires and limits.

The Indirect Route is when your sense of receiving pleasure is dependent on the other person's reaction when you touch them or vice versa.

If you're stuck in the Indirect Route dynamic, you won't be fully in tune with your own feelings but rather, be *feeding yourself through another's feelings*. This makes your Base unstable. Each person needs to have a strong connection to their Base (where they operate from) to know what their moment-to-moment needs are. To know when they're hungry, thirsty, tired, too cold, emotionally irritated and need to be alone, need a hug or whatever the present need may be.

When you notice the Direct Route your general awareness increases. Then, as this becomes more and more embodied, somatic inflow becomes the norm, constantly bringing you back to your own body—gradually becoming a stable default and intuitive setting, guiding you in the direction of self-responsibility and self-care.

Usually, when we're alone, it's easy to focus on self-care. We enjoy our own company, doing what feels right. When we're with others however, especially if with many people, we're consistently considering how to engage and tend to tip-toe around other people's needs, without fully acknowledging our own.

Without being grounded in self-care and having a sturdy Base, it's very easy to drop into the world of shadow dynamics. These are the survival strategies we use, such as specific words or behaviour we default to, to get our needs met. I'm sure we've all experienced this to some extent, when we go beyond our own boundaries to please the other—or we experience pleasing behaviour from them. Or we push others to fulfil our wishes. And what happens then? We blame, resent and react badly to each other, instead of realising that we've created the situation ourselves by not being connected to our needs, or by not taking responsibility for them.

It's especially easy to get lost in the Indirect Route and 'the story 'when you begin a new relationship.

Have you ever been in a situation based on telepathic agreements and assumption based relating?

How did that go for you?

When I was in my 20s, I went head-first into a relationship that was built entirely on assumption. It all started when I helped a girl I cared about to move house. Assuming I wanted a deeper relationship with her, she invited me around for dinner which led to us being intimate and me moving in with her. This hadn't been my intention at all but I jumped at the chance to sleep with her and one thing led to another. Neither of us discussed what we wanted nor took responsibility for our own self-care. I was thrilled by the notion of 'being wanted' but was never clear about my intentions. We both assumed what the other's needs and desires were, which led to all sorts of unspoken expectations, guilt, misdirected action and resentment. We argued often and split up after a short time. I'm sure most of us have been in a similar situation, where we only guess at what each other wants, don't take care of our basic self-care and base relationship purely on assumption. This lack of honesty to self and others is a breeding ground for shadow behaviour.

We'll go into the juicy topic of shadow relating in much more detail soon.

The bottom line is, when connected to your Base, you can easily determine if an action between two people is *for you* or *for them*. This enables you to relate in an *inter-dependent* manner with respect, equality and balance, free from false expectation and the disappointments that come from that. You neither remain independent and cut off from others, nor dependent on others to fulfil your every need, but wonderfully inter-dependent. You are grounded in self and function in relationship with others from a place of maturity. Here genuine intimacy and connection becomes possible.

Do you notice when it's time to take care of yourself and say no to something that would deplete your energy in those moments?

EXPLORING BOUNDARIES AND LIMITS

"Boundaries are to protect life, not to limit pleasures."
- Edwin Louis Cole

Everybody has boundaries, which start on a physical level, as the skin of your body. Your boundaries also describe the extent to which you are comfortable in any given situation. In the pyramid diagram, the edges of your Base define your boundaries. On a personal level, crossed boundaries are literally an indicator for people to notice, "Here's something I'm not comfortable with, Ok, I need to take care of myself".

Acknowledging and communicating your boundaries requires you to know what you *don't want* and be able to communicate that. If we don't know what we have a right to and responsibility for, our boundaries can be easily crossed. Although at times, paradoxically, it helps if our boundaries are crossed so that we're able to comprehend them and establish limits. A limit is the communicated line you draw, which says words to the effect of; "I'm willing to go until 'here 'with you and no further".

When two people engage, the level of encounter is largely based on cultural conditioning and how we've been taught we should behave with each other. General rules on how to behave never work. Our individual experiences throughout life guarantee that each person and their perception is unique. And so, what one person feels comfortable with, another may not. *Everyone has a right to how they feel.*

Let's look at an analogy about boundaries that most people can relate to;
Have you ever, while eating a bag of crisps, had someone reach into it without asking?
How did you feel and what did you do?
It isn't such a big deal right? Or is it?

So, there you are with your bag of crisps. You may feel a little 'splinter 'of discomfort at not being asked first—because you have a boundary, right? You may worry the other person will gobble up too many or dislike the idea of their hands in your food. Maybe you label that person as impolite or lacking respect. Maybe you think it's too little a thing to make a fuss about to risk being judged as stingy.

You probably have nothing against sharing, in fact sharing is a wonderful feeling—on your terms. But somebody sticking their hands into your bag of crisps without permission crosses a boundary. It reveals presumptuous behaviour and a sense of entitlement. It can bring up resentment at having that *choice* to share taken away from you. Being asked allows the space for you to respond from a place of genuine generosity.

It's entirely up to you if and how you share what's yours. Crisps or otherwise! If nobody is asking for permission, be sure you know your boundaries.

You can decide to eat your crisps alone.
You can move the bag away when someone reaches into it without permission.
You can go and get a bowl and share exactly the amount you want to.
You can express your boundaries and say "no" in an appropriate way.
Or you can ignore your boundaries, allow them to be crossed and get resentful.

No permission or agreements lead to unclear boundaries

If there is no communicated permission or agreement, it's very difficult to know where the other's boundaries are. This is shaky ground, as we may unwittingly interfere in someone else's Base. When we give our advice to someone without their permission or presume we can do whatever feels right for us, we may cross their boundaries without meaning to.

Acting without permission and giving unsolicited advice, however helpful your intentions are, can be translated as dictating what's good for the other to think, believe, do, not do, what to feel or not to feel.

Has anyone ever tried to tell you what to feel, think, say or do?
How did you feel about that?

Have you ever told others what to feel, think, say or do?
How did they react?

One of the most commonly breached boundaries is to tell another person 'who they are'. "You're selfish, lazy, annoying, negative, controlling, too this or that; or not fast, tidy, positive, spiritual (fill in the blank) enough". How can we possibly know who someone is, when we don't know ourselves in totality? Unless someone specifically asks for our opinion on them—doing so lies wholly within the realm of unsolicited, presumptive, pretty shallow, one-sided perception. *We can only know about ourselves.* We can only know how *we feel* and what is good or not good *for us*.

Imagine hearing the following two statements and notice how different they feel:

"You're too pushy..."

"When you say that, I feel pressurised and nervous."

Telling someone else 'who they are 'from our perspective is like a quack doctor's diagnosis and rarely feels good or rings true to the other. We'll talk about these dynamics in more depth in the Relationship Map.

A healthy level of engagement is, at its core, based on the agreement we have with each other. It can't be based on assumptions (a telepathic agreement), but on what is agreed upon (what both want within each person's limits). For now, know that when you can maintain a solid connection to your Base, you'll be aware of your needs, be able to communicate them—and in this way, open the possibility for intimate, interpersonal experience.

In other words, *you'll have a strong foundation on which to build healthy relationships in your life.*

MAP OF MIXED EMOTIONS

Recognising Feelings And Emotions

"Feelings are for dealing with what is now. Emotions are for healing the past."
- Clinton Callahan[31]

This Map focuses on the foundation of feelings and emotions—acknowledging that feelings are neither good nor bad—only feelings.

Just like primary colours, which can be mixed to produce all the other colours, we have just four core feelings in our limbic system that are mixed to produce all other feelings. These four core feelings are; fear, anger, sadness and joy. Through them, our nervous system steers us in our human quest to grasp onto pleasure and evade pain—in order to survive.

Fear

Fear is an instinctive reaction in the face of danger. It's our 'Survival Cocktail No. 1' at the root of 'danger induced 'feelings. Fear can cause changes in the heart rate, elevated blood pressure, night sweats, tremors and other physiological phenomena. It can even trigger the symptoms of cardiac arrest. As well-trained 'survival monkeys', we are hardwired to judge our environment and deal with external danger. So, paradoxically, fear *isn't* the problem. In its emotionally raw form, it keeps us focused and able to respond to danger. Therefore, in some situations, fear is our friend.

Common go-to belief of what fear is:

Fear is stressful, unstable, unprofessional, unreliable, unworthy, ridiculous, unpredictable and unproductive. It induces anger, is hysterical, wild, contagious, makes us feel small, powerless, vulnerable, insecure, a loser or a burden on others. It isn't credible, has no place and has to be overcome. We should hide it or risk being exiled or disowned.

Evolved go-to belief of what fear is: The Magician, Sorceress, Shaman and Creator

Fear helps us be aware of danger, to stay focused, gives us discernment to see more clearly so as to create opportunities and possibilities. It prompts us to pay attention, ask questions, demand information, explore research and take intelligent risks. It's an instruction to move and go nonlinear, to discover and improvise in creative ways.

Anger

Anger is agitation resulting from the perception of being violated, disrespected or wrongly treated. It stems from instinctive self-preparedness triggered within the nervous system. It causes your body to release adrenaline, your muscles to tighten, your heart rate and blood pressure to increase and your senses to feel more acute. This physical reaction arms us with a weapon to protect ourselves by fighting danger. Anger enables us to lash out in some way in order to unarm the perceived threat.

When we're angry, we tend to react rather than rationally act. Both active and passive expressions of anger are defensive. *Actively (directly)*, we express our defence verbally by shouting, insulting, threatening and 'bigging ourselves up'. Physically, we express our defence, for example by banging or throwing things around, hitting out or blowing the horn in traffic. *Passively (indirectly)* we express anger by ignoring, blocking, making snide comments and other forms of silencing or hinting. Anger signals to others that they aren't safe around you and that they should back off.

Common go-to belief of what anger is:

Anger is putting your stress onto others, disturbs the peace, is lost control, aggressive, wrong, hurtful, irresponsible, dangerous, untrustworthy, scary, the root of all evil, destructive, violent and starts wars. It's being a perpetrator, a psychopath, is uncivilised, animalistic, and savage.

Evolved go-to belief of what anger is: The Warrior, Doer and Maker

Anger is experienced by everyone. It's important to discern its cause with exquisite self-awareness in order to avoid blind reaction. Destructive anger occurs when it is used against those weaker, as a form of power over. Anger can also be channelled constructively, as an energy to create and protect, to provide discernment (as a bullshit detector), clarity to know what is important, focus to take action or a prompt to say stop or say no. It can be a catalyst to make decisions, to do what you care about, to change your mind, to change things, to set a boundary, to say yes and to make agreements.

Sadness

Sadness is the feeling of failure or loss. It can range from mild disappointment to extreme despair. Sadness is often triggered by endings and goodbyes such as the rejection of someone you value or the sickness or death of a loved one. It can arise through changes in aspects of identity within your home, social or working life and from disappointment through an unexpected outcome or missed opportunity.

Sadness can feel both painful or numb and can be expressed through a slouched, contracted or slumped posture, through tears and sobbing or withdrawn lack of expression. There is often an inability to focus or participate fully in life. Sadness serves an important role in signalling a need to receive help or comfort from others. It's a vital part of human social engagement so we can get support in order to survive hard times.

Old go-to belief of what sadness is:

Sadness is playing victim, is needy, childish, ugly, worthless, pathetic or pitiable. Men don't cry, it looks bad, is unproductive, unprofessional, emotionally unstable, unreliable, a party killer, incompetent, dysfunctional, not fun. It disconnects, drains others, attracts rescuers and is a melancholic black hole.

New go-to belief of what sadness is: Intimacy Journey, The Lover and Communicator

Sadness is being present, open, honest, eliminates resistance, lets things, people and situations go. It's releasing, softening and healing, helps find appreciation, acceptance and equanimity. It's transformative, alchemy, turns the pain of grieving into compassion, empathy, listening and support. It helps us find gratitude, generosity and creates intimate connection through vulnerability and surrender.

Joy

Joy is a state of pleasure, excitement, happiness, curiosity, contentment, comfort, well-being or playfulness. Joy happens when your nervous system feels safe. It can feel like an uplifting and open free-flow of being. A believing and allowing that all is and will be well. It can range from mild pleasure or amusement, through intense excitement, to an experience of relaxed and timeless bliss.

It can arise through delights experienced through our senses, personal accomplishment, good fortune, self-appreciation, connection through acceptance within social groups. Through love and support, a sense of freedom, connection to the natural world, excitement at the prospect of an opportunity, artistic expression and any other activity you are naturally drawn to take part in. When we feel some form of joy, our nervous system is in a state where healing, rejuvenation, trust and intimacy are possible.

Joy is expressed through smiles, laughter, shining eyes, a relaxed, upright, expansive and open posture, a soothing voice, humour and charisma. This radiates outwards to other people, signalling to their nervous systems that you are safe to approach, which makes connection possible.

Common go-to belief of what joy is:

Too much joy is stupid, selfish, childish, ridiculous, overbearing, entitled, unrealistic, disconnected, insane, delusional, irresponsible, drug induced, crazy, sick or naive. It shows too much energy and not enough work, is immature, unproductive, volatile, parasitical, irritating, dangerous, inauthentic, not serious or inattentive. It provokes envy, guilt and unempathetic reaction, 'how dare you be happier than I am'.

Evolved go-to belief of what joy is: King / Queen of Possibility and Surrender

Joy is a celebration of life, being in the present, innocence, self-wonder, appreciation, connection. It's flow, uplifting, inspiration and inspiring, empowerment and empowering. It's pleasure, awe, praise, grace, being fully alive, adventure. It's exploration, taking responsibility, nurturing, healing, collaboration, team building, sharing, generosity, playful, visionary, wisdom, genesis, source, communion, completion and surrender to all that is.

MAP OF MIXED EMOTIONS

3 MIX: AGGRESSION, JEALOUSY, GREED, GUILT, SHAME, BLAME, ENVY
4 MIX: BURNOUT, PSYCHOLOGICAL BREAKDOWN, COLLAPSE

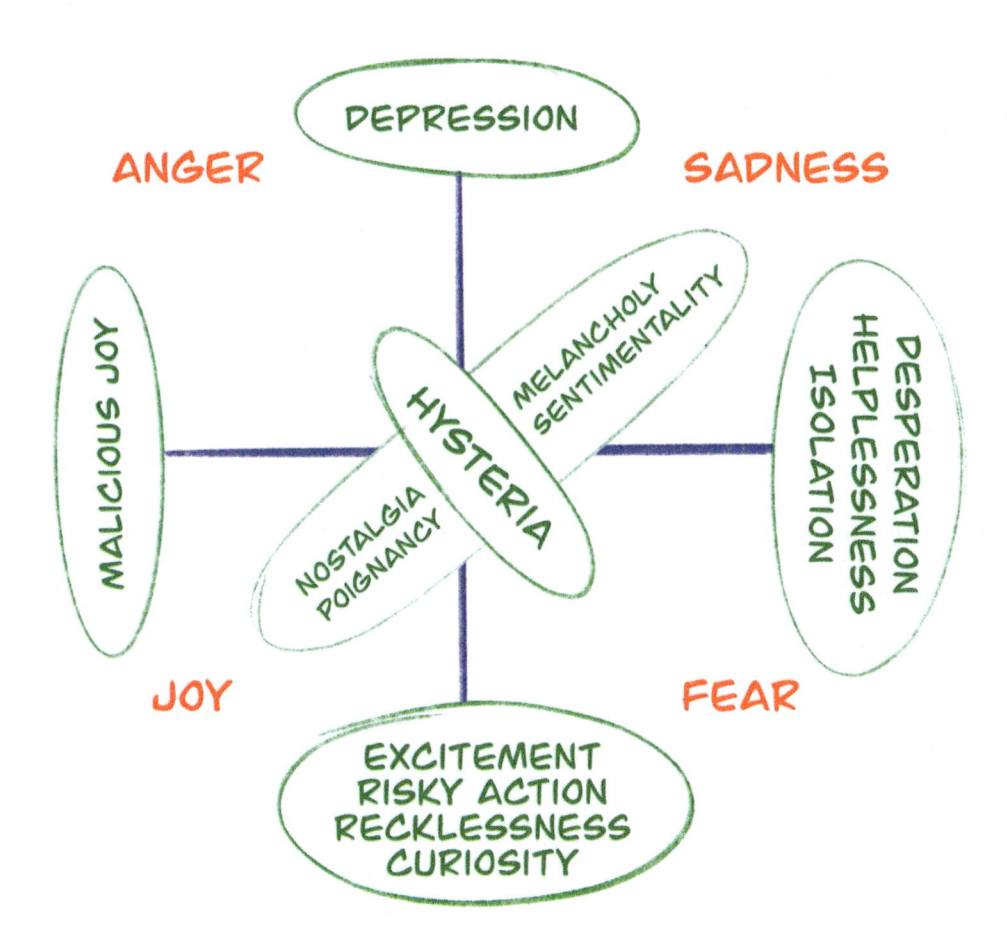

ANGER — **DEPRESSION** — **SADNESS**

- MALICIOUS JOY
- MELANCHOLY, SENTIMENTALITY
- HYSTERIA
- NOSTALGIA, POIGNANCY
- DESPERATION, HELPLESSNESS, ISOLATION

JOY — **FEAR**

- EXCITEMENT, RISKY ACTION, RECKLESSNESS, CURIOSITY

WWW.SOMATICCONSENT.COM

You'll have noticed that mixed feelings are common, a combination of either two, three or four of the core feelings. If we look at this map, we see encircled emotions which are a mixture of the core emotions on either side. An example of two core feelings mixed together could be anger and sadness which results in depression. Others combine to result in aggression, jealousy, grief, guilt, shame, blame, envy and so on.

The map makes your feelings and emotions more transparent, so that instead of them seeming like a kind of 'unconscious blur 'that you can't quite put your finger on—you are able to recognise and identify the core emotion involved. The core emotion is the one that feels the strongest. This is, more often than not, anger, which comes up in order to defend and protect yourself. It could also be sadness, joy or fear. It really depends on the individual.

Direct Route awareness increases interoception

Recognition and regulation of emotions require a coherent relationship with the self. This means effective communication between your body, thoughts and feelings.

Another word for tuning into your feelings is *interoception.* This is the awareness of sensations inside the body. Physical sensations including your heartbeat, respiration and satiety, as well as nervous system activity related to feelings and emotions. Mindfulness practices (especially those related to touch and sensation) wake up interoceptive awareness.

Sensations from the body underlie most, if not all of our emotional feelings, particularly those that are most intense and most basic to survival. Because interoception is a window to your emotional experience—being responsive to interoceptive information allows you to be aware of an emotion cue early. This means you are more able to process and choose a course of action at the onset of stressful events. It allows you to have a more integrated sense of self, so that self-regulation or co-regulation is an option before things spiral out of control.[32]

If you tune into your feelings, each one has its own clearly distinctive 'flavour'. When we're familiar with *how* each of these feel, we have access to their roots. We can more easily understand the cause of the emotional effect (the reason they arise). When we have more emotional awareness, we can more easily bring balance to our general health and performance, well-being and social connections.

The difference between feelings and emotions

Our feelings are for engaging with our environment in real time. Children are masters of this. They express their feelings as they come up, which usually takes about 1.5 - 2 minutes. When an expression of a feeling loiters longer than this time frame, it means you aren't dealing with a feeling at all —but an *emotion* from a past traumatic event. Many *feelings* we don't express for whatever reason, stay stored inside, only to rise up again as an *emotion* when we find ourselves in a similar situation to when they first occurred. You may feel something is 'getting on your nerves 'and that's accurate—because at these moments your sympathetic nervous system goes into activation (fight or flight).

Let's say someone forgets an appointment they made with you and you feel anger begin to rise. This is a feeling. It's only an emotion if it touches on a trigger from a past traumatic event, such as being dismissed and unappreciated. This can happen when, for example, another person let you down and had little responsibility for their actions—which resulted in you feeling disrespected or uncared for. This type of past experience caused a memory to form and be labelled as 'dangerous'.

When we deal with a feeling in the moment by saying for example, "Hey, I found it really inconvenient that you didn't show up...", the anger you're feeling has space to be aired, seen, heard, felt and acknowledged. This way the nervous system feels recognised, is able to relax and you can move on. When we can allow ourselves to do this, we can allow others to express their feelings too. The quality of our relationships increase as a result.

Other examples of emotions are experiencing overwhelm and disembodiment when asked to speak in public, feeling wobbly in a high place while looking down, or panicky when we're in water. Once we're aware of and able to express what we're experiencing, we can ask ourselves, "When did this first happen?" and are more able to trace the emotion back to its source. Some internalised emotions may require a form of therapy for them to be processed. There are different approaches for different people, types of trauma and expression of it.

It's especially useful within practitioner work to catch different cues of responses from clients. This way, the practitioner can guide their client's awareness of their feelings or emotions—which is a vital step within the healing process. Guiding others of course, requires personal commitment to self-development. Practitioners must heal their own experiences of trauma first. *We can only guide another person as deeply as we've gone ourselves.*

You have a right to your feelings

We are part of nature, though due to being consciously aware, we often see ourselves as separate from it. But really we're just complicated animals, trying to survive by getting our needs met in the most pleasant way possible. One way we do this is through our feelings and emotions, (a result of our nervous system gauging whether we're safe or not). We all also have a meaning making process, where we attach a story to our experience so that we can make sense of our environment. Feelings allow us to release tension in our bodies, enable us to bond with others and signal when we need support.

So, you need your feelings. They're not wrong, and they're not your shadows.

You have a responsibility for your actions

To build a solid Base of self-care—you have to know what you have a right to and what you have a responsibility for. Part of that is knowing you *have a right to* your personal thoughts, feelings and emotions. What you *have a responsibility for* is your behaviour—how you react to what you think and feel. Resisting, suppressing, hiding or blindly reacting in defence of your feelings and emotions is where shadows come into play—the behavioural, survival strategies that we all employ to get our needs met when we avoid our truth. We'll take a detailed look at the realm of shadow strategies later in this chapter.

THE SPECTRUM OF LIMITS

"True power arises in knowing what you want, knowing what you don't want, expressing it clearly and lovingly without attachment to the outcome."
- Leonard Jacobson

Have you ever experienced a "Hell Yes!" when asked if you want to do something that is exactly your cup of tea?

Have you ever experienced a "NO" (without hesitation) when someone asked you to do something strictly against your values?

When it comes to boundaries and expressing your limits, you'll have probably noticed a spectrum of feelings between a "Hell YES!" and a fierce "NO!" Many of us hesitate in the confusion between these two points, lingering in indecisive mode, avoiding committing one way or the other or lapsing into 'willing to 'without feeling comfortable doing so.

Have you experienced that place that's almost a "no" but you were willing to because you love someone? The Limits Map helps you to identify exactly how you feel and to express that authentically in real time.

LIMITS MAP

SPECTRUM FROM HELL YES TO FIERCE NO

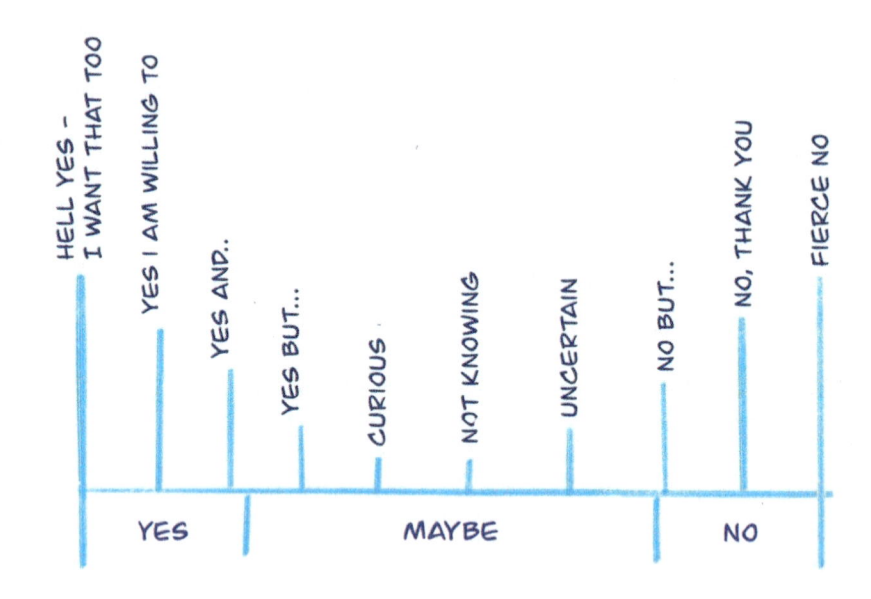

Positions along the spectrum:
- **YES**: HELL YES – I WANT THAT TOO | YES I AM WILLING TO | YES AND. | YES BUT...
- **MAYBE**: CURIOUS | NOT KNOWING | UNCERTAIN
- **NO**: NO BUT... | NO, THANK YOU | FIERCE NO

- YES IS A YES / NO IS A NO / MAYBE IS A NO AND NEEDS MORE INFORMATION / YOU CAN'T HAVE A CLEAR YES WITHOUT A CLEAR NO

- HOW DOES IT FEEL SAYING YES, WHEN YOU MEAN NO?
- HOW DOES IT FEEL SAYING NO, WHEN YOU MEAN YES?
- NO IS A FULL SENTENCE. IT DOES NOT NEED ANY EXPLANATION.
- NO IS IMPORTANT INFORMATION FOR THE OTHER PERSON.
- YOU CAN'T TRUST YOUR YES, IF YOU CAN'T SAY NO.
- HAVING CLEAR LIMITS AND SAYING NO IS SAYING YES TO YOURSELF.
- HAVING ENOUGH TIME IS ESSENTIAL FOR FINDING A CLEAR YES OR NO.

WWW.SOMATICCONSENT.COM

The more embodied you are, the more aware you are of the subtle differences along the scale of a yes and no.

Hell YES
If someone asks you to do something for them, (so it's their desire), and you feel a "Hell YES! I want exactly the same thing", it feels like it's for you too because you enjoy it, but it's actually for the person who made the request in the first place.

It could be a win-win situation, but still, it is *for the person who initiated*. So it can be a mixture between a request or an invitation—nevertheless, they get what they want and the fact that you get what you want too is secondary.

There is a spectrum between how you respond to a request. We tend to default to a YES, NO or MAYBE most of the time, though there are other possibilities.

Yes, I am willing to—just for you
"Yes, I'm willing to do that because I really love you."

Yes, and setting limits with a condition
It's a yes, and something else is important to add such as,
"Yes and… I want to go to the bathroom/eat/drink/make a call first."

Yes, but setting limits based on a boundary
It's a yes and you recognise your boundary and set a limit during the agreement.
"Yes, I can give that, but only to 'this 'point and no further."

Curious
You need more information to be able to make up your mind.
"Maybe, I don't know yet, I can't decide, can you tell me more about it?"

Not knowing
Again, self-care is necessary here, to know you have a choice and give yourself enough time to decide.
"I can't make a decision right now, maybe it's a no, maybe a yes but I can't tell you right now."

Uncertain
If something doesn't 'sit 'well, it is treated as a 'no 'unless you are sure you feel comfortable with the request.
"I'm not sure because it doesn't feel right."

No but
A clear no. Whatever has been asked for is something you're not willing to do or have done to you. But you are open to a different request or have an idea about something else you're 'willing to'. "No to what you asked for but would you like to ask for something else?" / "No, but I have another idea."

No thank you
This recognises that even if it's a clear no for you, you support the other in owning their desire. That their desire is still valid, even if you say no. "Thanks for asking but no, I don't want to do that."

Fierce NO
"No way!"

A fun exercise to experience your spectrum of limits

During the facilitation of cuddle parties I host, we always begin with an exercise to set a safe and fully aware 'container 'built on the principle of consent. All four rounds are played *without* going through with any action. The game is played to provide experiential insight into how a yes and no feels in the body, as well as to practise asking for what we want and answering requests authentically.

How to play:

I suggest playing The 3 Minute Game with touch only after playing the first four rounds below.

Round 1

Person A asks the question, "Can I (…)" / "Can you (…)" and waits for the reply. Person B *always* answers, "NO" even if it feels like a yes.

A few examples:
Can I hold your hand? Can I massage your feet? Can I scratch your back? Can I have a hug? Can I lick your face? Can I pinch your (…)? Can you suck my toes? Can I squeeze your thighs? Can I stroke your hair? Can I bite your (…)? Can you put your hand on my lower back?"

This is repeated for a few minutes with Person A asking different questions and Person B replying "NO" each time.

At the end of the round, Person B closes their eyes and reflects on all the questions asked. What felt like a "YES"?
What felt like a "NO"?
What felt like a "Maybe"? (a maybe is a no until it feels like a yes).
Did any other feelings from the spectrum map come up?

Round 2

Switch roles - Person B asks, Person A answers with "NO" - then closes their eyes to reflect as above.

Round 3

Person A asks similar questions - Person B answers all questions with "YES" also when they don't want what's suggested. (Remember - do not follow through on the actual touch, this game is purely for insight into how we internally feel when someone requests to touch us/asks us to touch them).

Person B then closes their eyes to reflect as above.

Round 4

Switch roles - Person B asks, Person A answers with "YES" - then closes their eyes to reflect as above.

Take a few minutes each to debrief your experience to each other. One talks for two minutes while the other listens and vice versa.

When each person is clear about what feels like a "yes", what feels like a "no" and other finer subtleties found in the Spectrum of Limits Map—and can express these feelings authentically, it's time to play The 3 Minute Game!

Download your Touch, Consent and Play App here:

Apple App   Android App

- Scan the QR code with your phone camera.
- For Android you may have to use a QR Code Reader app like 'Google Lens'.
- Choose your browser.
- You'll be directed to the webpage with the download.

EXPRESSING YOUR BOUNDARIES AND LIMITS

"No is a complete sentence."
- Anne Lamont

Within Somatic Consent, when it comes to giving and receiving, we take each person's boundaries and limits into account.

A **boundary** points to the extent to what a person is comfortable with. Everyone has a right to and a responsibility for their own boundaries.

A **limit** is the communication of that boundary *in the form of an agreement* or *permission* which clearly states how far you or the other is able to go. The core energy of having a boundary is the ability to express it by saying, "No, stop, that's as far as I am willing to go" and making an agreement as such.

So your *limits are defined by the agreement you make*. If there is no agreement, there are no limits and boundary crossing can happen easily.

The boundary in an agreement is a solid NO. The art of respecting somebody's limits is guarding and protecting their boundaries instead of trying to get a little more when it feels right for you.

You can identify your boundaries by noticing how you feel in any moment of engagement with another. Which emotion is present? Do you feel anger? Anger is a healthy expression of reaching the edge of a boundary. But feeling anger can be scary. Have you ever experienced a fierce, reactive "NO!" fuelled by anger at having your boundaries crossed in the past? We may worry that by feeling and expressing anger we could be overpowered or drive others away. We also tend to worry that by expressing our needs and limits to people who aren't coming from a place of care—but one of control, we make ourselves vulnerable by giving them the opportunity to see our weak spots.

The shadows of not expressing your limits, or of not respecting other people's limits is something we tend to avoid confronting. Overcoming the fear of confronting our shadows of automatic behaviour is a lifelong process. But we have to start somewhere. A good place to start is by acknowledging that we all have shadow survival strategies. They're part of who we are. And face them we must if we want to grow. Most of us have spent a large majority of our lives developing shadows to get our needs met. A more constructive approach would be to;

- Activate the sensory inflow to increase awareness of own experience —learning how to fully receive.
- Create a solid Base of self-care and know what we have a right to and responsibility for.
- Ask for what *we* want.
- Tune into how we feel when someone asks us for what *they* want— recognising our boundaries.
- Reply authentically and express clear limits.
- Make agreements within each person's limits.

Now let's take a deeper look at how to ask for what you want using a simple formula based on permission and agreement.

THE ENGAGEMENT ZONES: WHO IS IT FOR?

Permission And Agreements: The Four Doors To Desire, Pleasure And Consent

"The single biggest problem in communication is the illusion that it has taken place."
- George Bernard Shaw

The word *intimacy* comes from the Latin words *intimare* and *intimus* which mean 'to make the inmost familiar'. I also like the play on words 'into me you see'. But to be comfortable enough to allow someone to really see us, we have to feel safe, wouldn't you agree?

- We feel safe when the somatic inflow is activated, our nervous system is calm, we know what to expect and welcome it because we've consented to it.
- We get consent by making an agreement.

If you look at the next map, the four parts represent each individual's Engagement Zones. When two or more people engage, their Engagement Zones overlap in what I call 'The Space In-between'. Here, separate, responsible individuals (each with a solid Base) share their needs, desires and limits through honest communication.

The Engagement Zones are where *permission is granted and agreements* are made to create consensual interaction—and is where *true relationship* takes place.

The space in-between IS the relationship you share with the other

To make a consensual agreement about an action between people, we have to know;

- who the action is for
- what and where is it going to happen
- for how long

Key to personal and transpersonal development within Somatic Consent is practising the 'space in between'. This overlapping space of relationship where two individual people engage is where we practise awareness of sensory inflow of the nervous system, learn how to ask for what we want, establish our limits, ask for permission and come to empowered agreements so that a relational container of consent, trust and relaxed intimacy forms.

Do you want to stop guessing your partner's wants and needs and vice versa? Are you ready for transparency and harmony in your relationships?

The Engagement Zones Map is a visual aid to The 3 Minute Game and any other interaction you want to bring consent into. When you play, you practice expressing and communicating within the Engagement Zones.

To embody the Engagement Zones, play as much as you can with as many people as you can.

Let's look again at the questions in The 3 Minute Game:

How do you want me to touch you for 3 minutes?
How do you want to touch me for 3 minutes?

The Engagement Zones show how these two questions (which are both **offers**) open up *four* different dynamics enabling you to clearly define;

- **who is 'doing 'the action and 'who it is for'.**

ENGAGEMENT ZONES MAP

> YOUR ACTION: IT'S EITHER FOR YOU OR FOR THEM.
> THEIR ACTION: IT'S EITHER FOR YOU OR FOR THEM.

WHO IS DOING THE ACTION?
WHO IS IT FOR?
— TWO DIFFERENT THINGS.

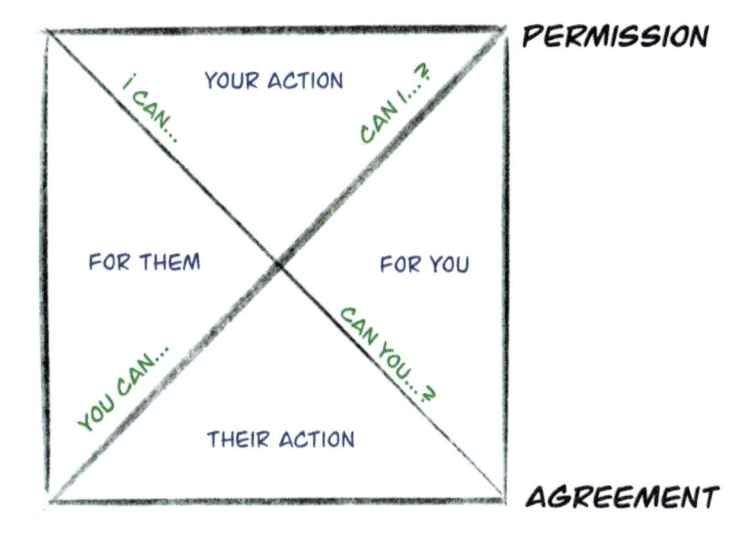

PERMISSION

```
          YOUR ACTION
    I CAN...        CAN I...?

  FOR THEM          FOR YOU

    YOU CAN...      CAN YOU...?
          THEIR ACTION
```

AGREEMENT

WHEN IT IS FOR YOU, EITHER YOU ARE IN ACTION OR THEY ARE IN ACTION

WHEN IT'S FOR THEM, EITHER YOU ARE IN ACTION OR THEY ARE IN ACTION.

THE ANSWER ISN'T TO DO WITH HOW YOU FEEL ABOUT THE ACTION.

IT'S TO DO WITH WHO ASKS FOR CONSENT.

WWW.SOMATICCONSENT.COM

How can we determine who the action is for?

Feeling pleasure is not the indicator of who an action is for—*consent* is the indicator.

Consent is made up of both **permission and agreement** between two or more people to determine what will or won't happen in an interaction. Within the Somatic Consent Engagement System, we determine 'who is doing the action '(your action / their action) and 'who it is for '(for them / for you).

We ask for permission on the **permission line** of the Engagement Zones. When permission is granted, the person doing the action is doing it **for their own benefit.**

We make agreements on the **agreement Line** of the Engagement Zones.
In agreements, the person doing the action is doing it **for the benefit of the other person**.

Asking for permission and making agreements are the end of shadow strategies such as;

When you can't ask for what you want (Taking what isn't yours to take / Expectation and entitlement)

When you can't say no (Pleasing to belong / Going along with something you don't like).

If there is no request or agreement, there is no action.

In every scenario you happen to be in your life, you'll notice that the action taken by someone is either for your benefit or for the other person's benefit. Although an action may seem like it is for both people at times, it is always either for you or for 'them '(the other or others). This covers the entire spectrum of human engagement, except when both are coming from an interpersonal 'space 'at the Apex, which we'll explore in the next section.

Imagine you're reaching your hand towards somebody.
The action is: YOUR ACTION

either
1) what you want - *for you*
or

2) what they want - *for them*

Now imagine that somebody's hand is reaching towards you.
The action is: THEIR ACTION

either
1) what they want - *for them*
or
2) what you want - *for you*

In other words:
You do what you want
You do what they want
They do what they want
They do what you want

Who an action is for is determined regardless of *who does the action*.
Your friend could bring you some apples from her tree, or you could go over and pick them yourself. In both cases the action is for you.

Understanding *for you* and *for them* depends on being able to distinguish between 'want to' and 'willing to'.

Want to: something I want for my own reasons because it brings me joy and it may or may not have anything to do with you.

Willing to: something I might not choose for myself, but I'm willing to for you because it brings you enjoyment and I care about you; it's a gift.

When it's for you: you are in your 'want to' of desire. You make requests

When it's for them: you are in your 'willing to'. You make limits and offers.

In order to experience the difference between the dynamics of *for you* and *for them*, you have to take them apart. That is, experience one of them at a time. We practise this within the Engagement Zones.

Verbal consent is made through permission and agreements

When people become aware of who an action is for, they realise how simple yet profound it is—and why it often feels 'off' when they're being touched by someone (who wants to do it for themselves) but can't own or ask for it.

It's important to remember that we've all been touched in ways we didn't like, before we could even walk or talk. We've all learned how to go along with it and accepted it as normal. This acceptance is embedded in our psyche and nervous systems—and takes time to rewire. Giving authentic permission is easy for some people and extremely difficult for others. This is in direct proportion to knowing you have a choice. Once you know you have a **choice**, you can relax and enjoy.

Embodying the Direct Route is key to opening up the **Permission Line**—and therefore the rest of the Engagement System.

Permission is *asked for* when an action is;
- **Your action for you** or
- **Their action for them**

Permission is *asked for*—by the person the action *is for*.
(It's for this person's benefit or pleasure).
For example, the person asking wants the cuddle and wants to do the action.
They ask; **"Can I stroke your hair?"**

Permission is *given* by the person being asked.
The action involves the person. Something is being done to them—and it is for the pleasure or benefit of the person asking.
For example, **"Yes, you can stroke my hair"**.

An Agreement is made when an action is;

- **Your action for them** or
- **Their action for you**

Can you...? Is a *request for an agreement* that someone does something **for**

you.

"**Can you** bring me a glass of water?"
"**Can you** walk the dog?"
"**Can you** wash the dishes?"

Each request for agreement involves communicating exactly what you want (such as describing the details of a massage, body parts, pressure and so on).
"**Can you** massage my back for 15 minutes?"
"Sure, how would you like me to massage you?"
"Wow, great, thanks! Really firmly, with your thumbs pressing into my shoulders, softer everywhere else, using the flat palms of your hands on my lower back?"

An agreement involves the possibility of negotiation.

The person asked to go into action for the other expresses any limits they have.
"Sure, but I don't want this leading to sex."
"Got ya, great, I'll go and lie down, will you come in when you're ready?"
"OK, give me 5 minutes to finish this… you want oil?"
"Yes, I'll get it".

Agreements are made based on the limits of **both people**.
Limits and agreements determine the level of relationship.

As already discussed, telepathic agreements or 'good guessing' is how most people form their relating with one another. There is no healthy relationship if limits aren't expressed and agreements aren't made because you'll constantly feel like your boundaries are being crossed.

The permission line

Your action for you / Their action for them

The Permission Line is a key part of the SCES—and the opposite of what most people are used to. We ask for permission when it is 'your action for you' or 'their action for them'.

Your action for you

Asking for permission can feel very vulnerable—because it puts us at risk of being rejected.

If you're granted permission, the other gives the gift of access to their body/Base.

Your action for you:

- Dismantles the assumption that your action is for them.
- If it is for you, you don't need to give anything to touch another person. What you need is their permission to feel them.
- You embody the dynamic 'your action for you' by learning neurologically how to feel pleasurable sensations with your hands.
- You learn that your wants matter and you are welcome.
- You learn to fill yourself up.
- You realise you don't have to use 'your action for them' as an excuse to get your hands on someone. As a result, 'your action for them' becomes clean and clear.

When you **ask permission**, you do two things at once:

1. **Put your desires first**
2. **Respect the other person's limits**

When you go into action for yourself, both your motor efferent nerves and your sensory afferent nerves work in unison. This powerful combination enables you to experience fully receiving a gift for yourself. When the gift is clear and the limits respected, you'll find you can more easily own your desires and relax into being you—following your natural impulses while enjoying the permission you have.

The art of 'your action for you' is:
When you become the guardian of their limits—you become trustworthy.
"Instead of testing their limits and trying to get a little more."

What people notice about the permission line - your action for you

"I feel guilty/ashamed/decadent/inadequate, this isn't for me."
"I'm relieved that my own action for myself is an option."

"I realise I'm responsible for my own feelings and actions."
"I love that I'm able to relax and focus on my own pleasure without multitasking."
"I'm used to thinking I'm giving when in action, this is nice but strange."
"It feels different, is it right?" (It takes practice to create new neural pleasure pathways).
"I didn't know I could feel so much pleasure for myself."
"I feel a lot of gratitude to the other for giving me their gift of access."

Their action for them

When you **grant permission**, you give someone the gift of access to your body/Base.
When you give a gift, you do two things at once:

1. **Put your desires aside**
2. **Stay responsible for your limits**

You must know you have a choice about where and how you'll be touched before giving permission. Feeling into what you are willing to give access to helps you to respect and communicate your limits. When you respect your own limits, deeper relaxation is possible and the doors to generosity open.

When you feel a lot of pleasure, it's easy to get mixed up about *who the action is for*. It can feel like it's for you, when it's actually *for them*. Feeling pleasure is not the indicator of who it's for. The gauge is who chose it.

In their action for them, you aren't choosing the action. You are choosing your limits. You also choose how much attention you bring to the sensation of pleasure in your body.

The art of 'their action for them' is:
The more responsible you become for your own limits, the more you access and experience relaxation, generosity, play, flexibility, freedom and joy.

> *What people notice about the permission line - their action for them*
>
> *"It feels so good to give a gift while not doing anything."*
> *"It felt strange to put my own desires to one side."*
> *"I loved hearing exactly what my partner wanted and giving permission from a genuine place."*
> *"It feels really good to be enjoyed by someone."*
> *"It's wonderful to surrender in deep relaxation because my limits are respected."*

The agreement line

Their action for you / Your action for them

The Agreement Line is used when it's 'their action for you' (they are in action and giving - you are receiving) or 'your action for them' (you are in action and giving - they are receiving).

When you want someone to touch you, you make an agreement with them to do so.

Their action for you

In this dynamic, you are **receiving**—which makes it inherently vulnerable. When you make an **agreement** to receive something from the other, you do two things at once:

1) Put your desires first
2) Respect the other person's limits

The key to receiving is knowing the difference between what you want and what you are 'willing to'. To make the difference crystal clear, make a request so that you can feel it land in your body.

Because it's 'their action', many people tend to go along with whatever the one in action decides to do. This is about your choice. What you want. You have to decide.
The question to ask yourself is not, "Why don't I like this?"

The question to ask yourself is, "What do I actually want?"

You'll find you're able to notice, trust and value your desires. Take all the time you need to ask for what you want in the simplest and most direct way. Communicating your desires will feel empowering because you'll believe it's for you. You'll find yourself stopping trying to take care of the giver in return. When you get exactly what you want you'll stop any habit of pretending or faking. You'll find it easy to change your mind and say stop whenever you've had enough or want to receive something different.

The art of 'their action for you' is:
Asking for what you want in the 'their action for you' dynamic.
Allowing yourself to enjoy as much as you want—and being grateful to them.

What people noticed about the agreement line - their action for you

"It's difficult to ask for what I want."
"What I want matters and affects everything."
"I felt like a freeloader/shameful/unworthy/a queen/deep gratitude."
"I can ask for exactly what and how I want it?"
"I didn't think that amount of pleasure was possible."
"I've never been asked what I want before."
"I felt fear about being judged for trying to control my partner."
"I found it hard to tune into what I want."
"I didn't realise it was possible to be touched exactly how I want to be."
"Now I understand the difference between 'want to' and 'willing to'."

Your action for them

In this dynamic, you are **giving.** The gift you give is your action.
When someone makes an **agreement** with you to give to them you do two things at once:

1. **Put your desires aside**
2. **Stay responsible for your limits**

The more you respect your limits, the more relaxed and generous you will find yourself becoming. The trap some tend to fall into in this dynamic is doing something to get the response you want. (Indirect Route). It's really important to remember that you are not giving pleasure to someone. Their pleasure belongs to them. You are adding to their experience of pleasure. You'll learn to give only what someone requests and stop giving when a request hasn't been made in order to please.

The art of 'your action for them' is:
Creating spaciousness, making it easy for the other to ask
for what they want and to change their mind whenever they like.

What people noticed about the agreement line - your action for them

"This is the end of guess work, it's so good to know what feels good for my partner."
"It is so pleasurable to give when I know exactly what's being asked of me."
"I'm starting to see how often I give when no request has been made."
"I noticed how much I think I'm giving when the action is really for me!"
"Giving is a beautiful and humbling experience."

The four different zones can create confusion. This confusion comes up if you only try to grasp the concepts using your rational and conditioned intellect (working part of the brain). The working mind cannot adequately create the experience—this is why it's so important to embody the *physical* experience within your nervous system by activating your hands and noticing the inflow of sensations. Your body will understand!

So, if you find all this confusing, you know what to do. Just practise until your body feels the "Ahh, there it is". I'm sure you'll agree that we can only deeply know something if we have our own experience of it, and we can only become an expert if we practise. Just like learning how to play an instrument, repetition makes the master, otherwise the skill isn't built on and depth and fluency isn't experienced.

And of course, continue to practise the Direct Route of somatic inflow with different objects. Let's say you're holding a pen in your hands. You're feeling the pen and bringing your attention to the skin on your hands. You're having your own experience, as you notice pleasant sensations flowing in from your sensory nerve endings. You're in action. You aren't giving anything. Just feeling it is *for you*. This is a somatic experience you can build on.

Initiating and being initiated

If you look at the Engagement Zones Map, you'll see four different parts or zones representing the four sides of the pyramid. You are always either on one side of a line or the other and are either the *initiator* or the *initiated*.

Depending on whether you are the one **doing** the initiating or **being** initiated, eight dynamics are possible (two per segment/question on the map).

For anyone beginning to put this map into practise, I recommend you try initiating from each of the four zones.

In the following 4 dynamics YOU are initiating

1. Your action for you - *Can I* (do s/t for me) = **request for permission** from them
2. Their action for you - *Can you* (do s/t for me) = **request for agreement**
3. Your action for them - *I can* (do s/t for you) = **offer to come to agreement**
4. Their action for them - *You can* (do s/t *for you* to me) = **offer** where you give permission to them)

In the following 4 dynamics THEY are initiating

5. Their action for them - **Can I** (do s/t for me) = **request for permission** from you
6. Your action for them - **Can you** (do s/t for me) = **request for agreement**
7. Their action for you - **I can** (do s/t for you) = **offer to come to agreement**
8. Your action for you - **You can** (do s/t for you to me) = **offer to** give you permission to do to them)

You will feel the difference when you're the one doing the initiating and when someone else is initiating you.

The difference between offers and requests

Most people prefer to make offers instead of requests. We often do this unconsciously, to avoid feeling vulnerable. Requests expose desires and needs which could put you into the position of being ridiculed or rejected. It feels easier to make an offer than to request something because it keeps us in a safer realm where rejection doesn't sting so much. To some, rejection may seem so lethal to their well-being that it provokes a fight or flight, or shut-down response within the nervous system.

When you make an offer—it's *for them*.
When you make a request—it's *for you*.

When they make an offer—it's *for you*.
When they make a request—it's *for them*.

It's important who initiates and you notice how it feels. When you initiate by making an *offer* **it feels completely different in the body** from initiating by making a *request*.

The offer: " YOU CAN / I CAN" (do such and such) feels very different than;
The request: " CAN I/CAN YOU?".

I recently had a session with someone wanting to have a small taster of Somatic Consent and how embodiment and empowerment feels. I suggested she have an *empowerment massage* which gives the client the choices to receive exactly what they want. She agreed with excitement.

I invited her to go to the massage table.
"How do you want me?" she asked.
I asked her to reflect on her question by replying, "Who would it be for if I was the one to choose how you sit, stand or lie down?"
She understood immediately and replied, "Oh, this is going to be fun." She then chose to take off her T-shirt, leave her bra on and lie down on her back.

I explained that it was her role to make choices by asking for whatever she wanted—without simultaneously trying to take care of my limits—because my limits were my responsibility.

She paused for a few moments then asked, "Anything?"

"Yes" I answered, "whatever you want".
A moment later she said, "You can touch my breast." I responded by asking her if she was aware that she'd just given me *permission* to touch her breast. "Oh did I?" she said surprised.
I then asked her to reflect on the difference between the words; You can... and Can you..?
At this point she began to cry, realising just how vulnerable and scary it is to ask for exactly what she wanted and risk me rejecting her by saying no. This realisation linked her to memories of the past of a controlling lover and how powerless she'd felt back then. After she'd had a good cry and released the emotions that'd come up, we continued with the empowerment massage where she practiced embodying the very different dynamics of offers and requests.

Making an offer means that either you or they will do something

Let's say you arrive home and your partner makes you an *offer*.

"Hon, you look tired, I just made dinner, would you like to eat?"

You may or may not be interested in this offer, for whatever reason (already eaten, don't like that dish etc.).

The following *offer* feels very different.
"Hon, you look tired, is there anything I can do for you?"

Now you can put your needs or desires into a *request* such as;
"Hey thanks, yeah, could you run the bath for me?"

Both situations are *for you*, but it feels totally different when you *initiate your need* by making a request, instead of being confronted with a closed offer.

You initiate by making an offer or request to another person
You get initiated by them when they make you an offer or request

Let's look again at the two questions of The 3 Minute Game.

Question 1: Their action for them - The permission line

You ask: "What do *you want* to *do to me*?" This question is an **offer** made by you.

This is in the **Permission Line** in the Engagement Zones labelled YOU CAN (do such and such *to me* to make *you feel good*).
It is **their action for them** (they're going into action for themself).

You'll find yourself in exactly the same position when the other asks;
"CAN I... (stroke your arm, touch your face etc.)".
The only difference is, in the YOU CAN dynamic, **you are initiating** and in the CAN I dynamic, **they are initiating**.

Question 2: Your action for them - The agreement line

You ask: "What do *you want* me to *do to you*? The question is also an **offer** made by you.
This is the **Agreement Line** in the Engagement Zones labelled as I CAN (do such and such for you, to make *you feel good*).
It is **your action for them** (you're going into action for the other).
You'll find yourself in exactly the same position when the other asks;
"CAN YOU... (stroke my arm, touch my face etc.)".
The only difference is, in the I CAN dynamic, **you are initiating by making an offer** and in the CAN YOU dynamic, **they are initiating by making a request**.

- When **you** make an **offer** you either give someone access to your body/resources, or you 'give 'an action for their desire.

- When **they** make an **offer** they either give you access to their body/resources, or they 'give 'an action for your desire.

- When **you** make a **request** you either ask for access to their body/resources or an action for your desire.

- When **they** make a **request** they either ask for access to your body/resources or an action for their desire.

THE BASEMENT OF SHADOWS

"We have in all naivete forgotten that beneath our world of reason another lies buried. I don't know what humanity will still have to undergo before it dares to admit this."
- Carl G. Jung

The word *shadow* immediately conjures up something dark or sinister, but I prefer the word to mean something slightly hidden, that gets in the way of optimal relating.

First thing first, please know that shadows are perfectly normal parts of every one of us and there is nothing intrinsically bad about them. As pair bonders and social beings, we tend to want to create harmony in the environment we're in. Shadows are coping and survival mechanisms we all develop in an attempt to get our needs met. They're behavioural strategies we revert to when we don't express what we desire and when we can't say no. We often use them in order to fit in and belong or to create a sense of balance or personal power. They not only stem from psychological needs but can be triggered by nervous system responses connected to past trauma. We are often unaware of our shadows, justify them in self-defence when we feel threatened, or suppress them due to the fear of not seeming like a good person (which could lead to rejection by others).

▢ BASEMENT / SHADOWS

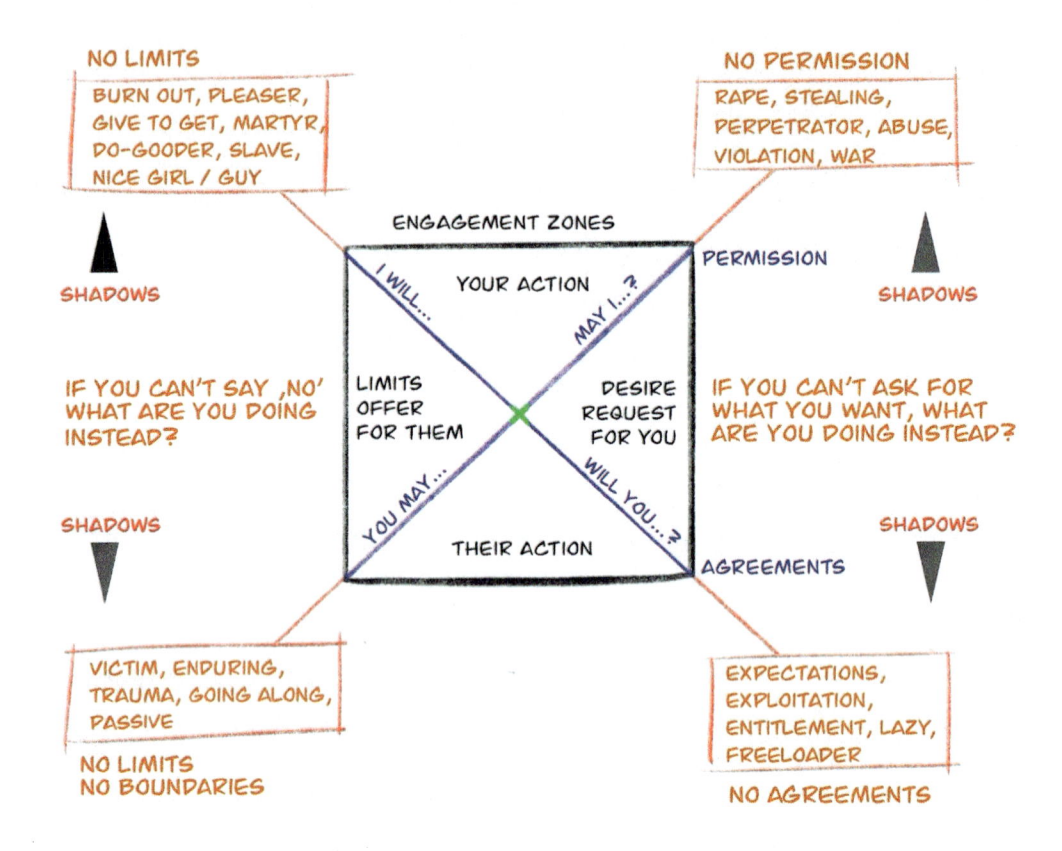

NO LIMITS
BURN OUT, PLEASER, GIVE TO GET, MARTYR, DO-GOODER, SLAVE, NICE GIRL / GUY

NO PERMISSION
RAPE, STEALING, PERPETRATOR, ABUSE, VIOLATION, WAR

▲ SHADOWS

▲ SHADOWS

ENGAGEMENT ZONES

- I WILL... — YOUR ACTION — MAY I...?
- PERMISSION
- LIMITS / OFFER FOR THEM
- DESIRE / REQUEST FOR YOU
- YOU MAY... — THEIR ACTION — WILL YOU...?
- AGREEMENTS

IF YOU CAN'T SAY 'NO' WHAT ARE YOU DOING INSTEAD?

IF YOU CAN'T ASK FOR WHAT YOU WANT, WHAT ARE YOU DOING INSTEAD?

▼ SHADOWS

▼ SHADOWS

VICTIM, ENDURING, TRAUMA, GOING ALONG, PASSIVE

NO LIMITS / NO BOUNDARIES

EXPECTATIONS, EXPLOITATION, ENTITLEMENT, LAZY, FREELOADER

NO AGREEMENTS

Shadow strategies can emerge in any situation in life. The ones outlined in the shadow map are common shadows we default to when boundaries, limits, permission and agreements are neglected. The situations they arise in are mostly within the following dynamics, with giving and receiving shown from YOUR perspective:

- **Receiving:** your action for you - Oppressing/Perpetrator Shadow
- **Giving:** your action for them - the Pleasing/Rescuer Shadow
- **Receiving:** their action for you - the Passivity/Victim Shadow
- **Giving:** their action for them - the Exploiting/Entitled Shadow

What we aim to do in Somatic Consent is to shine the light of awareness onto our blind spots to reveal these parts of self—rather than go into judgement of self and others. As long as awareness is present, we have a chance of knowing what motivates our actions and are more likely to be honest about how we relate with others.

Shadow dynamics are everywhere in society, within your family, relationships and professional structures, because most of human engagement is based on wanting something without being capable of communicating it.

You already know that if you want to go into action for yourself by touching another you need *permission,* and if you want someone to go into action for you, you need an *agreement.* **Permission and agreement make up** *consent* but obviously, getting permission and agreement each and every time we want to do something isn't a way to live our lives.

The Shadows Map is a tool to help us engage with others, so that we can be aware when permission or an agreement is missing. For example, when we aren't in alignment with what we actually want, or when the person touching us has an agenda and wants something out of us that we're not willing to give. It helps us to see where we can't say no or where we aren't setting limits.

Your action for you / their action for them

The oppressing/perpetrator shadow

When we don't ask for what we want, what are we doing instead?
We don't have permission but do it anyway.

This shadow manifests when you take action towards another person for your own benefit without that person's permission. This could be preying on others, being a perpetrator, stealing, bullying and abuse, any kind of force, violation, rape or war. It includes any kind of dominance, to have power over the other, including the wish to defend and protect them (which can feel overpowering, controlling and/or disempowering to the one being 'protected'—if they don't actually want it).

The passivity/victim shadow

If we don't say no, what are we doing instead?
We don't give permission and put up with it anyway.

This is the opposite of the oppressor shadow. We try to like what we don't like instead of changing what is happening. We don't say no, express our limits or give permission. But we allow it to happen anyway. The victim endures, goes along with things and is passive and shuts down, which creates trauma in the body.

Your action for them / their action for you

The exploiting/entitled shadow

When we don't ask for what we want, what are we doing instead?
We don't have an agreement but expect it anyway.

This shadow behaviour occurs when you want an action for you, but don't ask the other for that action. You believe no agreement is needed from a sense of privilege. This might manifest as having expectations (if you loved me you would do it), exploiting others, being lazy and expecting others to cater to our needs, freeloading, or being a pillow prince or princess in bed, expecting others to serve us.

The pleasing/rescuer shadow

If we don't say no, what are we doing instead?
We don't have an agreement and do anyway.

This is when we go into an action without having a request, doing something the other hasn't asked for or wants. It's the shadow of the do-gooder, the nice guy, the martyr or one who gives to get, I'll be good to you for something in return (seen in the service industry tip mentality). It is also the rescuer or wounded healer, the one who wants others to feel good all the time, who gives until they burn out.

Why can't you ask for what you want?

There are many answers to this question, and all stem from fear. The fear perhaps of seeming greedy or demanding, of not believing we can have what we want or of feeling exposed and vulnerable—the list is endless.

At workshops I often ask the questions, "Do you always ask for what you want? If not why?" The same answers come up again and again, irrespective of which age group, country or culture we're in. The answer to the first question is always no. The reasons why vary and include; not wanting to appear selfish, not wanting to be a burden, having a belief that it's better to wait until something is offered, that it's more holy or ethical to give than to receive, that it sounds pushy or strange, an unwillingness to appear needy and so on. At the root of all these different reasons is always the fear of rejection.

We all have basic human needs, which include touch and connection to others. When you perform an action of touch and it's *for you*—the sensory inflow that occurs as you touch is directly linked to getting this specific need met. If you can't clearly ask for what you want, it's difficult to get those needs met.

What happens if you can't ask for what you want? What do you do instead?

This is when the *shadow* comes into play. Because we all long for our needs to be met, if we don't ask for what we want—we consciously or unconsciously default to shadow behaviour to get what we want.

Answers to this question often include:

"I wait until it's offered."
"I go ahead and do it anyway."
"I drop hints."
"I get annoyed and blame my partner. They should know what I want by now."
"I try to convince myself I don't need anyone's help."

"I pretend I've transcended all my needs."
"I do things I assume they want (pleasing)."
"I suppress my desires."
"I do it myself without the other."
"I judge the other."
"I suffer in silence."

Why is it difficult for you to say no?

Reasons may include;

"They do so much for me."
"They'll think I'm weak."
"I like to be helpful."
"They need me."
"I want to be a good person."
"I don't want to hurt their feelings."
"I don't want to start an argument."
"Not realising I have the option to say no."
"Because I make myself responsible for their feelings."
"It's not spiritual."

If you can't say no, what are you doing instead?

Are you saying yes? Do you leave the other hanging without a clear decision? Go along with it? Push through your resistance? Suffer in silence? Pretend that you want and enjoy it? Give more than you want to?

And how does that work for you? How do you feel when you do this?
The inability to say no usually breeds anger, resentment, the urge to flee or chips away at our self-esteem.

What others say they do instead of saying no, and how it makes them feel.

"I do it and feel resentful."
"I repress how I feel and internalise my anger."
"I endure it but feel cornered."
"I disassociate and get more distant."
"I submit to what they want and remind them when I want something back."
"I lie, trying to convince myself that it's ok with me but feel dirty."
"I avoid my real limits and pretend all is fine, then regret it."

"I manipulate the other person to do what I want instead and feel guilty about it later."
"I block the other's request by staying silent and blame them for their desire/action."
"I go along with it and feel disempowered."

Again, if we're honest with ourselves, at the root of all these reasons is the core fear of being rejected.

In our early years, we were often not given any say or choice in decision making. We learned to adapt and change how we felt—rather than to trust our feelings. Due to this, as adults, many of us don't realise we have a right to voice what we want and don't want. We continue to endure, telling ourselves we can deal with what's happening or feel powerless to change the situation we're in. The adaptive survival strategies we all developed to avoid being rejected are at the core of most dysfunctional patterns of behaviour within relationship, whether between partners, family, friends, colleagues or in community. They are also at the root of oppression, racism, sexism and other 'isms'.

Because we become used to this during infancy, we may believe we are supposed to like or tolerate another's action and often go along with it to make them happy (and to fit in). The tendency to *push* ourselves rather than listen to the *pull* becomes the norm. In this way we abandon our needs, desires and boundaries (our self-care). We may even avoid being touched all together.

Shadows correlate with a child's responsibility or total lack of responsibility, which we'll go into in depth later. It is a realm in which there's neither genuine self-care nor authentic care of another being. When operating from a shadow dynamic our sensitivity is repressed and numbed. If we accept and endure unpleasant behaviour directed towards us, we can then direct it towards others around us.

In extreme cases, when someone is being or has been used or abused, sexually, physically or psychologically, they may have no reference point that it isn't acceptable and often go along with what's happening in order to avoid being rejected by their 'caretaker'. They try to like what they don't like instead of saying "stop".

We inherit the shadow of the victim from the time we didn't realise we had a choice. Out of this first shadow we develop many other survival strategies such as presuming we can do to others as they do to us. Hurt people tend to hurt people. Many step over from victim to bully as a sense of entitlement is established through feeling bitter and defensive about what happened to them in the past—demanding that 'the right thing' has to happen for them now and that others have to acknowledge whatever that is and provide it. This is when the abused becomes the abuser, producing action to get a reaction, for a response, gratification or a sense of power that they lacked in the past.

Our shadow strategies often support other people's shadows, for example, the shadow of a *pleaser* and the shadow of one who feels *entitled*. Or the *oppressor* and *victim*. Here we usually see the person with more perceived power within the engagement taking advantage of the other.

An example where shadows often emerge is when someone seems to be coming from a place of love and care, though is only pretending to provide action in the form of a gift *for you* (such as a massage) while actually having a hidden agenda such as pleasuring themselves. In this case they are in action *for themself* under the pretence that they are giving you a gift while in supposed action *for you*.

How the Direct Route helps you become aware of shadows

When the sensory inflow is *not* embodied, we're neurologically wired to go into action in return for approval and appreciation. We are more likely to 'give to get' and aren't so aware that we can ask for what we want. This is too challenging as it goes against everything we've learned through cultural conditioning. We feel too awkward asking for what we want and our survival strategies are all we know, are used to and what have 'worked' for us until this point.

The Direct Route is a kind of 'go to' landing pad that you embody within your nervous system. The somatic sensory inflow is the foundation for self-knowledge. It's always there to support, calm and ground you. It activates the noticing part of your brain so that you can bring your awareness to *what is* without putting a 'should' on top. When sensory inflow is embodied, you physically understand that you're *allowed to receive* for your own pleasure. You're more likely to know and ask for what you want. This challenges any shadow behaviour developed over the years by you or others to *indirectly* get needs and desires met.

What are your shadow strategies?

Do you take, steal or demand what you want? Suppress the desire? Pretend to be above your needs, too independent or spiritually advanced to care? Do you put up a wall of armour? Get pushy, moody, silent or sneaky? Give vague hints? Try to make the other feel guilty for not providing your heart's desire?

What examples can you think of from your own life?
What is your favourite way to be in the shadow?

Not being able to ask for what we want is really very similar to not being able to say no (what we don't want). Just as we all have a right and responsibility to ask for what we want, we all have the right and responsibility to ourselves to say no—by recognising our boundaries and expressing our limits.

Going along with touch you don't like

After my tantric awakening into the transformative space of pleasure, beyond the agenda of a goal—my nervous system became more adept at picking up subtleties of touch. One thing I became sensitive to was when someone went down on me with an agenda, either to please or in order to finish things off fast. Whenever it was clear that a lover was 'giving' me oral sex that involved the above actions or intentions on her part, my body would tense up. This was before I had embodied the neurological inflow of sensations via the Direct Route, and so, even though I didn't like it, I tried to like it by practising all kinds of techniques to bypass my body's responses.

Through embodying the Direct Route of pleasure, I realised that many people practise and provide oral sex with an intention to get a reaction—*without feeling much themselves*. Which was exactly what I didn't want to experience in my lovemaking with another. At this point, if someone wasn't able to feel themself via the Direct Route or were trying to please me with a goal in mind, I stopped pretending to like it.

Now that the Direct Route is my touching default, before being sensual or sexual with a partner, it's important to me that they've activated their Direct Route of pleasure too. I'm no longer willing to be touched by a beloved in the unawakened way. And although I sincerely want to touch, I only want it when the other is able to feel themself via the Direct Route and is really present in their body. It's also important to me that they are capable of being in tune with my body (via the Indirect Route) so that they know when their action is overwhelming me.

In later years a few of my clients asked for help because they didn't like their partner giving them oral sex. When they said 'giving' they meant 'doing', though because it was happening *to them*, they interpreted that as their partner *giving* to them while they themself were receiving.

They all asked how they could learn to like it, because they loved their partner. They all wanted to try and *learn to like what they didn't like.* Just as I had done previously, they were ready to abandon their actual, authentic desires and boundaries, to go along with what was happening. This meant they were only *willing* to touch and be touched.

- To be able to relate fluently with touch (have the capacity to fully receive) you have to want to be touched by the other person. This is a human need. Not *willing to*, but *want*.

- If you don't want to touch the other person and don't express your limits, you endure, in order to please in perpetual giving.

When you are only *willing* to be touched and the other person is only *willing* to touch you, both of you are trying to **give** something to the other. But if both are only willing to by giving, who is **receiving**? This is where both people are actually losing. It's a typical lose-lose situation. What I'm trying to bring across in this example is that when both are fully receiving what they want—*a winning situation is created for all involved.* This feels quite different in the body, especially when it comes to intimate relating between loving partners.

When somebody, while being attuned to you, can touch with their full presence in their own skin, when they don't perform to achieve a specific response, they will be relaxed and you will be able to relax with them. This is one type of co-regulation and leads to intimacy, surrender and the interpersonal experience of oneness.

Have you ever been touched against your will and tried to like what was happening?

Have you ever pretended you liked a specific kind of touch, to please the doer?

Have you ever faked an orgasm to end a sexual act because your partner was performing for your benefit without genuinely being tuned into their own tactile experience?

A lover's Direct Route experiment

Oral sex is obviously mouth to genitals. Based on the sensory fact that we have more nerve endings in our hands than even our mouth and genitals, it became clear that if someone hasn't activated the sensory inflow of their hands, they probably don't have the sensory inflow fully activated in their mouth either, and that through this action, it's much more likely that they have an agenda and goal in mind.

When your hands find the inflow, the rest of your body will too.

Here's a nice way to experiment feeling the inflow with other body parts after activating your hands. When practising oral sex with your partner try asking them; "Can I feel you with my mouth and my tongue?" This way, the intention focuses on feeling the sensory inflow and sensual pleasure instead of the agenda to prompt the end result of an orgasm. It's a practise of being with yourself, for your own pleasure, in-the-moment.

Are shadows wrong?

The personal and spiritual development of humanity is based on catastrophes and bad experiences, which we survived and learned from by acknowledging our survival strategies. In essence, it isn't wrong or bad to develop shadow strategies to enable survival. They are part of human engagement and we all have them.

Instead of beating yourself and others up about the survival strategies *we all use*, it's helpful to acknowledge that we never learned how to constructively ask for what we want or set limits in the first place. I'm sure you'll agree that if we dwell on our shortcomings (in any context) it just brings up more frustration, regret, guilt, resentment and so on.

If we don't acknowledge our own needs, and how we try to get them met, we'll have difficulty acknowledging that others have needs too—and their difficulties in getting them met. If we don't understand and have compassion for ourselves and our shadows, we won't have compassion or empathy for others' shadows. The understanding goes hand in hand. By being aware of shadow strategies that don't serve our personal and spiritual growth we awaken from the sleep state. We bring our actions from unconscious to conscious awareness. From drama to harmony, from not caring and not being cared for—to empowerment and choice.

Shadows are not something to avoid but to become aware of. They are juicy insights to human engagement. They provide an opportunity to learn about ourselves and others more intimately, which can be an extremely enjoyable process. I encourage you to look at your shadows with curiosity, just as you would unwrap a present. We're all so interesting inside. These inner insights are what enable us to grow.

Most people judge themselves when they become aware of their shadows. This is counterproductive. We don't judge ourselves for the dreams we have while asleep. It doesn't make any sense at all to chastise ourselves for being the product of all the unconscious input we've collected throughout our lives. We are who we are and everyone is perfectly imperfect. When we hold some kind of grudge against ourselves, it decreases the ability for us to relax into our being and form a solid Base of self-care. Part of self-care is taking responsibility for your thoughts, words and actions, awareness of what you want to change, self-forgiveness and willingness to move forward in growth. Uncovering shadows doesn't have to be dark, scary or serious. If we remain playful about the process we allow ourselves to have fun.

How to integrate shadows

"When there is integrity, there is impeccability."
- unknown

The great thing about shadows is, if one arises you know it's because you have a specific need for something—and this need isn't being met. Suddenly it shows you exactly what you *aren't* asking for or saying "no" to. When you become aware of a shadow, instead of shying away from it, suppressing it or being hard on yourself (which can result in you feeling fragmented, rather than whole), try instead to observe it, asking yourself; "Which need isn't being met here?".

Let's say, as an example, someone's giving their partner 'the silent treatment'. Clearly something is wrong. Ignoring stems from shadow. It is a rejection of the other and a form of punishment. In this situation the ignorer could ask themselves, "Which emotion is present right now? How do I feel?" If the answer is disappointment and frustration, because their partner didn't do something they wanted, then it begs the questions;

"Who is the action for?"

"Did I ask for what I wanted?"
"Did I express my need or just expect my partner to know or do what I want?"
"Did we come to any agreement about this?"

By asking these questions we come to the root of the unmet need—and the reason for shadow behaviour. We also avoid getting trapped in the loops of the 'story 'and our reaction to it. Naturally, it takes a certain amount of humility to take an honest look at ourselves. Sure, it can feel vulnerable and bring up other emotions such as embarrassment or shame. But these are just more juicy feelings to take a look at. When we begin this process, we open the door to the possibility of forgiveness, connection, intimacy and harmony within relationship.

If you are scared of asking for what you want, notice that and own it. When you notice, it can make it easier to take the leap and ask for what you want. For example, "I'd like you to slow down and notice I feel uncomfortable asking you to. Can you?"

Present moment engagement creates a window of transparency into our shadows. Shadows can show us, simply and easily, within each engagement we have with others, what *isn't being asked for*, *which boundaries aren't clear* and *what isn't being agreed upon*. This is in itself quite liberating. I encourage you to acknowledge the shadows you become aware of. Welcome them, especially when it comes to embarrassment and shame. Doing so will bring them to the light and allow the possibility for you to integrate this knowledge into your deepening level of relationship with self and others.

We don't have to 'work on 'our shadows, we don't have to heal anything, there isn't anything broken in you, nothing needs repairing or fixing. Just continue to let your skin do the work. Ask your partner or the person you want to connect with, "Can I feel you?" When you do this your neurological state begins to shift.

Is this a shadow or not?

Sometimes it may feel unclear whether a shadow has come up or not. Viewing a situation from the outside without knowing the details can cause us to jump to conclusions.

Once, while with a friend in a club oozing with heterosexual men hanging out to get some action, I took on the role as her protector. When I assumed a man was getting too close to her I threatened him saying, "If you touch her, you're in trouble!" She told me, "I'll tell you if he bothers me, otherwise, let him be." In this case, although my intention was to gift my power, my action took the possibility for her to stand in her own power away.

At other times it may seem that someone is in shadow and out of integrity when, in fact, they are giving a gift to the other—in order for them to explore their deepest truth about a certain thing.

During an exercise I was facilitating on receiving by choice, I began to observe one of the couples. To me, it looked like the person in action was trying to please the other. I checked with my assistant who couldn't tell for sure, though agreed it did look like 'pleasing'. I decided to ask. I went over to them and said, "That looks interesting, what's your agreement and who is it for?" The person the action was happening to said, "I want to clearly know how it feels when somebody is touching me while trying to please. I want to know the difference clearly in my body."

When we are the ones directly involved, it's also difficult to know whether we or the other is in shadow. Our nervous systems work hard to protect us, and our minds are often triggered by self-protective behaviour including pointing the finger in blame.

Consider the following scenarios:

Imagine, you're sitting in a plane and your neighbour falls asleep, leaning their head on your shoulder. If you have a prior bad experience of having your personal space invaded, it may bring up feelings of *victimisation*. You may endure, go along with it and blame the other for invading your space. But in reality the other is just tired and has fallen asleep. Is this person an *oppressor*? No.

Imagine another scenario. You lend your bike to a friend and ask them to put it back where they'd found it. They do it this time, but the next time they borrow it, you don't ask them to put it back in the same place and they put it somewhere else. When you go to use it, you can't find it, feel annoyed and tell your friend how you feel. They're surprised you're making a fuss, after all, it was only around the corner. Are you coming from a place of *entitlement* to expect your bike back where you'd left it? I would say it's a combination of common sense, adult responsibility and a sign of gratitude for your generosity to put it back where it was found.

Giving without permission or agreement
Love and care or shadow?

If you help someone without them asking you to, for example, when their shopping bag splits open, by picking up their things from the street; are you coming from a place of love and care, being a rescuer or a thief?

This is a tricky question. I've experienced a lot of rigidity within the consent community which leaves little room for the option of giving from a place of love and care (compassion and charity) when your action wasn't agreed upon. People, of course, can care for others without coming from the shadow of the 'rescuer'.

Would it be a shadow if the person you are helping accuses you of abuse because they haven't asked you for your help? It depends on the view of the beholder. This is the paradox that duality causes when the beholder doesn't perceive your action as a gift and instead views your action from their perception of feeling violated.

One day, while at the supermarket checkout, the person in front of me dropped their wallet. Their coins rolled in every direction including towards me. I bent down and began picking them up. The owner of the wallet started shouting and accusing me of stealing. Reflexively I opened my hands, dropped the coins and took a step back.

What had been my actual role in this scenario? Was I a thief? Was I being a pleaser or did I just feel compassion and want to help? I believe I was coming from a place of love and care. I assume the person who dropped the money perceived themselves as a victim, and so, automatically put me in the role of perpetrator.

Sometimes when we operate from a shadow we automatically put the other person in the opposite shadow, whether their action stems from shadow or not.

Let's say your lover begins to massage you. You might like and enjoy it, or you might not. But if you didn't request the massage or the other person didn't make an offer (and just started massaging you) you might think the other person is doing it for themselves—and because you love and care for them, you allow them to continue. At this point, you put yourself in a position of *enduring* and *going along.* As soon as you put yourself into the enduring *victim* corner, you put the other person automatically into the shadow of the invading *oppressor*.

Your lover now tries to do different things to get your appreciation (*pleasing*). The more action happens, the more you shut down as resentment builds and you blame them for being selfish (being in action for themself). This could lead them to feel resentful too. They see the rejection of their gift and service to you—perceiving you as *entitled*, never satisfied or taking their goodwill for granted.

This is a very common shadow dynamic between people.
Does it sound familiar?

Another example may be at a yoga class. Most instructors manually correct their students. If they have the best intentions, to correct others for their benefit—are they out of integrity, or are they coming from a place of support and care? The problem is most don't ask for permission before touching. I appreciate it if there's a 'do not touch me 'card next to the yoga mat these days and when the instructor respects my limits. I want the instructor to have my permission before touching me and appreciate being corrected when I don't put a card next to the mat.

The bottom line is, even when someone is coming from a place of altruistic compassion, support, love and care—consent is required. Of course, sometimes we reflexively touch without consent in order to protect someone. An example is a time someone fainted next to me. Without thinking I grabbed her to prevent her head from hitting the floor.

Under normal circumstances, each person must have the choice to accept and decline touch and other action. If you are coming from a place of love and care, maybe you aren't in shadow per se—but the other may perceive you to be, which will feed their shadows and cause confusion. If you are really coming from a place of love and care, then awareness of the possible confusion your action can cause is necessary, as is the compassion to ask for consent.

Simply offering your service of love and care provides choice. "Would you like any help?", "Do you want a hand?", "I'd love to give you a back massage to help you relax. Can I do that?", "Do you want my opinion? I think it may help."

The exception would be if you are in a flow state with your lover, in which case, agreements are made beforehand. We'll talk about this in more depth in the Relationship Map section.

Shadow dynamics of offers and requests

Everyone has a right to their basic needs; for water, sleep, food etc. If we have to ask for our needs to be met by someone else, we put them in a position of power, giving them the ability to decide whether they withhold or withdraw what we need. We make ourselves vulnerable on a survival level by creating dependency on the other (if they decide to abuse their role).

Let's say you need drinking water and have to ask someone for it. This happened continuously to a friend living at a remote place in Asia. Whenever the drinking water ran out, she'd ask her landlord to deliver some more. He sometimes didn't deliver the water for up to a week and often demanded rent money for the next month before doing so. So these dynamics are not just related to the structure of human engagement as lovers in the realm of intimacy, but can reflect a holistic imbalance of oppression, power over, control and manipulation in many other areas of life.

Another example is the time I was teaching in Hong Kong. This culture is based on *offers*. Giving and doing, over and over, bringing the other into a position of debt—so that the other has to finally ask you *what you want*. I told the organiser of the course that if I needed anything I would ask, and if I didn't ask, I didn't need anything—and to please not do anything unless I asked specifically for it. This confused the lady tremendously and shows how conditioned many of us are.

I'd like to briefly acknowledge here, that the avoidance of making vulnerable requests and instead, offering from a place of fear can *co-exist* with the desire to give a gift from an altruistic place of generosity.

OVERVIEW OF THE ENGAGEMENT ZONES & SHADOWS

WHO'S DOING THE ACTION?	YOUR ACTION	YOUR ACTION	THEIR ACTION	THEIR ACTION
WHO IS IT FOR?	YOU WANT TO TOUCH THEM – IT'S FOR YOU	THEY WANT YOU TO TOUCH THEM – IT'S FOR THEM	THEY WANT TO TOUCH YOU – IT'S FOR THEM	YOU WANT THEM TO TOUCH YOU – IT'S FOR YOU
WHAT TO ASK FOR OR OFFER	CAN/MAY I?	CAN/WILL YOU? WOULD YOU LIKE?	CAN/MAY I?	CAN/WILL YOU? WOULD YOU LIKE?
WHEN WE DON'T ASK / OFFER WE CAN'T GIVE PERMISSION OR MAKE AGREEMENTS	NO PERMISSION	NO AGREEMENT NO LIMITS	NO PERMISSION NO BOUNDARIES NO LIMITS	NO AGREEMENT
SHADOWS INCLUDE	PREDATOR PERPETRATE OPPRESSING BULLYING STEALING GROPING ASSAULT VIOLATION RAPE WAR	PLEASER RESCUER DO-GOODER NICE GIRL/GUY SLAVE GUESSING GIVING TO GET BURNOUT	PASSIVE VICTIM ENDURING TOLERATING DOORMAT PUSHOVER	EXPLOITING ENTITLEMENT EXPECTING FREELOADER LAZINESS ENSLAVING

Specific shadows often emerge in the following dynamics.

1. Permission line shadow: your action for you = OPPRESSING (perpetrator)
2. Permission line shadow: their action for them = PASSIVITY (victim)
3. Agreement line shadow: your action for them. PLEASING (rescuer)
4. Agreement line shadow: their action for you. EXPLOITING (entitled)

People often ask; "Can an action be for both people? Is it always either for you or for them?"

The answer to this question is yes, if it is what both want, it is simultaneous action at the Apex of the Engagement Zones for both.

It depends on if there is a giver and receiver. One person can totally enjoy giving a massage and the other can totally enjoy receiving this massage, but by definition a massage is *for the receiver* and an agreement has to be in place. Is your hand going where you want or is your hand going where they want? Most people have real difficulties speaking up about their boundaries and expressing their true desires.so What most likely happens in this case, is the emergence of shadow strategies such as expectations, entitlement or pleasing. That's why The 3 Minute Game is so useful. It makes this kind of scenario really transparent.

In Somatic Consent, giving is only offered from a 'clean 'place. A gift is generously given without attachment to outcome. We give from the interpersonal space at the Apex, the pinnacle of the pyramid structure where love and care is offered unconditionally as a gift to and from the world around us. Here we can experience the merging of separate people into an interpersonal 'we' space of togetherness in oneness.

THE APEX OF LOVE, CARE, INTEGRITY, GENEROSITY, GRATITUDE AND SURRENDER

"Out beyond ideas of wrongdoing and rightdoing, there is a field. I will meet you there."
- Rumi.

Humans thrive when we share our gifts and purpose with the world—and want others to share their gifts with the world too. This is a harmonious and mutually uplifting place, free of agenda and attachment where winning happens for all involved. It happens within friendship, in relationship between lovers, as a tribe, as a community. Here dwell the values of surrender, gratitude, generosity, the power of love and care and the genuine communication of *invitation*. It is what we access at the space I call the Apex.

The pyramid form of the SCES illustrates how to attain this state of interpersonal transcendence and bliss with another person. The Apex is the peak of the pyramid structure and represents the *state of being* we embody when the Engagement Zones are fully communicated and respected.

The Base represents the *foundation of self-care*. It encompasses what we have a right to and a responsibility for—i.e. ourselves.

The Engagement Zones are the space where *agreements and permissions* are made within relationship. They're a map leading you to the interpersonal space at the Apex.

The Apex is the transformative part, when we transcend conditioned action and simply rest in authentic being—and interpersonal experience occurs.

APEX

INTERPERSONAL, BEING A GIFT, INTIMACY, CONNECTION, TRUE RELATING, LOVE MAKING, FRIENDSHIP, PLAY, WIN/WIN

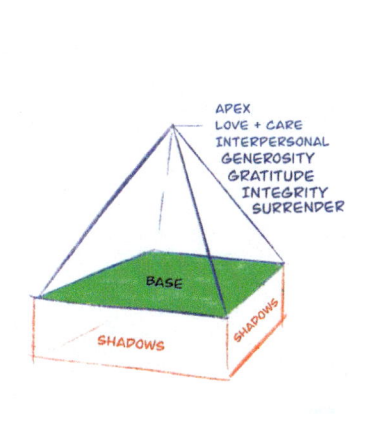

INTEGRITY: ALIGNMENT WITH OWN DESIRES IN WORD AND ACTION

GENEROSITY: UNCONDITIONALLY PROVIDING FROM ABUNDANCE WITHOUT NEEDING ANYTHING BACK

GRATITUDE: THE JOY OF FEELING GRATEFUL FOR THE GIVEN GIFTS, FREE OF GUILT RECIPROCITY

SURRENDER: FROM PLACE OF TRUSTWORTHINESS OF OWN LIMITS, TO A PERSON OR OWN EXPERIENCE

WWW.SOMATICCONSENT.COM

If we look at the Engagement Zones from above we see that the two lines crossing each other to show permissions and agreements have a point in the middle at which they meet. This is the Apex in 2D. In 3D we see this structure as a four-sided pyramid with the point of meeting being the Apex on top. This is where interpersonal action happens and where both people can be in action for both, whether that's between lovers, family members or friends.

Here our personal identification, shadows, survival strategies and defence mechanisms are transcended. There is a level of communication where invitation happens. It is a place of engagement where both people get what they want, and both 'win'. It is an agenda-less encounter, where both are having a good time and being good to each other through goal-less play.

We relate at the Apex with a combination of integrity in our action, generosity while giving a gift, gratitude when receiving and surrender to their action.

Integrity - in your action

- Acknowledging when there is something we want to do, and not pretending to be doing it for them.
- Alignment of your desires, words and actions.
- Awareness whether an action is either for you or them.
- Learning that you and others have limits.

Being at the Apex with another person only happens when both have a solid personal Base. This translates as; both knowing what their rights and responsibilities are as individuals, both understanding what the agreements are within the relationship, both respecting the other's limits, and both being aware of their own shadows.

When you are in alignment with your desires, thoughts and actions, you know if your action is *for you* or *for them*. This brings integrity to each action you make because your awareness is crystal clear.

You also have a deeper understanding of other people's motives and whether their actions are *for you* or *for them*. So, in every action, word, encounter, with whomever, wherever, whenever—you are also capable of knowing who it is for.

In any relationship, there are times when we get hungry, tired or overwhelmed. At times like these we can lapse into the assumption that the other has to do something for us, or that they've taken more than we want them to. Communication gets confused, misunderstandings occur, and all of a sudden the magic has gone. A lot of this has to do with conditioning and shadow survival strategies.

Once you reach the Apex, there will, of course, be times like this when you find yourself back in the shadows. The Apex is not a place of permanent enlightenment. We're all human.

When you become aware of a shadow, it's your choice and responsibility to head back up, from the Basement of shadow to the Engagement Zones, so you can work out what it is that hasn't been asked for (permission) and which agreement hasn't been made.

The more you practice the Engagement Zones, the more you increase your understanding of who an action is for, sharpen your skills of engagement with others—and the more fun it will be to explore. As your awareness increases, you will know that any disappointment comes from a *shadow*.

Then you can ask yourself;

What haven't I asked for?

Where couldn't I say no?

Where couldn't I express my limits?

Is it a gift that person is giving?

Am I giving a gift here or do I want something?

Am I disappointed because I want something but I haven't asked for it?

We never stop developing and discovering deeper layers of ourselves. We don't come to a 'final understanding' but grow and learn as we go along.

Through practice *with others open to these concepts*, we can learn how to engage more deeply by gradually allowing ourselves to be more vulnerable when expressing our desires, even though fear of rejection may be present at first when expressing something more honestly than we're used to.

Often we fail to engage in asking/granting permission and coming to agreement with others because we're afraid of the shadows in them and ourselves. But when we have the courage to do so, a great adventure in personal and spiritual growth is possible.

Generosity - when it's for them

- Generosity is giving the other access to your body or resources, giving permission to them, to do what they want to do.
- Giving or doing exactly what someone else desires (within your limits) while putting your own desires aside.
- Giving from a sense of abundance—without attachment to outcome or needing or expecting anything in return.

The Apex represents the peak experience of interpersonal love, care and connection where we are a gift to the other—with no attachment to outcome.

Just like a mother gives pure unconditional love and care, without expecting anything in return. This same state is experienced at the Apex, as we come into connection with our partner, others and the world around us from a place of embodiment without agenda.

In the *for them* dynamic you develop generosity as you unconditionally provide from a sense of abundance (without needing or expecting anything in return) being generous in your action to the other, giving or doing exactly what someone else desires (within your limits) while putting your own desires aside. You embody generosity when you give the other access to your body or resources, giving permission to them to do what they want to do.

Recently at the train station I saw a couple of women struggling to haul a large suitcase up the stairs. "May I help you?", I asked. This question usually asks for permission for something *for yourself*. In this context I was asking for permission to provide something *for them*. I could also have asked "Do you need any help?"

I was offering to give my gift of power from a place of care. I didn't want anything back, I didn't want to please or rescue in order to make myself feel good, I just felt an urge to offer that gift—because I could. Offering and giving a gift, then moving on, without any attachment to the answer is a tremendous skill to have. Can you think of ways you do this in daily life, when you offer and give gifts that are truly for the other, without any sense of disappointment if your offers and gifts are rejected?

Gratitude - when it's for you

- The joy of feeling grateful for the gifts you receive from either your action or their action.
- Being able to fully receive.
- Develops from the 'for you' dynamic.
- Free of guilt or need to give back.

When the *for you* dynamic is present in your awareness you will develop the spiritual quality of gratitude. Here you come into a space of gratefulness, receiving what is *for you*, either due to someone else's action towards you, or from your own action for yourself.

You will, no doubt develop a sense of gratefulness when given access to someone else's body (your action for you), or when receiving exactly the touch you asked for and needed (their action for you). Gratitude embraces being able to fully receive and is free of any guilt-driven urge to give back.

Surrender - when it's their action

- Surrender is experiencing ourselves as a gift and stopping managing the outcome.
- Surrendering to somebody's actions or to an experience, within your limits.
- Inner trust is required—when you know you have limits and can trust yourself to express them when they come up, you'll find it easier to let go and release control.
- Deep relaxation where you transcend all 'doing' and enter into a bliss state.
- Offering yourself to a power higher than yourself.
- Experiencing the gift of who you are, while knowing that this gift of self is not dependent on doing something to belong.

We experience the natural state of surrender during deep relaxation (when a part of the parasympathetic nervous system is engaged) and we allow ourselves to fully let go. Here, in this allowing state, we transcend all doing and just 'are'. In these moments, we 'offer' ourselves to a power higher than ourselves because we release our grip on control. In this absolute state of release, you feel immersed in pure bliss.

Surrender to their action for you

This naturally occurs as you let go. You are able to surrender to your own experience because it is exactly what you want. An example could be receiving a delicious massage, exactly where and for how long you want it, without attachment to outcome, agenda or any other story. You know you can ask them to stop, whenever you want to, due to the clarity of awareness and communication you've nurtured.

Surrender to their action for them

This is possible because you've made a choice as to what will happen. You can let go because your limits are clear and agreed upon—and you feel safe knowing they won't be crossed.

When you've made clear agreements and your partner respects your limits, you are able to enjoy **their** state of surrender to **your action for them.** For both this type of action and also when it's **your action for you,** you experience the sensations of flow and connection within your somatic sensory system via the Direct and Indirect routes of pleasure.

The *state of being* found in surrender provides the neurological need of feeling safe with another in a space of effortless love and connection. In this state we experience the gift of who we are, as we are, while knowing our gift of self is *not* dependent on doing something to belong. It is not only a deeply enriching experience, where rejuvenation occurs, but satisfies the deepest longing within—a longing to merge with others and the world around us beyond any concepts of duality. This call to connect in oneness is an intrinsic part of who we are. Most of us are deprived of it, suffering a kind of 'spiritual hunger'.

If you look at Somatic Consent from this perspective, you can begin to see it as a structure of personal development, guiding you to:

Know yourself deeply in an embodied way by awakening your body's tactile sensory capacity

Recognise your desires and limits

Unearth and integrate your hidden shadow survival strategies

Tend to your own self-care, self-responsibility and authenticity in expression

Learn to relax and let go by being fully yourself

*Surrender to the bliss of **interpersonal** merging with your partner*

*Develop this experience of being and fully awaken to your spiritual **transpersonal** self, where the oneness of all things is perceived*

Maybe you recognise this feeling of connection to things beyond yourself. Have you ever experienced something like this while alone? Possibly during meditation, dancing or walking in nature? A feeling of expansion, as if a door opened, allowing your soul to soar?

This is the state accessed at Apex, in surrender with another person to all you both are—in blissful oneness.

The direct route and surrender

In order to experience the Apex, we must be in tune with the Direct Route, so that we **land** in our bodies, are grounded in the reality of what is happening to us in-the-moment and can function in a holistically embodied way.

If we are cut off from the information coming in through our sense of touch, we reduce the ability of the nervous system to relax and feel safe, we produce less oxytocin, limiting our ability to connect and bond—and we default to the Indirect Route. This means we function in a disembodied way, identifying primarily with our conditioned thoughts, which leads us so easily into the realm of shadow behaviour.

CHAPTER 3

EMBODIED EMPOWERMENT & SPIRITUAL DEVELOPMENT

The Grounded And Spiritual Self In Union

"We are spiritual creatures - not spirits added to bodies, but embodied spirits."
- James H. Olthuis

Our nervous system isn't made to remain in only one state. There are many different ways to experience life, and there's a neurological state for each. These states change depending on the situation at hand, in order to optimise our survival and enable us to thrive. From an early age, while still dependent on our caregivers, we *co-regulated* with their help. We cried when we were hungry or uncomfortable. We were fed, made comfortable and soothed by them. They helped us to change out of dysregulated states until we were old enough to self-regulate alone. The challenge as adults is that the shift between nervous system states is often automatic, unconscious and based on past experience. This can hinder our ability to self-regulate at times of stress and trauma.

When we become more familiar with ourselves and all nervous system states, we can learn how to consciously change from one state to another, in order to self-regulate with more ease. This is an example of 'biohacking'. Making small, conscious changes that considerably improve your well-being. We can also learn how to help others co-regulate more easily in our presence—which is a great way of gifting our power so that others can live more fully.

THE POLYVAGAL THEORY

Surviving And Thriving

"If you want to improve the world, start by making people feel safer."
- Stephen Porges

Have you ever just been going about your day, maybe working, chatting with a friend or walking down the street, feeling yourself and relatively balanced when, suddenly, someone bumps into you and doesn't apologise, sends a rude email or makes a flippant remark?

Did that sting?

How did you react?
What did you say or do?
How did you feel?
Was your reaction instantaneous?
If it hadn't been so immediate, if your feelings had had time to settle… would you have reacted in a different, possibly more logical way?
Did you later feel disappointed with how you reacted?

I went shopping at the supermarket the other day and took along a bag of recyclable bottles to return. I remembered I had the bottles with me as I got to the checkout. I asked someone where to take them and he directed me to the back of the shop, on the other side of the checkout area. I hadn't yet paid so I left my shopping where it was next to the checkout, returned the bottles and came back. As I tried to pass through the checkout to get back to my shopping, the cashier began shouting at me aggressively, "That's forbidden, you're not allowed to pass through here, you have to go back to the entrance". It took me a few moments to collect myself, then in the quietest way I said, "no" and continued walking through the checkout to my shopping. Then, a loop of thoughts and feelings of fear arose. I really wanted to go and sit somewhere so I could digest the situation for a while.

Had I broken a rule or law?
Was I rude to ignore the shouting?
Did I want to complain to the manager?
Did I want an apology?
Did I have to apologise?
Did I want to leave and do my shopping somewhere else?
I ended up paying at a different checkout but the situation came home with me for a while, a running loop in my head and a knotty feeling in my belly.

When an external irritant takes place, I'm sure you've noticed that at times, yourself and others react immediately to them, without any thought process at all.

We've already talked a little about the amygdala and fear. When our brain identifies something as potentially dangerous, we have to be able to react instantaneously. Why we do what we do is therefore—*by no means always due to conscious choice.*

Sure, part of understanding and steering the enigma of self is knowing your subconscious shadows (what triggers you to feel threatened, as well as your particular 'flavour 'of reaction). But there's another cog in the human machine. It's called the autonomic nervous system. This system automatically controls your unconscious mechanisms. Things like your heart beat, breathing and digestion. It is, quite literally, hell-bent on your very survival.

Imagine. Suddenly a crazy storm appears on a sunny day. What do you do? Wrestle with an umbrella in the howling wind and pelting rain—or run for cover? And what happens if a powerful lightning bolt strikes the ground in front of you? In that split second, do you stop in your tracks? We **automatically** do whatever we need to, to stay safe. Because in safety we regain a sense of balance and well-being.

To really understand how we all tick at a very fundamental level, beyond our usual conscious control, let's look at The Polyvagal Theory from Stephen Porges. It'll shine a light in the struggle to know yourself in all your complexity. It'll let you off the hook for some seemingly irrational past reactions, when, at times, your body bypassed conscious choice in order to keep you safe. It'll give another layer of insight into the hurtful behaviour of others. It'll provide valuable tools for self-regulation (alone) and co-regulation (with the help of others) in times of stress and trauma. And, reveal the delicious and blissful state of being—beautifully and logically bringing together the scientific and the spiritual.

The three branches

Stephen Porges 'The Polyvagal Theory has only recently been acknowledged within the scientific community.[33] It is much more than an expanded understanding of how the autonomic nervous system works. It provides groundbreaking knowledge for a more evolved understanding of human nature. Key aspects explain why our bodies at times behave in ways we wouldn't consciously choose, taking us from the realm of *perception* to *neuroception*. It also provides incredible insight into *how we can influence* normally unconscious processes to greatly enhance our well-being.

Porges says that our cultures don't understand safety and don't focus on it. Instead, they tend to focus on threat. When we remove a threat, it isn't the same for our body as when it thrives in safety. We *need* cues of safety. We *need* refuge—and our nervous systems are wired to get that need met through social engagement. "Our bodies are not machines that need to be fixed, they are feeling organisms that need to feel safe in order to heal themselves".

In the past, the autonomic nervous system was described as having two parts: the parasympathetic and the sympathetic. The Polyvagal Theory more accurately points to three parts rather than two. This is due to the parasympathetic vagus nerve having two very different functions.

Vagus is the Latin word for 'wandering', an apt name because this nerve wanders throughout and is connected to all the body's systems. It begins in the brain and goes through the jaw, with one branch leading to the lungs and heart. The other branch continues down, connecting to the lower parts of the abdomen.

1. One part of the **parasympathetic system** is governed by the *ventral branch of the vagus nerve* which affects body functioning above the diaphragm. This branch serves the ***social engagement system*** which helps us navigate relationships. It leads directly to the muscles of the face and helps determine expression. It urges us to constantly seek safety in the environment we're in by initiating social contact through connection with others. When activated we feel calm, balanced and function as our optimal selves.

2. **The sympathetic system** is arousing. This branch functions in

times of stress (fight or flight) but is also responsible for mobilising the body during normal activity. The body needs the complementary parasympathetic and sympathetic functions in order to remain balanced and sustain normal function. Ideally they work in gentle collaboration.

3. The other part of the **parasympathetic system** is governed by the *dorsal branch of the vagus nerve*, a large, primitive nerve that affects the diaphragm and downwards to other organs. When the sympathetic system is over-aroused, the dorsal vagus nerve initiates the shutdown state of *numbness* that we commonly encounter in traumatic situations.

The Polyvagal Theory Map details the Triune Autonomic Nervous System. It is a down-regulation system, working sequentially from top to bottom based on cues of safety or danger.

There are two main functions of this three branched system.

1. **Survive**: this function operates under conditions of stress, enabling you to respond to a threat.
2. **Thrive**: this function operates under conditions of safety.

Whether we feel stressed or safe at any given time is, of course, relative, as it's based on an individual's past unique experiences and perception and therefore entirely personal. One person's 'safety zone' may feel terrifying to another.

How would you feel in the following situations? Would you feel some degree of stress, feel neutral or good (safe)?

A big spider is walking along your arm.

You're travelling alone in an unknown but peaceful country.

Your lover is embracing you.

Someone criticizes the work you put a lot of effort into.

A stranger approaches you on the street at night.

You're standing on the edge of a cliff looking down to crashing waves.

You jump from an airplane with a parachute.

You look at your beloved for a few minutes.

You look into a stranger's eyes for 3 minutes.

What kind of reactions did you notice in your physical body as you imagined the scenarios?

However you reacted, know that your body is watching out for you, even if it is a little over reactive at times! Your nervous system is wired to automatically respond to keep you safe.

POLY VAGAL THEORY MAP

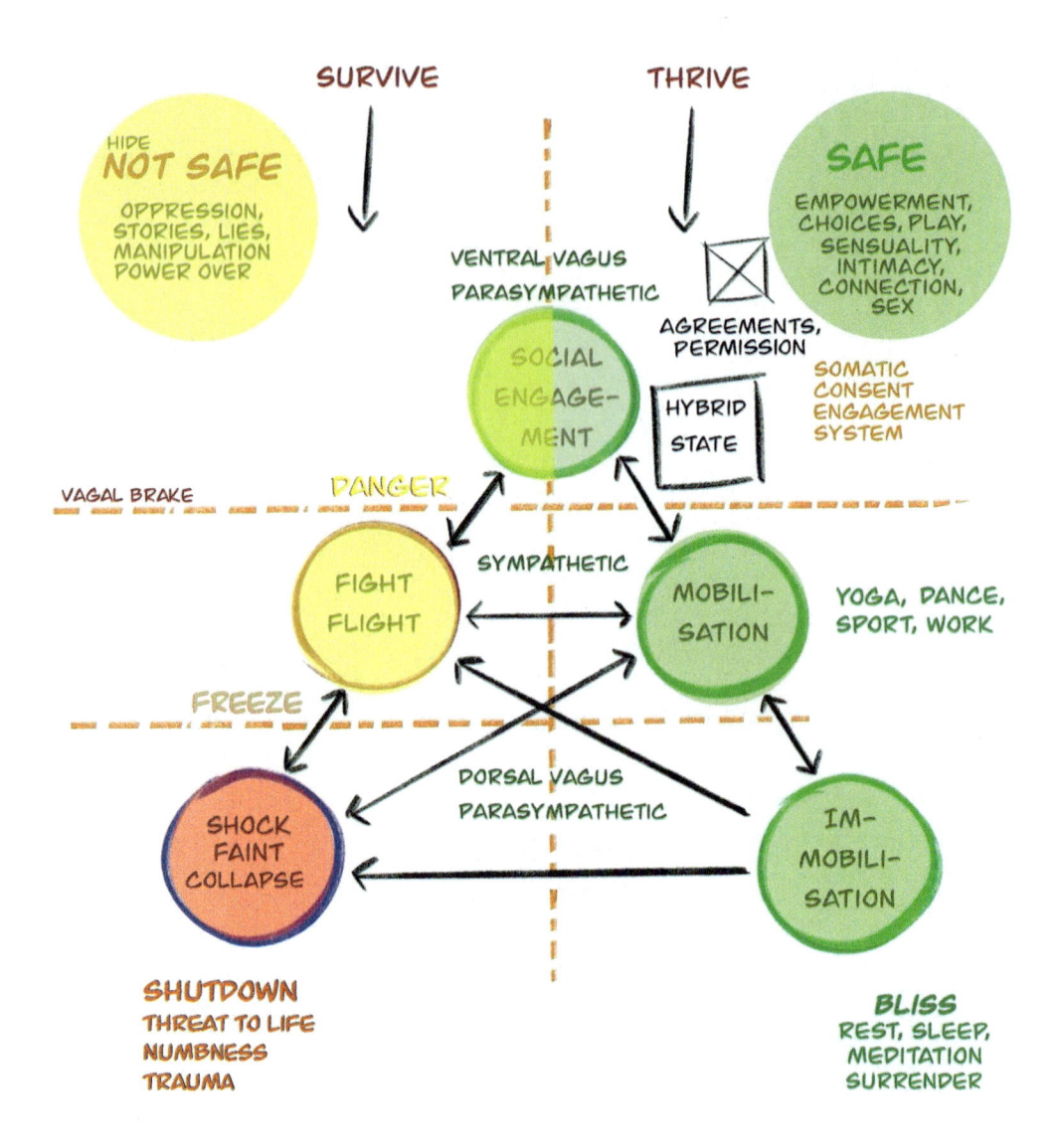

SURVIVE → **THRIVE**

NOT SAFE (HIDE)
OPPRESSION, STORIES, LIES, MANIPULATION, POWER OVER

SAFE
EMPOWERMENT, CHOICES, PLAY, SENSUALITY, INTIMACY, CONNECTION, SEX

VENTRAL VAGUS PARASYMPATHETIC

SOCIAL ENGAGEMENT

AGREEMENTS, PERMISSION

HYBRID STATE

SOMATIC CONSENT ENGAGEMENT SYSTEM

VAGAL BRAKE — — — **DANGER** — — —

FIGHT FLIGHT ← SYMPATHETIC → MOBILISATION

YOGA, DANCE, SPORT, WORK

— — — **FREEZE** — — —

SHOCK FAINT COLLAPSE

DORSAL VAGUS PARASYMPATHETIC

IM-MOBILISATION

SHUTDOWN
THREAT TO LIFE
NUMBNESS
TRAUMA

BLISS
REST, SLEEP, MEDITATION
SURRENDER

WWW.SOMATICCONSENT.COM

Primal instinct - the human animal and neuroception

Despite our more advanced consciousness, we have similar primal instincts to other mammals. The **vagus nerve** uses a mechanism called *neuroception* to process sensory information from your environment. In this way it scans for signs of safety and signs of danger. Each time we meet someone new or experience a new situation, our bodies use neuroception to determine whether they are safe or dangerous. Neuroception is responsible for much of that gut feeling we get that we like to call *intuition*. Sometimes we get it right, sometimes we don't. Our bodies have a bias to recognise danger, even if it may not be real, in order to increase our chances of survival.

If we imagine this in the context of traffic lights; your nervous system reacts depending on how it determines the new encounter:

Safe = green, all normal, go ahead.

Dangerous = amber, high alert, retaliate or run away.

Life Threatening = red, shutdown and 'simulated death'.

This survival mechanism is an *instantaneous and automatic process*, changing in order for you to respond, adapt and stay safe. It affects everything. Not only your heart rate and breathing, but *how you perceive* all your sensory signals. Sights, smells, sounds, taste—**and touch**. This means that you perceive the very *same situation completely differently, depending on how safe you feel*. If you're feeling safe, someone may seem pleasant. If you're feeling unsafe, that very same person may seem dangerous. A feeling of safety is dependent on many things. It's influenced not only by your personal history, but by the situation you're in, your general state of health and whether certain needs are being met or not.

Have you ever said yes to an invitation to go out and socialise, when you'd rather have spent some quiet time alone? Were you able to connect and function as you would if you'd have been 'in the mood'? Were you less tolerant of certain things such as crowds, loud music or remarks people made?

Let's look at the three branches of the autonomic nervous system, beginning with the first branch of social engagement, a place of safety where we all aim to be. Then we'll look at both the unsafe (survive) and safe (thrive) sides of the other two branches.

Social engagement

When the social engagement system is active, your *ventral vagus* parasympathetic nervous system is dominant. When there is a neuroception of safety, the ventral vagus nerve inhibits the fight or flight trauma response of the sympathetic nervous system to activate the social engagement system. In non-stressful situations, your body and emotions feel in a happy state as you go about your day with others. You're relaxed and your physiology is calm. You feel safe and good. Your heart rate slows down, your digestion is in equilibrium, the cranial nerve activates your facial muscles so that you can connect to others through face-to-face engagement using emotional expression and eye contact. You'll speak with a soothing or melodic voice. The middle ear muscles also activate, enabling you to pick up frequencies associated with human voices, even in crowded environments.

Humans are intensely social for a reason. We absolutely need safe interaction with others in order to thrive. One very important function of the *social engagement system* is to motivate us to seek support and connection. This is its built-in mechanism for stress resilience.

Imagine a group of gazelles grazing peacefully. With no apparent threat in their environment, they interact with the rest of their herd, eating, drinking, moving calmly and playfully. It's similar when we humans feel safe. Through social contact and especially through touch, oxytocin is released. As a natural anti-inflammatory, oxytocin protects your cardiovascular system by helping your blood vessels stay relaxed during times of stress.

Oxytocin also primes you to do things that strengthen close relationships by fine-tuning your brain's social instincts. It enhances bonding and empathy —making you more willing to help and support the people you care about. So, when you reach out to others for help or to help someone else, you release more oxytocin. In this way your social engagement system enables you to not only survive, but to thrive in co-regulation.[34] Though bonding and connection with others, your capacity for playfulness increases. Connection supports choice, intimacy and empowerment. You more easily listen to and understand others, you eat and sleep well, and feel open and curious about life in general.

Without social engagement/ventral vagus activity, we cannot bond and feel *safe*. If we're continually disconnected from the experiences of face-to-face and touch interaction, the lack of safety renders us unable to relax, rejuvenate, heal or function with balance. This means that in times of social isolation, when we're consistently disconnected from others, the nervous system automatically functions in a chronically unsafe state. At times like this, the simple biohack of tuning into the inflow when touching an object can be a literal life saver.

When we touch mindfully, the afferent neurons relaying information from our skin activate the ventral vagus and release of oxytocin. This creates the sense of safety needed to relax, rejuvenate, heal and function with emotional balance. If you find yourself in isolation, it is essential for your wellbeing to have face to face time, even if this is online—and to awaken the afferent nerves in your skin by feeling an object with your hands or feeling somebody else's hand. Wearing a mask and washing hands is always an option.

Generally, if your neuroception signals a potential hazard (whether from a real or perceived threat), you leave your Window of Tolerance (comfort zone) and your nervous system primarily reacts by operating within *Social Engagement* in the form of communication. In stressful situations that lie between social engagement and sympathetic activation, we often see protective and defensive behaviours such as appeasement, oppression, denial, lying, manipulation, control and passive aggression.

Survive

Let's now look at how your nervous system functions when you feel threatened and go into the differing forms of survival mode.

The vagal brake between social engagement and fight or flight (hide)

The urge to hide is a state on the verge of ventral vagal social engagement and fight or flight. It occurs when we aren't feeling comfortable with a situation and it starts to feel overwhelming. It is a psychological state which brings with it a feeling of being seen when you don't want to be seen and a sense of shyness. The shyness could stem from a sense of embarrassment or self-judgement. What this state also contains is the capability to be vulnerable. Due to this capacity, there is a huge opportunity for intimate connection and engagement if we choose it.

When we can acknowledge the urge to hide and choose to allow vulnerability, we welcome acceptance of self and integrate discomfort. This can guide us into an expression of suppressed beauty, joy, pleasure and self-acceptance.

Survive/unsafe - sympathetic nervous system (fight or flight)

If self-regulation or communication and co-regulation with others fails to bring the body back to a sense of safety, adrenaline is released which triggers the *Sympathetic Nervous System's* hyperarousal response. Your heart rate speeds up, your pain tolerance increases, your face becomes less expressive and, interestingly, the middle ear muscles shut down. When this happens, you can focus on very high or low frequencies associated with predators and distress signals. Think of a panther sneaking through the undergrowth or a person screaming in pain. Your body is on high alert to recognise danger and it's capacity for diplomatic peace-making conversation is decreased.

This doesn't only happen when we're confronted with a life-threatening situation, but also in situations where we aren't yet sure if we are safe or accepted. An example could be getting a kind of stage fright, when it's our turn to do something such as introduce ourselves to strangers or speak in public. This, despite the social pressure to have it together and appear embodied and confident, is a very natural process. You may notice that your heartbeat quickens, or your verbal centre prevents you from vocalising as you usually would when you feel safe. There's nothing wrong with you when that happens! This is the vagal brake—as your nervous system drops into sympathetic activity.

The stress response itself isn't necessarily the enemy. It prepares you to meet and rise to a challenge. Stress chemicals help mobilise energy and increase alertness. However, during chronic stress our bodies become flooded with these chemicals. This results in prolonged dysregulation of the nervous system and the many problems, both physical and mental that result from this. Depending on the person and situation, *fight or flight* is the impulse to defend yourself by fighting back or to get out of the situation by physically leaving/running away.

Adrenaline causes air passages to dilate so that muscles are provided with the oxygen they need to either fight danger or flee. Adrenaline also triggers blood vessels to contract which re-directs blood toward major muscle groups, including the heart and lungs. Cortisol is released, which curbs functions that would be nonessential in a fight or flight situation and floods the body with glucose, supplying an immediate energy source to large muscles and enabling the full range of movement of the torso and limbs.

When the unsafe side of the sympathetic nervous system is active, the rational working mind attempts to resolve the situation logically. This is like trying to drive a car with one foot on the accelerator (hyperarousal) and one foot on the brake (the working brain's rationale). Your metabolism can only cope with this overwhelm to a certain point.

I remember creeping into a neighbour's garden as a kid with a friend. We were happily helping ourselves to apples when the owner ran out of the house shouting. If we'd been cornered by a fence or a dog, our nervous systems would have gone into freeze. We started running and he began chasing us. We rounded a few corners and eventually lost him. Jumping down into a little ditch, we hid inside a bush there. My heart was beating nineteen to the dozen. I was shaking and scared to death. I remember holding my breath so I wouldn't make a sound. Then, something really intense happened. My breath stopped for a while and I had the feeling I became the sound of the wind in the leaves in the bush above me. It was absolutely amazing and peaceful. Now I realise this was the shutdown state of the ventral vagus nerve. I can't remember how long we were there but at some point we started whispering to each other and carefully moved out of the bush to run home.

Survive/unsafe - parasympathetic nervous system (shutdown)

If the fight or flight response does not create safety, if overwhelm escalates or the situation becomes life-threatening, the reptilian brain's dorsal vagus nerve activates the hypoarousal *Parasympathetic Nervous System's* shutdown response. This is the point when a person's nervous system can't hold the sympathetic tension anymore. It comes on so strongly that it overwhelms sympathetic arousal and the person collapses, going into a state of immobilisation.

We can witness the *shutdown* response whenever an animal is trapped as prey in a predator's jaws, such as a gazelle caught by a lion. The gazelle may appear dead but is, in fact, very much alive. It is unresponsive because its nervous system has gone into the state of shutdown, to give the impression of being dead, to reserve energy for a possible escape, to rest vital organs and to block pain. If the lion drops its prey, the gazelle's nervous system switches back into sympathetic arousal and it responds in flight, running away.

It works exactly the same way in humans. This is the state the nervous system goes into during **trauma**. In situations we can't fight or flee from, just as a hedgehog rolls into a ball when threatened, trying to make itself invisible, we may hold our breath, or, especially in chronically abusive situations, partially shut down. Children of abusive parents often 'become invisible 'this way in order to stay safe.

The shutdown state is our built-in survival mechanism, keeping us alive in life-threatening situations. It blocks pain, preserves energy and rests the body as much as possible so that we have a chance to escape or otherwise survive the experience.

It's vital that more people understand this. How often have judges declared that people haven't been assaulted because they didn't fight—and instead 'allowed 'their attackers to do what they wanted?! Many survivors may even believe this themselves. **This is completely false.** This is not how the nervous system works. Many people may think they would act in the fight or flight mode if attacked, because they are familiar with how this state feels. It's impossible to really know how the shutdown state feels unless you've experienced it yourself.

Shutdown is a disruption in the body-mind Window of Tolerance (explained fully later in this chapter) and happens automatically. It is *completely involuntary*. The person is unable to decide what to do consciously. The nervous system decides.

When we go into shutdown, the neocortex (working brain), responsible for making choices and decisions, is switched off. When this happens, we're unable to think clearly, make rational decisions or remember the logical narrative order of events. It can affect someone partially, such as feeling constriction around the throat. It can immobilise parts of or the whole body. It can be momentary, short term or permanent.

One example of partial shutdown is *vaginismus*, the involuntary contraction of vaginal muscles when penetration is attempted. Vaginismus doesn't interfere with sexual arousal, but it can prevent penetration or make it very painful. This happened to a friend of mine at age 24, and didn't resolve until she'd ended the relationship she'd been in. She recalled, "I was pretty clueless back then, but even so I knew this was my body shouting, "NO!" to so many things I didn't want and didn't verbally express. In that relationship, no permission was ever asked for, power-over dynamics were out of control, no limits were ever expressed and no agreements ever made. My general shadow was one of *going along*. I was incredibly unhappy, confused and overwhelmed. Years later, I'm very grateful that my body reacted that way. It gave me the insight to radically change my life for the better."

At the point of shutdown, we may *disassociate* or faint as the body switches off. You may be unable to think clearly and access words or emotions. Emotionally, it can feel like numbness, dizziness, hopelessness, depression, a sense of feeling trapped, out of your body or disconnected from the world. Your eyes may be fixed on one point or look spaced out. Your heart rate, blood pressure, breathing rate, facial expression, sexual and immune response systems decrease. You may feel nauseous or throw up, spontaneously defecate or urinate, and feel low or no pain at all, even when seriously injured.

It's important to note that all of these states are well-functioning survival mechanisms that operate involuntarily to bring you back into a state of safety or to prevent you from feeling pain in the face of death.

Thrive

Now let's look at how your nervous system functions when you feel *safe*.

By implementing the steps within Somatic Consent, you can access a *Hybrid State* which enables you to remain in, or more readily access the safe parts of the nervous system. We'll talk about the Hybrid State in detail soon.

Thrive/safe - sympathetic nervous system

The safe side of the Sympathetic Nervous System is activated when you engage in activities within your Window of Tolerance (comfort zone) that mobilise the body such as working out, yoga, sport, dancing and sex. When you feel safe, sensual pleasure and physical connection are possible. This safe mode of sympathetic action is called *mobilisation*.

Much of the dynamics of healthy play and fun depend on our ability to move with ease between the states of social engagement and safe sympathetic activation.

Thrive/safe - parasympathetic nervous system

The body can fall into an immobilised state where you experience rest and rejuvenation during sleep. You are also able to enter into deep relaxation and ecstatic states through meditation, cuddling, love making, massage, gentle touch and connecting deeply with another person—both as the nurturer and the nurtured. In this parasympathetic state, your system can rest in the most exquisite way. This mechanism is pre-verbal and belongs to all humans. You always have the ability to tap into it, independent of your belief system.

Within dorsal nerve immobilisation, a state of *surrender and bliss* can also be accessed. Here, in the vulnerable state of immobilisation, we encounter the same nervous system state as shutdown. The only difference being that it takes place in a situation of **safety** rather than a **life-threatening** one. Due to this, the noticing brain is still active and we are able to observe and retain our full rational capacity to make choices.

In surrender, interpersonal and transpersonal connection takes place. We relax our whole identity to the point of ego death and are able to experience interconnected one-ness with our partner or further—with the whole of existence. This experience has been documented and taught for thousands of years by eastern schools of philosophy.

Porges says he has much respect for ancient wisdom that was conveyed in ways different to our contemporary terminology.[35]

Prakriti in yogic philosophy, is the name given to all of material nature (including ourselves). It is made up of three qualities called *Gunas* which are present in everything we experience in life. They describe the changing nature of the body, mind and environment in a very similar way to the three neural branches of The Polyvagal theory.

Sattva serves to illuminate: its qualities are calmness, lightness, clarity, harmony, buoyance, lucidity, joy and understanding. *This describes the ventral vagal complex of social engagement.*

Rajas serves to activate: it is the capacity to mobilise and has the qualities of energy, excitement, turbulence, pain, anger and agitation. *This describes the sympathetic nervous system of fight or flight and mobilisation.*

Tamas serves to restrain: Its qualities are stillness, indifference and delusion but also those of stability or groundedness. *This describes the dorsal vagal complex of shutdown or surrender.*

There are many other aspects of ancient wisdom that parallel our current, modern, scientific understanding of the human body. That fascinating topic, however, belongs in another book. Let's now look at how you can learn to consciously shift your nervous system state for increased well-being.

SHIFTING STATES

Dysregulation, Self-Regulation And Co-Regulation

> *"Co-regulation is a lifelong need. A child is born with a sympathetic nervous system. Parasympathetic regulation happens through the mother. Because of its evolutionary ties, human to human co-regulation is the most powerful calming agent."*
> - Gabor Mate

Depending on the situation and environment, the nervous system can change and shift from one state to another depicted by the arrows in the Polyvagal map. It *isn't possible* however to switch from sympathetic fight or flight, or the dorsal parasympathetic shutdown state—directly into immobilisation (the bliss state). If in shutdown, you first have to go through the sympathetic state via mobilisation and your limbic system, so as to access, activate and express feelings and emotions. You can only enter the bliss state from the safe side of social engagement and the sympathetic activity of mobilisation—via the neurological pathways of the limbic system. Remember, the *limbic system* is the area of the brain responsible for emotion and memory. Its structures include the hypothalamus, thalamus, amygdala and hippocampus. The hypothalamus plays a role in activating the sympathetic nervous system, which is part of any emotional reaction.

This is a very complex subject. If you're interested in studying it in more depth, I highly recommend Stephen Porges 'fantastic research[33] as well as this interview.[36] His research is also deeply backed up by his wife, Sue Carter's research on oxytocin and the development of the social engagement system.[37]

You can **dysregulate** when, for example, you're suddenly triggered while socially engaging, resulting in fight or flight or shutdown if overwhelmed. You can also dysregulate while in the bliss state which could happen if you need to get up, go to the bathroom or see to any need such as eating and drinking, or if, of course, your environment becomes physically threatening.

You can *self-regulate* (alone) when, for example, you're in a state of sympathetic fight or flight (unsafe side) by choosing to *mobilise*.

Have you ever noticed, whenever you feel dysregulated in some way—worried, nervous, sad or scared—that you feel better if you begin to move? That your whole mood *shifts*? By going for a walk, doing yoga, dancing, exercise, playing sport or another activity—you are self-regulating. In this way you are able to shift your nervous system from sympathetic (unsafe) fight or flight to (safe) mobilisation.

I remember getting triggered at a sexuality workshop I was assisting at by something the main facilitator was doing that I didn't agree with ethically. At the time, all I wanted to do was to leave. I felt rooted to the spot, almost frozen. Then, I chose to slowly stand up and walk out of the room, pretending to go to the bathroom. Outside on my own, I shook my whole body and stamped my feet. It took about two minutes to feel the calmness return to my system. I was then able to walk back into the room, where I chose to participate by observing what was happening.

You can sometimes even self-regulate from the shutdown state—though this takes much more effort and time, by communicating your feelings as you notice them. This is only possible if your noticing brain is active due to it being wired to do so, (for example through the practice of mindfulness or through embodying the Direct Route). If the noticing brain isn't active, we lose the ability to think and communicate rationally.

The shutdown response can affect you in various ways from numbness and confusion to falling unconscious with no ability to respond whatsoever.

David Livingstone, a man who survived a lion attack, said that until a ranger rescued him, he'd been hanging in the lion's jaws, totally aware of what was happening but had completely lost the capacity to feel pain or physically move—and that he'd been in a dream-like state of what he called awe, agreement and surrender to death.

You can *co-regulate* (with the help of another person) when, for example, you ask for help when in a dysregulated fight or flight state so that it's possible to re-enter the safe zone of social engagement. Co-regulation also happens if someone helps you back from a state of shutdown to sympathetic fight or flight, or mobilisation.

Have you ever had sex after an argument with a loved one? This is an attempt at co-regulation, back into love and connection.

Once, while out dancing, a person I'd just met and been talking to spotted their former partner across the room. They felt enough trust in me to share the fact that they felt insecure. I asked whether I could support them in any way. They shared their story briefly and asked for a hug in order to feel more grounded—then were able to go over to their former partner and connect with them.

Different types of therapy and healing methods can help to restore the body-mind connection. They are able to change these neurological states of dissociation to aid health, rejuvenation and healthy relationship to self and others. The best way to assist someone in a dysregulated state is to help them *choose for themselves*, instead of imposing any action *we think* is best for them. This fosters self-empowerment. We go more deeply into this soon in The Window of Tolerance and in Chapter 5 for practitioners.

Understanding the dynamic of The Polyvagal Theory, specifically bonding through oxytocin, is crucial in knowing how safety and connection is established within the nervous system. But again, grasping these concepts rationally or intellectually with your analytical working mind isn't enough. Embodied awakening has to be experienced with your body to fully understand how each state feels. Saying that, you've probably experienced most of the different states your nervous system is capable of at some time during your life and will be able to recognise them with practice.

THE HYBRID STATE

"Expanding our capacity to talk, particularly when we face critical choices, is a life-enhancing skill. I believe that there is no faster way for us to evolve than through the process of interacting with one another."
- Sarah Rozenthuler

The SCES focuses on the safe mode of the nervous system in the area between social engagement and sympathetic mobilisation. This is a *hybrid state*. Only when this hybrid state is active can we feel a sense of safety, which prompts connection to others. When we feel safe and connected we relax. In this relaxed state of is-ness, play is possible and sexuality, sensuality and intimacy happens naturally.

You are in the hybrid state when you practice the SCES by playing The 3 Minute game. The game helps you to create clear verbal agreements that establish a sense of safety and connection. This guides physical action with absolute clarity on who is doing the action and who it is for. Because the dynamics of The 3 Minute Game have a unique influence on the nervous system, it is not just a concept, to believe in or not—but an opportunity to notice and live your truth.

Neuroplasticity and the hybrid state

Habits are nothing more than things we believe or are compelled to do, because past experience has wired the brain's synapses to respond in this manner (so that we behave that way). Any new habit you repeat, whether perceived positive or negative, causes rewiring to happen in the brain (neuroplasticity). Examples could be any way of thinking or action that become habitual, such as brushing your teeth, believing you are good or bad at something, driving a car, a new exercise routine that you get into, a tendency to worry or developing a taste for vodka.

Functioning in the *hybrid state*, (which includes being aware of the Direct Route) connects you to your authentic desires. This rewires your brain, as you make new habits of receiving for your own pleasure and joy, and choosing the touch you want.

This kind of touch, combined with awareness of the direct inflow of sensory sensation and subsequent release of oxytocin, results in experiencing pleasure when feeling others, intimacy and loving connection. This new embodied habit replaces the old habitual strategies of pleasing others to make them happy (to make you happy), or waiting for affirmative responses before feeling good about yourself.

The 3 Minute Game fits perfectly into The Polyvagal Theory. As long as two consenting people have the mutual desire to go there together, deep experience is possible. Because the game fosters playful arousal and restorative surrender, it has great potential in leading you from the hybrid state into the bliss state—the dorsal vagal/parasympathetic state of interpersonal surrender with one other.

THE BLISS STATE OF IMMOBILISATION AND SURRENDER

"Surrender is to give oneself up to the original cause of one's being."
- Ramana Maharshi

Shutdown can almost seem like a kind of death. Many trauma survivors have been known to report feeling they came back from an experience of near death, when what they experienced was this state.

We often confuse the state of deep relaxation with that of the shutdown response. Most people are afraid of being powerless, and do their best to avoid it. As a result, they rarely allow themselves to go into immobilisation, where the safe side of the *parasympathetic nervous system* engages, and a state of *surrender* is accessed. Here, the sweetest transformation can take place. Instead, many remain in the sympathetic nervous system's unsafe fight or flight mode, pumped with adrenaline and completely wired or in the state of mobilisation, without any deeper experience.

If we look at immobilisation as 'bad', we believe we can't go there, otherwise we'll 'die 'and therefore we create mechanisms to avoid the experience. Within immobilisation there is no death of the body of course. The reptilian brain is active in the state of surrender.

This parasympathetic state kills the 'ego-self 'and awakens the state of being or 'is-ness 'known as super-consciousness. It is the state of being where interpersonal and transpersonal experience occurs.

The death we experience in *surrender* is that of ego death—as our individual sense of self expands beyond our contained ego and connects to something bigger than ourselves. This happens at the Apex when we experience *inter-*

personal connection with another person. Beyond this state is *transpersonal* experience, where we realise our infinite nature and feel connected to all that is—in oneness.

In relation to sex, in the moments of climax, also known as 'la petit mort '(the little death), it's interesting to experience how super-conscious we can be. During climax, the *parasympathetic nervous system* experiences an explosion to infinity, without ego identity.

Another option is to stay present, retaining this potential spiritual energy, choosing not to climax but to follow the 'internal road', utilising sexual energy as a kind of 'rocket fuel 'to energise the whole system, connecting the body and mind to this experience of oneness.

We'll go more deeply into this subject in the section, Being on the Edge.

NOTICING AND MEANING

Connecting The Dots

*"When you become comfortable with uncertainty,
infinite possibilities open up in your life."*

- Eckhart Tolle

The Noticing and Meaning Map enables you to identify *what is* in any given situation so that you are able to train yourself to be fully present and *fully be* with what is. It's a ticket into awareness and spiritual development. It shows how we can connect parts of the brain that often work against each other, to positively transform our experience of life.

NOTICING AND MEANING MAP

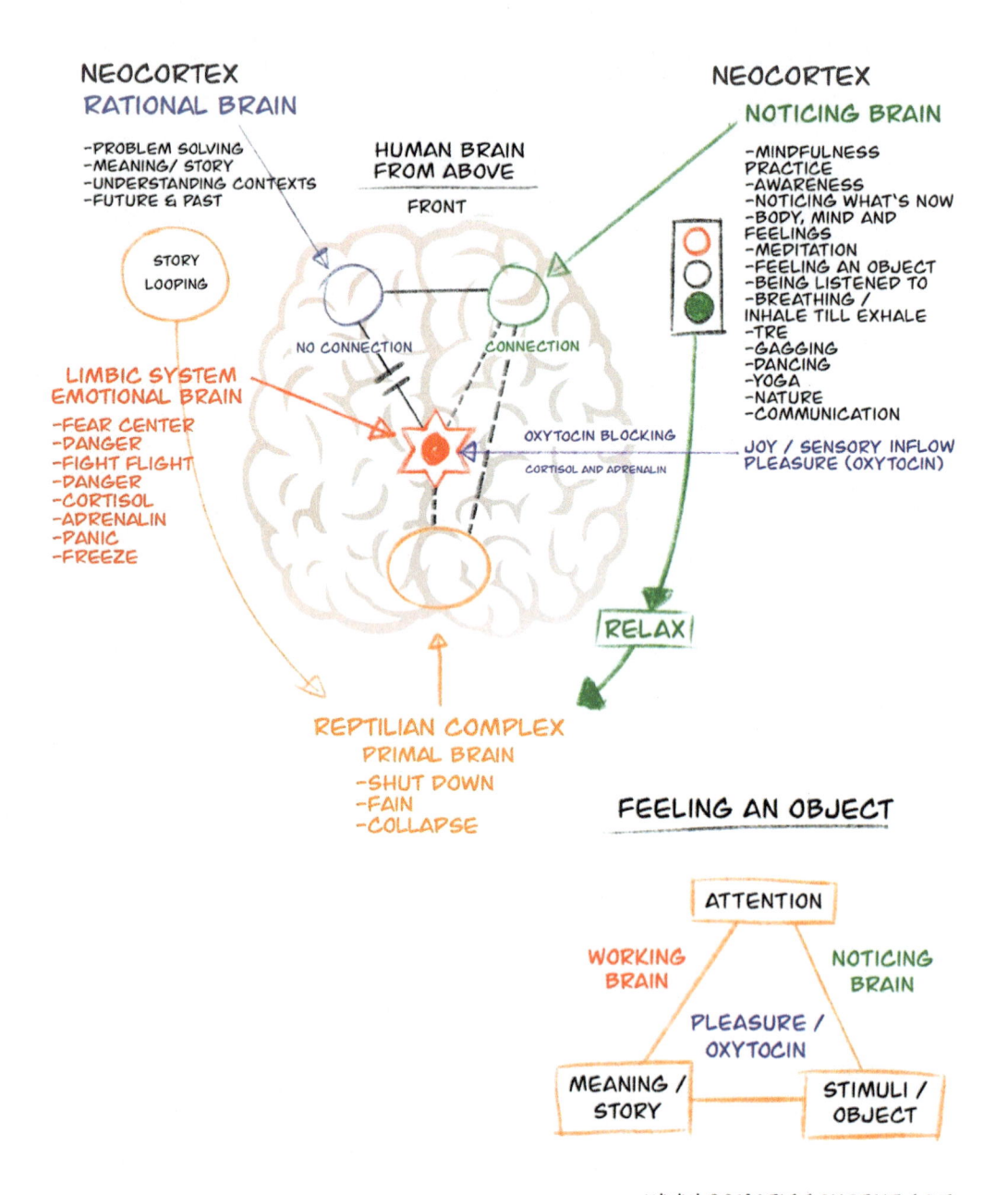

NEOCORTEX
RATIONAL BRAIN

- PROBLEM SOLVING
- MEANING/ STORY
- UNDERSTANDING CONTEXTS
- FUTURE & PAST

HUMAN BRAIN FROM ABOVE
FRONT

NEOCORTEX
NOTICING BRAIN

- MINDFULNESS PRACTICE
- AWARENESS
- NOTICING WHAT'S NOW
- BODY, MIND AND FEELINGS
- MEDITATION
- FEELING AN OBJECT
- BEING LISTENED TO
- BREATHING / INHALE TILL EXHALE
- TRE
- GAGGING
- DANCING
- YOGA
- NATURE
- COMMUNICATION

STORY LOOPING

NO CONNECTION   CONNECTION

LIMBIC SYSTEM
EMOTIONAL BRAIN

- FEAR CENTER
- DANGER
- FIGHT FLIGHT
- DANGER
- CORTISOL
- ADRENALIN
- PANIC
- FREEZE

OXYTOCIN BLOCKING
CORTISOL AND ADRENALIN

JOY / SENSORY INFLOW
PLEASURE (OXYTOCIN)

RELAX

REPTILIAN COMPLEX
PRIMAL BRAIN

- SHUT DOWN
- FAIN
- COLLAPSE

FEELING AN OBJECT

ATTENTION

WORKING BRAIN   **NOTICING BRAIN**

PLEASURE / OXYTOCIN

MEANING / STORY   STIMULI / OBJECT

WWW.SOMATICCONSENT.COM

There are three parts to the brain.[38]

- **The neocortex / neomammalian** (human or rational brain) which houses the **working brain**—responsible for conscious, logic and abstract thought—and—the **noticing brain,** which gets its information from the senses and has the ability to observe our experience.

- **The limbic system / paleomammalian** (mammalian or emotional brain) houses the subconscious mind with our memories and related emotions, as well as the fight or flight response. It aids bonding and survival by urging us to avoid pain and repeat pleasure.

- **The reptilian complex** (the lizard or primal brain) acts out of instinct, with survival as its focus. It responds to the stimulus of changes within the limbic system. The shutdown response happens when the limbic system is overwhelmed.

The working brain

The *working brain* (which craves context) creates *meaning* within the present moment. Here we process thoughts such as, what happened yesterday, what might be tomorrow or reflect on our experiences. It blends information (new sensory data and old memories and emotion), categorising it and putting it into structures. We use our working brain 90 percent of the time.

There are three levels of mind within the working brain.

- The reactive mind (triggered when the present is connected to past suffering)
- The personal construct mind (how we perceive / how beliefs are formed)
- The linear mind (the rational, problem solving mind)

The reactive mind

The reactive mind sources from the memories of multisensory input you've received since you were developing in the womb. All the sights, sounds, smells, tastes and tactile information. It is based on your lifelong experience of this information and how you perceived it. Whenever a memory is triggered which involved trauma, behaviour can show up as reactive and defensive.

When triggered, due to increased blood delivery, the reactive mind is 20 times faster than the linear mind. It serves to protect and resist repeating old, uncomfortable memories.

I often notice my reactive mind activating when I speak in public, especially when I feel challenged by questions that (I assume) are asked to show a gap in my knowledge.

After 10 years of public speaking and reflection on this challenge, I'm well aware of its origin. It stems from the memory of forgetting words for a presentation I had to recite in first grade. I stood there, frozen and crying. The memory is connected to strong emotions of embarrassment and loneliness.

These days, as an adult, whenever I feel that trigger, I deal with it by riding it through with awareness. I allow my heart to beat a little faster and I 'own' my feelings by just noticing and expressing what is going on within my body and sharing it with the audience in real time.

This honest, moment-to-moment relating allows me to express the emotions that are real for me, rather than suppressing them. As the emotions triggered in this case stem from the fear of rejection, it's always interesting to notice that never happens. In fact, people can often relate, which instead creates connection.

The personal construct mind

The personal construct mind is based on repetitive experience which leads to the formation of a construct or belief. These constructs begin as soon as we're born. An early example is a baby's feeding time. After many repetitions of crying when hungry—which resulted in being fed, the construct of 'feeding time' is formed. This works well until crying doesn't lead to being fed.

We all have many constructs wrapped in expectation that our minds have developed throughout our lives. Do you remember learning to ride a bike, to play an instrument or smashing the tennis ball over the net uncountable times—before the right movement was learned?

I think the best example I have related to touch is an assumption I once had with previous partners before the 'era of consent'. Back then, I was sure that I had permission to touch, based on the fact that they'd welcomed it the first time and I'd touched them in that way so many times before. My continuous assumption and repetitive behavior formed the belief that I am always allowed. This is what happens in most relationships. The feelings of frustration, pain and abandonment I felt when touch was not welcome was contrary to my own personal construct.

The linear mind

This is our rational, planning, problem solving mind, the one we usually identify with as our mind. It deals with definitions, ideas and context. It allows us to plan and execute tasks. If you want to go on a business trip, you decide on the date, book a flight, go to the airport check in, board the plane, get a taxi from the airport, drive to the hotel and go to the meeting. If you want to make juice you wash the fruit, chop it, put it in a juicer, pour it into a glass and drink, or you go to the juice bar around the corner and order one so that someone else does the linear thinking for you.

Have you ever tried to resolve a feeling of emotional discomfort by trying to think of a solution for it to stop? How did that work out? When the nervous system is in a dysregulated state, often, there is no connection between the rational, thinking and the emotional limbic parts of the brain. However, when you are tuned into your body you tend to notice what its needs are in-the-moment and are able to follow its wisdom. In this way we are able to break the link that causes our linear minds to 'loop', going around in circles without a solution.

210   ORGASMIC BLUEPRINT

MIND MAP

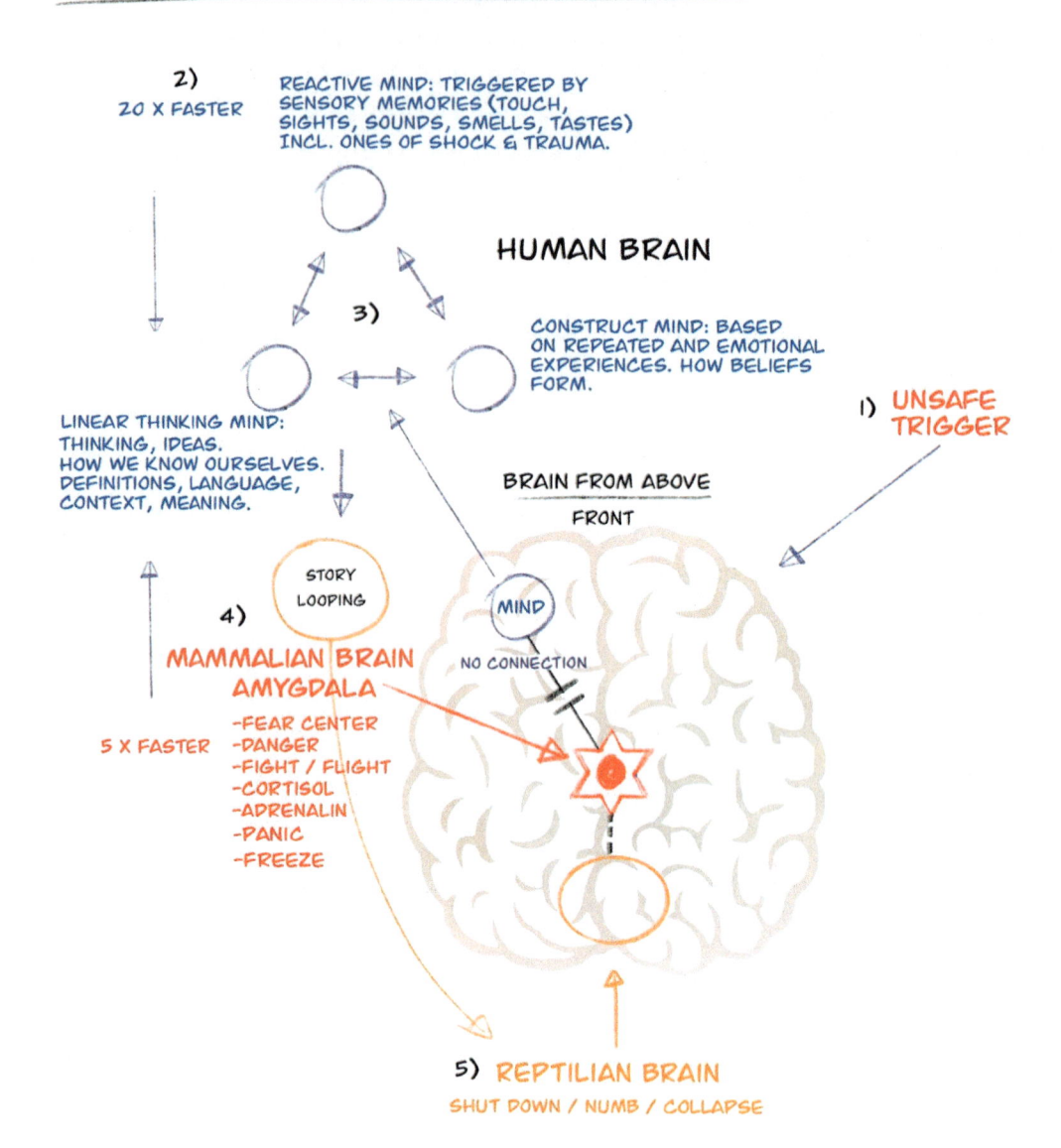

2) 20 X FASTER

REACTIVE MIND: TRIGGERED BY SENSORY MEMORIES (TOUCH, SIGHTS, SOUNDS, SMELLS, TASTES) INCL. ONES OF SHOCK & TRAUMA.

HUMAN BRAIN

3)

CONSTRUCT MIND: BASED ON REPEATED AND EMOTIONAL EXPERIENCES. HOW BELIEFS FORM.

LINEAR THINKING MIND: THINKING, IDEAS. HOW WE KNOW OURSELVES. DEFINITIONS, LANGUAGE, CONTEXT, MEANING.

1) UNSAFE TRIGGER

BRAIN FROM ABOVE
FRONT

STORY LOOPING

MIND

NO CONNECTION

4)

MAMMALIAN BRAIN AMYGDALA

5 X FASTER
- FEAR CENTER
- DANGER
- FIGHT / FLIGHT
- CORTISOL
- ADRENALIN
- PANIC
- FREEZE

5) REPTILIAN BRAIN

SHUT DOWN / NUMB / COLLAPSE

WWW.SOMATICCONSENT.COM

Without awareness of these three minds and their function, they can easily confuse and contradict each other. It's usual for the construct mind to have many beliefs about self and others. The reactive mind will most likely try to defend what it came up with, whether accurate or not, and the linear mind will no doubt try and rationalise. When this happens, thinking is unreliable.

Our feelings and emotions are recorded as memories and stored in the subconscious within the limbic system. This is the fuel for the *reactive mind*.

All our repetitive experiences are stored as memories here too and develop into constructs and beliefs. This is where the *construct mind* gets its information.

1. If something in your present environment connects to a similar memory of past emotional pain, you get triggered (warned and prepared to get out of potential danger).
2. This is like an alarm going off as your nervous system responds on high alert (fight or flight) and your *reactive mind* takes the lead.
3. If there is a lack of awareness about the cause of the trigger, the *construct mind* usually supports the reactive mind.
4. As this response is different from functional problem-solving, *the linear mind* tries to work out the emotion/feelings and fix the confusion.
5. If the situation escalates and the sympathetic nervous system becomes overwhelmed, shutdown occurs.

Interestingly there is often *no conscious connection* between the working brain and the limbic system's subconscious due to a filter called the *conscious critical faculty*. This filter only opens when our brainwaves slow down, we're relaxed and the noticing brain kicks in (which is what happens when we tune into sensory input via the Direct Route).

Because of this disconnection, the working brain can't usually process present-moment emotional responses. In an effort to work out the confusion, this part of the brain begins to rationalise, by looping the stories within our personal belief system (our perception of reality). This includes our personal conditioning and past experiences and all the 'shoulds' and 'should nots' we've been programmed to believe. This looping is, in effect, like having one foot on the accelerator—the limbic system's high alert, fight or flight response—and one foot on the break—the working brain's rational, which gives the opposite message of, "let's work this thing out" / "don't do anything" / "control yourself".

During this process, stress is produced due to the release of adrenaline and cortisol, which wreak havoc on the entire body. The metabolism can only deal with this to a certain point. As overwhelm increases to beyond this point, we drop from flight or flight into complete dorsal vagal *shutdown*.

As mentioned in The Polyvagal Theory, at the point of shutdown, we may go numb or faint as the body switches off. This can happen during a devastating event, when something is overwhelmingly painful. This extreme survival response is made possible due to the medulla oblongata (which has 12 cranial nerves) inhibiting nerve impulses reaching the brain. This not only numbs somatic feeling but switches off the working mind.

Resetting associations of touch

The brain's parietal lobe has many functions and although multisensory in nature, it is primarily responsible for processing information about bodily sensations and touch. It is also involved in explicit memory, the conscious, intentional recollection of factual information from previous experiences. These include somatic memories associated with shock and trauma.

If we've had a past traumatic encounter linked to touch, the present experience may associate with that memory and classify it as 'unsafe'. When a triggered memory emerges, we may feel exactly the same emotions we did at the time of the original traumatic event or shortly afterwards.[39,40]

The mind is a defence mechanism to protect against any touch that is mediocre or based on bad experiences such as going along with touch while not having given permission, or even being asked at all. The good news is that we can reset these traumatic memories through a fully embodied experience of touch which triggers safety within the nervous system.

The way this works isn't by trying to fix an existing system, i.e., the mind's resistance to protect, but rather to create a new memory so that the old memory can rest. When we wake up the hands and use consensual questions such as, "May I touch you?" —over time, we create an experience that liberates the original memory, by replacing it with a new one. Biohacking, or neuroplasticity[41] takes place when an experience is repeated and has an emotional flavour. In combination with language, the rewiring happens whenever touch feels pleasant, so that a new concept of touch without the triggers of past traumatic events is created.

In order for neuroplasticity to take place, we must be embodied while touching and being touched. To do this, it is crucial we begin to feel, rather than be directed purely by our minds. We do this from the outside in. In this way, we gain the capacity to 'drop into 'ourselves with presence.

The way to begin the process is by differentiating between noticing and thinking. Then we are able to slow down the working mind's chatter, gain some clarity and be grounded in our experience in an awareness continuum.

Everything we can possibly notice comes from three places

- All that is exterior to you
- Your own body
- Your own mind

Noticing is easier when we bring our focus to one of these at a time—in this order.

1. Awareness of what is happening externally to your body right now. The place you are in and all the sensory input pouring in from it. The light and shadows, the distant and close by sounds, any scents or taste.

2. Awareness of what is happening on your skin and inside your body right now. The places your body is in contact with your environment. All the sensations and locations of touch, tension, tingling, numbness, discomfort, pleasure, heat or cold.

3. Awareness of what is happening in your mind right now. What the three parts of your mind are relaying to you—and the contradictions. When you do this you'll notice your reactive mind thinking one thing, your construct mind another and your linear mind possibly thinking something entirely different.

If you notice a resistance to experiencing these layers of awareness, know that this is due to thinking your way around the situation. When you think, your mind creates thoughts about the situation you are in. Awareness on the other hand is when your attention is focused on the situation by simply *observing* what you see, hear, feel, smell and taste, without attaching opinion to the experience. Thinking separates you from your direct involvement in the situation.

When we begin to notice, we slow down the three parts of the mind and become fully aware of what is—in each moment—feeling and fully embodied in our 'is-ness'. This leads to a more balanced perception and ability to more accurately navigate our way through life.

The noticing brain

Unlike the emotional limbic system, the noticing brain *has a connection to the working brain.* The noticing brain **has the potential** to be aware of **how** the working brain is functioning in-the-moment. It can notice how the working brain formulates words and thinks. It can simultaneously tune into our limbic system of feelings, needs and desires. It can also notice the nervous system's responses and tune into the reptilian brain, being aware of any numbness or waning energy before shutdown occurs.[21] Unfortunately, most of us have unlearned the capacity to use this part of our brain fluently, due to our learned focus on the rules of social conditioning.

When we embody somatic experience (awareness of sensory inflow via the Direct Route) the noticing brain *regains its full capacity.* We become aware of deeper aspects of ourselves—of the connected body and mind, of our emotions, feelings, ego, needs, desires and shadow strategies. It enables us to gain insight and empathy. To connect the dots. To consciously explore the manner in which we operate as we engage with the world.

As we tune in, the noticing brain is also capable of being aware of nervous system dysregulation. So that instead of automatically escalating into *shutdown* during a traumatic event (or intense triggers of past trauma), we can learn to self-regulate by moving away from the threatening environment or *co-regulate* by asking for help.

One of my own early experiences of the fear response happened when a former lover invited me to go rock climbing with her. She loved it, and, remembering how fearlessly I'd climbed trees as a kid, I accepted and went along. She began to climb and when she was about 20 metres up, she gave me a sign to start. I began climbing as enthusiastically as a child—and at about a height of 5 metres, I looked down. Suddenly, a fear of falling rushed through my body and I completely froze, grasping onto the rock and unable to move. I remember experiencing feelings of shame. Back then I didn't realise I actually had the choice of telling her that I'd had enough and wanted to go down. So, I gathered all my energy together and screamed up, "Give me a minute, I can't move." She responded with a very relaxed, "Take all the time you need, the weather's good, there's a great view up here". The fear in my body was pretty intense, my legs were shaking and I was close to tears. That was the first time I really noticed the power that fear provides to keep us focused on survival. I realised that tears and sadness couldn't help me out, but the energy of pure anger could. By focusing this energy I was able to move my body up the rock face step by step. It felt like I was fighting my way up. I didn't fall. I made it to the top, but I didn't enjoy it at all. My body was stiff and I felt I'd just about escaped with my life.

After this experience I tried climbing about five more times with the same result. Fear and anger induced by sympathetic fight or flight and bouts of freezing—with a looping of self-judgmental thoughts about how stupid I was to repeat the experience. There was only ever a feeling of pure survival. No joy or fun, no enjoyment of being in nature or exhilaration from the act of climbing. One positive was a deep learning within my nervous system and my noticing brain. My response was to stay focused within my fear and to channel my anger so that I could move—thereby avoiding collapse by self-regulating away from freeze and the verge of shutdown, back into fight or flight.

Can you relate to this? Have you ever had a similar experience?

The noticing part of your brain is only activated through awareness and/or safety, and usually switches off as soon as you feel you're in danger. However, by tuning into the sensory inflow, you train the noticing part of your brain to *remain active*. This expands your ability to remain focused during unease, to the point where you're not afraid of the consequences, even while experiencing fear. This is an 'awakening state' into deeper personal and spiritual growth and why somatic experience through the Direct Route is so important. By activating your Base through the sensory inflow, you become aware of what is going on in your body, where the sensations are and which emotions are present.

"I notice a tingling feeling in my stomach, a nervous feeling."
"I feel disassociated, unable to focus, not grounded, in shock".
"There's discomfort in my chest, I feel restricted and resentful."

An interesting reference to this can be found in David Lynden's book, *Touch: The Science of Hand, Heart and Mind*.[42] Lynden delves deeply into the functionality of specific neurons connected to touch and their effect on our entire nervous system.

There are many practices that can increase your powers of self-awareness by activating the noticing part of your brain and encouraging a dialogue between it and the working part. These include any mindful practice but especially ones that slow down the brain waves to a relaxed Alpha or Theta state **as waking up your hands does**. Others include meditation, hypnotherapy, yoga nidra, sound therapy, shamanic drum journeys and so on.

When you tune into the sensations by feeling an object in your hands or touching another human being, there is the *additional bonus* of oxytocin release and with it, nervous system regulation.

- For reference, the definition of ego in this book is the subjective experience of self in regard to personal separate identity, formed and based on mediation between conscious thought (neocortex - working brain) and automatic subconscious impressions (limbic system).

THE WINDOW OF TOLERANCE

Personal Growth

"Your comfort zone is a beautiful place, but nothing ever grows there."
- Unknown

The Window of Tolerance is where we can engage in being social with one another in our day-to-day encounters and function most efficiently. Here, we're in the familiar realm of our comfort zone. We're calm, cool, collected and connected. Within this space of relaxed consciousness, you have the ability to soothe yourself via emotional *self-regulation*. It's possible to think rationally, reflect, express yourself clearly and make choices and decisions calmly, without feeling overwhelmed or withdrawn in response to the demands of everyday life.

However, this feeling of safety can easily get shaken by events that push us out of our comfort zone. This happens whenever you experience anything distressing. This can be due to a present threat or originate from your limbic system's subconscious memory store, and be a trigger connected to a past experience. In both cases your nervous system responds in an effort to take care of you.

When we leave the comfort zone of our Window of Tolerance we can enter *dysregulation*. This can be a nervous system state *hyperarousal*, where we have a fight or flight response or *hypoarousal*, where we go into shutdown.

Hyperarousal is often associated with hypervigilance and feelings of anxiety, panic, overwhelm, racing thoughts, emotional outbursts, anger, being reactive, aggression, obsessive compulsive behaviour, rigidity and impulsivity. The sympathetic nervous system is active in this state of danger.

Hypoarousal is associated with emotional numbness, emptiness or paralysis. Here we disassociate and disconnect. The parasympathetic nervous system state of shutdown is active in this state of danger and threat to life.

Both of these states, being beyond our range of tolerance, hinder the ability to be mindful in the present moment—meaning within these states, we can no longer make rational choices. This is largely due to cortisol excess inhibiting hippocampus function and diminished function of the limbic brain, which is involved in symbolisation and contextualisation.[43]

Awareness of the fear response

When we experience fear we tend to either 'F*ck Everything And Run 'or 'Face Everything and Recover'. So, in truly dangerous situations, the fear response helps us to survive. The problem is, although we've evolved a great deal since the time we lived in caves, the amygdala hasn't really adapted to our modern environment. Back in the past it was necessary to be hyper-vigilant, to constantly check the environment for danger to ensure survival. To be able to fight or run away. Nowadays, life isn't usually this intense, but the amygdala still functions in the same way. It overreacts to situations that aren't necessarily dangerous, but ones that trigger social or psychologically embarrassing or painful emotions. I call this 'False Evidence that Appears Real'.

Have you ever felt your pulse racing during a job interview? Felt the fighter in you rear up when someone cuts you off in traffic? Felt like running when you have to speak in public? And were any of these situations really a danger to your survival?

About a decade ago, I had an experience that taught me something simple yet profound—to focus my fear where the actual danger is. This was the first step in moving towards expressing my emotions in real time, instead of allowing my imagination to run away with me—which triggered my emotions to do the same. While fear is almost always fed by the imagination and somewhat illusory, danger is very real. It's important to focus on what is real so that you can respond appropriately. If we don't, we get caught up in our imagination which can make the situation much more threatening than it actually is.

The situation that gave me this insight began one sunny day in the middle of my tantric journey into sexual liberation. As part of this awakening, one of the ways I'd chosen to challenge myself was to allow myself to feel sexual while outside in nature. On this particular day, my partner and I were sunbathing in the archipelago outside Stockholm. We were naked, very relaxed and facing a little rock formation towards the water, not far from where the big ferries from Stockholm passed by towards the Baltic Sea.

We both began to get aroused although didn't intend on having sex. We were just enjoying each other playfully and time slipped by. Then suddenly, I noticed that one of the big ferry liners, which had been sailing in the distance was coming towards us relatively quickly. At the same time I noticed the little fear response in my body—a discomfort at the thought of being seen naked and aroused. Nevertheless, I chose to stay there, naked, feeling my sensual sensations while, at the same time, observing the fear rising within me.

The moment the ferry got really close I chose to close my eyes and investigate my shame, fear and embarrassment. I visualised people standing on the railing pointing towards me, a person of ridicule, indulging in inappropriate behaviour, naked and sexual out there in the open, and I started to panic. This inner vision became so overwhelmingly scary that I wanted to jump up and run away. When I opened up my eyes I saw the real facts. Not one person was on the deck of the ferry. No-one was looking or pointing a finger towards us. It was then I realised the inappropriateness of my emotional response. The entire situation had been dreamed up by me. It came from my internal, home-made, conditioned response to perceived danger.

I choose to - Face Everything and Recover.
Can you recall having a similar experience at some point in your life?

States of *dysregulation* create an overall sense of discomfort and vulnerability which makes us feel unsafe and exposed. Over time, the nervous system begins to perceive danger more readily and our Window of Tolerance narrows. This is a survival strategy of the nervous system to protect us from possible and diverse threatening situations. When the Window of Tolerance narrows we become imbalanced and our ability to make choices in a conscious and calm manner decreases.

By expanding your Window of Tolerance—rather than just returning into it—you increase your sense of calm and overall well-being, which enables you to deal with stressors in a more adaptive way.

How do you expand your window of tolerance?

Without hyper or hypo-arousal, we stay within the Window of Tolerance but don't learn to expand it. We neither thrive nor evolve.

When you know where the edges of feeling comfortable are in any given situation, you can expand your Window of Tolerance while feeling relatively safe. There is a field of learning, just at the edge of the Window of Tolerance, just before leaving and entering the realms of hyper or hypo-arousal. Here we are able to *dysregulate* and then *self-regulate* back to our *comfort zone*. It's important to have experience of different neurological states and to know the responses of the limbic system (the emotional body), then we can understand how *dysregulation* and *self-regulation* feel and recognise each as they happen.

WINDOW OF TOLERANCE

HYPERAROUSAL
FIGHT / FLIGHT / FREEZE
DYSREGULATION

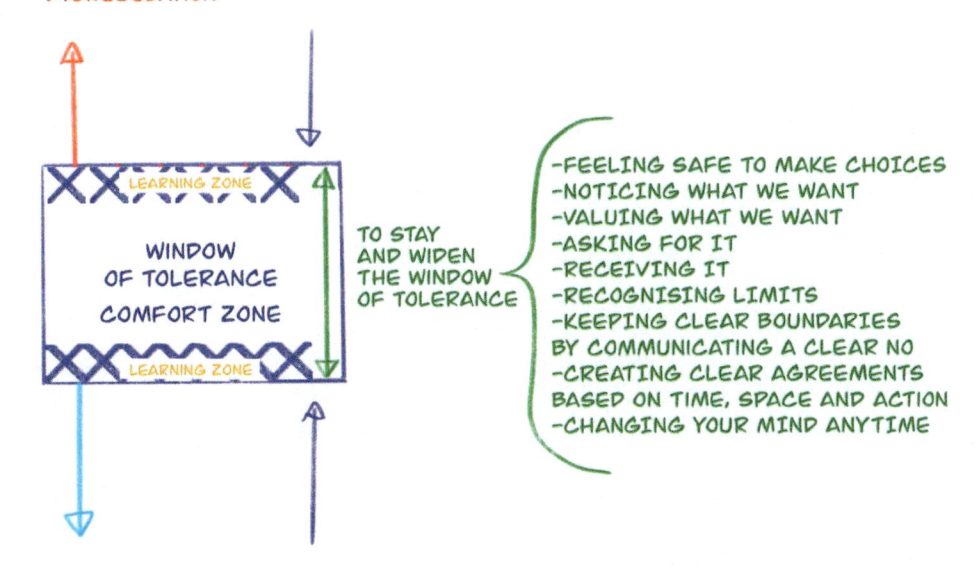

LEARNING ZONE

WINDOW OF TOLERANCE
COMFORT ZONE

LEARNING ZONE

TO STAY AND WIDEN THE WINDOW OF TOLERANCE:
- FEELING SAFE TO MAKE CHOICES
- NOTICING WHAT WE WANT
- VALUING WHAT WE WANT
- ASKING FOR IT
- RECEIVING IT
- RECOGNISING LIMITS
- KEEPING CLEAR BOUNDARIES BY COMMUNICATING A CLEAR NO
- CREATING CLEAR AGREEMENTS BASED ON TIME, SPACE AND ACTION
- CHANGING YOUR MIND ANYTIME

DYSREGULATION
HYPOAROUSAL
HIDE / FAINT / COLLAPSE

SOMATIC CONSENT ENGAGEMENT SYSTEM

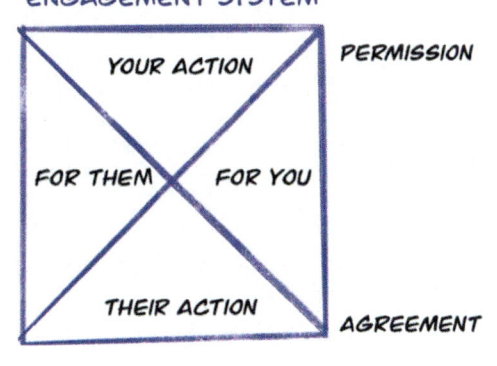

YOUR ACTION — PERMISSION
FOR THEM — FOR YOU
THEIR ACTION — AGREEMENT

WWW.SOMATICCONSENT.COM

Do you remember when we talked about following the *pull* and how it feels different to a *push*? Have you ever felt the *dysregulation* in your body when you pushed yourself to do something, although you felt the situation was too much and you actually needed to withdraw?

Have you ever taken yourself out of a situation that felt unsafe, and by doing so, were able to ground yourself again? Maybe you left the scene to go to the bathroom, or for a walk, and in those moments alone, were able to return to calmness. This is *self-regulation.*

Have you ever experienced a *pull*, excited about trying out something that feels daring but safe enough to take a quantum leap into the unknown and possible transformation?
This is what it means to have one foot in your Window of Tolerance while you expand your comfort zone.

My younger sister once invited me to go parachuting with her. She was quite advanced, having already jumped over a hundred times. Although I was scared to death, I didn't want to admit it and soon found myself on a plane, 4000 meters above ground level. When the time came to jump, like a lamb being led to the slaughter, I followed the instructor to the open hatch. Before jumping I remember looking at my little sister and (needing to prove my bravery) said, "Everything's fine, don't be scared." When I jumped I felt numb. When the parachute opened, I nearly passed out—and when we landed I was close to shitting myself. It was the worst experience I'd ever had.

That was a definite 'push'.

Years later, on a road trip in New Zealand I saw a sign for the highest bungy jumping bridge in the country. The plane jump memory flashed before my eyes. I immediately felt butterflies in my stomach, tingling feet and sweaty hands—but I also felt an urge to try it, without the fake bravado. I felt like doing something exciting, just for myself.

When it was time to jump, the instructor told me I had to count down from five, and jump on zero. I told him I wanted to do it a different way. To wait until I felt the impulse to jump. We agreed on a maximum of five minutes.

I remember standing there and feeling the *push* of the pressure to jump. Simultaneously I also began to feel a *pull* to find my impulse to *want to jump*. It was the first time I'd consciously noticed the pull and the push within my nervous system. And how different they felt. I began to feel the joy of excitement as I followed the pull. The push from the instructor blended into the background. The cocktail of fear and joy propelled me forward. I felt the impulse to walk to the edge, several hundred metres over a riverbed. And, in what seemed like slow motion, I chose to jump in the moment it felt right.

That was a 'pull'.

Within a professional context, there are many incidences of clients coming to me because of a push instead of a pull. Over the last few years, many women have come to sessions believing that something within them was broken. Some felt the pressure to 'heal 'through cervical de-armouring, having heard claims from others or via self-help groups that every woman needs it. Following the 'push 'of group pressure, they assumed they needed it too, to get fixed, and also belong to the club.

Whenever this seemed the case, that they were there due to a 'push', I refused to do cervical work, offering instead an empowerment session, so that they could learn to choose what they really wanted. Some became angry with me, feeling disappointment due to unfulfilled expectations of me doing the 'right thing'. Others agreed to the empowerment sessions, where many realised that they didn't in fact, want their cervix touched at all—and felt hugely relieved to own that fact.

I recognise a real 'pull 'when clients come from a very vulnerable place, asking for help and close to tears. Perhaps having difficulties reaching orgasm or feeling numb. They say words to the effect of; "I'm scared but I really want to do this to get my power back". They are often, although afraid of receiving a cervical session from a male practitioner, very centered in their vulnerability, choosing every step of the session.

SELF-REGULATION AND TRAUMA RELEASE

"Trauma is a fact of life. It does not, however, have to be a life sentence."
- Peter A. Levine

The body is miraculous. We all have a tremendous capacity to self-regulate, from a state of shock and shutdown, back to sympathetic mobilisation (shown by the arrows in the Polyvagal Map). I'd like to illustrate the body's ability of this enormous intelligence with a personal story.

When I was five years old I could climb like a little monkey. One day I climbed about three metres up into a tree. I felt very safe and confident until my father saw me and told me to come down, otherwise I might fall. When I heard his fearful voice, my body suddenly contracted. I felt clumsy and no longer confident. Usually, I slid down and jumped the last metre or so without thinking too much about it. But now I was afraid. My nervous system dysregulated to freeze.

My father told me to let go and jump into his arms. In my confusion I let go without releasing my legs from the tree trunk and slid down, badly ripping the skin on the inside of my legs and groin. There was a lot of blood and I spent the next week lying flat on my back with my legs spread widely open. It took a long time to heal and I couldn't walk properly for weeks afterwards. A childhood mishap I forgot all about until a lover asked me where I'd got the scars from.

At the beginning of my tantric journey, I did a lot of yoga and, due to the pain it induced, always had a problem with the butterfly pose (lying on the back with the knees to the sides and feet together). Soon after my lover had mentioned the scars, I decided to try it again, this time relaxing into whatever came up. I held the position for about 15 minutes, then closed my knees. At this point, my entire lower body began to shake involuntarily like an earthquake. Instead of freaking out I just let it happen while observing the process, during which, all the memories, pain and emotions from the tree accident came up. I allowed my body to shake and the emotions to surface. Relaxing in the butterfly pose had led to a kind of metamorphosis, leaving my body feeling wonderful. Intrigued, I did some research to figure out what had happened. I soon came across something called *TRE* (tension and trauma release exercises). These exercises assist the body to produce involuntary impulses, a self-regulating mechanism via the brain stem which releases deep muscular patterns of stress, tension and trauma. I later met the developer of *TRE*, had a private session, then went on to complete the instructor's training.

Sometime later, while at a quodoushka retreat, I fell, crashing my pelvis on the edge of the pool. The impact was intense. Luckily I didn't break anything, but the pain was excruciating. People ran towards my screams and wanted to help by calling an ambulance. I remember repeating over and over, "Please don't touch my body, let it do what it needs to do", "I'll be fine", while flipping and shaking on the ground like a fish out of water for about 30 minutes. It must have looked weird and a little scary. After the intense tremors had subsided, my body gave a deep sigh. I lay there for a few more moments, then stood up and walked to my room. I'd successfully self-regulated my nervous system, from a state of shock (dorsal vagal) to mobilisation.

This mechanism belongs to all mammals including us humans and is profound in its ability to transform trauma. Long-term emotional suppression leads to excess energy being trapped in our bodies, resulting in chronic physical tension and mental distress. Most mammals don't get post-traumatic stress disorder (PTSD), writes trauma therapist Peter Levine, in his book *Waking the Tiger*. This is because they release tension in their bodies automatically. You may have seen your pets do this from time to time, shaking as they stretch. There are two instances where conditioning results in unlearning this response to release tension. One of them is found in civilised humans and the other in caged animals. We humans however tend to try controlling this natural urge to shake off tension, in an attempt to remain looking calm and composed. This means the tension remains trapped in our bodies.

You can self-regulate more easily and return to your Window of Tolerance by being mindful of your physical sensations as they happen—and voicing how you feel in the moment. (We'll talk more about that soon in the section, The Numbness Bar).

CO-REGULATION AND TRAUMA RELEASE

"Immobilisation without fear is what we call 'intimacy'; all our defences are gone when we hold each other and are near each other. We don't need words because our bodies conform and feel safe with each other."
- Stephen W Porges

To widen your Window of Tolerance in co-regulation (with another person) you need to cultivate a sense of safety within your nervous system. You can do this by being tuned into the Direct Route and playfully engaging with the other using the Engagement Zones. This process creates intimate and genuine connections, training your nervous system, over time, to have a much higher capacity to adapt when challenging situations occur, so that it remains in balance.

The process of co-regulation in regard to past trauma guides you to the states on the right side of the Window of Tolerance map. Before it comes to any kind of action, we create an agreement about time, space, what's going to happen, who is the one doing and who it's for, as well as other relevant parameters. Then we can engage—and as part of the agreement—go beyond the Window of Tolerance with the other, so that each person can learn to self-regulate back into their comfort zone.

When clients come to their first session, I can often sense their nervousness and insecurity due to uncertainty about what will happen. It's vital to address this nervous system state and to establish an environment of safety before anything else takes place.

I usually invite them to choose one of the two available chairs, before sitting down and engaging in a very casual way. I then encourage them to express how they feel in their body at that moment, describing any sensations they notice. When someone is very dysregulated, I invite them to take part in a short breathing exercise utilised by Stephen Porges. We then breathe together, exhaling longer than the inhale, intentionally exhaling to the end of the outbreath, until the inhaling impulse occurs by itself. The inhale is accompanied by any sound that feels natural to them. I do the same, sighing out loud on the exhale together. This simple process stimulates the parasympathetic complex and is a very effective practice in co-regulating the nervous system.

Following this, the most effective mechanism I've observed to gain a sense of embodied safety is to practise feeling an object with the hands. When feeling pleasure with the hands, oxytocin is released, which, even in a group situation, leads to such relaxation within the nervous system that people can fall asleep. When working with a client one-on-one, this exercise helps them to drop so deeply into their body that all nervousness dissolves.

What kind of experiences have you had when confronted with fear and how did your body react? It doesn't have to be an extreme experience, an example might be if someone you don't feel comfortable with asking if they can hug you. This could trigger fear (in one form or other).

Were you aware of the processes while they were happening or did they feel automatic?

Were you able to self or co-regulate?

How did you do that or how did others help you to do that?

If your Base is intact and you're fully conscious of your internal processes, you will be able to notice the warning signs of fight, flight and threat of shutdown, acknowledge your inability to say "no" and either self or co-regulate.

THE NUMBNESS BAR

Repression And Expression Of Feelings And Emotions

"Unexpressed emotions will never die. They are buried alive and will come forth later in uglier ways."
- Sigmund Freud

It's been a tough period of time during the pandemic and many of us have experienced emotional upheavals in our bodies. The immune and emotional responses are two connected reservoirs in equilibrium with each other.[44] Repressed emotions weaken the immune system, creating symptoms of disease (unease and illness). And let's be honest, who likes to show that they aren't in control? And when we go down the path of trying to control our emotions—suppressing them with organisation, food, humour, entertainment, substance abuse, porn or whatever your 'distraction go to' is, if you pretend you're sailing on calm waters when there's a storm raging inside you—does it really help?

To some extent, feeling your feelings seems wrong for most people. We all grew up being taught that feelings and emotions are not okay to have, especially if they're 'negative'. To avoid dealing with them therefore, it seems easier to suppress them as they arise. The problem is, by doing this, we *decrease our ability to feel*. We allow them to enter our cognitive minds and numb the rest of ourselves from the neck down. This is the abandonment of the experience of our physical body and is represented in The Numbness Bar.[31] The Numbness Bar Map shows the four core feelings/emotions. Fear, Anger, Sadness and Joy. Generally speaking, most people's Numbness Bar is around 65-80%. When our Numbness Bar is this high or higher, we avoid emotional relationships with others and are unable to engage on a level of really *being* together.

NUMBNESS-BAR MAP

FEELINGS ARE FOR DEALING WITH THE NOW
EMOTIONS ARE FOR HEALING THE PAST

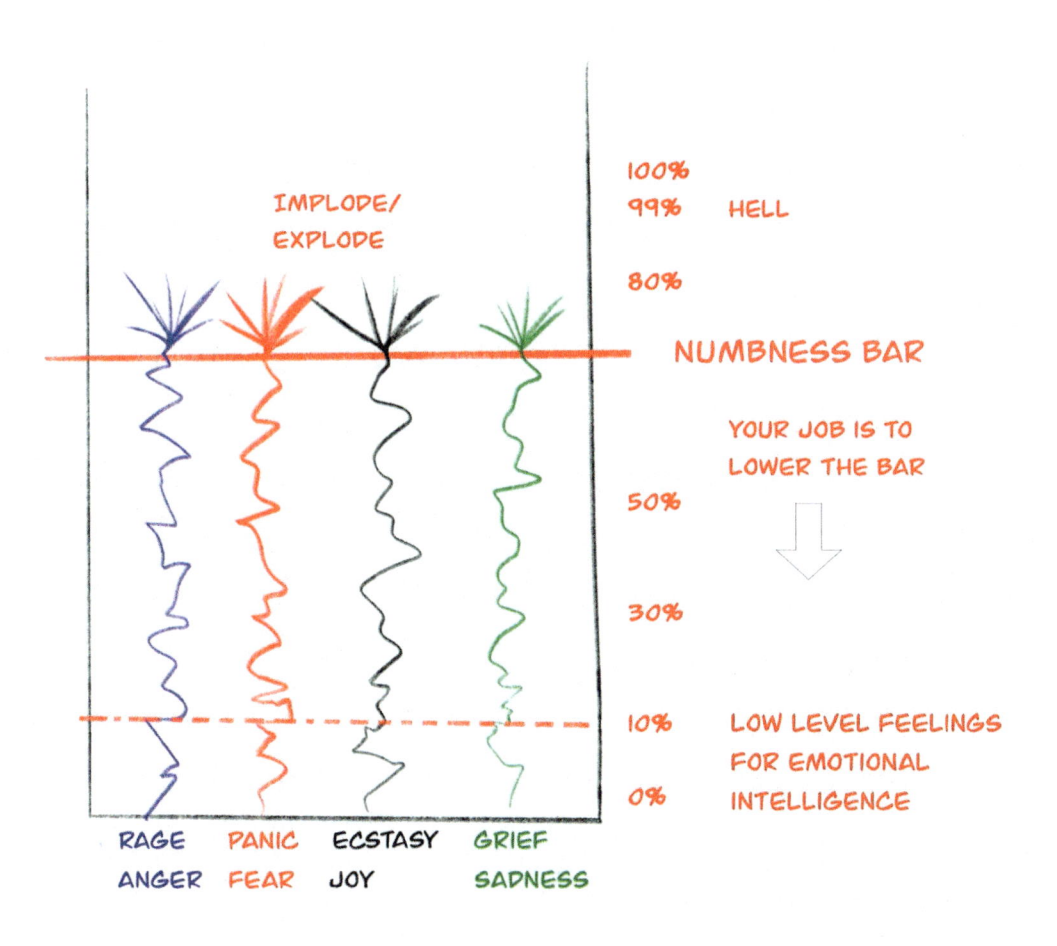

IMPLODE/EXPLODE

100%
99% — HELL
80%

NUMBNESS BAR

YOUR JOB IS TO LOWER THE BAR

50%

30%

10% — LOW LEVEL FEELINGS
0% — FOR EMOTIONAL INTELLIGENCE

RAGE / ANGER
PANIC / FEAR
ECSTASY / JOY
GRIEF / SADNESS

WWW.SOMATICCONSENT.COM

When we get triggered by other people or situations in our environment, the natural expression of anger at a low-level isn't usually aired. We very rarely tell others; "I feel a little annoyed at the moment". And we just as rarely hear the reply; "Okay, thanks for sharing that".

When we suppress our emotions they stay within, darkening our perception and spilling out of us when we can no longer contain them, rearing their head again in unconstructive bursts of anger, sadness and so on. Looping again and again. We usually allow an emotion to simmer, then cook until we can contain it no longer. It then rises up inside, eventually boiling over into explosive rage. It's the same for all emotions we suppress. Fear usually explodes into panic, joy into ecstasy and sadness into pain, tears and sobbing. When the pressure rises this far, we need to explode or implode to release it. Ways in which we can implode include self-hatred, depression, contraction, physical and psychological illness, feeling numb, collapse and shutdown.

When we suppress our emotions, the pressure may ebb, but will, without doubt, reappear later, the next time a similar situation triggers that emotion. When we allow this to happen, we feel generally numb most of the time, and experience regular episodes of implosion or explosion.

As you now know, being tuned into your somatic sensations releases oxytocin. When oxytocin is released during stressful times, it increases empathy, trust and connection. In doing so, oxytocin 'nudges' you to tell someone how you feel. So that instead of bottling your feelings up, you are able to vocalise, release emotion and get the support you need. This is part of our built-in social engagement system and how our nervous systems work. The release of this neurotransmitter also enables you to notice when others close to you are struggling, so that you are able to support each other.[45] When we do this, it is co-regulation from a place of love and care at the Apex.

How to release internalised emotion

In order to drop the mental loop that tries to control your emotions, allow them to happen.
It may sound scary, but dropping into an emotion helps you bring awareness to any need that isn't being addressed, as well as release the pressure that's built up through its suppression.

We can take a core emotion out of the equation by expressing it as intensely as possible for about 90 seconds.

> *First tune in by noticing how the emotion physically feels and its location within your body.*
>
> *Then take off the brakes, resisting the urge to suppress. By doing this you'll no doubt have a few minutes of discomfort—I invite you to allow yourself to feel what wants to come up.*
>
> *Express the emotion as exactly as you can, in a physical and exaggerated way. This way you're sure to find the 'sweet spot'. If you feel sadness, express it by crying or sobbing. If you feel fear, express it by shaking. If you feel anger, express it by screaming (you could do this into a pillow to avoid alarming the neighbours), and, if you feel joy, express it in some kind of jubilation such as jumping and yelling out a "YES"!*
>
> *Observe as the feeling of discomfort is released—just like opening a pressure valve.*

Expressing low-level feelings in real time

When we, however, acknowledge low-level feelings in-the-moment, we can increase our capacity to express them authentically in *real time*. The more we lower the Numbness Bar, to around 5-10%, the more we can be honest when we feel anger or another emotion, so that we don't explode/implode when the Numbness Bar is reached.

Anyone who engages with another person, whether as part of a couple, as a friend, family member, practitioner, within a team and so on, must be able to acknowledge that feelings are *always present* and they need to be expressed. When you engage with your feelings in the present moment, by noticing where this feeling sits within your body, you can express it or make adjustments. Then it won't be suppressed, simmer, cook and at some point implode or explode.

We can even lower the Numbness Bar to below 10% with practice. Let's say you're sitting at the computer and can feel discomfort. Maybe you can more easily identify the physical element first, such as tension in your back. Maybe the emotional sense of discomfort is stronger.

Which emotion is the physical discomfort causing or vice versa?
Where does the emotion you can identify sit within your physical body?
Is there low-level anger or frustration?

Now you are aware of your physical discomfort and the connected emotion, it's possible to consciously decide to take a break, have a stretch or find a more comfortable position. After doing so, you can check in with how you feel again and notice whether the emotion has diminished.

At any time, notice which feelings are present when you tune in.

You'll usually notice different levels of different feelings. Name the most prevalent feeling, is it anger, fear, sadness or joy? Where is it sitting in your physical body? Give it a percentage according to its intensity. Then notice why it is present, for example;

"I feel 10% anger when you say the word 'stupid'."
"Right now, I feel about 15% fear in my stomach because I can't keep up with my work."
"I feel 30% sad because you left without saying goodbye."
"I feel 20% joy waiting for my lover's visit later this evening."

This may sound trivial, but it's a very important skill to learn. We need to be able to recognise our low-level feelings to be able to increase our emotional intelligence. The more we bring the Numbness Bar down, the easier we can express our feelings as they happen in the moment. Here you learn to notice your desires, your limits, your body and how to express yourself in a relational dynamic with others more fluently.

When you feel vulnerable

A common emotion to experience is unease while speaking in public or socialising. Maybe you can relate? How do you feel? Nervous? Disassociated or lost for words? I'm guessing vulnerable in some way.

Realistically, in situations such as this, there isn't always an option to take five minutes out alone in order to self-regulate. As I already shared, one thing I do whenever I feel nervous while speaking in public is to own and express how I feel, in-the-moment. I notice my feelings and share them in real time. Doing this enables me to let out any build-up of discomfort and I find myself suddenly back to where I want to be, sharing my topic in an articulate way. This is a very empowering way to self-regulate. Some may shy away from this method, worried what people will think, and focus instead on keeping up a facade of strength. By showing your vulnerability, you in fact show a rare strength. And, by showing yourself, as you are, comes the possibility of connection.

There are different ways of bypassing vulnerability. One is when we don't ask for what we want and resort to shadow behaviour to get our needs met. Another example is the shallow small talk of conventional socialising, when we talk about superficial things to fill in the gaps of uncomfortable silence. I really find it difficult to engage in this kind of conversation without feeling awkward. It's a state I don't want other people to see in me. When this happens, what I occasionally do, instead of being honest about how I feel and showing my vulnerability, is default to talking about my ideas on certain concepts I've learned.

About a year ago I spontaneously chose to be more honest. I was travelling on a train from one airport terminal to another, when the man next to me struck up the kind of conversation common in the US to have with strangers. "Hi", he said loudly, "how are you doing today and where are you going?" Immediately a sense of awkward shyness materialised within me. I replied with a couple of words and imagined he expected to be asked back in return. Instead of doing that, I decided to express my genuine feelings in the moment. "I have this uncomfortable feeling in my body when I don't respond in the conditioned way to meaningless conversation, when I go against the grain. I feel kind of shy, with the hope that we'll arrive as soon as possible at the terminal, so I can avoid feeling what I feel." His answer surprised me. He said, "Yes, I feel the same way, but I can't stand the silence and need to fill the gap with something, to avoid the awkward feelings." I thanked him for sharing that and told him it made me feel relaxed to hear it. I went on to say that throughout my life I'd learned that this shy, awkward feeling was a weakness and I needed to hide it at all costs so as not to be judged. He nodded in agreement. Then I suggested, "How about we allow ourselves to just be seen in our awkward shyness that we have an urge to hide—just allowing ourselves to be with our feelings and acknowledge them silently until we get to the station?" He smiled and agreed. We were in this together. And it felt like an eternity. When we arrived we both agreed that it had been both the worst and the nicest transit ride ever. We thanked each other and shared a hug before continuing our journey in different directions.

Lowering your Numbness Bar is a key to unlocking the door of awareness. When you can be in constant connection to how you feel, know your desires and limits and intelligently express low-level feelings, you'll be able to connect more deeply with others you encounter.

Obstacles to pleasure - the pleasure ceiling

Some people find it difficult to feel pleasure for themselves directly, relying solely on the Indirect Route via the confirmation of other people's pleasure (whether in sounds, words or gestures). Sometimes this is due to having a high Numbness Bar of joy. When we reach a certain level of feelings we can get overwhelmed, even when it comes to pleasure. For this reason, many have learned to push this feeling down too. The result is we feel less or nothing at all.

Why would we push away joy? Well, a little bit might be nice but too much could evoke feelings of gratitude. The pure joy of gratitude is challenging for many people to feel without dropping into the shadow of guilt, duty, fear of appearing needy, dependent or vulnerable or the urge to reciprocate.

You may notice you can only take a certain amount of feeling coming in from the inflow before getting overwhelmed, and having to stop. I call this reaching the 'pleasure ceiling'. You may also notice that by allowing yourself to feel a little more each time and by welcoming the feelings that come up, your capacity to feel pleasure more exquisitely increases. This expands your *pleasure ceiling* and lowers your Numbness Bar of joy.

It's good to remind yourself that within the process, there is no meaning, goal or destination. It's only about being present in your skin and following your pleasure. This can be challenging for many who associate pleasurable sensual touch as foreplay leading to sex.

Numbness of the genitals

This can be an indicator of partial neurological shutdown, a nervous system response in order to protect against intense feeling and emotional memories that result from trauma.

About 10 years ago I began to practice kegling (pelvic floor exercises). But I did it to such an extreme that I became so numb, I couldn't feel much for three months. It was pretty scary.

From my personal and professional experience, I consider kegling good for women after giving birth, to help create new muscle tone. However, these exercises which voluntarily control the muscles of the pelvic floor (during sympathetic mobilisation) are generally misused to teach women to get tight, in order to please men. So that men can feel better for themself.

I've talked to midwives on the subject who all agreed that a normal workout practice such as walking or dancing is enough to tone the pelvic floor (in general and after giving birth) and that extreme exercises promoted by some 'experts 'can create muscle tension. You may wonder what the difference is between muscle strength and muscle tension. A strong muscle is not tight but relaxed. Tighter does not equal stronger. It's just tighter[46].

To recap:

When we utilise the Engagement Zones, we can actively create a safe environment. When we feel safe the noticing brain is constantly activated and connected to all levels on the safe side of our nervous system, as we saw in The Polyvagal Theory.

The noticing brain remains active and observes processes within the following:

- **The social engagement system:** ventral vagus part of the parasympathetic system.
- **Mobilisation:** the safe side of the sympathetic system.
- **Immobilisation/bliss state:** dorsal vagus part of the parasympathetic nervous system.

When the noticing part of the brain is activated, it connects all the information from the working brain (logic), amygdala (emotions) and reptilian brain (shut down mechanism). Can you imagine how much insight we can gain when this happens? It truly is an awakening in itself.

Whenever you notice shadow survival strategies coming up, it's also important to acknowledge that you're in survival mode and that they are involuntary activity. What we want to aim for is authentically engaging with others—in the moment—by acknowledging our shadows and expressing our desires and limits. If we look at our shadow strategies as wrong, bad or something to avoid, we miss out on the opportunity to learn from them and to heal. Through avoidance we bypass the capacity we have to grow through past experience of trauma.

Not being aware of our shadows is a kind of slumber and the opposite of the awakening process. When we develop our capacity for somatic experience we process our experiences, integrate our learnings and grow. With a stable Base of self-care, we are able to face any shadows that become apparent, and aren't afraid to dig deeper into what is profoundly possible. When we don't avoid the pain of our shadows, we integrate them into self-knowledge. We expand and evolve.

We can integrate our shadows by acknowledging and accepting them, then retraining our unconscious responses. We do this by lowering our Numbness Bar and engaging in feelings at the time they occur.

First we acknowledge our feelings to ourselves, such as, "Something's going on right now, I'm not sure what, but this is how I feel. My heart's beating more rapidly, my legs feel shaky, I can feel a burning sensation rising up".

Just like an early warning system, when we're aware of the internal response of feelings that come up moment-to-moment and the resistance we feel inside (towards certain people or types of behaviour), we can trust the impulse and approach the subject that triggered the feelings immediately.

Then, however we express our feelings, we find relief. We have an informed choice and can make rational decisions to behave a certain way, such as leaving the situation that's causing us distress or engaging and expressing how we feel. An example may be, "This makes me feel really sad, I need a moment to reflect on how I feel, can you give me a little time?" It is then possible to move on without having to go into survival mode.

If you can't express yourself or you're in a situation that you can't easily leave, you can observe your feelings and remind yourself that the situation is temporary, breathing through it for this limited time, and recalibrate afterwards.

When you lower the Numbness Bar, overwhelm doesn't happen. You can widen your Window of Tolerance because you're in connection with your feelings and you'll have a much better idea of how long you're able to tolerate a certain situation. By noticing how it feels for the nervous system to go through different neurological stages without dysregulating, shutting down or going into rage, you maintain conscious awareness *as your survival mechanisms begin to kick in*—and *before* they take over.

When we do this, the hybrid state is accessed due to feelings of safety, compassion and openness between people during social engagement. Each person knows and expresses how they feel in the moment. Each knows and expresses their desires, asks for permission, recognises their boundaries, communicates their limits and respects the other's desires and limits. Personal and interpersonal growth happens through play, fun, connection and intimate relating. This really is a lifelong practice of ever deepening richness.

EMPOWERMENT AND CHOICE

"Empowered people empower people."
- Unknown

Antoine de Saint-Exupéry, author of *The Little Prince,* once said, "If you want to build a ship, don't drum up people together to collect wood and don't assign them tasks and work, but rather teach them to long for the endless immensity of the sea".

Empowerment happens through an individual's longing to be complete and is the process of exploring all you need to feel whole, while **knowing that you have a choice**.

When it comes to touch, instead of going along with something that feels mediocre, the magic formula is having enough time to; NOTICE, TRUST, VALUE and COMMUNICATE your desire when in the receiving role. As the giver it means being true to your limits while allowing the receiver to let their body find and express desire in the most authentic way *for them.*

EMPOWERMENT & CHOICE MAP

CHOOSING IS MORE IMPORTANT THAN ACTION

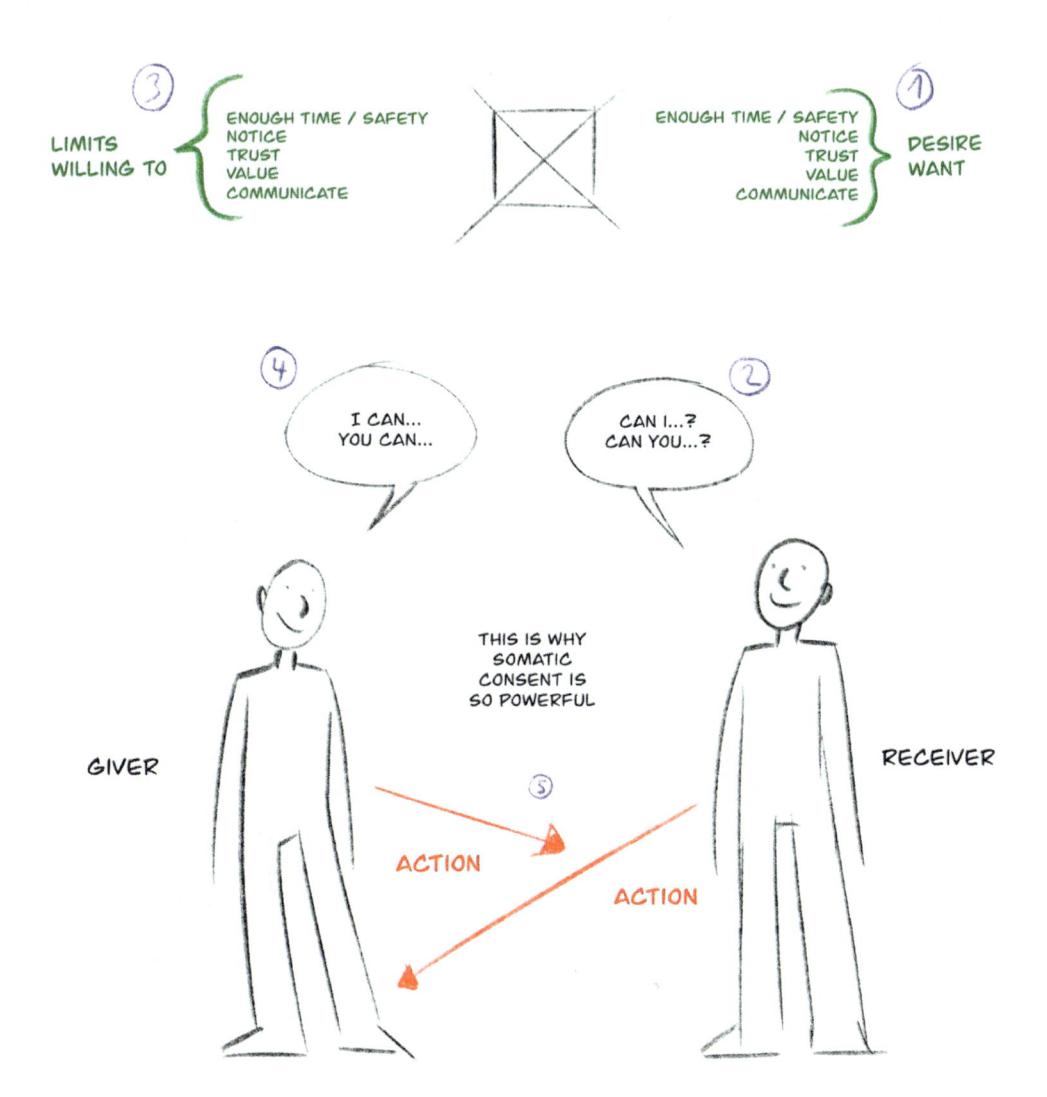

③ LIMITS / WILLING TO
- ENOUGH TIME / SAFETY
- NOTICE
- TRUST
- VALUE
- COMMUNICATE

① DESIRE / WANT
- ENOUGH TIME / SAFETY
- NOTICE
- TRUST
- VALUE
- COMMUNICATE

④ "I CAN... YOU CAN..."

② "CAN I...? CAN YOU...?"

GIVER — RECEIVER

THIS IS WHY SOMATIC CONSENT IS SO POWERFUL

⑤ ACTION / ACTION

WHEN YOU CAN CHOOSE WHAT YOU WANT — THERE ARE ENDLESS POSSIBILITIES FOR ACTION

WWW.SOMATICCONSENT.COM

We often presume that we have to intuitively know what the other person wants, or we do something in order to belong. One of the biggest 'aha' moments in the *giving* role, as you go into action *for them*, is when you realise you *don't have to guess* what the other person wants anymore. You don't have to pretend that you know. You don't have to invent anything. This can come as a huge relief, wouldn't you agree? With this lack of pressure to 'second-guess' also comes the supreme clarity and ability to focus on your own experience.

Most of us also presume that when we give something, we *do* an action. That giving and doing are conflated, one and the same thing. What the Empowerment and Choice Map does is take these presumptions apart. As you can see below, when we are in the role of the *giver*, actually, the last step of the map (step 5), is the action.

Step 1
As the giver, you allow the *receiver to* have enough time and to feel safe enough to recognise their desire/tune into what they want. This is a vital process in itself. When we feel safe and connected, a part of the frontal lobe (in the neocortex) allows us to notice our desires and make rational choices. We trust that our desires are real, we value them and can communicate them. *This first step is the foundation of empowerment.*

Step 2
Next is communication. The receiver notices their desire and bases the request on permission, i.e. "Can/may I do that?" or on an agreement, i.e. "Can/will you do that for me?" These questions literally become the mantra of receiving. Without communication, there is no request, and therefore, no action.

Step 3
Then the giver goes through the same process. We usually react quite quickly to requests, but as the giver, you also need time to feel safe enough to know what you're willing to do—by *noticing, trusting, valuing and communicating* your *limits*.

Step 4
The answer could be, "Yes I can", "Yes you can", "No you can't", "Ask me for something different".

Step 5
Now you'll find you can slowly relax into *giving* with presence, while fully enjoying whatever you're doing. You're doing exactly what the other asks

you for (within your limits). If they want something different, they will tell you. You can then reassess your limits if need be at that time. So, the receiver 'steps into 'the place of noticing first and each person takes responsibility to communicate their desires and limits, using the map as a tool for expressing their needs. This turns the situation we usually default to around, so that the giver is no longer *responsible* for what the receiver receives.

> ***On the path of empowerment, choice and communication are more important than the action itself. When you can ask for what you want—every action is a bonus.***

---

*When I'm the **receiver**, I own my desire **without need or attachment to getting it**. Even if the other says "no", there is gratitude to them for knowing and expressing their limits.*

*When I'm the **giver**, I own my limits, and even if I say "no", there is gratitude to the other for owning and expressing their desires.*

When we rewire the nervous system back to wholeness we *shed* man-made structures, largely based on rules within social groups and cultures. We *satisfy* the spiritual longing we all have—to return to our true nature. A state of bliss.

Experiencing a state of bliss requires equilibrium of body and mind. The balance of each person's body and mind is influenced by the state of their nervous system. The SCES shows how to achieve this balance in logical, practical steps.

- Waking up the hands - re-establishes the Direct Route's sensory inflow of your moment-to-moment experience of touch. When you're fully aware of the somatic inflow during touch, you're also aware you're going into action for yourself. This knowledge develops integrity in your actions.

   Tuning into the sensory inflow of the Direct Route calms the nervous system, bringing you into a more relaxed state of being. It increases physical awareness which rewires your nervous system back to its natural capacity to receive pleasure independently. It enables you to be more aware of your feelings, emotions, needs, desires, boundaries and shadow strategies. It releases oxytocin which blocks stress hormones (cortisol and adrenaline) and increases your ability to feel empathy and bond with others.

- The Basement - awareness of the misalignment of shadow engagement. This provides the ability to gain deeper knowledge of self by observing which needs you're trying to meet with these strategies, what isn't being asked for and which agreements aren't being made.

- The Base - where you function from the sturdy foundation of being grounded in self. The bridge between your motor and sensory route is activated. You are awake— know what you have a right to (your basic needs) and take responsibility for your own self-care, thoughts, feelings, emotions and actions.

- The Engagement Zones - where you practise authentically communicating what you want and don't want. Here you can clearly see *who is doing an action, who it's for*, ask for permission and come to agreement within each person's limits. When a difficulty arises within relationship, the Engagement Zone map helps to clarify and provides a quick and effective way of solving miscommunication and blind spots. The combination of the Direct Route and the clarity of this kind of engagement relaxes the nervous system.

- The Apex (interpersonal state) - the state of pure being, where you do something to/ for others from an altruistic place of love and care. Integrity is in place due to self-knowledge, self-responsibility and honest engagement. There is generosity because you feel abundant. There is deep gratitude for self and the other as you feel the gift of who you are, as you are—and who the other is, as they are. There is no agenda or any urge to do something in order to be accepted and to belong. Here the nervous system is in a relaxed state of social engagement with the other person. When in this safe, connected, intimate state, we are able to surrender to something bigger than our identity of separate individuality (ego)—and experience a merging with the other in oneness and bliss.

- Above the Apex (the transpersonal state) is the realm of further merging beyond the experience of interconnection with your loved one —that of an unlimited connection with the rest of life. This is often referred to as Nirvana, Samadhi or Enlightenment, a complete spiritual awakening, as we fully realise (not just grasp a concept with the mind) but experience *being Source Consciousness.*

OM AND SPIRITUAL CONNECTION AT THE APEX

"I am the medium, the channel, and I cannot become the channel unless my surrender is complete."
- Paramahamsa Satyananda

The dynamics within the SCES can be seen within the symbolism and structure of the OM, so that we can interpret the symbol as a similar development map.

SPIRITUAL DEVELOPMENT MAP

OM

- TRANSPERSONAL VOID / BINDU
- APEX INTERPERSONAL ALL IS ILLUSION
- ENGAGEMENT ZONE REALISING DREAMING WHILE AWAKE
- THE BASE / FOUNDATION STATE OF AWAKENING
- DEEP SLEEP CONCSIOUSNESS SHADOWS BASEMENT

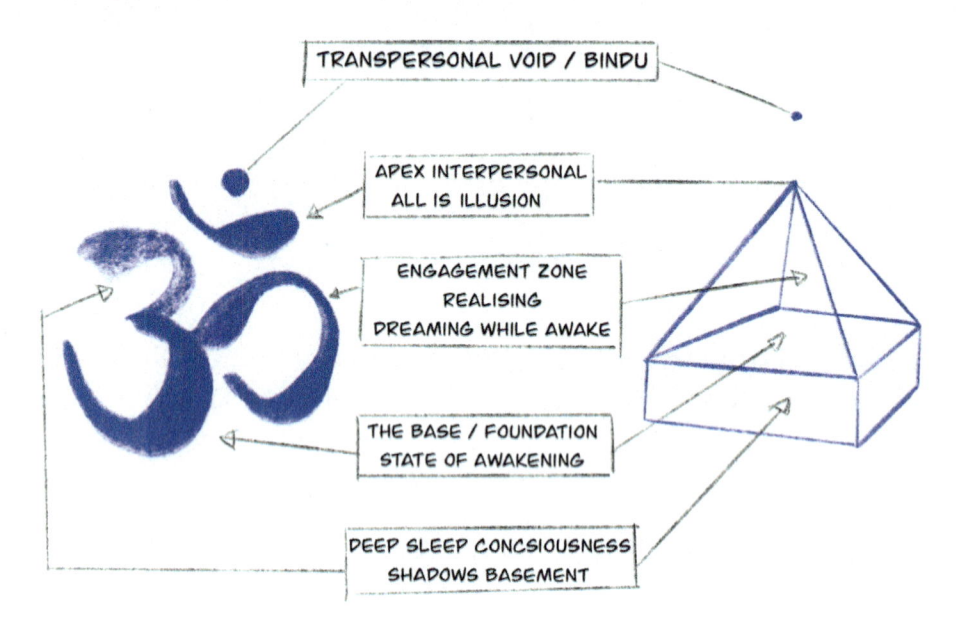

WWW.SOMATICCONSENT.COM

- The Basement (upper curve) represents 'deep sleep', living in the illusion of shadow strategies, where we are unaware and function automatically.

- The Base (lower curve) shows self-responsibility for self-care, where the bridge of awareness between the sensory and motor route provides a foundation for choice.

- The Engagement Zone (curve to the right) represents the permissions and agreements you make with those you relate with.

- The Apex (curve on top) represents pure interpersonal transformation.

- The transpersonal space above the pyramid structure (*Bindu*, the dot on top) represents source consciousness, the void, where we don't identify with the individual sense of self but with pure spiritual, shared consciousness.

When we embody the three dynamics of the OM symbol, making a solid base of self-care, being aware of our shadows and developing truthful communication within the Engagement Zones—we can transcend the sleeping state/illusion of separateness (*Maya* in Sanskrit).

Here we access interpersonal connection and dissolve into oneness with the other. This is the Apex, the interpersonal space of play with the other where love making happens. A place of mutual desire, mutual play and mutual feeling. It is an orgasmic place of pure connection without goal or agenda.

Transpersonal connection

This work emerged through 25 years of personal experience, research, practice and playing with concepts and ideas. I didn't just put them together as a theory, but lived them.

These spiritual teachings are transparent and accessible. The concepts aren't new but found in ancient Tantric scripts about consciousness; within the dynamics of Shiva and Shakti who represent the union of immaterial consciousness and material nature. Of Kali who symbolises mastering the animal nature while maintaining enough power to stay in connection and presence. It's a philosophy, with no limits or end. It's about *being* bliss—your true nature. Although there is a deeper understanding that *everything* is temporary aside from connected consciousness, it's about being fully embodied (grounded in your body) while flowing with the daily tasks of life. It's not about ascending into disassociation and leaving the body, but being here, now, in the totality of each breath in each moment, even within suffering.

When you see life as an 'Earth school', lovemaking becomes so incredibly good because you 'team up 'together. There is no chance for sex or the relationship to become ego based. It has to become a collaboration, otherwise it doesn't work. Just like tuning into a radio frequency, both need to be on the same wavelength for connection to happen.

SPIRITUAL BYPASSING

Seeing Beyond Self-Trickery

"Spiritual Bypassing is a tendency to use spiritual ideas and practices to sidestep or avoid facing unresolved emotional issues, psychological wounds, and unfinished developmental tasks."
- John Welwood

The state of transpersonal spiritual connection is often misunderstood. Many believe that to access this 'space', we only need to be positive, to love, care and smile our way through life, and that this alone will give us an experience of oneness. This however can be termed *spiritual bypassing.* It avoids or bypasses the fact that we are in a human body, living a human existence with very human emotions. Not being aware of how the mind works, as well as suppressing emotions rarely enhances our ability to grow and awaken.

SPIRITUAL BYPASSING

CONNECTION,
INTIMACY,
SAFETY,
SOCIAL ENGAGEMENT,
SENSUALITY,
VENTRAL VAGUS,
LET YOUR SKIN DO THE WORK

DIRECT ROUTE OF PLEASURE

ARTIFICIAL TRANSFORMATION

MAKES PERSONALITY WRONG, JUDGING EGO

FIGHT

PERSONALITY
MEANING   IDENTITY

INDIRECT ROUTE TO PLEASURE ONLY

DEFENSE   CONDITIONING
EMPTY   ARTIFICIAL STIMULI
YANG   STORY AND FANTASIES
SHADOWS   PRETENDING, PERFORMING

HUMOUR, FUN, COSMIC JOKE, DIGGING DEEPER

RELAXATION   TRANSCENDENCE
MATURITY   SENSUALITY   GROWTH
DEPTH   SENSITIVITY
LOVING CONNECTIONS   REAL TRANSFORMATION

INFINITY, VOID

WWW.SOMATICCONSENT.COM

I based the Spiritual Bypassing Map on my own experience of illusion. Prior to discovering the Direct Route, I focused on the Indirect Route where I pretended and performed for other people's pleasure and created mental arousal through fantasy that had nothing to do with what my body was actually experiencing. I was consumed by conditioned pretending and performing. I call this 'empty yang' or artificial stimuli, and I overdosed on it.

At the time, I believed I was spiritually aware, when in actual fact I was practising spiritual bypassing based on my intellectual grasp of what I believed it was. All I had done was to create a type of 'artificial transcendence' in my own mind. My mind juggled the concepts of what it meant to be spiritual but was still judgmental. Whenever anyone around me pointed this out, I would respond in defence, always in fight mode if I got criticised or felt threatened. I would also, as part of my defence, make their personality 'wrong'. I knew this was my ego desperately trying to defend itself when it got triggered and was hard on myself for that.

Most of us either suppress or try to 'crack the nut' of our 'wrong' personality during therapy by using force. This 'biting through' of our own defence mechanisms can create huge emotional resistance and make matters worse. From this place of imbalance, many attempt to access a higher state of consciousness. This is what I understand as 'artificial transformation' or spiritual bypassing. Instead, I believe we have to integrate our shadows in order to transform.

You know when you've avoided being aware of your shadows when, for example, you find the personality structure of others to be wrong, getting defensive when people push (fight) against your own personality. You may make some progress on the spiritual path, and it may feel good, but it'll be a limited transformation. I did this myself for a long time, but the more people criticised or pushed against me, the stronger my ego became.

When I realised that the positive development of personality structure was based on *connection* (achieved through feeling safe and tied to the function of the ventral vagus nerve and the social engagement system), I knew the only way to develop spiritually was to let my skin do the work. When I tuned into my real-time experience of sensory input, I began to wake up. The more I activated the sensory inflow of pleasure, the more I experienced a 'softening', a relaxed presence, an embodied sensuality with genuine tangible feelings of connection to myself, others and the world around me—*in the moment.*

This experience was like allowing love to slowly drop into a crack in the rock-solid state of my personality to create a new foundation, from where I could feel and relate differently, in a more expanded, natural way. It opened a previously unknown place where I began to engage with others without an agenda, without focusing on a goal, without needing or wanting anything connected to any 'meaning 'I'd placed on it. It created a different level of depth, one based on integrity, alignment, truth, connection and 'being'.

Whenever I experience difficulties, I always go back to these roots based on touch, connection and oxytocin, so that I'm able to tune into my genuine self at any given moment. Because of this connection within myself, based on the inflow, I'm no longer dependent on identification with my personality structure and its usual reactions to unconscious triggers. This new dimension of self allows shadows to come to the light so that whenever I get triggered, I notice, "Oh yes! It feels really awkward when such and such happens!" and I'm able to understand why.

The massive potential to dig deeper into myself became fun. It became a playful game. I can now engage with my shadows with humour, light-heartedness, acceptance and ease—and allow others around me to do the same. Here I've experienced real transformation and transcendence with maturity and depth. I don't have to fight against anything or protect my shadows anymore. I live in a broader truth and know my infinite nature. The self has deep waters. By diving into what is real, we find transformation and infinite possibility to experience our spiritual identity. This becomes a lifestyle, a continuum of connection to god/divinity/your higher self (or however you prefer to call it). Not as a concept, belief or religion, but as a pure experience of is-ness—through your own somatic perception, interoception and neuroception of *being* in the present moment. This is how I dropped into the present moment of being—and there's no way back.

> *"When you are kissed by that once—you are ruined forever"*
> *- Rumi*

Sharing this experience with a loved partner at an intimate and sexual level is the best thing in the world. You don't have to be in solitude if you can share it with someone who wants to share it with you. You can grow together simultaneously. You can always be alone, but I find transformation can be limited that way. Human beings are pair bonders and therefore, through physical connection and oxytocin-based intimacy, our transformation occurs within the very nature of our is-ness together.

I think we've all struggled to understand the other within relationship despite our best intentions. We all perceive so very differently. Without both partners fully embodying the Direct Route and practising the Engagement Zones, being in the Apex together on an interpersonal level is difficult to achieve.

Tuning into the Direct Route is the core practice, the cornerstone and the Holy Grail of the entire Somatic Consent system. By practising it you're clear that an action isn't based on getting a reaction from the other, but on your own experience of feeling. You can then go about getting permission from others to practise **for yourself**. Practicing with consent builds deep trust within the nervous system, which is necessary to experience surrender and the awakened state.

The apex and shadows

*"Kindly let me help you or you will drown,
said the monkey putting the fish safely up a tree."
- Alan Watts*

A lot of knowledge comes from learning and embodying the teachings of the SCES. Any new learning brings empowerment—and with that power, comes the responsibility to use it wisely.

Earlier in the book we talked about giving from the Apex without permission. I'd like to expand on this subject a little more here. It's good to regularly check in with yourself as to whether, when you believe you're at the Apex, you are giving your gift of power from a place of love and care in order to support the transformation of others; or whether you're doing it for some kind of personal gain. This scenario may transpire, simply because it feels so good to give. It can also happen if we are invested in or convinced about a certain method, tool or technique, to the point where we force it upon others without their permission. In this case, ask yourself who the action is really for. Another possibility is being in love with the feeling of 'power over 'someone else. In all these cases you may be using your skills and knowledge to manipulate others, in order to get more of what you want.

The interpersonal space can co-exist with active shadow strategies. One person may be in the interpersonal Apex space with a full heart and see the other struggling. Even when you may sincerely care for them and want to provide an action for their benefit, the action provided could still be perceived by the other in an entirely different way than intended.

What feels like one thing for one person can feel completely different to the other, and so, misunderstanding can occur. When we come from a sincere place of love and care at the Apex we want the best for the other. This means we often want to gift our power of loving resonance in a desire to lift the other up. At times this may be really helpful. At other times, instead of providing support, it can take the power away from the other to figure out something essential for themselves (in order for a personal transformation to happen).

Have you ever been in a situation where you did something for another person because you cared, but in retrospect, it was the worst thing you could have done for them at the time?

It's also common to trigger others by well-intended actions and instead, re-traumatise them, so that they perceive our action as invasive, as a shadow within us. This often happens when the other has not asked for our help or we haven't properly communicated an offer of help and given them a chance to refuse it.

This unclarity is confusing to the receiver who more often than not will go along with the situation, become resentful and thereby place themselves in the role of the victim.

We all have the tendency to go along with things—allowing things to happen to us—because we learn throughout life that what happens is more important than how we feel about it.

When one person provides a gift and sincerely believes they are coming from an altruistic, generous place, and the other feels it is not needed but neglects to express their boundaries, the doer (person in action) is perceived by the other as a perpetrator.

This perception of an action does not mean it is true. If someone is doing something to or for you from a place of love and care, and you place yourself in the role of the victim, you automatically put the other in the place of *'no permission'*. When one person is in one shadow, we tend to place the other in the opposite role. This is the *meaning* that is given, whatever the intention may be. We presume things which may not be true and instead of rising together to the Apex, a relationship can end up in the shadows—with nobody having a clue how it got there.

I'm sure you'll agree that we can get pretty mixed up if we aren't clear and honest with each other.

Have you ever thought you knew what was best for a loved one and provided that thing for them? Then realised that they didn't necessarily need or want that thing and were just allowing you to do it, in order to please or not upset you by rejecting your gift?

Have you ever pleased others by pretending you like the way they touched you, so that you wouldn't disappoint them by rejecting their attempt at making you happy?

Who do you think is receiving in these dynamics when both are giving?

You guessed right—nobody!

Intuition might be a blessing or a curse. The bottom line being that however intuitive we are, we never really know about another person unless we ask. All you need to do whenever there could be a speck of doubt, is to check in and ask the other person, "Is that really what you need?" or ask yourself, "Is this within my limits?"

This opens space for permission, reflection, choice and feedback. If both people are in touch with their own experience through Direct Route activation and if honest communication is practised within the space-in-between (the relationship), it's possible to come to a mutual agreement where no presumptions can be made and no ulterior motives to get needs met can exist.

CHAPTER 4

INTIMATE RELATING

The Real You Sees The Real Me

When I formed the dynamics of the SCES into the Base, the Zones and the Apex, *The Four Pillars* became a logical agreement guide for functional, intimate relating.

THE FOUR PILLARS OF RELATING

"The whole point of intimacy is to serve each other in growth and love, hopefully in better ways than we can serve ourselves. Otherwise, why engage in intimacy if your growth and love are served more by living alone? Intimacy is about growing more than you could by yourself, through the art of mutual gifting."
- David Deida

The Four Pillars are agreements for core engagement and relating which crystallised over the last four years while practising The 3 Minute Game.

The Four Pillars of Relating Map is specifically for lovers. The map can, however, be adapted to guide agreements in any situation in life.

Do you have clear agreements when you relate with others that allow you to be intimate and connected on a level that supports engagement in a positive way?

4 PILLARS OF RELATING

1. WE ARE FEELING AND SENSING BEINGS AND COMMITTED TO STAYING OPEN. I AM RESPONSIBLE FOR MY FEELINGS AND YOU ARE RESPONSIBLE FOR YOUR FEELINGS.

BASE: SELF-CARE, DOMAIN, BOUNDARIES, LIMITS, INFLOW

2. I GIVE YOU PERMISSION TO TOUCH AND FEEL ME ANYTIME, ANYWHERE AND I WILL TAKE CARE OF MY LIMITS. I ASK THE SAME FROM YOU.

PERMISSION NO VICTIM

3. IF I WANT / NEED SOMETHING, I WILL MAKE A REQUEST, IF I DON'T ASK, DON'T DO ANYTHING. SAME IN RETURN.

AGREEMENT NO PLEASING, NO EXPECTATIONS

4. BEING A GIFT, GIVING A GIFT FROM A PLACE OF ABUNDANCE AND GENEROSITY. WITHOUT NEEDING ANYTHING IN RETURN.

APEX: LOVE+CARE, INTERPERSONAL, MAKING LOVE, WIN/WIN, PLAY

WWW.SOMATICCONSENT.COM

Don't look for a good relationship, look for good agreements.

Within a lover dynamic, consistently giving permission creates rigidity. Pillar 2 provides unspoken permission to let the other 'just be 'while you take care of your limits. The 'general 'permission is an *allowing* where you can be yourself as a living invitation.

What is the quality of being a living invitation?

It is neither a passive nor an active way of being. It is an openness to whatever may unfold. It guides towards altruism, while maintaining an awareness of the shadow of giving more than you have to give and therefore becoming a victim. Limits are spoken about in real time as boundaries become clear.

Nowadays, I personally create clear agreements using an adaptation of the four pillars with anybody I engage with, whether with a friend, colleague or relative. While my own actions towards others are still defined by asking individual permission for each action—this promotes any kind of interaction (not necessarily touch related). It allows others to be *as they are* while I take care of my limits, remaining grounded in *being a living invitation* so that people feel comfortable to reach out and approach me with whatever they want.

RELATIONSHIP

The Zone In-Between

"To know oneself is to study oneself in action with another person."
- Bruce Lee

I'm a relationship person, I love to relate, to feel people and be felt. Although I've played sensually with thousands of people, intercourse has always been special to me, a more intimate experience I've chosen to share with less than 50 partners.

I've experimented in the Kink, BDSM and tantra scenes, been to swinger clubs and other hedonistic environments such as The KitKat Club in Berlin and had anonymous sex through online dating sites. I've cheated on my partners and been cheated on. I was faithfully married for eight years, have been in monogamous, polyamorous and open relationships. I've also been single for long periods of time in-between, with no sexual encounter at all. I would call myself a sex-positive person. I feel very relaxed while experimenting with ideas of intimacy, love and connection, ever learning more about relating with others in a joyful and meaningful way, for the purpose of growth and transformation.

One of the most important things that I've learned in life is that when a relationship is based on assumption and framed by telepathic agreements, it isn't really a relationship at all. When we *assume* we know the other and their motives we never really get to know each other in any depth or create real intimacy. We base our knowledge of the other entirely on our own perspective and wishful thinking of 'how things 'should 'be. We presume, expect, get disappointed and feel justified in our disappointment. This leads to frustration, anger, resentment and reactive patterns of behaviour. In this dynamic, no-one feels truly safe enough to let go and reveal themselves.

There is no should/shouldn't in relationship

We were all conditioned by the societies we grew up and have lived in. Each culture has its very own social norms, the behaviour it accepts or rejects, its unspoken 'shoulds 'and 'should nots'. While some societal rules are in place to protect the citizens within them, many stem from repeated age-old traditions that aren't necessarily true and remain largely unchallenged. Many of our beliefs are based on oversimplified assumptions masquerading as timeless common sense. If we look a little deeper, we can see that many of these rules are actually fake 'wisdoms'. When we accept them without question, they can shape our view of the world, lulling us into accepting things that are actually false and foolish.

Would you agree that each one of us has a different experience of life?

How many of your acquaintances, brought up in a similar background as yourself have very different values, beliefs, likes or dislikes from your own?

How often have you clashed with members of your own family due to contrasting opinion?

Can you think of an incident from your youth that influenced you to have a fear or a strong belief you carried through to adulthood?

Did all your friends have that very same experience?

Our personalities are just like pieces of jigsaw puzzles, largely made from our experiences that result in very different images. We only have our own picture of life, our perspective, formed from our own unique experiences. If this is true, is it logical to assume others 'should 'behave in a certain way? In reality, strong reactions to how others 'should 'or 'shouldn't 'behave come about when our own personal boundaries are crossed. Something another person does or says that isn't in-line with what we are personally comfortable with.

Meanwhile, the other has their own personal outlook, based on their own perspective, derived from their own experience of life. This is how most misunderstandings happen between people. We're all multi-layered and complicated. Presuming others act in certain ways for reasons which seem clear to us, is very uncertain territory. No-one is right or wrong. Presuming someone should or shouldn't act in a certain way without actually voicing preferences and coming to agreements is expectation based on thin air.

What kind of unagreed-upon expectations have you brought into relationships with family, friends or a lover?

How do you expect them to behave and react? How do you feel when they don't fulfil these expectations?

How often have you pointed the finger at someone, labelling them as 'wrong' because their behaviour triggered an emotion unique to your own personal experience?

How often did this result in blame and reactive action on your part?

Have you ever told someone they should or shouldn't behave in a certain way?

There is no should or shouldn't in relationship. Just different perspectives that need clarifying through agreements. If that can't be done, real connection or intimacy won't happen.

We're all motivated to protect ourselves

Safety is a basic human need. It's the primary motivating factor in each person's life. When our safety is threatened, the sympathetic nervous system switches to fight or flight mode, so that we can fight to protect ourselves or run away from the threat.

What kind of people are you drawn to? We usually like people who are like us. This basic principle enables us to feel safe. But can we expect others to be carbon copies of ourselves, with the very same belief systems, values, likes, dislikes, idiosyncrasies and opinions of how things 'should 'be?

How do you communicate when you feel uncomfortable with someone else's actions? Clearly, when this happens, one of your boundaries is being crossed. This usually results in feeling unsafe, though if you haven't made your limits clear, can you expect the other not to cross them? More often than not, we blame and shame the other when this occurs.

With this in mind, consider how the following two remarks would feel if someone you cared for said them to you. If you have experience in non-violent communication, authentic relating or radical honesty, this will already be familiar to you.

Scenario 1: Blame and shame

"You shouldn't do that, it's... rude/ annoying/ disgusting/ hurtful/ not how a mother/ friend/ son/ daughter/ lover behaves, and so on.

Scenario 2: When you do that, I feel...

"When you do that, I feel... embarrassed, resentful, annoyed, disappointed, insecure, unappreciated, jealous etc.

Notice the difference? When we point the finger in blame and tell someone their behaviour is wrong, their natural instinct will be to defend themselves. Announcing shoulds and shouldn'ts is like passing a guilty verdict before a trial has had chance to take place. It feels very threatening to the accused and often prompts some form of retaliation, or them fleeing from the scene entirely.

When we, on the other hand, point the finger at ourselves, explaining how we feel, it takes away the accusation that the other is in the wrong. Yes, their behaviour affects us, however, that is due to our own individual experience of life and perception; of what triggers our emotions and doesn't align with our likes, dislikes, beliefs and values or fails to meet an expectation we have. When the other doesn't feel like they've been accused, when it's clear that *you take responsibility for your own feelings*, it is so much easier for them to reflect and empathise. Then it's also easier for both to navigate emotional responses within relationship, define limits and come to agreements.

Communication through an exchange of information using 'I statements' has to be there before love making.

- "I feel anxious when you say that. How do you feel?"
- "I can empathise with that feeling/ thanks for sharing that, I had no idea...".

The structure of a relationship is built by the people creating it. It's a container held together by the glue of their agreements. When agreements are made, a sense of safety is established. When we feel safe we let go. There is no need to build walls. Both can stand truly naked before one another, and intimacy happens as a natural result.

RELATIONSHIP MAP

ENGAGEMENT ZONES

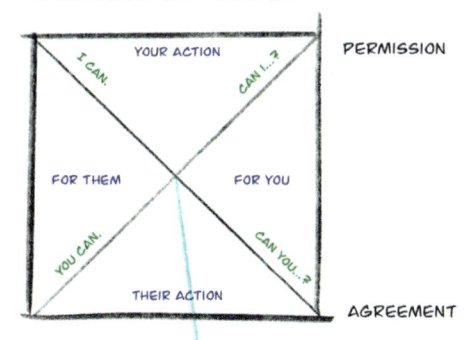

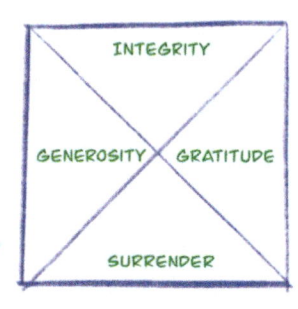

```
         YOUR ACTION      PERMISSION
    I CAN.  │  CAN I...?
      ╲     │     ╱
   FOR THEM │  FOR YOU
      ╱     │     ╲
    YOU CAN.│  CAN YOU...?
         THEIR ACTION     AGREEMENT
```

```
         INTEGRITY
           ╲ ╱
   GENEROSITY × GRATITUDE
           ╱ ╲
         SURRENDER
```

TEXT

APEX

④ I AM A GIFT AND GIVING A GIFT WITH NO ATTACHMENT. IT'S FREE.

③ IF I WANT YOU TO DO SOMETHING FOR ME, I WILL ASK. NO REQUEST NO ACTION. SAME IN RETURN. **AGREEMENT**

② I GIVE YOU PERMISSION TO FEEL ME.
I ASK FOR PERMISSION TO FEEL YOU.
WE TAKE CARE OF OUR LIMITS.

① I AM RESPONSIBLE FOR MY FEELINGS.
YOU ARE RESPONSIBLE FOR YOUR FEELINGS.
WE ARE COMMITTED TO STAYING OPEN. **BASE**

Pyramid labels: APEX, AGREEMENT, PERMISSION, SELF-PLEASURE, SELF-LOVE, INFLOW, SELF-CARE, BASE, SHADOWS

WWW.SOMATICCONSENT.COM

The Relationship Map correlates directly with the Engagement Zones (permission and agreements through making offers and requests, and the Four Pillars of Relating).

The Somatic Consent Engagement System invites us to create agreements within relationship by making clear requests or offers: formulating verbal consent by being aware of and clarifying:

> *What is going to happen? Where and when? Who is doing the action? Who is it for? And for how long?*

The Relationship Map shows how to create this container using the four layers of the SCES.

Layer 1. Base (self-care)

I'm responsible for my feelings, you're responsible for your feelings. We're both committed to staying open and noticing our own truth.

The first layer of encounter is establishing each person's Base. Every individual has to know their own Base so that their system's default setting is one of connection to self and self-care. Clarifying that, "I'm responsible for my feelings, and you're responsible for your feelings". In other words, you don't have to take care of me and I don't have to take care of you. Because if we can't take care of ourselves, how can we take care of others without burning ourselves out?

Making agreements that take into account our limits are determined by and dependent on our boundaries. If we are not aware of our boundaries or we haven't agreed upon limits, we constantly feel that our boundaries are being crossed. And if we don't know how to ask for our desires, we don't get our needs met. To know what our boundaries and needs are, we have to come back to our Base, again and again and again. We have to check in with ourselves with awareness, whatever the situation we're in or experience we're having, and ask;

"What's going on with me emotionally?" so that we know when we're tired, hungry, need a break, to stretch or lie down, to be alone, need a change or to relocate. Only then can we make a conscious choice in how we can take care of ourselves optimally. To act in self-care is the foundation of health. It gives us a stable Base and with it, the ability to function as grounded individuals.

Layer 2. Permission line

When permission is granted, the person doing the action is doing it for their own benefit.

Whenever we have a desire that includes another person, we have to ask for what we want.
The only healthy way to do this is as a request, asking; "Can I do that for myself?"

I give you permission to feel me, I ask for permission to feel you. Both people take care of their personal limits.

Asking permission to do something, "Can I...?" or giving permission for someone to do something for you, "Yes, you can..."

Permissions are clarified with the other person and limits respected.

If you are in someone else's space, make it clear what you have permission to do and be specific by asking, for example;

"Do I have permission to do what I like in this space?"
"Can I open the cupboards, go into your bedroom and lie or sleep on the bed?"
"Where are the limits of what you're comfortable with?"
"Are there places you don't want me to go to?"

When engaging with a friend or lover, you can suggest going on a journey for a specific period of time together, maybe a few hours, the night or longer. Here you could ask for example;

"Do I have permission to touch you?"
"What are your limits?"

An answer may be, "I don't want any sexual, genital touch", "no exchange of body fluids", I don't want intercourse", "I just want to stay close", or "you can touch me anywhere except my ears".

With this clarity you know the other's limits and therefore what the *limits of engagement* are. Whenever you're not sure where the exact limits are, you can be specific.

"Can I touch your neck?"
"Can I stroke your hair?"
"Can I lean against your shoulder?"
"Can I touch your leg/play with your foot/rub your back".

You could also use the second step of the Four Pillars of Relating, giving the other, for example, infinite permission to touch/ do what they want to, however they want to—and tell them you'll take care of your own limits, letting them know as they arise within the established container or frame of a time agreed upon.

Layer 3. Agreement line

In agreements, the person doing the action is doing it for the benefit of the other person.

If I want you to do something for me I will ask. No request, no action—and vice versa.

Asking someone to do something for you, "Can you…?" or agreeing to do something for someone, "Yes, I can…"

The agreements we have with others will differ depending on the established container, either long or short term, personal, social or professional.

When we come into a new environment with new people we have no idea what their limits are. We have no idea of their 'dos and don'ts'—and so, we tend to tip-toe around others to avoid conflicts. We may, for example, generally want guests who come to our home to feel good—and possibly feel under stress to take care of them. To make the 'community experience' easier, it's good to consciously communicate about your limits and desires and create agreements about what is going to/ not going to happen.

"If you want me to do something for you—ask me".
"If I want you to do something for me—I'll ask you".
"If I don't ask, don't give".
"Feel free to make yourself a drink, use the bathroom, put your feet up and change the music. Please don't go into my bedroom though. If we both make a mess, then I'd prefer we both clean up".

Layer 4. The Apex (giving a gift / being a gift)

I am a gift and giving a gift with no attachment. It's free.

If we have a compulsion to make others feel good, then we have to ask ourselves why. Is it coming from a genuine place of generosity? From a space of 'beingness' without expectation of receiving something back in return? True gift giving is a choice that comes from a space of altruism. This 'clean' giving can feel similar to the shadow side of giving, such as giving in order to be accepted—and they can also co-exist. The shadow comes up when there is an agenda. An expectation and attachment to outcome. Altruistic giving comes from a place of, "If I give a gift it comes from a free place of generosity. I don't want anything in return. What you do with it is your choice. I don't have any expectation that you'll do or behave a certain way if I give you a gift".

This is giving a gift from a place of love and care. It's not about recognition for your efforts. It's not that you do something to receive. When I make a cup of tea for someone I do it *with love* for them. If we look at giving in this way, your love is not less if the other doesn't want a cup of tea.

Relationship or relation-shit?

Most people's level of relationship can be humorously referred to as a 'relation-shit' because the lack of authentic relating leads to so much disharmony. Most relationships are assumption-based with many actions resulting from vague deductions, without a clear 'container' about what is going to happen and who it is for.

Before beginning a deeper relationship with a new partner in the past I suggested we hang out together and play The 3 Minute Game. Plato once said that we can learn more about someone from an hour's play than a year of conversation, and that's so true. In a small amount of time, it's possible to feel how much someone is in touch with themselves and to discover common ground in a fun way.

So, for the first stage of our new relationship, we decided to play by creating a 'one night stand' time frame, where we agreed to meet and play with each other for a specific amount of time (14 hours), after which, we closed the 'container' and ended this phase of our relationship with each other.

Before playing, we made our limits clear and agreed that our encounter during the game wouldn't be about climaxing/ having an orgasm or getting the other person "off". That however high the desire was there would be no intercourse or exchange of body fluids.

How we played with the four pillars of relating

First Pillar - The Base
We started with the relationship agreement of self-care at the Base, by committing to staying open to noticing our own experience and truth and agreeing that; "I am responsible for my feelings and you're responsible for

your feelings". We intentionally agreed not to play with shadows, i.e. no dominating or pushing, but just to spend time together because that's what we both wanted.

Second Pillar - The Engagement Zones
We both expressed mutual permission; "I give you permission to feel me, however you want to—while I will take care of my limits," and "I ask your permission to feel you—while you take care of your limits".

We agreed we didn't want to do something to get a reaction (pleasing the other for our own benefit)—rather we wanted to *feel ourselves* by focusing on our individual sensory somatic inflow simultaneously. This was already an invitation to the Apex (to do this at the same time).

Third Pillar - The Engagement Zones
We both agreed; "If I want you to do something for me, I will ask."
"If you want me to do something different, or something specific, you'll ask".
"If there is no request, there is no action (except for gift giving)."
If we chose not to ask for anything, it meant we didn't want anything.

Fourth Pillar - The Apex
We then agreed; "If either you or I want to give a gift, it's free". There is no attachment to an outcome. What we do with the given gift is each person's choice. We don't need to give anything back. Therefore, if I want to give you a back massage, because it looks like your shoulders are aching, I'm giving it as a gift because I have the capacity to give. No more, no less.

This is exactly what I help people to embody when I offer a course on relationship. Any kind of encounter is more or less based on these dynamics. This is the *foundation* of relationship. The agreements you have with another person, specifically when it comes to intimate relationship between lovers.

When my present lover and I began our relationship, we discussed exactly these points.

Our relationship is still based on these four pillars, and whenever we begin to struggle we pause to honestly look at what's going on in that moment. To take a look at ourselves and understand why we've encountered a glitch.

It's easy to deconstruct when using the 4 Pillars of Relating Map. We ask ourselves, "So, did I ask for something that I wanted you to do, or is my perception influenced by a *shadow*, for example, taking without permission /

not voicing my limits / my no?" Do I feel frustrated or disappointed because I'm basing my expectation on an assumption / what you "should do?"

The apex within the relationship map

We embody the space at the Apex by practising connection. When each person takes responsibility to stay open to their present sensory inflow, wants to, asks for and has permission to touch the other, we can make connection physically, sensually, intimately and possibly sexually.

Transformation (arriving at the Apex) then happens automatically because you're able to recognise yourself as a gift. That you, simply being here, being you, is enough (without having to do anything to belong).

So, the Apex is a *natural state of being.* You are a gift as you authentically are, without doing anything. And the love you receive is not dependent on providing anything.

There are so many different possible pathways leading to the state of merging experienced at the Apex. This altruistic place of connection, of simply being and sharing the gift of yourself with the world. No pathway is any better than another. Just as there are different people drawn to different things, a specific path will resonate more with you personally than another might. Within the Somatic Consent teachings, you can *feel* the gradual transformation and embodiment of this state as you practise.

Honesty with self and the other is how it works. You make an agreement that you'll share how you feel. Therefore, when two people (who want to spend time with each other) practise the Direct Route, but one gets confronted by feelings of vulnerability, they can say, for example; "I'm hesitating to ask you for a back massage because I'm afraid you'll say no."

When we share our vulnerability, the other can see themselves more easily in you. They may also be holding back and finding it difficult to ask for what they want—in the fear of possibly being rejected. With this kind of clarity, we can relax and agree on an exchange such as; "How about a 30-minute massage each?" This kind of open relating only ends in bliss. There is no guesswork, no tension, no fear. This is where the beauty in relating really is, when we feel open and connected. Your love is amplified within this kind of space.

LANGUAGES OF LOVE

Shadows, Base, Engagement Zones And Apex

*"I am amazed by how many individuals mess up every
new day with yesterday."*
- Gery Chapman

In 1992, Gary Chapman published a book entitled; *The Five Love Languages: How to Express Heartfelt Commitment to Your Mate.*[47] It points out that, as unique individuals, we all have a preferred love language with which we communicate. When our significant others don't share that same 'language', but communicate in their own, we may not understand or interpret it as love. This is when love gets 'lost in translation' and miscommunication, not feeling appreciated and resentment can happen. Of course, we may have a number of love languages, or prefer to give and receive love in different ways.

What are these five different love languages and how do they look in practice in relation to the SCES? Find some examples below, which are by no means exhaustive. I'm sure you can think of more!

Giving gifts

Gift giving is depicted in Chapman's book as one of the love languages, though within the SCES, all ways of expressing love are regarded as such. The Apex represents the interpersonal space of *being a gift* where altruistic love happens, whatever the form.

If gift giving is your thing, you'll probably notice what people say they need. Gift giving really doesn't have to be elaborate or costly. It's about thoughtfulness and creativity.

How do you feel when someone gives you a gift? Would you be disappointed if nobody bothered to get you a birthday present?

While some love receiving gifts, some may feel uneasy, believing that the other is trying to buy their love or feel pressured to give back in return.

Shadows

Which shadows are you aware of in yourself and others when it comes to gift giving? Do you ever order, arrange or organise without the other's consent? Anything else?

Can you categorise your shadows? *(entitlement/oppressor/victim/pleaser)*.

- Expect or demand gifts from others? *(entitlement)*
- Give because you think you 'should'? *(pleasing/rescuing)*
- Manipulate or exploit to receive gifts? *(oppressing)*
- Ever give to get? *(pleasing)*
- Take other's gifts for granted? *(entitlement)*
- Pretend you like what others give when you really don't? *(victim/pleasing/rescuing)*
- Arrange a gift that requires the other's time—without asking them first? *(pleasing/rescuing)*
- Are you ever attached to what someone does with your gift? *(entitlement)*

The Base of self-care

Do you gift yourself experiences or treats? This could include alone time, time with friends, a wellness day, a walk in nature, a material item, a holiday, a ticket to an event, a relaxation day, a meal in a restaurant and any other 'gift to self' that nourishes you or feels good.

Engagement Zones: *permission and agreements lines*

Can you make requests for the gifts you'd like to receive?
Do you offer or invite before you give?

The Apex *(giving a gift / being a gift)*

- Giving gifts altruistically, without expectation of something in return.
- Noticing, remembering and giving what people say they need.
- Surprising your loved ones with thoughtful gifts you know they could

do with.
- Creating things to give to others.
- Gifting things that reflect thoughtful consideration of someone's individual tastes.
- Giving to ease a burden on others.
- Giving to see someone light up in some way.

The ultimate gift is to give oneself effortlessly to another, fully recognising and being the gift that you are in your essence. When you give this gift of self, you are a living invitation that allows another to fully be themselves too. This gift of self includes letting others choose how to use the gift you give for their good—as you simultaneously take full responsibility and care of your limits.

Words of affirmation

Do you like to hear sincere words of kindness and affection? Does hearing appreciation for who you are/ your efforts feel like rain to a garden?

How do you feel when someone acknowledges their love in words to you? How do you feel if these words are absent?

Shadows

Which shadows are you aware of in yourself and others when it comes to words of affirmation? Do you ever say nice things so the other will like/ love you? Anything else?

Can you categorise your shadows? *(entitlement/oppressor/victim/pleaser)*.

- Expect or demand the words you would like to hear? *(entitlement/oppressing)*
- Shut down or blame when these words aren't said? *(entitlement)*
- Blame yourself for being unlovable if your loved ones don't express their affection in words? *(victim)*
- Give your 'love' as unsolicited advice? *(oppressing)*
- Find words of affirmation untrustworthy? "How could anyone love me?" *(victim)*
- Cut others off instead of listening because you think you know what they need to hear? *(oppressing)*

- Not tend to express your love in words, due to the fear of being rejected? *(victim/pleasing/entitlement/oppressing)*
- Say things you don't mean because you think you 'should ' or to give yourself an 'easy way out'? *(pleasing)*
- Avoid words of affirmation for fear of manipulation/ entrapment/ not being in control? *(oppressing)*

The Base of self-care

How do you speak to yourself? Do you;

- Speak down or up to yourself?
- Remind yourself of the progress you've made?
- Congratulate yourself on a job well done?
- Thank yourself for acts of self-care?
- Forgive yourself for mistakes, misguided choices or whatever went wrong in the past?
- Tell yourself how valuable and lovable you are?

Engagement Zones: *permission and agreements lines*

Can you;
- Ask for what you need to hear?
- Make requests instead of demands?
- Set limits when you feel uncomfortable?
- Respect their limits of what they are willing to say?

The Apex *(giving a gift / being a gift)*

- Whispering loving words to your partner.
- Leaving little written notes for them to find.
- Sending messages of appreciation.
- Writing poems to your lover.
- Telling people what you appreciate about them.
- Saying what you're grateful for without expecting the same in return.

Whenever I have the loop of self-judgement running in my mind, I ask my partner if she can tell me that it's totally fine to feel stupid, ridiculous, worthless or however I feel at the time. "Yes," she says, "it's totally fine to feel that way", then I like to play with the dynamic a little, asking her to tell me that I am stupid or ridiculous or worthless. She tells me. Then I ask her, "Can you tell me in a loving way that I'm also intelligent, creative and have value?"

Voicing all this out loud helps me to integrate these feelings as it takes the emotional charge out of the loop. I know she's coming from a place of love and care and feel immediately released.

Quality time

Do you crave more presence from your loved ones—or get asked to be more present? And if the latter is the case, what does that actually mean? Quality time is being together, paying attention to each other, noticing, sharing something meaningful, listening and communicating below the surface of small talk and pretence.

Shadows

Which shadows are you aware of in yourself and others when it comes to quality time? Do you ever avoid the request for deeper conversation without explaining why? Anything else?

Can you categorise your shadows? *(entitlement/oppressor/victim/pleaser)*.

- Expect constant attention when with a friend or loved one? *(entitlement)*
- Arrange to meet someone then watch TV or constantly check your phone? *(entitlement)*
- Say yes when you'd rather be alone or with others? *(victim/pleaser/rescuer)*
- Nod your head when listening but are somewhere else entirely in your mind? (pleaser, enduring)
- Be with somebody to please them and can't wait to leave? (pleaser)

The Base of self-care

Do you;
- Gift yourself the time you need to rest and rejuvenate?
- Have a day or an evening alone with yourself?
- Gift yourself time to pursue an interest?
- Go on an adventure alone?
- Give yourself time to just be?

Engagement Zones: *permission and agreements lines*

Do you:
- Have ideas about how you'd like to share quality time with your loved

ones?
- Make requests for these desires?
- Ask for and agree on time you can spend together?
- Agree on a date night or set aside a specific time each week to connect?
- Set limits when you need to be alone or want to do something else?

The Apex (*giving a gift / being a gift*)

- Making food together with your loved ones, talking while preparing and eating.
- Sharing plans for the future.
- Spending time creating something together.
- Making slow, fully present love.
- Looking into your lover's eyes as you touch.
- Listening and noticing what's said.

Long before the five languages of love were written, when I was married and lived with my wife and children, we were pretty busy as I'm sure you can imagine. Studying and working. Kindergarten activities and other commitments took up a lot of time. Nevertheless, no matter how turbulent the week was, we had an agreement we stuck to. Once a week, we hired a babysitter so that we could spend at least 2-3 hours to just be and share these moments together, fully committed to being in loving connection.

Acts of service

For some of us, actions speak louder than words. Acts of service are actions that ease the burden of responsibility. Acts such as cooking, shopping, cleaning, construction, repairing, decorating, organising, gardening, driving or technical tasks such as sorting out a computer problem.

Do you feel cared for and supported when someone's actions provide a concrete difference in your life? How do you feel when others ask you to show your love through acts of service?

Shadows

Which shadows are you aware of in yourself and others when it comes to acts of service?
Do you ever agree to help then fail to fulfil the promise? Make an offer then not provide it? Give to get back something in return? Anything else?

Can you categorise your shadows? (*entitlement/oppressor/victim/pleaser*).

- Presume or demand that your partner gives their time and energy this way? (*entitlement*)
- Expect certain acts such as cooking or DIY? (*entitlement*)
- Do more than you have the energy or time for? (*victim/pleaser/rescuer*)
- Do because you feel you 'should'? (*victim/pleaser*)
- Resent lack of action without expressing your desires or needs? (*victim*)
- Sit back while your partner 'does it all'? (*entitlement*)

The Base of self-care

Do you;
- Say no when you don't want to?
- Act in service for your own self-care, whatever that may be?
- Give something a try to foster self-empowerment?

Engagement Zones: *permission and agreements lines*

Do you;
- Make requests to be supported in this way?
- Offer your services when you notice they are needed?
- Voice your limits when they come up?

The Apex (*giving a gift / being a gift*)

- Providing acts of service for the greater good without an agenda.
- Making a drink or running a bath for someone.
- Making breakfast in bed for a loved one.
- Repairing something you noticed was broken without being asked.
- Gifting your partner 'time off' while you do the chores.
- Cooking for the special people in your life.

A friend told me a great example of an act of service. She'd mentioned to her lover that she wished she had a place to put her cup of tea while taking a bath. He went outside, sawed a plank of wood, came back and placed it over the bathtub.

Physical touch

Touch, as we've already begun to explore in depth, can be the most effective way to gift your love, because it calms, heals and reassures at a neurological level.

Do you enjoy hand-holding, hugs and caresses? Do you like it or recoil when touched during a conversation with your lover, a friend, an acquaintance, a stranger? Are you in your element when you're offered a massage? Do you only like to be touched by certain people? Those who love to give and receive touch thrive when the Direct Route is nourished.

Shadows

Which shadows are you aware of in yourself and others when it comes to touch? Do you ever expect someone to want to be touched in a certain way because they've been willing to in the past? Anything else?

Can you categorise your shadows? *(entitlement/oppressor/victim/pleaser)*.

- Expect your lover to meet your physical needs without an agreement? *(oppressor/entitlement)*
- Take without permission? *(oppressor/entitlement)*
- Manipulate by giving to get? How? *(oppressor/entitlement)*
- Allow touch that feels mediocre, uncomfortable or painful? *(victim/pleaser)*
- Say yes to touch or intercourse when it's really a no? *(victim/pleaser)*
- Touch or 'perform 'sexual acts because you think you 'should'? *(victim/pleaser)*
- Feel entitled to touch whoever you like? *(entitlement/oppressor)*
- Expect others to want to be hugged, shake your hand or be touched without asking? *(entitlement/oppressor)*
- Ask, but immediately go ahead before hearing a clear yes? *(entitlement/oppressor)*

The Base of self-care

Do you;
- Gift yourself direct pleasure through your sensory inflow?
- Touch and explore objects around you?

- Feel the ground under your bare feet?
- Touch the textures of nature? Run your fingers over wood, stone, sand?
- Hug a tree or cuddle a pet?
- Explore your own body and find the sweet spots?
- Gift yourself a self-massage?

Engagement Zones: *permission and agreements lines*

- Do you make requests for specific touch for you?
- Do you offer specific touch for them?
- Can you say no to touch that you don't want?
- Do you make requests for specific touch you want to do?
- Do you offer specific touch for them?
- Can you set your limits to touch that you don't want to have done to you?
- Can you put yourself aside for their desire?
- Do you ask for the exact touch you need right now?

The Apex *(giving a gift / being a gift)*

Do you:
- Offer touch such as a massage, without an agenda?
- Touch a loved one to reassure them?
- Squeeze a friend's arm, shoulder or hand if they're upset?
- Invite your partner to follow their desire?
- Give your power as a gift to play-wrestle with somebody and let them win?

Touch, I'm sure you're not surprised to hear, is my primary love language, along with quality time. I once had a partner whose primary love languages were gift giving and acts of service. It was somewhat of a mismatch. My need for physical connection was not fully met, and so, I filled my cup by touching *for myself* (with her permission). But because her language was not touch I missed out being touched by her.

What's your love language?

To feel really loved and connected, some people are more sensitive to gifts and actions, some to physical touch, others to time spent together, while some respond to encouraging, affirming words. You may find that a combination of two or more appeals to you personally.

Whatever your preferred love language(s), the SCES guides you to ask for exactly what you want. To make requests, offers or invitations so that it's a win-win for all involved.

When the difference between giving and receiving is clear through neurologically embodying the difference, it also becomes clear how we want to receive and how we want to give. When we make sure we fill our own cup through self-care and our partner does the same, we are able to do everything within our limits.

Whether your love language is **time, service, touch, gifts or words**—all five can be accessed, expressed and experienced through practising The 3 Minute Game and dynamics of the SCES. Here we are all able to experience love as it feels natural to us—at the Apex. This is where play, laughter, creativity and lovemaking happens.

For further reading I recommend a book called *Ritual Play* by Marina Kronkvist[48] which provides creative, transformational ways to engage at the Apex through the art of play.

LOW AND HIGH DRAMA

Lifting The Unconscious Veil

"Low Drama creates only more Low Drama, so nothing ever really changes."
- Clinton Callahan[31]

The Low and High Drama Map shows a Low Drama Triangle of *disempowerment* on the left, which runs on unconscious emotions, and a High Drama Triangle of *empowerment* on the right which runs on conscious feelings.

Within relating, there is often a triangle of disempowerment, where blame and finger pointing coincides with the roles of the victim, the persecutor and the rescuer. Here someone always pays the price and loses. When we take ownership of our feelings and emotions, the Low Drama triangle can evolve into a High Drama triangle. Here, intimate relating through expressing our genuine feelings provides possibilities to create and manifest a new reality. Here winning can happen for all involved.

LOW AND HIGH DRAMA MAP

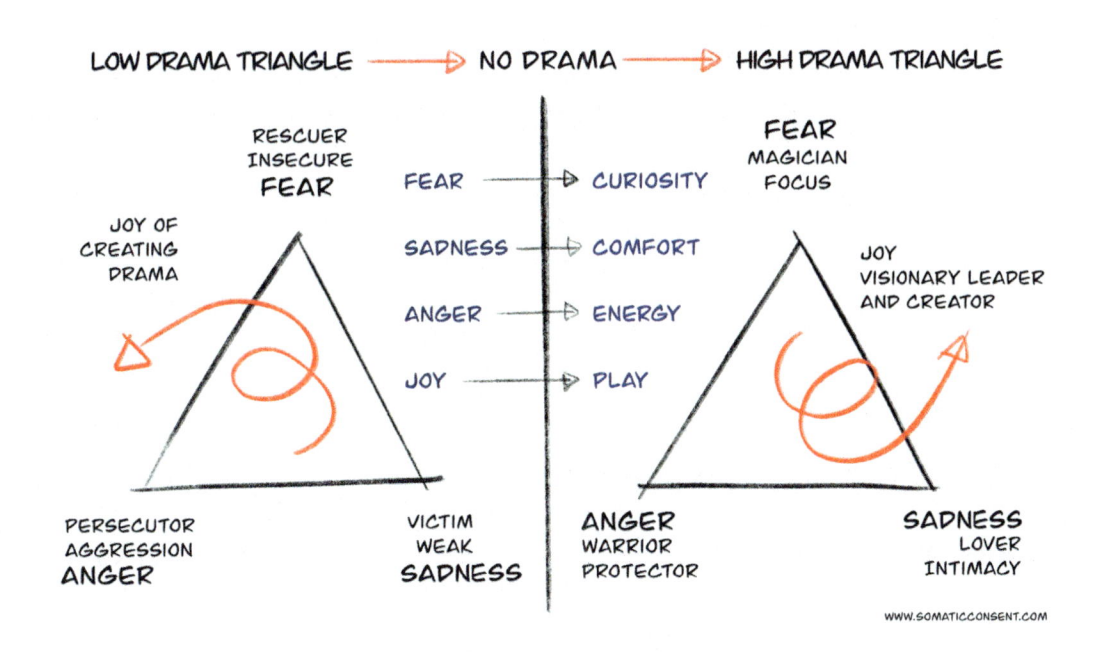

LOW DRAMA TRIANGLE → **NO DRAMA** → **HIGH DRAMA TRIANGLE**

Low Drama Triangle:
- RESCUER / INSECURE / FEAR (top)
- PERSECUTOR / AGGRESSION / ANGER (bottom left)
- VICTIM / WEAK / SADNESS (bottom right)
- JOY OF CREATING DRAMA

No Drama:
- FEAR → CURIOSITY
- SADNESS → COMFORT
- ANGER → ENERGY
- JOY → PLAY

High Drama Triangle:
- FEAR / MAGICIAN / FOCUS (top)
- ANGER / WARRIOR / PROTECTOR (bottom left)
- SADNESS / LOVER / INTIMACY (bottom right)
- JOY / VISIONARY LEADER AND CREATOR

WWW.SOMATICCONSENT.COM

The low drama triangle

Low Drama comes about when people have difficulty accessing their feelings and emotions or interpreting them well. It happens when our Base isn't intact and is related to the shadows of *projection*, when we make others responsible for how *we feel* i.e. "You make me feel…" It doesn't involve 'ownership' or personal responsibility for our feelings or emotions, usually because we're unconscious of what is really motivating our thoughts or actions. When there is a lack of awareness about the *cause* of the effect (shadow behaviour), we convince ourselves that our actions are justified.

Until awareness is raised and the veil is lifted, until we can identify which needs, desires and limits we aren't being truthful about (first to ourselves, then to others), the shadows of the Low Drama Triangle—which we employ to get our needs met—will persist in a continuous loop. Not being aware of the cause of your actions leads to taking the responsibility of a child, or none at all.

Do you recognise when you connect with someone that every feeling you have belongs only to yourself?

You have the choice at any given moment to either stay in the world of no drama, drop into the low drama realm (making the outer world responsible) or enter high drama, where you take full ownership of your inner world, get creative and manifest what you want to experience in your life. Each dynamic, whether Low Drama, No Drama or High Drama, is always accessible through the power of choice.

Within the SCES, the foundational agreement in relationship is:
I am responsible for **my** feelings and **you are** responsible for **your** feelings.

I'm responsible for staying open, knowing how I feel in the moment. In relation to my Base, I feel what is going on within myself and take ownership for that. I can't make you responsible for how I feel—and vice versa. We acknowledge that we all have four core feelings. We all feel anger, sadness, fear and joy. They aren't negative, wrong or bad. They all have their own importance, belonging to our 'emotional body' and our limbic systems.

The Low Drama triangle occurs when we irrationally express or deal with what is through shadow behaviour. You can see that the Low Drama Triangle is made up of the three shadow roles in relationship with each other. The **victim**, **persecutor** and **rescuer**. These roles are connected to the four core feelings: Fear, Anger, Sadness and Joy.

This triangle can happen in all sorts of relationships and a myriad of situations. During workshops and sessions, I've witnessed many couples falling into Low Drama dynamics when one tries to please the other without clear offers and agreements. One example could be when someone learns tricks to make their partner orgasm. When one puts themselves in 'rescue mode' as a pleaser or do-gooder, their partner puts themself in the position of enduring and letting it happen. Because the action hasn't been asked for and no offer has been made, the conclusion could be that the one in action is doing it for themself.

When the victim state of 'going along' becomes too much to bear, the one being 'done to' accuses their partner of using them for their own pleasure—placing them in the position of the perpetrator. The one in action then becomes the victim, defending themself for not being able to fulfill their partner's expectations or do the right thing. The end result is usually a relationship that ends in 'bad sex'. When the one in action then gives up, their partner may try to rescue them by reverting back into the role of the victim, enduring and allowing their partner to do whatever they want.

When in a Low Drama triangle, we identify with one of these feelings and make them wrong, possibly because we feel judged, fear being rejected or find them inappropriate ("I should get myself together"). Not many of us welcome this kind of discomfort and therefore tend to suppress it by not allowing ourselves to feel whatever we feel. We are all hard-wired to avoid pain, though everyone needs to feel. Suppression of emotion doesn't make emotional discomfort go away. It just leads eventually to its implosion or explosion when our personal level of tolerance (Numbness Bar) is reached. We need to both feel and understand our emotions in order to evolve.

Do you ever avoid facing your feelings and emotions? Which tactics do you use?

Roles in non-ownership and rejection of feelings

The Persecutor - *anger* - but the belief is that anger is wrong.
When people don't 'own' their anger. The persecutor has the shadow of leaking aggression such as in passive-aggressive comments.

The Victim - *sadness* - but they believe that sadness is weak.
They don't 'own' their sadness—instead blaming others for it, "You make me feel that way" / "It's all your fault". The *victim* has the shadow of wanting help from a *rescuer*.

The Rescuer - *fear* - which creates insecurity.
Fear can be utilised as supportive energy to stay focused and present, but the rescuer operates from an inner place of insecurity. The rescuer usually has a history of not being taken care of, in a situation of danger in their past. They've suppressed their fear and so create drama in order to feel 'something'. This results in the unhealthy projection of feelings and emotions. The *rescuer* has the shadow of always making sure others feel good, as well as making the *persecutor* responsible for how the *victim* feels.

The Low Drama triangle also has a 'joy factor' which is accessed through creating drama. Each of the roles create the feeling of joy for themselves by believing their behaviour is *justified*. Within the Low Drama triangle, one or more of the people involved is benefiting from the drama by getting something back, and therefore a little 'blast of joy'.

An example could be;

The persecutor abuses the victim and feels joy at feeling in control/having the power.
The victim gets joy from the rescuer's support and by blaming the persecutor for them feeling 'this way'.
The rescuer feels joy by righting the wrong situation by punishing, pressurising or excluding the persecutor.

Can you recognise yourself in any of these roles?

It's common to automatically default to a different role with the different people in our lives. We may, for example, find ourselves being 'the victim' in our closest relationships, a rescuer with friends and a persecutor towards colleagues or strangers.

Are you always aware when you're in one of these roles? Do you ever automatically put others in one of the roles based on very limited information? Maybe going off a hunch, perceiving others based on your own insecurities or relying solely on something someone else said? The truth is, we're often unaware of the role we may be participating in and what we project onto others as we go about our lives.

In order to make the triangulation dynamics more visible, I like to initiate a playfully insightful exercise within the safe 'container 'of a workshop setting. This has the advantage of speeding up the awareness of personal 'ahas' in a limited time frame.

The idea is to notice feelings of fear and the shadow dynamics that emerge, while in a safe, playful setting. To notice how we project danger onto other people. To notice how most people aren't aware of being viewed as a predator in other people's eyes—and to notice how much we make ourselves 'prey 'by putting others in a predator position. The outcome is learning to own and express our feelings without projecting them onto others by blaming and rescuing or victimising oneself.

The exercise goes like this:

I invite people to stand up and walk around while imagining that they are some kind of prey (victim), such as a rabbit or gazelle. Then, without pointing at anybody in the room, to choose one person as their predator and another person as their rescuer. Once this is done I ask everyone to move through the room, making sure their rescuer is always between them and their predator. It always results in very funny and chaotic movement, with everyone running around without any obvious result.

I then ask people notice:

- How it felt in their body to be in the victim state.
- Whether they were aware that they'd been someone's rescuer.
- Whether they were aware that they'd been someone's predator.

Almost nobody is ever aware that they'd been chosen as a predator or rescuer —while fully identifying with the role as the prey (victim).

The confusion of victim shaming - what it is and is not

When I talk about the victim dynamic, I'm referring to the general tendency or habit to go along with things. It's when we allow things to happen to us that we by no means want. When our limits aren't obvious to ourselves or clearly expressed to others, we tend to endure until resentment builds. The role of the victim is apparent when we make others responsible for our resentment (for *how we feel*) without taking responsibility for our own part in the experience (of not having spoken up about our limits). Being responsible for our own self-care (the Base) includes recognising where our boundaries are and giving clear consent.

What I'm *not referring to* when I talk about the victim dynamic are the times when someone is in an abusive situation that they cannot react to or escape from (due to nervous system shut down). In these instances of trauma, as mentioned earlier in The Polyvagal Theory, the decision-making part of the brain is switched off. When this happens, rational choices aren't possible and self-care is reduced to basic survival.

Victim shaming is when accountability is put onto a victim experiencing the *shutdown* state.

Have you ever given your power away to someone by being nice to them so that you won't be harmed in some way?

This is when a victim befriends the persecutor in order to stay safe. This could happen in a variety of situations, domestically within families, at the workplace and within the community. A severe example results in *Stockholm Syndrome*, a psychological condition that occurs when a victim of abuse identifies or bonds positively with their abuser. It was originally observed when kidnapped hostages not only bonded with their kidnappers, but also fell in love with them.

It's a true step into empowerment when we build a community that allows us to stand up, speak out and be listened to about misuse, abuse, suppression and oppression. When we are allowed to be honest and own all of our feelings, we can develop neurologically, personally and spiritually—and move forward with support into the joy and creation of High Drama.

Then we have the possibility to transform;

Fear into curiosity.
Sadness into being comforted and letting go.
Anger into creativity.
Joy into play.

No drama

When we begin to come into ownership of our feelings, we might find ourselves in a place where there is no drama, where nothing much happens. We may not relate or engage with people emotionally, and dwell in a kind of void. This can also have a shadow element, a lack of connection prompted by choosing to keep our feelings to ourselves or by cutting ourselves off from others.

We can also find ourselves in a place of no drama by avoiding feeling. Have you ever been in solitude for a period of time, choosing to avoid connection with others and the outer world, in order *not to feel?* It can be extremely peaceful with few ups and downs, but it can also lead to unconscious dissociation. People need people. We need the opportunity to express ourselves as well as touch in order to remain regulated.

The high drama triangle

The 'drama' in this triangle doesn't refer to any devastating or dramatic engagement, but the *high frequency* of manifestation and creation.

The High Drama triangle shows that when we transform archetypes, we raise our vibration to one of creativity.

Anger—from the perspective of the *persecutor* transforms to **the warrior** and **protector**.
There is a big difference between the protector and the rescuer. The rescuer tends to look for situations in which to interfere, in order to feel better about

themself. The protector's focus is generally on protecting when they see injustice concerning children, the sick, weak and old of the 'tribe'. They offer support from an empathic place of love and care.

Fear—from the perspective of the *rescuer* transforms to **the magician**. One who focuses like a laser point on what's next. Then the fear becomes neither negative nor positive, just an energy flow of focused presence.

Sadness—from the perspective of the *victim* transforms to **the lover** who creates intimacy and connection where vulnerability is allowed in the moment, so that feelings are expressed.

Joy—from the perspective of **shadow, of duty, justification, survive and 'have to'**. This is the joy of creating drama and separation, like a child destroying another kid's sandcastle and having fun seeing them upset. Or the joy of controlling others, of being right when winning an argument, or of seeing others getting into trouble when making mistakes. Can you relate to this kind of joy? It can be transformed into the **visionary leader** and **creator** which guides directly to the Apex. In this space we can collaborate with others in creation.

If you look back at the Noticing Map, you can see that we're able to break through these shadow perspectives by using the *noticing brain*. This enables us to become aware of our thoughts, actions, feelings, emotions and 'shut down mechanisms'. We can then tune into the stories we tell ourselves, understand what causes them and become responsible for them.

When we gain awareness and own our feelings and emotions, we make the transition from Low to High Drama because we function with an intact Base. We begin to communicate in the 'I 'form, i.e. "I feel this way, I feel that way", implementing this understanding and communication into our conscious daily lives.

This way we stop projecting our feelings onto someone else's Base or allowing them to interfere with our own, dropping the 'game 'of making others responsible for how we feel. We go from the *child responsibility* of "all your fault" to the *high* responsibility of, "I take responsibility for my feelings and want to create beyond the status quo with others who also own their feelings". Taking responsibility for ourselves in this way opens a crystal-clear space, making it much easier to direct our energy towards our personal life purpose and co-creation with others.

THE THREE POWERS OF RADICAL RESPONSIBILITY

"Where there is great power there is great responsibility, where there is less power there is less responsibility, and where there is no power there can, I think, be no responsibility."
-Winston Churchill

The Radical Responsibility Map is about taking full responsibility for our lives, whereas what we're mostly used to doing is taking the responsibility of a child.

What does radical responsibility actually mean and how is it interpreted and expressed in our day-to-day lives? In order to honestly answer this question, we must ask ourselves if we really take full responsibility for ourselves and own the instances in which we don't.

Inspired by Clinton Callahan's *Possibility Management*[31] and specifically his 'Expanding the Box 'training, taking radical responsibility allows us to break out of the oppressed and oppressive cultural ideologies we were born into, in order to empower ourselves and others.

If we look at the left side of the map we see the word 'people', meaning people in general, individuals or societies. Along the bottom we see the differing amount of responsibility taken, from none to that of a child, adult, high level and radical.

RADICAL RESPONSIBILITY MAP

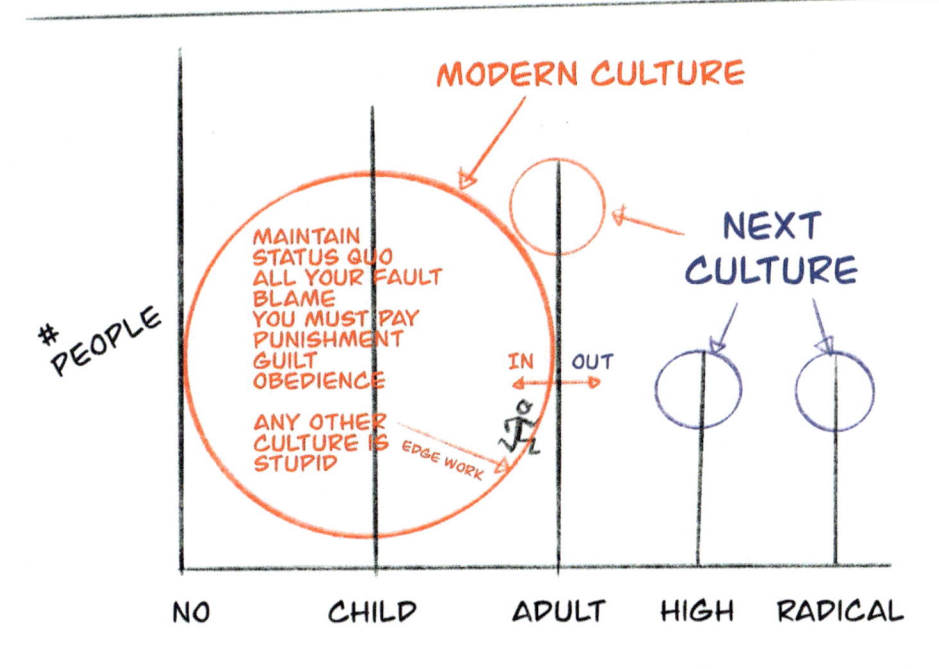

MODERN CULTURE

MAINTAIN
STATUS QUO
ALL YOUR FAULT
BLAME
YOU MUST PAY
PUNISHMENT
GUILT
OBEDIENCE

ANY OTHER
CULTURE IS
STUPID

IN ← → OUT

EDGE WORK

NEXT CULTURE

PEOPLE

NO | CHILD | ADULT | HIGH | RADICAL

LEVELS OF RESPONSIBILITY 'TO CHOOSE'

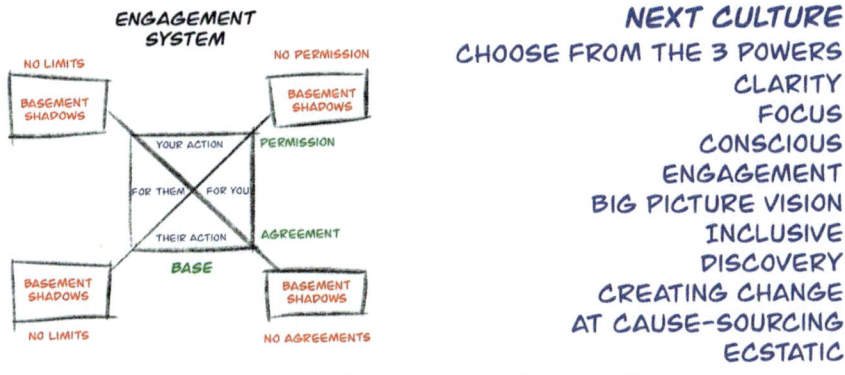

ENGAGEMENT SYSTEM

- NO LIMITS — BASEMENT SHADOWS
- NO PERMISSION — BASEMENT SHADOWS
- YOUR ACTION / FOR THEM / FOR YOU / PERMISSION
- THEIR ACTION / AGREEMENT
- BASE
- BASEMENT SHADOWS — NO LIMITS
- BASEMENT SHADOWS — NO AGREEMENTS

NEXT CULTURE
CHOOSE FROM THE 3 POWERS
CLARITY
FOCUS
CONSCIOUS
ENGAGEMENT
BIG PICTURE VISION
INCLUSIVE
DISCOVERY
CREATING CHANGE
AT CAUSE-SOURCING
ECSTATIC

THE 3 POWERS

1.) ABLE TO CHOOSE: FROM OPTIONS THAT ARE NOT ON THE MENU

2.) ABLE TO ASK: QUESTIONING ANSWERS THAT EXIST IN A DIFFERENT REALM

3.) DECLARING: TO BE ABLE TO SAY WHAT 'IS'

YOU ARE RADICALLY RESPONSIBLE FOR YOUR BASE   WWW.SOMATICCONSENT.COM

No responsibility

Taking no responsibility is akin to being an outlaw. These are people who don't ever take responsibility for their actions such as a criminal with no principles or ethics.

Responsibility of a child

Most of us are used to functioning with the responsibility of a child.

We live firmly within the realms of our culture. Our belief systems are largely based on its structures and enslaved to its ideals. This is where most of us were born, were conditioned and still live. Here we dwell, consumed by thoughts of maintaining the status quo. We tend not to be connected to our bodies or individual sense of self and presume the values we've been taught to accept were actually chosen by us.

When something happens, we don't voice or own our feelings, instead, we make others responsible for our misery by blaming and shaming them; "You make me feel…", "It's all your fault…" and so on. We live in a conditioned loop with the mindset of how things 'should be', often believing without question that if you've done something 'wrong 'you must pay for it. We guilt-trip or shame others about what they 'should or shouldn't do', criticising and bullying them about how they 'should 'behave, how they should dress, who they 'should 'love, what they 'should 'do with their bodies and so on, picking on anything which stands out from the norm (which differs of course, depending on where in the world we are). We state, "That's not normal", when clearly, no unanimous version of 'normal 'exists.

Here there is obedience to the imbalance of a hierarchical system. We accept we must obey those in a higher position of power than ourselves. We assume that being wealthy equates to more rights, privilege or entitlement to oppress others beneath our financial status. There is no equality, solidarity or belief that we are all fundamentally equal. These conservative structures of 'how life should be 'automatically make any different, alternative or new culture faulty, wrong, bad or dangerous.

Examples of taking a child's responsibility are:

I don't do good work because I don't like what I do.
I expect to get government support if I choose not to work.
I stay in my known environment during my holidays because anything un-

known seems violent and dangerous. I know this from the media.
If I have an accident or make a mistake, I look for a reason to blame others for it.

Adult responsibility

Some of us have an epiphany at some point. Some of us wake up. We question this reality and begin to think outside the box. Many of those who awaken from the confinements of programmed structures often work within professions I call, 'edge-workers', working outside the generally accepted system. Examples are sexual and energy healers, visionaries, any kind of artist, creator or inventor.

When we realise we can go beyond the framework we were born into, we can create a new culture, *based on* the rules of our culture, but at the edge of it. One example is the *Burning Man Festival*, a 'next generation culture' where people have broken out of their society's structural norm and implemented other rules based on progressive ideas such as creating community that celebrates artistic expression, knowledge sharing and the release of social stigma. New ideologies like this are created but remain based and dependent on traditional structures. People who break out of their culture tend to flip back and forth, often not knowing where they belong.

Examples of taking adult responsibility are:

I get up in the morning to go to work because I choose to, maybe doing a job that I don't like, in order to pay my rent and support my family.
If I damage something belonging to someone else, I tell the owner and offer to pay for it.
I choose to explore other countries to get first-hand experience of the world.

High responsibility

The next level of evolution shows a high level of responsibility that is more distant and independent from your culture's status quo. An example is *The New Earth Movement* in Bali, who've created an infrastructure using exchange as currency and grow their own food for self-sufficiency.

Their environment has its own structure of rules and community according to how people are and want to individually be. Each person takes ownership of their beliefs and choices. However, this type of system still maintains a hierarchical structure. It seems like a win-win ideology, but someone is still losing, or both lose something through compromise. In most cases of presumed 'win-win 'a compromise happens for one party or the other, by letting go of a specific desire so that the other benefits in some way—or because common agreement can't be found in the expression of what both desire most.

An example of compromise could be taking a job during an economic crisis which doesn't pay the standard rate you're used to, or isn't worthy of your level of training or experience. We often compromise within our partnerships. Sometimes it can't be avoided. Compromise is healthy, as long as it comes from a place of 'willing to', limits are expressed and agreed upon and it isn't continually one sided (the same person compromising most of the time). Better is finding *middle ground*, where both get their needs met. An example could be on a holiday you want to go on together. One may love and one may dislike tropical weather. One may love and the other dislike modern cities. The *middle ground* may therefore be a holiday on a Greek island. When true winning happens for both, it opens up a completely different realm of connected engagement.

Radical responsibility

My **entire relational wisdom** is based on the *first agreement* or Pillar of Relating along with the *radical responsibility* of carrying that agreement out.

"I will remain open to my sensory experience and build a solid foundation of self-love and self-care. I am responsible for my feelings".

You take radical Responsibility when you take radical self-care of yourself. You're clear about who you are and the direction you want to go in. Your behaviour and choices aren't based on what you think you 'should 'do. You create a new structure based on impulses occurring in-the-moment, which are completely in tune with your own values. You step fully into your life purpose and creator mode, empowering others to become creators too. In this way you surrender your power to something greater than yourself. In radical responsibility, it's a win-win situation for everyone.

With radical responsibility we consciously engage with others based on responsible choices and ownership of our feelings. Here, there's a bigger inclusive vision, without separation or segregation due to age, skin colour, race, gender identity or religious belief. You come from a place of joy because you're fulfilling your life purpose. This isn't based on resistance against the old—but creation of the new. You choose to follow an ideology based on love, care and connection, rather than on guilt and shame. You choose to focus on evolution—rather than revolution.

Examples of communities attempting radical responsibility are; The Possibility Management Community and the Global Ecovillage Network.[49,50]

> *"You never change things by fighting the existing reality.
> To change something, build a new model that makes the existing model obsolete."*
> - Systems theorist, author and architect
> Buckmeister Fuller.

When you take radical responsibility, you embody the three powers

1. *The ability to choose*: to see beyond the structure of our modern framework. To be able to choose from an option that *isn't on that menu*. To creatively choose in accordance with one's own values and ideas as a result of creative and independent thinking.

2. *The ability to ask*: to be able to ask questions that uncomfortably challenge the status quo. Questions that dispute conclusions that have been explained and accepted 'en masse'. Going to the roots of conditioned belief, and when people give answers from a conditioned place, being able to question them. Here we know how to ask for and point out deeper truths. We own our actions and take full responsibility for them. We choose to change our behaviour in order to create valued change within the collective.

3. *The ability to declare what is*: Usually, when we make mistakes or come to the edge of our capacity, we tend to fall into the obedience or oppression of our culture's *child responsibility*. We are apologetic, tending to make ourselves small or stupid; "I don't know what to do...", "I'm sorry...", "I'm a man...", "I'm over 50...", "I'm German...". We may pressurise others into seeing our point of view, so that they collude with our lack of responsibility; "Can't you be empathic?", "Haven't you ever been in a similar position?", or we make others responsible for our failure; "It's your fault".

This third power enables us to declare; "I did that, yes, it was my mistake and I take full responsibility and own it". We make conscious choices to become aware of and change certain behaviour. We work towards creatively changing our environment. And we have fun doing this because we source our energy from a place of ownership of the many layers of who we are, as well as the urge for positive change and connection.

The somatic consent engagement system and personal responsibility

When you embody the structures outlined in the SCES you become empowered. How you use that power determines whether you function with adult, high or radical responsibility. The three powers of radical responsibility are fully accessible within the system. It's up to you how much you implement them into your life.

The basement

Shadows refer to the *child's responsibility* or *none at all*. Shadows are unconscious survival strategies employed in order to get needs met and to belong. They are reactionary behaviour stemming from established cultural programming, driven by the fear of rejection.

No responsibility corresponds with the bully, manipulator and perpetrator shadows. Taking what we want, when we want, without owning the consequences of our actions and without respecting other people's limits. The *child's responsibility* includes hinting towards wishes or manipulating others to do what we want them to do for us, without being able to ask consciously and openly for what we desire.

The entire relationship dynamic of western culture, the Walt Disney style romantic dream, is based on a child's level of responsibility. Here Prince Charming makes the Princess happy (if she's pretty and cute enough) and they both live happily ever after. This is not taking responsibility as an adult. It's based on 'you have to make me feel good and if you don't you've been watching the wrong movie'. 'You have to do things to make me feel good', is a jump into the shadow of exploitation and/or entitlement. It assumes that someone else is doing something *to me* and *has to do the right thing*.

The base

Forming our Base begins when we step out of the *child's responsibility* into *adult responsibility*. It's when you know what you have a right to and responsibility for. Here you take responsibility for your thoughts, feelings, body and experience of life. Taking ownership of your experience is specifically related to the Direct Route of pleasure. You fully own your desires, limits and everything you want in the present moment. You empower yourself by owning your choices and actions. By acknowledging boundaries and limits and being able to respect the other's "No" as a full answer, you prevent abuse of power and its expression in any form. You also recognise where you lose yourself (drop into shadow behaviour) and acknowledge and integrate these aspects of yourself honestly.

By embodying the somatic inflow via the Direct Route, you take a quantum leap of owning your experience. You know you can go into an action towards your own pleasure. You know you have to ask others for permission if it's *for you* and involves others. You're able to distinguish between *giving* and *receiving*.

When we make others responsible for how we feel by going into victim mode, blaming them (for being a perpetrator), then we're not taking responsibility for our part in that experience. When relating with others, if we make them responsible for our feelings by saying, "It's all your fault…", "you make me feel…", "you're responsible for making me happy…", "you have to pay for my misery…", then we *haven't embodied our own Base*. When the Direct Route 'lands 'in the nervous system (when we've fully embodied it), we can't possibly go back to telling another person that they're responsible for making us feel good.

When we know what we have a right to and take responsibility for ourselves, we stop taking advantage of others from a place of privilege (invading their Base), because we know that we don't have permission to take their resources. We clearly recognise when others are doing this to us and are able to say; "Stop, no further".

* Of course, this doesn't apply to those in a repressed environment of neglect or abuse. If someone is living in survival mode, they aren't able to make rational choices or healthily express their boundaries.

Expressing boundaries comes from ownership of anger. This means we *have to be in an environment that is safe* in order for us to gauge and express our anger. When this is the case, we are able to set boundaries and say, "No".

During a workshop for women on accessing boundaries and voicing their "no", almost all shared that they'd been in a past situation where saying no would have been more dangerous than going along with what was happening. Until then, from my white, heterosexual male and privileged perception, I hadn't realised how commonly women experience this kind of situation. It was a big eye-opener for me, to understand that so many had been in a position that negated the choice to act in the way I prescribed. Drawing a line would be too dangerous in such situations. Fear and shutting down would be the only neurological option—the involuntary nervous system response we talked about in The Polyvagal Theory.

The engagement zones

When the Direct Route and Base are embodied, the experience we have rests on the agreements and permissions we give to each other in order to have a fulfilling time. We have integrity, being able to differentiate within each encounter who an action is for; "Is it for me or is it for them?" We're able to differentiate because our Base is intact. When two or more people come together within this structure of consent, *high responsibility* has to be taken in order for each person to come into their own power and break out of programmed cultural norms based on 'doing to belong'.

The level of responsibility increases with the level of power we gain through embodiment of consent. We can go into action, ask for permission and we don't take advantage so that people can't say no. The more power we have, the more responsibility we carry.

Communication within the Engagement Zones is authentic. When two adults are consciously and openly communicating, they are taking *high responsibility* for themselves. They are fully in tune with their desires and boundaries, are able to make requests and offers, express desires and limits, respect and acknowledge boundaries and limits without making the other wrong for saying 'no', and come to agreements together. They are aware of shadow strategies when they surface, acknowledging and integrating them into their exchange.

When the Engagement Zones are embodied, we share from a place of generosity and gratitude because we source ourselves from a higher ideal. This enables us to create an environment which is sustainable for everyone, and not just a group of privileged people.

The apex

The Apex is the interpersonal state where we can provide, give and bring about change because we have accessed our resources and use them where we want the change to happen. The 3 Minute Game played from a place of love and care at the Apex enables us to choose options that aren't on the menu. These are possibilities that involve creative thinking outside the usual 'box' of options. Here in *radical responsibility*, we declare 'what is' while remaining empowered. We're able to ask questions that are uncomfortable and can question the answers because we aren't influenced by the fear of rejection from others. We remain aware of shadow strategies when they're triggered in-the-moment and can playfully and spontaneously adapt, according to our values and limits.

At the Apex we use our power to empower others (into their own power), therefore surrendering our power to something greater than ourselves—rather than trying to gain more power for ourselves. We interact through invitation with others and give ourselves as a gift, unconditionally to the world. We function from the interpersonal space in a dynamic all parties can engage in, exploring mutual desires and wishes without compromises, based on *how all want to live*. Here the possibility of experiencing the transpersonal state unfolds. What we are motivated by and create means winning happens for all involved.

COMMUNICATION

Bridging The Gap

"Good communication is the bridge between confusion and clarity."
- Nat Turner

The three basic levels of communication

1. The informational level *is an exchange of information.*

We do most of the time. It includes all the facts of daily life, in the past, present and future. What happened, is happening and will happen to who, when, where and so on.

Examples: He caught the train at 6pm. She called me after dinner. I saw a fox in the garden today. Can you pass the salt? I'll visit you at the weekend. I'll send them an email. He got a new job. This is how the app works. They're having a party on Saturday. The government introduced a new law.

2. The feeling level is *an exchange of feelings.*

This is the personal level, it's about saying how you feel and what you notice about yourself. When we communicate at the personal level we express how we feel while the listener listens.

Examples: That makes me feel amused / connected / lucky / sad. It made me smile. I'm excited / annoyed / bored / feel unsettled. I have butterflies in my stomach because I'm nervous. I felt a pang of envy.

3. The relational level is *an exchange of empathy.*

This is the level of communication which connects and forms intimacy. You talk about how it feels to tell the other how you feel/ what you notice between you both and how it is to have deeper interaction with each other.

Examples: I feel connected when you say that. This feels cosy and familiar. It feels uplifting sharing with you. I feel nervous expressing that to you. I feel vulnerable sharing that part of myself. I feel you. I hear you. I can relate to that. I feel worried / concerned / helpless hearing that. I imagine you feel anxious, is that right?

Usually, people have a tendency to try to fix a problem or give advice. This is neither the personal nor the relational level. It is purely the informational level.

Apex and Shadow dynamics within the Informational level

I'd like to point out an exception to the Engagement System structure which may, on the surface, seem like a shadow strategy of control or expectation. Usually, we'd ask for something we want and the other would reply while considering their limits.

However, where the time factor would either save or lose lives, such as in medical, fire and other emergency situations, we see a necessary chain of command. In these cases, the language used often includes demands or orders. We all know that a surgeon or firefighter isn't going to waste precious time asking each individual co-worker whether their request is within the other person's limits.

The bigger picture allows us to see that these demands aren't for the personal benefit of the speaker. They come from a place of care and necessity. The people taking action in response to these demands, will either have agreed to do so in advance, acknowledging them as part of their duty or be acting in willingness to help, in whichever emergency situation they find themselves in.

And that's all well and good. However, the same pattern of communication would feel like a shadow in a personal relationship. Difficulties arise when people get stuck in this hierarchical level of communication with its clear line of information. When they take it away from a work scenario and into their daily lives. This can result in difficulties relating on a more personal level.

In these cases, the types of dynamics that may come up are:
- Difficulties communicating on deeper levels (expressing and hearing feelings)

- Inability to empathise with others who feel threatened by a demanding tone
- Lack of empathy for anyone having difficulties expressing their limits
- Arrogance, believing they are better, more important or evolved than others
- Domineering shadow tendencies of inflated ego

As you can see, the *informational level* of communication can be a parallel reality of both care, and at other times, shadow. What is really life-saving and heroic in an emergency situation, is in daily life unloving, uncaring and void of intimacy. People who work professionally in these situations need to train their ability to switch between being attentive to the demands of an emergency, as well as fostering their ability to communicate at a personal and relational level.

The communication map

The Communication Map shows that when we're in survival mode and relying on shadow strategies (dwelling in the Basement), we communicate in a substandard way. We don't clearly relate with the other person, but instead give hints, orders and commands. We dictate, coerce, push, manipulate and use 'should or have to' statements. This comes from 'power over', oppression and from taking the *child's responsibility*.

If we look at the OM symbol, the *Shadow* domain is seen in the first upper curve and represents lower levels of consciousness. The Base is the foundation of the pyramid structure and is represented in the OM symbol as the second, lower curve. Here we take responsibility for self-care, for our limits and boundaries, for saying, "no", and not allowing shadow communication to happen. If someone, for example, begins trying to manipulate us, we stop them immediately. The Base is also where we communicate boundaries and limits, where we say, "This is how far you can go and no further".

COMMUNICATION MAP

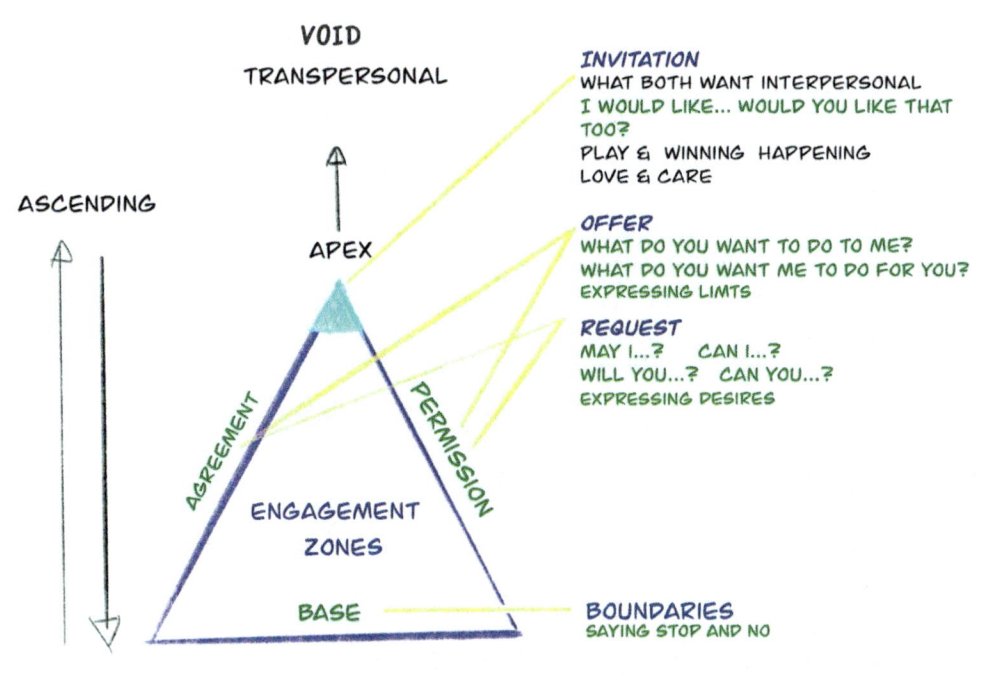

VOID
TRANSPERSONAL

ASCENDING

APEX

AGREEMENT *PERMISSION*

ENGAGEMENT ZONES

BASE

DESCENDING — BASEMENT / SHADOWS →

INVITATION
WHAT BOTH WANT INTERPERSONAL
I WOULD LIKE... WOULD YOU LIKE THAT TOO?
PLAY & WINNING HAPPENING
LOVE & CARE

OFFER
WHAT DO YOU WANT TO DO TO ME?
WHAT DO YOU WANT ME TO DO FOR YOU?
EXPRESSING LIMITS

REQUEST
MAY I...?   CAN I...?
WILL YOU...?   CAN YOU...?
EXPRESSING DESIRES

BOUNDARIES
SAYING STOP AND NO

DEMAND
HINTS, ORDERS, COMMANDS, DICTATING, COERCING, PUSHING, MANIPULATING, YOU SHOULD STATEMENTS, HAVE TO & NEED TO STATEMENTS

SHADOWS
BASE

VOID TRANSPERSONAL
APEX / INTERPERSONAL
ENGAGEMENT

WWW.SOMATICCONSENT.COM

Next on the Communication Map are the Engagement Zones. This part (between the Base and the Apex) is pretty much limited to either making a *request* or an *offer*. If we want to lift up from the Base, we have to own our desires and be capable of requesting what we want.

When you have conscious communication between two consenting adults (who take high responsibility for their conversation), each is capable of knowing; 'If I want you to do something for me or to me, I have to ask you first and respect your limits.'

Therefore, if I ask you to do something beyond the limits you've voiced and we've made an agreement on, I'm not respecting your limits or taking responsibility for my desire. Of course, I could try and get my needs met by hanging out in the shadow realms of hinting or using manipulation, but again, this would be taking the responsibility of a child.

If we look at the Engagement Zones within the Communication Map, you can see that the giver either makes an offer or a request.

Wrapping up your request in the guise of an offer

Often we don't voice our desires due to the vulnerability of showing ourselves and the risk of rejection; instead, we wrap up our request in the guise of an offer. When we avoid making a request, we often offer things that **we would like to receive** or **in the hope of receiving something back.**

Every offer with a hidden agenda is due to a request being avoided. What the *receiver* does with the gift of an offer is, of course, their choice. So, if you feel disappointed when the receiver doesn't want what you offer, it's a good indicator that you actually have an *agenda* (an attachment to a specific outcome/ an expectation) usually to get something back in return. What you want back may not be obvious to you. We often give to receive appreciation, acknowledgment for our thoughtfulness, time and effort, or to be accepted and loved. Whether done consciously or unconsciously, this belongs to the shadow and can feel like manipulation.

A few years ago I was invited to Hong Kong to teach consent on a somatic level. Here a large part of the culture is built on 'giving to get'. To me, it appeared that the bigger the gift, the higher the level of expectation was, to figure out what the giver wanted back. While there, a few people became offended when they gave me a gift and I didn't ask what they wanted in return.

During the workshop, it was difficult for most people to experience the Direct Route of sensory inflow through the waking up the hands exercise. When it dropped in and people started to feel for themselves—the entire dynamic *of going into action to get something for themself* went out of the window.

They became stuck again when I invited them to place their hand on somebody else's.

Here, most lapsed back into the belief that their action had to be for the other, and that the other had to do something in return for them. Recognising boundaries and expressing limits was difficult for all. Even when something wasn't pleasant, they felt they had to pretend to like it, to avoid shaming the other person. The cultural belief was embedded so deeply, it took a whole day of returning to the inflow exercise of feeling an object with the hands before some 'ahas' began to take place.

When we clean up our offers, it's like a quantum shift. How do you make that shift? First of all, while learning to master this new approach, stop giving and drop into your receiving role. Ask for what it is you really want—and you'll never have to put a hidden agenda in an offer again. You'll get your needs met when you ask directly for whatever your desire is.

By knowing that communicating your needs is achieved through a request, you know how to do so by asking; "Can I do this for myself?", or "Can you do this for me?". This level of communication literally allows us to shift to a higher level of conscious awareness.

Making an offer is giving a gift

When an offer is made, it's done from a higher state of consciousness *towards* the altruistic state at the Apex. We offer to give something that someone else needs or wants. We give something because we have it and can. An example such as, "Would you like me to give you a massage?" is only a genuine gift if given freely, without attachment to the offer being accepted or getting something in return. Reciprocity is not a necessity in making an offer. Some cultures see this differently, such as the Chinese culture, but again, this is a cultural construct.

Personally, if I lack energy or am feeling burned out, I don't offer anything to anyone, because I have to focus on my own self-care. However, if my batteries are charged and I have no present needs or desires, I ask, "What would you like? Is there anything I can do for you?".

This is specifically important when it comes to work. Would I offer my skills and gifts if I didn't like what I do? I would only do this if I desperately needed to survive, otherwise I wouldn't be offering something from an empowered place but from a suppressed survival mechanism.

COMMUNICATION

WHAT DOESN'T WORK SO WELL

- **STATEMENTS:**
    I WANT... / YOU SHOULD... / DO THIS / WE DO } **POWER OVER!**
        HINTS, ORDERS, DEMANDS
        COMMANDS, DICTATING

WHAT WORKS
(WITH NO ATTACHMENT OF GETTING OR GIVING IT):

- **BOUNDARIES:** SAYING STOP OR NO!

- **OFFER:** EXPRESSION LIMITS WHAT ARE YOU WILLING TO GIVE
    WHAT WOULD YOU LIKE?
    IS THERE ANYTHING YOU WANT?

- **REQUEST:** ASKING FOR WHAT YOU REALLY WANT
    MAY I...? / CAN I...? - PERMISSION
    WILL YOU...? / CAN YOU...? - AGREEMENTS

- **INVITATIONS:**
    BOTH ARE BRINGING THEIR DESIRE FORWARD
    FOR WHAT THEY WANT
    WANT/WANT / HANG OUT / WIN/WIN / PLAY

POWER OF LOVE!

WWW.SOMATICCONSENT.COM

Offers and requests in the 3 Minute Game

By embodying the dynamics of offers and requests in The 3 Minute Game, how good communication works becomes very transparent. Due to your increased awareness of receiving and giving, you can hear when you or others aren't communicating clearly. You notice when you're not clearly expressing what your desire is and instead making an offer (motivated by getting something *you want*).

You notice when you're being manipulative to get a certain response or reaction. And when you notice, you have the opportunity to ask yourself, "Wait a moment, what is it I haven't asked for that I actually want?" Getting clear on how to communicate therefore continuously unravels layers of self. It increases awareness and self-discovery.

At its roots, the 3 minute game is an offer game

We offer by asking, "What do you want to do to me for 3 minutes?" and "What do you want me to do to you for 3 minutes?"
We play within the Engagement Zones by making offers and requests where one *wants to* and the other is *willing to*.

Though for play to happen at all, both have to want it. And so, by asking someone to play, it is also an **invitation**.

Person A: "I'd like to play a game, would you like to play too?"
Person B: "That sounds fun, it could be nice, what's the game about?"
Person A: Explains the rules.
Person B: Decides whether they want to join you in the game: "Yes please / no thanks / maybe another time".

The language itself is really transparent, and so, when I ask for what I want, you can say "no" to the entire thing but I'm still able to express and own my desire. This is very empowering in itself. With this or any power comes the responsibility to function from an interpersonal space, rather than manipulating or taking advantage of the other through shadow engagement. There is responsibility to give the gift of our power to others, so that they can find their own desires. When we do this, it becomes a very transformative experience.

Invitation happens at the apex

At the Base there's the level of communication where you're capable of saying no, keeping your boundaries clear and taking responsibility for your own self-care.

The Engagement Zones are where we make requests, offers, ask for permission and come to agreement.

Invitation happens at the Apex. Here we come from the interpersonal space where it's about what *both want*. When one wants something and the other feels a *pull* towards it too. Both act without agenda or attachment to outcome. Both are in a state of flow. It's less about making offers or requests and more about *invitation* from a higher level of consciousness.

The Apex is an altruistic space of love and care, where we offer support, feel and show empathy and compassion and are empowered in co-creation for mutual benefit. It's a playful space of conscious communication, intimate connection, safety, friendship, relating, lovemaking, listening to hear, authentic responding and body language. When both lovers have activated the Direct Route, they can follow their impulses and be much more 'fluid 'in their movements with one another.

A good example of authentic communication through body language is *contact improvisation dancing*. For those who've never experienced this, it's a kind of meditative dance. Although it's good to know how to support others safely, there are no pre-learned steps. The mind doesn't direct the body. Sometimes there is accompanying music and sometimes silence.

The idea is that dancers tune into their bodies and move, spontaneously and intuitively according to the genuine way their bodies wish to move, while in contact with another person or people. When people dance in such an embodied way, each moment of contact holds a clear signal. It can feel as though your body can 'read 'the other's energy. The dancers tune into the feel of the other, supporting and allowing themselves to be supported, flowing with the natural pull of their body's impulses. It's clear when someone doesn't really connect—if they're only tuned into themselves—and push without feeling your signals, intent on domination and power over. It's also clear when there's a lack of resistance, when someone can't meet you in an empowered way, allowing themselves to be pushed around. These interactions feel very different from the playful push and pull of authentic connection.

The speed of movement differs; sometimes a spontaneous stillness occurs. Movement and connection have many flavours depending on who you dance with and how both feel in the moment. It can feel fast, lively, playful, funny, slow, sensual, intimate, edgy, freeing, exhilarating, grounding, peaceful and more. Due to the ease, grace and beauty of these natural movements, an onlooker may be mistaken in presuming they're choreographed and rehearsed.

Communicating an invitation

The most important conversation at the Apex is communicating what it is that *you want* and what it is that *I want* as an *invitation*.

"I want something here, what do you want?"
"I want this, do you want it too?"
"What would you like? I would like this. And you, what do you desire right now?"
"Well, I'd just like to do this, can we find *middle ground* where we both get our needs met?"

Communicating at the Apex is about finding a win-win situation and isn't about compromise at all. Here, winning happens for all involved. You create invitation and agree on what both parties want. This, of course, isn't always easy to find and can require a high level of 'investigation'. In radical responsibility, you have to ask the right questions (the three powers) to find out what's important to the other person. You stay in relationship, owning your own desire, while being capable of investigating someone else's world.

I'm highly motivated to work with people in win-win exchanges. While working on the SCES course content, apps, website, marketing, translations and this book, I invited people to build structures with me that they are good at and like to do. These skill exchanges are paid and are also about mutual learning, sharing and growth. I couldn't have done all this work without others who were interested in, invested in and benefited from the content of the SCES structure. Due to the openness of idea and experience exchange, where all parties are encouraged to express their truth, this project continues to result in an upward spiral that touches and enriches hearts and lives from a joyful place of *invitation*.

Being at the Apex doesn't mean that life will be 'happily ever after'. If we look at the *ascending* and *descending* arrows on the Communication Map, they show an upward and downward possibility of movement from the Base to the Apex and vice versa. It's clear that when we constantly engage with new people in new situations and environments, we will have to establish our Base again and again. The more we practise, the more fluent we become in these dynamics. When you begin to master the SCES, it becomes clear if there are no functioning agreements. You know when you haven't clearly or appropriately communicated, when you're guessing and are in the shadow of taking your assumptions for granted.

With practice you know when something doesn't quite sit right and you need a conversation. When shadows emerge or something hasn't been properly communicated, there's a continual up and down process of relating, from the Basement of shadows, through the Engagement Zones to the Apex and back. This way you find out what's going on and where you both are (the desires and limits of both) in any given situation, so that you are able to re-establish connection.

WHO IS TALKING AND WHO IS IT FOR?

Listening And Communicating

"It was impossible to get a conversation going, everybody was talking too much."
- Yogi Berra

Whenever we're together with others, we make an effort to listen. Or do we? If you're honest with yourself, when someone else is talking, how much of your attention is on what the person is saying? And how much attention are you focusing on your own opinions while formulating a response—so that *you* can be listened to?

How often have you been in a 'one-sided 'conversation with someone who's intent on absorbing your attention, while they talk about their experiences and opinions or teach and preach without asking you if that's ok?

One example from my childhood springs to mind. I remember sitting as a kid in my grandmother's living room, looking at endless boring holiday photographs and having to listen to stories about people and places in the photos that I had no connection to. All the while I sat there with ringing ears, knowing that at the end of the ordeal I'd get my five Deutschmark pocket money.

The SCES isn't limited to navigating consent in relation to touch but is a powerful tool for all sorts of day-to-day situations. The Who is Talking and Who is it for Map gives an overview of the Engagement System in relation to communication. It shows how communication sounds when we have permission, make agreements and express our boundaries, and which shadows come up when we don't.

The Engagement Zones clearly show *who the action is for*. In this case, *talking* is the action. When we know who the talking is for, we access many opportunities to engage verbally on different levels. This makes it easier for people to listen and be listened to. For co-creative counselling sessions, it also makes it easier to guide someone into the kind of conversation that provides insight, helping them move out of a place they may be stuck.

When there is an action, who is it for?

During conversation, the action is in the form of *talking*. So, we first look at who the talking is for. When we know who it's for, we know who is in the role of **giver** and who is in the role of **receiver**.

During The 3 Minute Game you experienced the 4 basic dynamics during any exchange.

- You go into action for you.
- You go into action for them.
- They go into action for them.
- They go into action for you.

Ask yourself;
When do **you** need to *ask them* for permission and when do you need to make an agreement?

When you are talking it's for you or for them.
If you are talking and it's for you, you need permission.
If you are talking and it's for them you need an agreement.

Ask yourself;
When do **they** need to *ask you* for permission and when do they need to make an agreement?

When they are talking it's for them or for you.

If they are talking and it's for them, they need your permission.
If they are talking and it's for you, you need an agreement.

The Practice

*"We cannot solve our problems with the same thinking we
used when we created them."*
Albert Einstein

This map isn't meant to replace normal conversation. It's a tool to bring more awareness into how we communicate. If you're keen to bring more conscious communication, openness and intimacy into any relationship, be sure that it'll take a bit of practice. We're all so used to fighting to be listened to.

WHO IS TALKING AND WHO IS IT FOR?

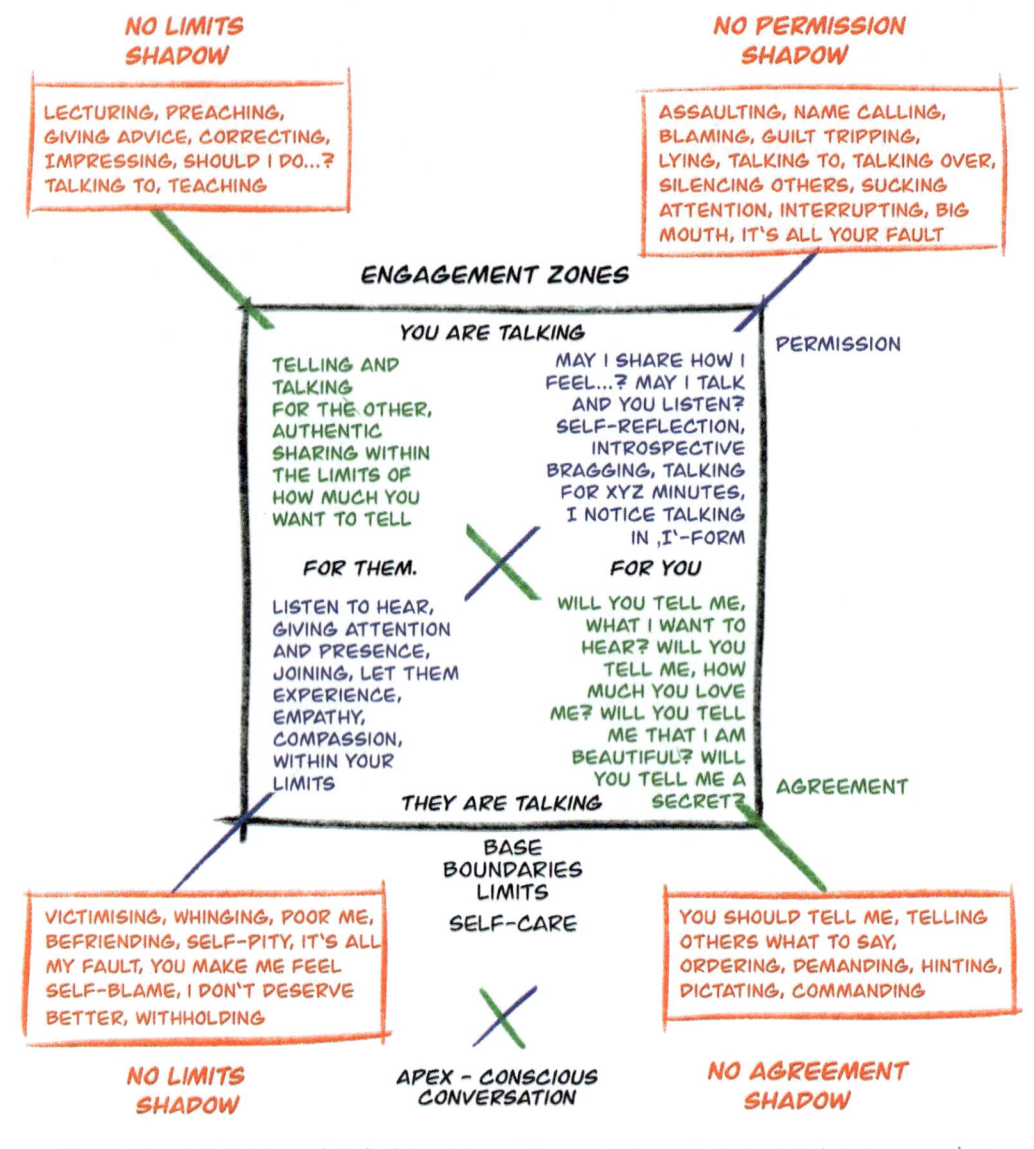

NO LIMITS SHADOW

LECTURING, PREACHING, GIVING ADVICE, CORRECTING, IMPRESSING, SHOULD I DO...? TALKING TO, TEACHING

NO PERMISSION SHADOW

ASSAULTING, NAME CALLING, BLAMING, GUILT TRIPPING, LYING, TALKING TO, TALKING OVER, SILENCING OTHERS, SUCKING ATTENTION, INTERRUPTING, BIG MOUTH, IT'S ALL YOUR FAULT

ENGAGEMENT ZONES

YOU ARE TALKING

FOR THEM: TELLING AND TALKING FOR THE OTHER, AUTHENTIC SHARING WITHIN THE LIMITS OF HOW MUCH YOU WANT TO TELL

PERMISSION: MAY I SHARE HOW I FEEL...? MAY I TALK AND YOU LISTEN? SELF-REFLECTION, INTROSPECTIVE BRAGGING, TALKING FOR XYZ MINUTES, I NOTICE TALKING IN 'I'-FORM

FOR THEM: LISTEN TO HEAR, GIVING ATTENTION AND PRESENCE, JOINING, LET THEM EXPERIENCE, EMPATHY, COMPASSION, WITHIN YOUR LIMITS

FOR YOU: WILL YOU TELL ME, WHAT I WANT TO HEAR? WILL YOU TELL ME, HOW MUCH YOU LOVE ME? WILL YOU TELL ME THAT I AM BEAUTIFUL? WILL YOU TELL ME A SECRET?

THEY ARE TALKING

AGREEMENT

BASE BOUNDARIES LIMITS SELF-CARE

NO LIMITS SHADOW

VICTIMISING, WHINGING, POOR ME, BEFRIENDING, SELF-PITY, IT'S ALL MY FAULT, YOU MAKE ME FEEL SELF-BLAME, I DON'T DESERVE BETTER, WITHHOLDING

APEX – CONSCIOUS CONVERSATION

NO AGREEMENT SHADOW

YOU SHOULD TELL ME, TELLING OTHERS WHAT TO SAY, ORDERING, DEMANDING, HINTING, DICTATING, COMMANDING

THIS IS NOT REPLACING CONVERSATIONS, IT IS A PRACTICE TO LEARN HOW TO COMMUNICATE AND LISTEN

> EXCHANGE LISTENING TURNS – FOR XYZ MINUTES EACH DAY, WEEK OR MONTH

WWW.SOMATICCONSENT.COM

The four dynamics of listening and talking

When you are talking and it's for you
You ask their permission. They agree within their limits.

Can/May I share how I feel? Can/May I talk while you listen?

You decide what you want to say. It can be about self-reflection/introspection, including body sensations, feelings and emotions. Or you can share what you're struggling with, how well you're doing, or what you've achieved.

You always talk in the 'I 'form. "I feel..." sharing what is meaningful to you.

When you are talking and it's for them
You make an offer. They ask your permission. You agree within your limits.

Here you tell and talk *for them*, saying whatever someone else wants to hear. You do this authentically within your limits.

"Is there anything you would like me to say?"
"What could I say to help you feel more heard?"
"Can I say anything that will make you feel better?"
"Is there anything you want me to tell you about myself?"
"Is there anything you want me to say that would help you right now?"

When they are talking and it's for them (you listen)
They ask your permission. You agree within your limits.

You listen to hear. You give your full attention and presence for the agreed upon amount of time so that the other person has the opportunity to talk about themselves.

You bring empathy and compassion to their story (where they presently are) by allowing them to have the experience of what they want to share.

When they are talking and it's for you
You ask their permission. They agree within their limits.

You can request exactly what you want to hear.
I like to do this with my partner, especially when I'm feeling bad about

something.

"Can you tell me what I want to hear?"
"Can you tell me exactly the words that are important for me to hear right now?"
"Can you tell me you love me?" / "Can you tell me I'm beautiful?"
"Can you tell me a secret?"
"Can you tell me what you appreciate about me?"

The shadows of conversation

This map shines a light on our automatic survival strategies while communicating. When familiar with the map, you can literally hear yourself and others functioning from a shadow, and notice which. During a conversation, shadow dynamics are often based on 'power over', fear, contraction, control or manipulation.

It's so easy to be triggered by the ways others communicate and to blame them for it. This often happens when people give unsolicited advice; when there is no permission and the 'advisor' tells the other what they 'should' do. From their point of view, it seems like they're helping, when, in actual fact, they are actively taking the power away from the other—to help themselves from an empowered place. Another common shadow comes up when we don't give someone permission to dominate a conversation, and instead go along with it. As a result, we may feel drained or not heard and blame the speaker.

What happens when you exceed your listening limits?

One student of Somatic Consent reflected on the time her sister came to visit after not seeing her for a while. Though she was happy to see her sister, the constant attention and presence necessary to listen to a waterfall of words during the catch-up overwhelmed her and brought up resentment. It's easy to feel ambushed if we can't take care of our limits, no matter how much we love someone.

When there is no permission (purple line)

There's an expression in German that translates as: 'Speaking like a waterfall'. This, as I'm sure you can visualise, refers to incessant rambling, talking without a pause, when words—just like water—pour without end out of someone's mouth. Usually, when this happens, the speaker is oblivious to whether they are being listened to or not, whether they are boring the other person or bleeding their energy dry. It points to a lack of awareness of or interest in the fact that they are **taking without permission.** When someone's talking feels like they're taking, when it's draining, attention-grabbing and not contributing to anything in a shared way, you may feel you're in the audience of an event someone forced you to go to. It's your responsibility in this case to make your limits clear.

Other shadows in this category include any kind of assault such as name calling, blaming, "It's all your fault", guilt tripping, lying, talking at or talking over, exaggerating our own importance, interrupting or silencing others. These are all typical of someone coming from a place of 'power over.'

Whinging also often happens when there is no permission. This is the domain of the victimised self where we make ourselves small; "It's all my fault", "poor me", "I feel bad" "I don't deserve" (from a place of self-blame). This shadow also includes 'befriending the enemy '(Stockholm syndrome, when people who are being abused bond with their abusers).

When there is no agreement (green line)

Here we assume we can invade other people's personal decision making or self-expression, telling them what they 'should 'or 'shouldn't 'think, say or do. It includes ordering, demanding, commanding, dictating, lecturing, preaching, teaching, educating, hinting and correcting. This shadow realm also includes an expectation that others talk, when no agreement has been made; when we tell others what to say, putting words in their mouth that we want to hear (that they don't want to say). "You should tell me what I need to hear", "You have to know what I need to hear.", or "If you loved me you would say the right thing."

Before practising I suggest you each take some moments to feel an object in your hands and wait for your physiology to switch into the parasympathetic state of relaxation.

> *Just like The 3 Minute game, but specifically focused on talking and listening, each of the 4 dynamics above can be explored for a set amount of time.*
>
> *When you are talking and it's for you*
> *When you are talking and it's for them*
> *When they are talking and it's for them*
> *When they are talking and it's for you*

A clear time frame is necessary so that no one dominates the conversation. If, at any time you lose track of who the talking is for, I encourage you to ask your partner:
"Can we pause for a moment?" This way you can both take a step out to reflect and clarify together.

Regular talking and listening buddies

This exchange is a conscious experiment in communicating and listening awareness.

I have a regular talking and listening exchange buddy. We get in touch once a month for a set amount of time. While one of us talks, the other listens and vice versa. Sometimes I'm not aware of all the layers of thought, emotion or sensation in my mind and body until I verbalise them. It makes the dynamics of communication more transparent. It's really interesting to observe what comes up and to be fully observed by the other. It can be used as a form of therapeutic self and co-regulation.

You don't even need to be in the same country to play. It's perfect to do as a face to face call on your mobile or computer.

Want to play?

Both decide how often you want to exchange and for how many minutes each time. I suggest once a week, fortnight or month, depending on the relationship, and having a full 15 minutes each to talk.

Start by deciding who would like to talk first and who would like to listen first.

In this exercise:

The talker is the *receiver*: they *receive* the attention of the listener.
The listener is the *giver:* they *give* their attention to the talker.

The dynamics of 'you go into action for them 'and 'they go into action for you 'is *not applicable in this particular exercise.*

You have an equal amount of time each to talk. When it's your turn to talk, you speak about what's important to you. You notice what you feel and speak in the 'I 'form.

It's not about entertaining or educating the other person or explaining something you think they want to hear. It's about practising radical self-reflection, where you use someone else's attention *for you* (for your own benefit). It's a form of introspective, cathartic meditation.

When you're the one talking - it's for you

When you're talking, you're going into action (talking) for your own benefit. So, you get to practise going into action for yourself.
You're **receiving** the other person's attention *for you.*

Similar to noticing the Direct Route, you're going into action for yourself. Just like when you ask for permission to touch someone else, you utilise the other person as a resource so that you can reflect or feel something *for you.*

You notice what's going on inside yourself and voice whatever comes up. You tune into your interoception (how your body is feeling physically and mentally). Examples could be your breathing and heart rate, hunger level or temperature. You might notice restlessness, tiredness, lack of focus, having a slight headache, feeling rushed, flushed, having tension in your shoulders, feeling nauseous, bloated and so on.

Also take the opportunity to tune into your present feelings. How do you feel? Do you feel relaxed or stressed? How you feel could be related to new feelings in the moment or old emotions showing up. It could include any of the core or mixed emotions such as anger, sadness, fear, joy, frustration, shyness, excitement, anxiety, playfulness, jealousy, nervousness, feeling up-lifted, confused, depressed and so on.

You can say anything of meaning and importance to you, what you're presently disappointed, fearful or excited about.. What you share is totally up to you.

If you find it difficult, what can really help the first few times is 'bragging' by sharing something you're really proud of yourself for, such as any breakthroughs or achievements, or about something that's going well in your life. While talking about the 'good stuff', try noticing which body sensations and other feelings come up. This helps train interoception while providing a doorway to express what you notice.

Listening turns have the added bonus of breaking loops of destructive communication patterns such as interrupting and making comments to get attention, or the habit of having conversations that sound like a Ping-Pong game, centred on outwitting others or blaming and 'you' statements like, "You make me feel" and "It's all your fault".

When you're the one listening - it's for them

When you're listening, it's their action *for them*. You provide access for another person to go into action *for themself*.

The listener **gives** the gift of listening and **doesn't take away** by interrupting or distracting the talker. You're lending your ears. You're **giving** your undivided attention, *your total presence*, so that they can **receive** *for themselves*.

Stephen Porges says listening is essential for our nervous system. Listening is also part of any meditation. When we listen, we become the objective and compassionate witness. Porges says that when we listen with focused attention and presence, we activate the nerves in the face and head as well as the vagus nerve to the heart. This is vital for social engagement so that our bodies receive the crucial feedback mechanisms we need to survive and thrive.[51]

Debriefing

When you've both had your turns to talk and listen, have a debriefing. It's good to set a timer for an agreed upon amount of time, for example, three minutes each, but it's entirely up to you both.

The debriefing isn't about asking questions or giving advice to the other.
It isn't a conversation with the other person at all.

It's another personal monologue that the talker has *with, about and for themselves*.

Examples of things to debrief:

What did you notice while you or the other were talking?
What was difficult for you.
What triggered you?
How was this related to your or the other's shadows?

When it's your turn to talk, do so in the 'I' form.

"When I said (XYZ), I felt... (vulnerable / shy / angry / proud / silly / small / excited / confused / childish / scared / expansive / playful / melancholic / carefree / amused") and so on.

"When you said (XYZ), I felt... (a connection / included / jealous / annoyed / loved / appreciated / uplifted / nervous / afraid / sad / empathy / turned on") and so on.

What to consider when listening

Any reflections of thoughts and feelings are completely personal. Everyone is entitled to feel however they feel. Feelings aren't to do with the other person *per se*. They aren't about criticism or to be taken personally, and they *aren't an invitation for advice*.

When I started listening turns a few years ago I often had the urge to say something to help fix the other's problems. I had to catch myself so as not to interrupt; to focus only on noticing and feeling what was being said. When I managed that, the door of empathy magically opened. I was able to just be with the talker and feel with them.

In most cases of deeper connection, there's a healthy exchange at the Apex where mutual, uplifting, empathetic and compassionate relating occurs. Here, communication flows. We are, however, all human and all conditioned, so shadows are bound to come up. I encourage you to acknowledge these shadows in curious and playful light-heartedness as part of the journey of intimate relating with yourself and others.

When we listen to someone fully in their vulnerability with an open heart, so much becomes possible, because we see the other person as they really are. We might see that they have good intentions, that they feel confusion and sadness and fear and anger and joy; that they feel much of what we feel ourselves. We notice the unique and special parts of them we might have missed before—the gift of who they are, as they are. The attitude of love improves our ability to listen, to gain empathy, trust and intimacy.

We all know we need to be nurtured and loved, and we all have a tendency to build metaphorical shields to protect ourselves. Our need to connect and *give love* is, however, who we are at our core. Most of us suffer from an inadequate chance to express the huge capacity we have to love and to nurture. There is much love inside us all that rarely gets expressed. When we allow it to happen, we reach the Apex of our potential—together.

THE SIX LEVELS TO BLISS

"If you suffer, it is because of you, if you feel blissful, it is because of you. Nobody else is responsible - only you and you alone. You are your hell and you are your heaven too."
- Osho

When I talk about bliss it's related to The Polyvagal Theory Map. When we feel safe we can enter immobilisation, activated when our nervous system is in the parasympathetic surrender state. This is our natural state of bliss, one of the sweetest spaces to be, where the experience of oneness with unified consciousness becomes possible.

The Six Levels to Bliss is like a staircase to this unity and oneness, the transformative, transpersonal state above the Apex (the bliss state).

6 LEVELS TO BLISS

WORKS LIKE A TORUS – ASCENDING – DESCENDING

L6 — TRANSPERSONAL, NON-DUAL, BLISS STATE, ALTERED STATE OF CONSCIOUSNESS, SPIRITUAL ONENESS, UNITY

L5 — INTERPERSONAL, LOVE + CARE, ABUNDANCE, BEING A GIFT, NO AGENDA, NO ATTACHMENT, GRATITUDE, GENEROSITY, INTEGRITY, SURRENDER, INTUITION, INTIMATE CONNECTION, PLAY

L4 — ENGAGEMENT ZONE: AGREEMENT: CAN YOU...? / I CAN. REQUEST/OFFER

↕ | WHO IS DOING THE ACTION & WHO IS IT FOR? | ↕

L3 — ENGAGEMENT ZONE, PERMISSION: CAN I...? / YOU CAN. REQUEST/OFFER

L2 — SELF-CARE, BOUNDARIES, LIMITS, SELF-PLEASURE, DIRECT ROUTE, PLEASURE, RIGHTS AND RESPONSIBILITY, NOTICING, CHOOSING, SAFETY, SELF-REGULATION, HONEST COMMUNICATION

L1 — SHADOW: RAPE, PERPETRATOR, STEALING, VICTIM, ENDURING, GOING ALONG, ENTITLEMENT, EXPECTATIONS, EXPLOITATION, PLEASING, RESCUER, GIVE TO GET, ORDERS, HINTS, STATEMENTS-YOU SHOULD BURNOUT, POWER OVER

WWW.SOMATICCONSENT.COM

At level 1: We acknowledge our shadows

To experience a state of bliss, we have to acknowledge that we have all these levels within us, and all of the shadows too. We are all; perpetrators, rapists and thieves who take what we want without permission and victims who go along with things. We're all entitled little princesses and princes expecting things for free. We're all full of expectations, we please others, we rescue others in order to feel self-worth and we all exploit others. We give to get, we order others around, we make statements from a place of entitlement and expect others to react. We demand and long for power, and we all get burnout.

This is all part of the human experience, the mud of our humanness. We aren't here to ascend away from that. It's part of who we are. It's not wrong or bad. Just a fact. You have to acknowledge that everyone dwells in the Low Drama Triangle from time to time, and that doing so is OK. Nobody is a saint. So, I invite you to take a breath and admit to these parts of yourself, while forgiving yourself and others in the process. There's no point in dwelling on our shadows with regret or guilt. We need to look them squarely in the face and acknowledge them. We need to accept them so that we're able to integrate them into our awareness, give ourselves a break and move forward in playfulness, good humour, self-care and acceptance of ourselves and others.

Years before the #metoo campaign reached the tantric scene, as a sexual bodyworker, I realised from an ethical and energetic perspective and due to the differentiation of power dynamics—that sexual intercourse with a client on their request was something I didn't want.

I posted words to that effect to my public profile on social media, owning up to having crossed that line in the past. I also shared I'd recognised it as a shadow strategy in order to feed my need for intimacy. I wanted to invite other male bodyworkers to see my point of view. A few months later, Maya Yonika, an acquaintance, published a book to expose her experiences with a man offering sexual service within the tantra scene. Her book is definitely worth a read. It's called, "No Mud No Lotus".[52] Reading it made me realise that we are all dwelling in muddy ground to some degree, wading through the dirt to find truth and to evolve.

Biohacking empowerment by integrating shadows

When it comes to shadows, here are some practical ways to shine a light on what's going on below the surface. By experimenting you'll gain clarity about your habitual survival strategies and may find it surprising to discover new elements of self. It can feel very liberating and be a lot of fun, it can also be a little embarrassing or even painful. In order to reach the level of freedom it offers, I invite you to biohack your road to empowerment by trying out the following;

It's essential to have a safe container to make these exercises possible. Remember, self-honesty is vital, as well as a little humour and humility.

OPPRESSING / PERPETRATOR:
1. Feeling an object.
Most people with the power-over shadow have a strong attachment to the Indirect Route, and therefore require a little more effort to tune into their sensory inflow. This shadow is used to going into action for themselves, while recklessly bulldozing over others. There is often a lack of willingness to be vulnerable, which deters from accepting and practising the Direct Route, instead, labelling it as weird, stupid, boring, unnecessary or just for 'softies'.

There is a difference between;
a) the Direct Route (receiving for yourself) and
b) going into action for yourself (while recklessly bulldozing over others)

- When you *receive for yourself* via the Direct Route, you are able to feel yourself physically and emotionally and the other too (through empathy).

- When you *selfishly go into action for yourself*, you aren't able to feel yourself in any great depth, and you aren't able to 'feel 'the other. This inability to feel is often accompanied by pretending to feel something, or needing to get a reaction from the other to feed a sense of power and control.

Becoming more embodied (tuned into yourself physically and emotionally) needs practice, practice and more practice. It could be especially difficult for men who've experienced trauma due to circumcision. In his research, Gregory J. Boyle states that infant circumcision may cause adverse changes to brain structure and function in the prefrontal cortex that impact adversely on a child's personality development. In their study into *alexithymia* (the inability to identify and describe one's own emotions), Bollinger and Van Howe (2011) reported that circumcised men are 19.9 percent more likely to exhibit dysfunction in emotional awareness. Forty-one percent of participants reported impeded emotional intimacy with partner(s) that resulted in sexual dysfunction.[53]

2. For a period of three weeks, practise asking for and getting an agreement or permission, every single time you want someone to do something *for you* or you want to do *something for yourself* (which involves the other). Also notice how a rejection feels (and deal with it) whenever you receive a "no". Keep in mind that a rejection isn't about you *per se*; it's about what the other person isn't 'willing to'. Try to notice that your desire is still valuable and valid, even if the other says no.

PASSIVITY / VICTIM:
Have regular 'Empowerment Massages', which we talk about in Chapter 5.

EXPLOITING / ENTITLED:
Play the *Master and Servant game*. Stay in the role of servant three quarters of the time!

Master and Servant Game: The purpose of this interaction is to deepen the *your action for them* dynamic by feeling into the difference between a 'want to ' and a 'willing to ' and making an agreement, while having fun in the process!

Choose who wants to be the Servant first.
This person (who'll be in action) asks the Master;
"What do you want me to do *for you* for 5 minutes?"

The Master asks for whatever they want. They play with as many different requests as they can think of, change their mind often and experiment with demands and orders.

Examples could be:
"I want you to rub my feet..."
"I want you to get me a glass of water..."
"I want you to jump up and down until I say stop..."
"Go and ask those other people across the room to stop what they're doing..."
"Crawl around the room and act like a dog..."

The Servant tunes into whether they feel a 'want to ' or a 'willing to ' or a 'no'. If they feel a 'no', they say "no" and ask the Master to make another request. If it's a 'want to ' or 'willing to', they are responsible for their limits.
After 5 minutes swap roles.
When you've finished playing, have a de-briefing where both of you reflect and share your insight:

What did you notice about yourself while in the role of Master?
Was it difficult to ask for what you wanted in a demanding way?

What did you notice about yourself in the role of Servant?
Was it difficult to say no? Did you notice and express your limits or find yourself going along with things you were uncomfortable with?
Was it difficult to go into action at all when being told what to do?
Could you feel resistance?

PLEASING / RESCUER:
For a time period of three weeks, practise by stopping any action whatsoever *for others* without first having had a request. Also, whenever you presume you're giving a gift from the Apex, stop offering when you realise you're getting frustrated because the other person doesn't want whatever your action is. (This can include 'fixing 'tactics such as offering advice or trying to change another person's mood). You'll soon realise when your action is, in fact, something you want, rather than a gift given from the Apex.

Play the *Master and Servant game*. Stay in the role of Master three quarters of the time!

At level 2: We make the foundation of our Base

Our Base is built on self-care and self-love. We know what we have a right to and responsibility for. We know our boundaries and limits. We have access to the Direct Route, can self-pleasure and know that somatic embodiment is the foundation of growth and development. Our noticing brain is activated so that we can clearly choose our desires. We can create safety for ourselves and self-regulate. We are honest with ourselves and authentically communicate what we feel and what comes up for us.

Personally, I know that I'm responsible for my feelings. By activating the sensory inflow, I create possibilities for the foundation of relaxed arousal and ability to recognise when a shadow comes crawling up from the Basement. My Base is my landing pad. It doesn't matter how lost I get. Whenever I fall, from here I can reinvent myself in any given moment.

With mastery at this level, we go onto the next.

At level 3: We ask to go into action for ourselves
We get and give permission - Engagement Zones

At this level we get confident asking for what we want and making offers. We know how to make a request and the difference between a request (such as "May I feel your chest?") and an offer (such as "How would you like to touch me?"). We know the difference between asking for permission and an agreement.

Using impulses of desire to ask for what we want to receive has been for myself and many others, the essence of empowerment and the cornerstone of liberation and intimate connection. Here the notion of making others responsible to do something that *I need to feel*—dissolves.

At level 4: We ask others to go into action for us We make agreements - Engagement Zones

At this level we fluently communicate within the Engagement Zones. We have personal integrity and are clearly aware of the direction of the gift. We are neither purely focusing on ascending qualities nor trapped within a descending dynamic.

People whose only focus is on *ascending* to a high spiritual realm become absent and unconscious of their physical reality, ungrounded, disembodied and lack the ability to feel. They often pretend they don't want or need anything to be content. People who predominantly focus on a *descending* dynamic tend to bury their head in the sand. They avoid the possibility of personal development or the reality of spiritual connection. In actuality, both *ascending* and *descending* dynamics coexist simultaneously in our human condition. We have a physical body that we need to feel in tune with —grounded and embodied in this aspect of self. We have shadow behaviour which needs integrating into our awareness and we have the capability for altruistic, spiritual and transpersonal experience.

For most pleasers and rescuers, burned out from giving more than they have to give, this level is about liberation from any duty to provide something without first being asked. It is the entry point into living a free life.

At level 5: We dwell at the Apex

Here we thrive in awareness within an interpersonal space of love and care. This is a place of abundance where we're in gratitude for the gift that we are —just as we are. Doing isn't a duty, there is no agenda and therefore no attachment to outcome. We're in celebration of our being-ness.

We're generous and have integrity because when we're in action, we have an agreement made in awareness—so it's clear whether it's for you or for them. We can determine whether we are giving something out of generosity or from a place of shadow. From this space we create with authenticity.

We function with 'the power of love 'rather than the 'love of power'. Rather than using 'power over 'as abuse to misuse people with less power than ourselves such as with oppression, sexism and racism, we use our power as the strength and gift of leadership. We give our gift of power, to empower and enrich others and our environment.

The Apex is the art of being while holding awareness of all the levels below it—as integrated levels of self. It's where lovemaking happens through light-hearted engagement. It's where action flows playfully with ease. It's a state of bliss where we share mutual togetherness. In this state we aren't seeking or granting consent for each individual action; nevertheless, this doesn't mean action is based on shadow dynamics.

In the past, before I fully understood what I share here about consent, I witnessed and also created so much rigidity around the concept. Some may believe that if there is no agreement between people, and an action takes place, then the action automatically falls within the realms of shadow. This isn't the case. Worrying about that just makes people stiff, afraid of making mistakes.

Examples could be, cooking, cleaning or building together, or just hanging out with friends. We are expressing care and love. This is the joy of being. Each action is a win-win *for us*. When we are in full integrity and coming from a place of love and care—we are at the Apex, not the Shadow Basement. Though we all get tied up in shadows sometimes. When I experience the Apex, I'm not afraid of shadows coming up. On the contrary, I love to learn new things about myself and others.

At level 6: Transcendence to the bliss state

At level 6 we experience a merging back into unified consciousness—to oneness. There is no need to identify with the separate individual you call "I' because *we are already complete*. We dwell in pure reality. We don't have to go anywhere or be anybody. Here, creation manifests through us effortlessly.

All these levels are active at all times. We dip into and out of the shadows and also the enlightened state. It's a continuum of living; a constant evolving through day-to-day engagement.

I remember many glimpses and joyful, infinite moments of bliss. I love whenever I enter this state and dissolve, grateful for the miracle of life itself. I haven't been able to 'capture 'any of these experiences with more than a subtle sense of residue in my cellular memory. There may be many higher spaces to experience for the mystic explorers of life, bliss and love to discover.

RELATING DYNAMICS

Brother, Sister, Lover And Polyamory

"Once intercourse has happened there is no going back, brother-sister transforms to lovers and ex-lovers."
- From a former lover

I can personally recall each woman I've had sexual intercourse with as if there's a memory imprinted with the energy of those connections. I believe when we cross over to the realm of lovers, there's always a shift, not only on a physical and emotional level, but on a spiritual one too.

BROTHER, SISTER, LOVER

RELATING

BROTHER AND SISTER:

PLAY, INTIMACY, RECREATION, REJUVENATION, SEXUAL PLAY, SEXUAL ENERGY, GENITAL LEVEL, INNOCENT, SENSUALITY, CUDDLING, NO CLIMAX INTENTION, NO INTERCOURSE, NO EXCHANGE OF BODILY FLUIDS, STD FREE, BASED ON AGREEMENTS, WHO YOU WANT TO PLAY WITH, INDIVIDUAL CHOICE, GENDER FLUIDITY, INTERPERSONAL, TRANSPERSONAL, TRANSFORMATIVE, HEALING, INTIMATE RELATING

LOVERS:

SAME AS BROTHER AND SISTER INCLUDING INTERCOURSE AND EXCHANGE OF BODILY FLUIDS, MIGHT INCLUDE CLIMAX AND PROCREATION, MIGHT INCLUDE PARENTING, DEEP SPIRITUAL JOURNEY POSSIBLE, CONSCIOUS RELATING AND COMMITMENTS TO SELF AND OTHERS.

POLY OPEN, POLY SENSUAL, POLY SEXUAL:

BASED ON THE AGREEMENTS OF INDIVIDUAL LIMITS AND DESIRES, HONESTY AND TRANSPARENCY, DON'T JUST FUCK AND CLIMAX AROUND THE BROTHER AND SISTERHOOD, INCLUDE AND INTRODUCE A POTENTIONAL SEX PARTNER TO YOUR LOVER, IF YOU HAVE ONE, LET YOUR LOVERS FIND BROTHER / SISTERHOOD WITH THEM BEFORE YOU HAVE SEX

WWW.SOMATICCONSENT.COM

The brother-sister dynamic

The brother-sister dynamic involves intimacy with a recreational flavour. Fun and joy are experienced with or without sexual energy, but no bodily fluids are ever exchanged. When we engage with someone without intercourse it's within the realms of this brother-sister dynamic. There's an innocence similar to the relationship we had while hanging out with our siblings and friends when young. There is no intention to have intercourse or come to a climax. You probably have a similar memory to me, of playing doctor as a kid and it being innocent, clear and clean. The brother-sister dynamic is based on play, what both want, individual choices and intimate relating with clear communication of limits and agreements. It can be personal, interpersonal at the Apex, transpersonal, transformative and very healing.

Generally, through discussion and coming to agreements, we can be sure to know whether it really makes sense for us to go into the realm of lovers by making a decision with conscious awareness. When we learn to play in the context of the brother-sister dynamic and exclude intercourse and exchange of body fluids, we avoid unnecessary regret while opening up infinite possibilities of play and engagement.

When it comes to intimate relating and embodied empowerment, it's important to understand and come to agreements about which relating dynamic is happening. It's not necessary, for example, to be lovers to play The 3 Minute Game. You can play it with anyone. It doesn't have to be sexual or lead to sex. Even if sexual energy is involved within the brother-sister dynamic, a very clear distinction is made. You play with that energy, choosing to enjoy it as it is, without going further. You decide not to bite the apple.

The lover dynamic

The lover dynamic is exactly the same as the brother-sister dynamic but, of course, with the inclusion of intercourse and/or exchange of body fluids. It may include climax and procreation (having a family). Here, the Direct Route has to be fully embodied in order for us to be able to make fully informed choices. Solid agreements are made which respect boundaries and limits. Each person functions with radical responsibility for their actions. The interpersonal space at the Apex offers transformation of consciousness together.

Being lovers is a different spiritual journey to one within the brother-sister dynamic. Once you become lovers, it isn't possible to go back to the innocence of brother-sister. Even if a friendship continues, it's different to the one enjoyed before sex. In many cases, the whole relationship breaks down. As soon as you have intercourse with someone, it changes the dynamic of the relationship. It involves a change of commitment to self and the other person which often brings a deeper responsibility due to the possibility of having children.

Nowadays I very consciously choose who I have intercourse with and take a minimum of three months to be sure it's really appropriate. There is so much exploration and play possible with another person before shifting into the dynamic of lovers.

The polyamourous dynamic

How people form their personal relationships is an individual choice of course. There is no black and white, and it's entirely up to the individual to find what feels best for them through trial and error. Poly-open, poly-sensual and poly-sexual dynamics offer other levels of relating and can involve both the lover as well as the brother-sister dynamic.

To be clear, here, the definition of *polyamory* is not synonymous with 'poly-fucking'. There's nothing wrong or bad about the latter—it's just very limiting. When we have a relationship based on the *Four Layers of the SCES* (self-care, permission, agreements and being/giving yourself as a gift) it requires an investment of energy. As an analogy, imagine the energy you share as a laser beam. Are you capable of directing this laser beam of energy towards multiple people within the lover dynamic? Is it possible to divide it into a number of different streams while still remaining in integrity within the Engagement Zones? Are the others in relationship with you able to do that too? Are you really living in polyamory or is there a certain amount of 'poly-agony' involved? Only you and your partners can answer these questions.

> *"The root of suffering is attachment."*
> *– The Buddha*

Many drawn to polyamory believe it to be the practice of non-attachment—and this may, for some, be the case. The spiritual concept of non-attachment requires taking *high/radical responsibility*. When the concept gets confused, there's a risk that we shift into taking the responsibility of a child.

Non-attachment in a spiritual context means allowing things to be—as they are. This results in balance. It's about accepting the present moment. Of course it's fine to have goals, *as long as there is contentment within our present situation.*

According to the Buddha, attachment leads to suffering. It happens when we:

Run from potential pain
This could manifest as running from awkward, embarrassing or other emotionally painful situations, running from the personal responsibility for our actions, worrying about rejection / intimacy / the result of our actions, and

so on.

Grasp onto pleasure
This could manifest as 'I want it all my way'/ 'I'm never satisfied with what I have and always want more', for example running after multiple partners or concepts such as cohabitation or marriage, in order to quench our insecurity.

'Non-attachment' and 'detachment' are often confused.

Detachment within relationship is taking child's responsibility

Detachment is an uninvolved state, a lack of investment, an unfeeling withdrawal. When we're detached, we don't feel accountable. It includes manipulation of others in disregard of their boundaries. Detachment is clinging to our pursuit of personal pleasure in disregard to the agreements we've made with others.

Non-attachment in relationship is high/radical responsibility

Non-attachment is about letting go of the thoughts and emotions that create suffering. It isn't about running from awkward, embarrassing or other emotionally painful situations. It's the opposite of having a lack of responsibility for our actions. *Being able to do this requires taking immense responsibility for yourself.*

Non-attachment is releasing control on events and how things 'should' be and our tendency to want to control (by running away from pain—or grasping onto pleasure). We practise by allowing events to unfold while relating to ourselves and others honestly and authentically *in-the-moment*. We consider and respect what all want / don't want and make agreements, neither suppressing emotions nor fuelling low drama. When emotions and shadows come up, we face, own and integrate them. We allow pleasure and pain to arise, and let go when they dissolve.

Personally, although I have the right to have sex with whoever I want to (with consent and absolutely not at the professional level), I choose to be with one person in a committed 'container'. Within my personal relationship in the context of the *lover dynamic* I'm also committed to staying open to knowing how I feel in the moment, which means I'm capable of being in love with more than one person. By 'staying open' I mean I'm aware of what I feel and own these feelings. The feeling of 'being in love with more than one person' can be a confusing concept. Rather than being polyamorous in my sexual life, for me, it's more of a realisation that I *am love* and therefore able to feel love for many.

In my private life and professionally, due to the nature of my work within the fields of sacred sexuality and tantra, I also engage with many others on a poly-sensual level within the boundaries of a clear brother-sister dynamic.

If polyamory appeals to you and you want to stay in integrity within the agreements made with your partner (while avoiding 'poly-agony'), transparency is vital. High and Radical Responsibility never involves sneaking around, hiding, withdrawing without clear communication or lying. Polyamorous relationships require a *very high level* of conscious engagement, which means that your own feelings and those of your partner have to be explored together *before* your relational dynamics with a new person changes from brother-sister—to lover.

If you have a regular partner and you're both open to introducing a new person into your relationship, honest communication includes everything that is real and true for both you, your partner and the new person.

Depending on the dynamics, it's necessary to check out whether it is possible for your partner to form either a brother-sister or a lover relationship with the new person. If you and the new person want to form a sensual/sexual connection which excludes your present partner, in order for your partner to feel safe, the ability to form a brother-sister dynamic is vital. Within polyamory, the intention of the new connection is to deepen the existing relationship—not to weaken it.

As mentioned earlier, a huge factor which is rarely understood or acknowledged is that women's bodies need to feel safe in order for their nervous systems to allow the state of surrender.

PROCREATION

Goal-Driven Sexual Agenda

"Once you realise that the road is the goal and that you are always on the road, not to reach a goal, but to enjoy its beauty and its wisdom, life ceases to be a task and becomes natural and simple, in itself an ecstasy."
- Sri Nisargadatta Maharaj

The hormone cocktail of reproductive oriented sex

When touch and encounter begins, oxytocin increases. Then comes dopamine, which signifies the wildness or horniness of sexual arousal. Serotonin is then released, which brings with it the feeling of pleasure and expansion.[54] At the moment of climax, contraction occurs within both the brain and the genital area. At this point, serotonin begins to drop, and prolactin is released. This is the hormone responsible for the sleepy feeling after orgasm. Post orgasm, all these hormones drop and stop being released, which create new neurological shifts in stages as the oxytocin, responsible for connection and intimacy, shuts off. When people have a goal-driven sex life, they experience a constant imbalance of the release of hormones oxytocin, dopamine, serotonin and prolactin. The 'hangover 'effect caused by the drop in these hormone levels can last between two hours and up to seven days.[55]

As long as people are stuck in this goal-driven state of mind, they'll have trouble finding the inflow of the somatic nervous system. This is because your nervous system needs to pick up signals from your skin during slow touch. If you can't relax into the now and be slow, tuned in and present—if you are instead, focused on getting to the goal or whatever it takes to get there—you'll experience an inability to feel deeply.

This creates a repetitive loop of disconnection that many are unaware of.

Ninety percent of couples fall into this category.

Please keep in mind that whenever differentiating between gender I refer to how a person's body, especially the nervous system initially developed and is still wired and not to gender identity.

PROCREATION

THE BODY'S CHEMICAL COCKTAIL OF CLIMAXING AND PEAK ORGASM

SEXUAL AROUSAL

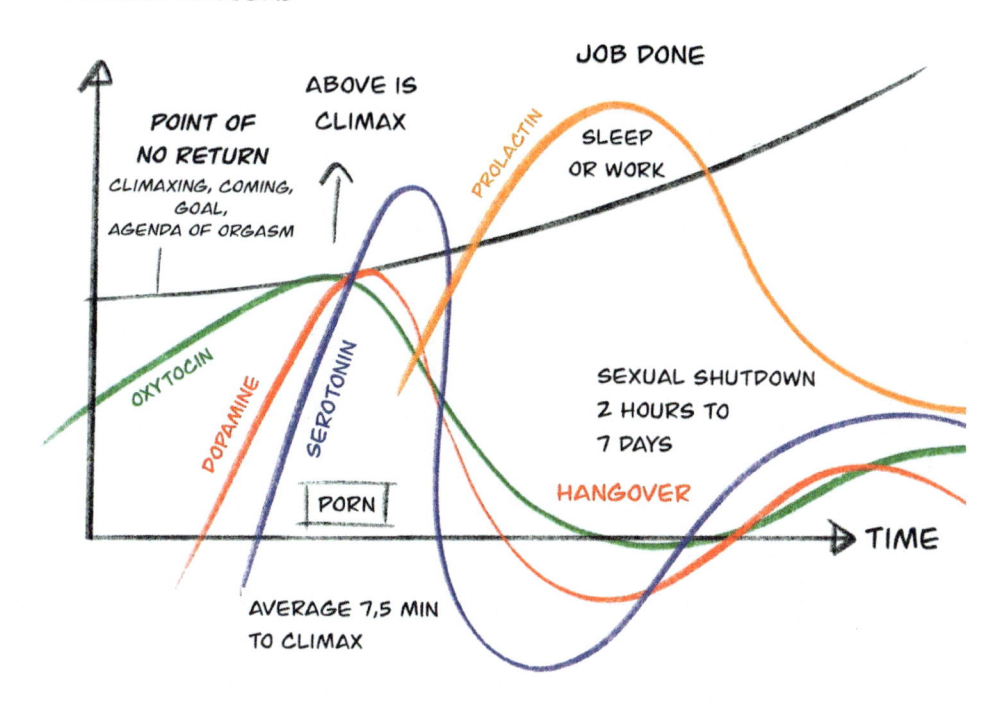

POINT OF NO RETURN
CLIMAXING, COMING, GOAL, AGENDA OF ORGASM

ABOVE IS CLIMAX

JOB DONE

PROLACTIN

SLEEP OR WORK

OXYTOCIN

DOPAMINE

SEROTONIN

PORN

SEXUAL SHUTDOWN 2 HOURS TO 7 DAYS

HANGOVER

TIME

AVERAGE 7,5 MIN TO CLIMAX

WWW.SOMATICCONSENT.COM

The Procreation Map is based on a graph by Marnia Robinson and Gary Wilson, who did much research into hormone and neurotransmitter levels during different sexual and sensual states.[56]

Women are more profoundly wired

Let's take a deeper look at how men's and women's nervous systems are differently wired. Whether you are in a man's or woman's body crucially affects your experience of life. If we look at the tenth week of gestation, we're still cellularly very alike—with one exception. This is the point when a foetus develops into a male or female body. And at this point, the social engagement system and the dorsal vagus nerve wires differently, depending on whether their genitals are inside or outside the body.

In a female body, the dorsal vagus nerve is *directly connected* to the uterus, specifically to the cervix. It remains dormant until activated. During his research on pain with paraplegic women, neuroscientist Barry R. Komisaruk and his colleagues used functional magnetic resonance imaging (fMRI) to determine how genital sensation was signalled to the brain in women without an intact spinal cord.[57] Imaging revealed that when internally penetrated, an alternative pathway was activated through the vagus nerve which led to orgasm. The female body, therefore, through this different 'wiring' has a deeper capacity for spiritual transformation than that of a man's due to the state of surrender the dorsal vagus induces.

In relation to intercourse and penis/cervical touch, *due to vagus nerve wiring*, it is much more vulnerable and dangerous to be in a female than a male body —and for this reason, the uterus is much more finely tuned. This fine-tuning detects cues as to whether the person you want to have intercourse with is safe or not. If her body isn't safe, it says "no". Even when her mind says "yes", if the body says "no", the experience will not be optimal.

When it comes to sexual encounter, it is crucially important for women to feel connected and safe in order to have the capacity of being open and receptive. During intercourse, a woman's body is extremely vulnerable, because neurologically, her body is in a place of immobilisation where any danger or threat would put her at risk.

On the other hand, most men are sexually 'wired' such that their sexual encounters are driven by the urge to spread their sperm and fertilise as widely as possible, which is exactly what the procreative peak orgasm is about. Men are hard-wired at the cellular level to 'get the job done' as soon as possible, which is actually on a world average, only 7.5 minutes. Therefore, when his sense of sexuality is based on the agenda or goal of a climax, the capacity for spiritual transformation during sex (which comes about through allowing being/is-ness to occur moment-to-moment) is extremely limited.

Of course, some men have more stamina than others, but the goal of climax is programmed at a cognitive level through porn, social conditioning and past experience. When a man's sexuality is based on seeing pleasure as foreplay, with the purpose of getting turned on enough to have sex—which leads to the goal of climax as soon as possible—deeper connection or transformation isn't possible. In his research, Garry Wilson talks of the release of an enzyme called 'deltaFosB' that programs the reward centre into a pathway of 'sexual habit' that runs like a highway, so that once established, sex starts with arousal and ends with a climax—and it's fast.[58,59]

Specifically, because a woman's body is neurologically wired for infinite expansion and multi-orgasmic realisation, if anyone touches her, sensually or sexually with the agenda of this orgasm goal, it will be, neurologically, a completely different and limited experience. Because our entire society is so male dominated, goal orientated and indoctrinated that we have to get the results, otherwise there won't be any benefit, women too are conditioned by society in the same way—to aim for climax/peak orgasm.[60,61]

Have you heard about relaxed arousal?

Relaxed arousal is the blissful state that's possible to us all when we slow down, stop performing and focus on our own body's sensations as we touch another person. Everything becomes play. When we think of foreplay, we presume that the main thing comes later. It doesn't have to be like this. When we initiate touch with a curious, non-goal driven attitude, we can reach an orgasmic state in which we experience a high level of arousal and pleasure without climax.

What's going on inside our bodies during relaxed arousal?

When we maintain this state, the brain releases a delicious cocktail of neurochemicals and hormones which stay in the body, regenerate cellular structure and re-establish neurological balance. What's also possible is the release of DMT, a naturally occurring compound which mimics the chemical structure of serotonin. Also known as the 'spirit molecule', DMT has the potential to bring us into a blissful state of expanded connection with Source Consciousness. Imagine sharing this experience of oneness together with your lover.

Staying in this state requires self-restraint because it invites a fundamental shift in our perception of experiencing pleasure through climax. However, you've already started the necessary foundations by waking up your hands and being present to your own somatic experience, and so, I'm confident that what took me around 10 years to learn can be accessible to you in a few months.

After my tantric awakening I realised that during my 'age of ejaculation 'as a teenager, I'd trained my brain's reward system into orgasmic addiction. I was so hooked back then that I made sure I got my 'shot 'as quickly and often as possible. Infused by porn and other teenage friend's opinions, my understanding about sex was very limited to the agenda of climaxing. I often suffered a post orgasmic hangover due to the release of prolactin and remedied this low feeling by masturbating again and again to keep my system filled with my 'drug of choice'.

I remember being in bed with the flu when I was 14 and feeling pretty terrible. The arousal during masturbation made me feel better. And the hormone cocktail released at climax felt great. After my little shot, I felt really sick again. Back then I didn't realise how rejuvenating sexual energy is when kept within your system and its correlation to health, energy and well-being.

Doing this not only created an orgasmic reward circuit but trained my body into premature ejaculation before I was an adult. I remember masturbating a few hours before having sex with my first girlfriend, so that I'd have the stamina to perform longer than a few minutes. Performance is the key word here. Sex was disconnected and lacked feeling.

Barry Long talks about this in his book, *Making Love: Sexual Love the Divine Way,* about how we create separation between one another during goal-oriented sex and create connection when engaging in non-goal driven lovemaking.[62]

I'm happy I got to connect with my early lovers with some hours of cuddling and connection, but I'm not sure anymore whether that was possible because I'd already had my climax 'fix'.

Earlier in the book I shared the story about 'the beginning of the end 'of my 'I'-dentity, when I had a breakdown, collapsed, desperately crying until only two concepts remained in my consciousness—Love and Tantra. This experience marked my quest to change everything about how I related sexually and spiritually with myself and the Divine within all of us. This was the beginning of my tantric awakening and journey beyond known concepts of relationships, romance and eros—to *become love and life*, speaking truth from the place of *being love*.

Learning the tool of sublimating (redirecting sexual energy) took around 10 years with little success at first. At the beginning I tried clenching and kegels to bring awareness to the urethral sphincter, pelvic floor muscles and anus in order to control ejaculation. I later learned that clenching muscles to control orgasm is an oxymoron. The peak climax is a neurological contraction. Trying to control contraction with contraction will cause the contraction you are trying to control. I then learned the relaxed arousal and expansion approach in under a year along with experiencing trauma awareness, de-armouring and further embodiment.

Contraction of muscles is a neurological response to avoid feeling. Controlling ejaculation by tightening muscles through contraction does not allow the muscle tissue to be receptive to feelings/sensations or conductive of energy. De-armouring, on the other hand, releases the contraction patterns held within the muscle and allows people to relax and come back into feeling. During relaxed arousal we stay in the realm of feelings, feeling the inflow while being connected to the oxytocin pathways of expansion.

I'm sharing this because I believe if I'd known all this and embodied the Direct Route as a teenager, life could have been easier and transformative earlier. It would have been like striking gold in personal development. I see so much repetition of what I went through and worse these days. Youths are hooked and conditioned into procreative climaxing even before they've kissed someone, not to mention the lack of education and acceptance to reassure kids that it's good to feel themselves for the sake of intimate self-connection without being sexual.

RELAXED AND TRANSFORMATIVE SEXUALITY

Being On The Edge And Becoming Orgasmic

"Being on the edge isn't as safe, but the view is better."
- Ricky Gervais

You can compare sex without a goal to playing music or dancing. When playing music, it's about the moment, wouldn't you agree? You play music to enjoy it—as it unfolds. You dance to the rhythm of the music, feeling your body in motion. You don't play music or dance to aim for the end of the song or to reach a particular point in the room.

The Being on the Edge Map shows what becomes possible when we tune into the somatic experience and energy within our bodies during *relaxed arousal*. As we play and enjoy without aiming for the goal of climax, we are able to relax into the is-ness of our being state within timeless moments.

The key to relaxed arousal is a constant flow of oxytocin.

Oxytocin is the *foundation of connection*, just as the Direct Route is the *foundation of the somatic system*.

BEING ON THE EDGE (NO CLIMAX) BECOMING ORGASMIC

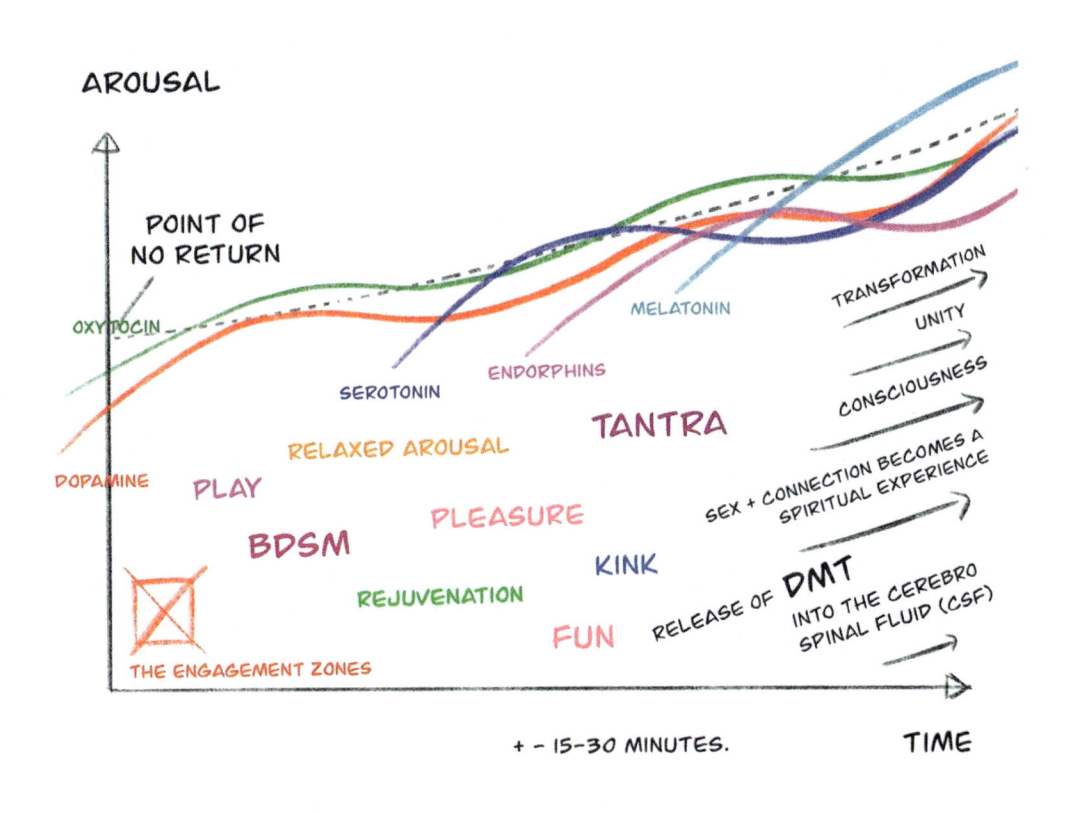

AROUSAL

POINT OF NO RETURN

OXYTOCIN

MELATONIN

SEROTONIN

ENDORPHINS

DOPAMINE

TANTRA

PLAY

RELAXED AROUSAL

BDSM

PLEASURE

KINK

REJUVENATION

FUN

TRANSFORMATION →
UNITY →
CONSCIOUSNESS →
SEX + CONNECTION BECOMES A SPIRITUAL EXPERIENCE →
RELEASE OF **DMT** INTO THE CEREBRO SPINAL FLUID (CSF) →

⊠ THE ENGAGEMENT ZONES

+ − 15-30 MINUTES.   **TIME**

WWW.SOMATICCONSENT.COM

Most of us think that, when it comes to sex, we have *to do* so much. Many go through the motions of 'getting the other turned on 'as if pushing buttons on a machine. Others focus on fetish-action to get themselves and their partner going. Here there is no relaxed arousal and instead, something I call 'empty yang'—techniques we use if we're not able to feel very deeply. It burns out fast like a bushfire without kindling. Here, we focus on performance, on sexual stimuli and pretending.

When it comes to a spiritual approach, we embody sexuality as a resource for connection and feeling each other. We stay aware of our sexual energy, dancing with it, instead of focusing on increasing stimulation with the goal of climax.

The action of the sympathetic nervous system is dopamine-driven and based on reward. To get turned on, you need to have dopamine in your system. Without it, your reward system isn't active. Dopamine is an important part of the feeling, 'I want to stay here as long as possible because it feels really good, exciting and enjoyable'. Dopamine doesn't, however, build the height of arousal. It's a vital part of arousal—but it doesn't run the show. We don't climax because we need a dopamine rush.

The Being on the Edge Map shows the level of arousal your body can handle before climax. When arousal becomes too high, you reach the *point of no return..* This exists within everybody's nervous system. To maintain relaxed arousal at this point, we have to slow down. When you slow down, a healthy, steady level of connection through oxytocin, arousal through dopamine and pleasurable expansion through serotonin **remain continuous**. I call this experience 'surfing orgasmic waves'.

Having awareness around the *point of no return* state allows us to slow down when we notice the build-up to orgasm—and to relax once more into the connected state of is-ness.
Tantric practices are based on this level of relaxation, bringing presence and awareness into this connection as we weave a blissful relationship.

Relaxed arousal has a sweetness of its own. You don't have to bring it to completion. Even at the point of near climax, you can choose not to go there because what you're experiencing in being relaxed and aroused is already amazing. When sexual energy occurs, there is no reason to be compelled into action. During *relaxed arousal*, it *isn't necessary* to get anywhere. It's just a feeling of 'we are safe here, connected, feeling each other, with no agenda, no duration, target or goal'. It's a state of *being desireless at the peak of desire.* This is an experience of interconnection with another at the Apex and exactly why the Somatic Consent Engagement System, which leads you to this place, is a map for exquisite transformation.

Men's bodies are usually in the sympathetic mobilisation state during sexual activity. When action is stopped, (so as not to go beyond the point of no return), the nervous system either goes back into the *social engagement* state through interaction such as talking—or into the safe dorsal vagal parasympathetic state of *immobilisation*. During this time, because each person is aware of the subtle inflow of sensation, micro movements in both partners keep the penis erect.

Most people find it difficult to enter a state of relaxed arousal due to carrying tension in their body which tightens and contracts the muscles. In the presence of tension, sexual energy gets stuck and can't conduct. Bodywork and de-armouring can help to release that tension so that contraction is reduced and conduction of energy is possible.

At the beginning, when men stop ejaculating, most find they go through a period of 'blue ball syndrome', a slang expression for *epididymal hypertension* which refers to aching or painful testicles. This happens because, over decades, most have trained their bodies to release semen through ejaculation and orgasm. As a result, the lymphatic system in the genital area is incapable of reabsorbing the sexual fluids back into the body (needed for the DMT cocktail described below). I have helped many to remedy this with de-armouring methods I personally developed through self-exploration.

Women too have similar difficulties in accessing relaxed arousal, knowing orgasm only through high-speed rubbing or vibrator stimulation and having learned (both during sex and as a 'sleeping pill') to squeeze their vaginal and pelvic muscles to cause tension for clitoral orgasm. This, of course, leads to the reward of a hormone cocktail as well as a release of body tension at climax.

This is known as a *contractive climax* and is very different from relaxed *orgasmic* arousal. The first centres on the agenda of climaxing, which is rapidly over. The latter is an experience of *being orgasmic* without an urge to reach a 'peak'—because you are already and continuously *in an orgasmic state*.

Relaxed arousal is possible when the dependency on contractive climax is overcome. This can require a physical sexual detox from three weeks to three months. De-armouring can also be very supportive as well as becoming more present and embodied by activating the sensory inflow of external stimuli.

In the presence of oxytocin, you remain feeling safe, connected, aroused and relaxed—together. Then everything is possible. It doesn't matter what you do, including BDSM or kink play. Within tantra, kink, BDSM or any other kind of play, when both partners are responsible for themselves (the Base), when somatic, sensory inflow is open and both can meet without the agenda of a goal, sensuality and sexuality becomes incredibly delicious. At this interpersonal state at the Apex, both enjoy each other as 'a gift'.

When we utilise the Engagement Zones, we say what we really want. To know what we want while engaging in transformative sexuality—the deeper questions to ask yourself are:

1. Does the desire to climax come from a conditioned agenda—from the imprint of the procreative, addictive, gratification of climax and ejaculation?
2. Can I get over the conditioning of this obsession with the goal?
3. Can I be aware of using sexual energy as a transformative dynamic to take me into the spiritual realm of interconnected consciousness?

When the Engagement Zones are fully embodied during sexual engagement and *the point of no return* maintained, a neurological cocktail of hormones which include endorphins and melatonin are present. When we continue to play within this realm for 15 - 30 minutes, micro doses of DMT are released into the cerebral spinal fluid from the pineal gland. In the presence of DMT, *transformative experience always occurs*. Here we perceive reality in a very different way—as we connect with the essence of our very nature.

Is climaxing bad?

Climaxing has nothing to do with right or wrong. While I'm 'addicted 'to edging, others may be 'addicted 'to climaxing.

Right or wrong, good or bad, the best or worst way of doing anything—are oversimplified principles of duality. Sometimes people feel offended by the emphasis on sex without agenda. Angry feelings of protection, defence or 'goal guilt' may arise.

If you feel similar, I invite you to look a level deeper into the powerful pull towards unconscious attachments. Climaxing is a reproductive feature of nature. Its function enables our species to survive. Climax gives us a huge reward. That's why it feels so good.

Climaxing is the fundamental root function of any drive towards the bliss of feeling connected—to self—to others—to the world. This is what all addictions aim to provide. Any addiction is a substitution of this primary drive, to the feelings climax gives.

The Solution is not sobriety, the solution is: *Connection Based Bonding.*

When you practice Somatic Consent's core exercise of Waking Up The Hands, you open up your sensory inflow while in action. Here you connect much deeper to yourself and the possibility to feel intimate and make love without a goal becomes natural again.

There is no need to think about concepts and whether they're right or wrong. You have your own experience of being complete in the here and now.

The unconscious pull towards climax—evaporates.

Here there is no duality.

There is no goal.

Only the exquisite experience of bliss and connection.

It's up to you whether experimenting with edging is worthy of this deeper experience.

CEREBROSPINAL FLUID AND THE APPEARANCE OF "I AM"

"Fluids come together and the 'I Am' appears."
- Nisargadatta Maharaj

Sri Nisargadatta Maharaj was an awakened guru of non-dualistic philosophy called Advaita Vedanta. By awakened I mean he had a 'complete experience' of what he taught.

He said;

"In order to find out who you are, you must first find out who you are not."
"Everything you think you are, you are NOT."
"There is only one substance".[63]

What does that mean?
He described the possible perception of 'I AM 'in two ways;

1) Through your intellect, which happens when you attach your identity to thoughts, i.e., whatever your mind identifies yourself with, such as, "I AM good, a giver, a receiver, intelligent, excited, impatient, not (...) enough" and so on.

   Here you perceive I AM as your 'intellect-body'. You have a separate sense of self, with your own individual consciousness—external from Source Consciousness. By identifying with thoughts (which are only 'perceived reflections 'of Source Consciousness) a veil is created by the ego-mind ('I') which obscures the pure 'no subject-object 'of your true connected essence.

2) Through your experience of 'being 'as *you are in essence*. Here you don't identify with any thought. You just are. With the experience

of pure be-ing or is-ness at the Apex 'you 'recognise that the I AM of your body, is a *condensed* (material/solid) form of Source Consciousness, and therefore both a container of Source Consciousness AND a part of it. This second perception is referred to in ancient texts as, "I AM THAT". It is the experience of interconnected, interpersonal and transpersonal love and bliss.

Cerebrospinal fluid (CSF) has been known for thousands of years in Eastern traditions as a gateway for transformation. It is understood to be a conductor of Source Consciousness. Through it, we can become aware of our true nature (I am that).[64]

Yoga, Tantra, the Kabbalah and Taoism each describe a psycho/sexual/spiritual energy called Prana, Kundalini, Chi and Shekinah respectively, which travels through the centre of the brain at the third and fourth ventricles and the central canal of the spinal cord (known as the *Sushumna nadi* in Sanskrit).

Many age-old traditions believed CSF to be part of the 'step-down 'process of condensing from Source Consciousness to physical form (described in the quote above, "Fluids come together and the 'I am 'appears"). This process was thought to begin in the pineal gland.[64] The pineal gland helps regulate many of the body's systems and natural cycles. It is sensitive to electromagnetic forces and contains the same cells as eye retinas, which respond to light.[65]

The pineal gland participates in the circulation of CSF.[64] It is located at the third ventricle, a chamber filled with this fluid. In ancient texts, this place is referred to as, 'The Crystal Palace 'and 'The Cave of Brahma. '(Brahma being one of the names of 'God/Source Consciousness'). Most esoteric spiritual practices now refer to this place as the seat of the third eye which represents inner insight.

Stem cells, characterised by self-renewal and ability to become any cell within an organism, are responsible for healing and rejuvenation within the body. Cerebrospinal fluid regulates the production and migration of these cells.[66] CSF is also home to many neurotransmitters providing an elaborate range of biological functions.

Adults produce around 500ml of CSF daily. It bathes the entire inner and outer surface of the brain and spinal cord. From here, at the back of the third ventricle, it coagulates into a thread-like structure known as *Reissner's fiber*. This hollow fibre extends the entire length of the spinal cord's central canal.

Lawrence Wile M.D., author of, *Reissner's Fiber and the Neurobiology of Mysticism*,[67] writes about Reissnner's fiber as a basis for scientific investigation into mystical experience, stating that this little-known structure in the centre of the spinal cord, is identical with the anatomical entity described as the *Sushumna nadi* by Kundalini yoga. His research focuses on the parallels between expanded states of consciousness and modern physics which he hopes will, "reconnect us to our inner-directed feedback systems" so that we can "take the last steps toward realizing the mystical quest for meaning, love and truth, illuminated by the light of science".

We generally tend to think we have five senses. Wile states that neurobiological features of Reissner's fiber suggest it can function as a central sense organ. The fiber is a highly specialised conduction path with a similar gel-like membrane to that of the inner ear. Just as hair vibrations transmit signals to the auditory nerve to produce sound, similarly the vibrations of the cilia that touch Reissner's fiber transmit signals to the CSF, contacting neurons to produce inner sensory experiences.

Theos Bernard, one of the first westerners to be initiated into tantric yoga practices by the highest lama in Tibet, wrote in 1940 about the inner conduction of conscious energy. In his memoir, *Heaven Lies Within Us*, he wrote, "Inside this central (Sushumna) nadi, the Yogi identifies an invisible nadi known in the West as the fibre of Reissner, but which is known here as *Chittra* (the Heavenly Passage)."[68]

Relaxed arousal and DMT

DMT is present in large concentrations during birth and death to ease these potentially traumatic experiences. At birth, it enables us to transition out of the uterus—and at death, out of life.[69] DMT-containing plants are commonly used in indigenous shamanic practices. It is one of the main active ingredients of the ceremonial drink, *ayahuasca*. Those who take part in these ceremonies report feeling a sense of timelessness and 'ego-death 'as the 'I 'ceases to exist through their experience of oneness with the entirety of existence.

There is a growing consensus among contemporary researchers that traditional spiritual practices can enable people to experience this state naturally due to the DMT present within CSF. Rix Strassman, *DMT the Spiritual Molecule,* reports on experiments with people who took DMT and the transformational experiences they had. He quotes that people practising tantra get the closest to this transformation.[70]

Tantra and other ancient traditions that focus on raising consciousness, talk of a 'by-product 'of this experience. When we experience ourselves as Source Consciousness, special 'powers 'known as *Siddis* become accessible to us. These powers aren't special, however. They are natural states of being that usually evade us, due to our conditioned, preoccupied, distracted and analytical minds. Telepathy or 'being able to read people 'is one of these abilities or 'powers', not because you are able to read their minds, but because within this experience there is no distinction between your consciousness and theirs. When you are aware of 'being 'Source Consciousness—you *share* it.

This can be observed during professional sessions utilising a tantric approach. Some practitioners who have already had the experience, focus purely on activating kundalini (vital spiritual energy) within other people. These practitioners maintain a connection to Source Consciousness and have cultivated their own energy systems for years. When laying hands on someone's body, the kundalini release within the other's nervous system clearly increases.

I've encountered many of these experiences personally and call it 'the liquid light'. I've also experienced it many times during sexual edging sessions where the intention and approach was to raise sexual energy for transformational purposes. Many other practitioners I know working in the field of transformative sexuality have shared similar experiences with clients. There is a high state of physical sexual arousal with a level of involuntary shaking similar to TRE, except with an expanding sense of safety and joy.

When you bathe in your essential self (I am that), you feel energised. Your nervous system isn't dependent on survival strategies. The need to hold onto pleasure due to a fear of loss is obsolete and you don't function through other people's needs. It's a phenomenal awakening.

These findings relate to the Being on the Edge Map and transformative sexuality—which show how to consciously direct energy within the body to move away from procreative, goal-driven sex. Here you surrender to a power greater than yourself. Perceived boundaries between the individual 'I' and others dissolve—resulting in the being/bliss states of interpersonal and transpersonal connection.

The ascending and descending dynamics of spiritual experience

The state of transcendental oneness has been written about for centuries in one form or another depending on the culture. However, after observing that many people found it difficult to grasp and embody, I began to focus my personal and professional work on understanding; how neurological processes work, how emotions work, how we engage, how we create connection, what connection is actually about, what oxytocin is for and how the nervous system is wired. My big picture vision was to create a clear method of relating which takes place in a field' *in between*' where individual people fully meet and experience transformation together. The result was the Engagement Zones—which shows how to engage with each other authentically, providing a map to the Apex of interpersonal merging.

Because of the different ways male and female bodies are wired, there are different dynamics at play that lead to spiritual awakening and merging as one. I call them *ascending* and *descending*. As mentioned earlier, and generally speaking, we all have a little of both ascending and descending within us, though women often seem to go from spirit to sex, from an ascended space—and *descend* into their bodies—whereas men usually go from sex to spirit, from being embodied and *ascending* towards the spiritual space.

Female bodies can only go into the realm of unity (with the phallus inside) while feeling fully in connection, open hearted, safe, supported and held by their partner. In his book, The Polyvagal Theory, Porges talks about nervous system immobilisation and the female capacity to surrender in sexual activity.[72]

The Polyvagal Theory explains two types of immobilisation: one triggered by fear (the shutdown state) and the other triggered by connection and love (the immobilisation of surrender). Mammals need to *feel safe* in order to digest food efficiently, to sleep and to mate. In humans, Porges' research points to oxytocin modifying the function of the dorsal vagus nerve, so that the immobilisation state induced by loving connection occurs—rather than the shutdown state triggered by fear.

For women, intercourse, being entered and the internalisation of sexual energy connects to many factors. In order for a woman to be truly ready for intercourse—to be receptive, open and able to surrender—she has to feel safe enough to be able to relax her body. For her to feel safe and to relax enough, she must be in a place of trust and connection by bonding with her partner each time before penetration happens. As you can see, there is a neurological and emotional component to this activation.

When this is the case, penetration triggers vagus connection to the uterus —initiating the surrender state—opening the realm of transcendental oneness.

The nervous system wired within a male body, however, seems to enter the realm of oneness by going beyond mere sensation and movement in the sympathetic mobilisation state. This happens by slowing down to activate the ventral vagus parasympathetic branch, to establish connection and safety with a partner (social engagement). Then learning to be without a goal—remaining on the edge, 'surfing' the cocktail of hormones (which produce a continuous orgasmic wave). This triggers the dorsal vagal state of surrender, opening up the transcendental realm of connection/oneness.

We cannot stay in this transcendental realm permanently. To function as human beings, we must be grounded in our bodies. Focusing only on the *ascending* quality isn't realistic—we become ungrounded and easily scared of our shadows, falling into the trap of spiritual bypassing. Only focusing on the *descending* quality would be like restricting ourselves to digging in the mud of existence and survival. Life is hard without love and the experience of spiritual truths radiating light in the darkness.

The somatic experience of the Direct Route in connection with the Indirect route is a vital part of being able to relate with awareness, insight and authenticity. Much of my work is now based on teaching singles, couples and practitioners about this process: when goal orientated sex is dropped and the neuro-physiological cocktail created by the body is combined with healthy sensuality and sexuality—transformation occurs.

Overview of nervous system states in female and male bodies during arousal and intercourse

A woman's experience during intercourse depends on which nervous system state is active.

Female parasympathetic social engagement (ventral vagus)
Connection and bonding through gentle touch (release of oxytocin) communication and eye contact is essential to form trust and safety so that dorsal vagus activation of the safe side of immobilisation and surrender occurs.

Female sympathetic mobilisation (*splanchnic nerves)
When a woman puts herself first (while respecting the limits of the other) it's possible to go fully into sexual action for herself.

Female sympathetic fight or flight (*splanchnic nerves)
When a woman allows intercourse to take place due to a sense of duty, inability to change the situation or say no, or due to fear, past trauma, habit or abuse, her nervous system will be somewhere on the unsafe side including *shutdown*. Fight mode during sex can manifest as performing/acting and/or channelling anger through dominance, pushing around, showing who's boss and so on.

Female parasympathetic shutdown (dorsal vagus)

If a woman feels unsafe, whether that's due to lack of bonding, a habit of going along with unwanted touch, fear of pain, abuse, actual abuse/rape or past trauma, her body can enter the state of *shutdown* in order to reserve energy and decrease sensory stimuli and pain—which increase chances of surviving the incident. When in this state, no logical decision making is possible, unless trained in self-regulation.

Female parasympathetic immobilisation (dorsal vagus)

When ventral vagus activation through *social engagement* occurs, a woman can form a connection with her partner which enables a feeling of safety. Penetration can then lead to dorsal vagal activation and immobilisation. Here, choices and decisions remain possible and total relaxation leads to surrender into the bliss state. This is a very rare state for most. If the dorsal vagal parasympathetic nervous system of *safe immobilisation* doesn't occur for a woman through social engagement, then trust, relaxation and surrender won't happen either.

Male parasympathetic social engagement (ventral vagus)

When a man embodies his Direct Route of pleasure, he is present and connected to himself in-the-moment. He is then more able to connect and bond to his partner emotionally. Intimacy and slowing down increases the chance of edging to happen which opens the realm to spiritual interpersonal connection.

Male sympathetic mobilisation (*splanchnic nerves)

When in *sympathetic mobilisation*, a male body is geared towards procreative, goal-oriented sex, control and power over. Sympathetic tone is necessary, though in the absence of awareness, the limbic system dominates his experience. The key for a deeper experience is to access the limbic system (feelings) and not to get lost in an agenda (procreational climax).

Male sympathetic fight or flight (*splanchnic nerves) or parasympathetic shutdown (dorsal vagus)

In instances of rape a man's nervous system will, of course, also be either in sympathetic *fight or flight* or parasympathetic dorsal vagus *shutdown*.

Male parasympathetic Immobilisation (dorsal vagus)

While a female body's parasympathetic dorsal vagus nerve is activated during intercourse, if a male body doesn't have access to the full potential of the Direct Route (including their genitals and any feelings (stimulated through sensory experience in the moment), relaxed arousal doesn't happen. Sexual turn on is then limited to sympathetic nervous system action, control and power over. With embodiment of the Direct Route, a man is aware of sensations in-the-moment and is able to remain on the edge in relaxed arousal and experience the bliss state of dorsal vagal *immobilisation*.

*Sympathetic activation is regulated by cardiopulmonary, thoracic, lumbar and sacral splanchnic nerves.

◆ ◆ ◆

During workshops consisting of 6-7 day journeys, (where working with highly transformative energies is part of the agreement at the beginning), the participants also agree that they will have no peak orgasm experiences. Sexual tension is allowed to increase, so that after 5-7 days, the participants feel a transformation that they often claim they've never experienced before.

They then go back to their daily lives. As a result of going back to their usual habits, they reported that their frequency lowered. It isn't usual to function in our conditioned society on a higher vibration. The question is; how can you remain 'as high as a kite 'and simultaneously remain grounded? How can you live fully within your body and also remain fully switched on at this transformative level? How can you get on with your daily life while being tuned into Source Consciousness—connected to everything and everybody in oneness?

I and others have experienced this phenomenon by practising boundaries and limits, communicating our "no" and asking for what we desire, by giving permission and creating agreements based on authentic needs, by respecting limits—and by being aware when ourselves or others operate from the shadow parts of personality.

In the environment this creates, we can find bliss, as we finally understand the cosmic joke that life—just 'is'.

CHAPTER 5

TRANSFORMATIONAL LEADERSHIP AND FACILITATION

Being The Gift

*"Leaders become great, not because of their power,
but because of their ability to empower others."*
- John C. Maxwell

Facilitation literally means to make something easy. Our job as facilitators is to make it easy for people to have the experience they choose to have, as well as make certain experiences more accessible to them. Facilitation is not therapy. As a facilitator, we don't have to get to the bottom of everyone's issues or to protect clients from any unpleasant feelings that may come up during a session or workshop. However, it is our responsibility to show respect, care and a willingness to be there with them.

Activity and experience

It's helpful to distinguish the difference between activity and experience. As facilitators, we guide an activity. How the participant feels it, integrates it and digests it, happens in their inner world and is up to them.

Though we are not responsible for someone else's inner experience, there is much we can do to encourage and support them—so that they are able to have the experience that is most helpful *for them*. Our job as facilitators is to guide activities and respond to the needs of the participants so that their inner experience becomes more easily accessible.

TRANSFORMATIONAL HANDS-ON WORK

"We are our choices."
- Jean-Paul Sartre

I feel blessed to do transformational hands-on work. I feel honoured when someone asks for help from a place of pain or numbness and puts their trust in me., I feel humbled each time I see their empowerment switching on, when they open up in vulnerability and I see the *pull* for change.

I've learned from the best teachers a man can have—women. They were midwives, medical doctors, therapists and lovers. After being a 'tantric lover' for many years, I thought I had a pretty good idea about what I was doing, until the day my lover told me I didn't have a clue. I thought I was doing what she wanted. I remember my insecurity and feelings of inadequacy. She was a sexologist and very experienced in yoni mapping, de-armouring, g-spot massage, orgasmic meditation and sexual pleasure massages. She knew her body.

Long before I'd heard about somatic work in relation to consent, I was blessed to learn from her by following her instructions into her sexual, physical and emotional landscape. I'd already studied many modalities and had much insight into embodiment, anatomy and sexuality—but this was the true initiation to my journey as a sexual bodyworker and practitioner.

For many years, my practice had been very treatment oriented. It was based on one-way touch where I, as the practitioner, had to know what to do and how to do it. I read cues and followed my intuition through empathically feeling into the receiver's expression. Over time I'd begun to receive positive feedback from clients about the presence they felt in my hands and the pleasure they received through my touch. Results seemed good as clients reported having new experiences of embodiment, pleasure and sexual activation.

At this point I only knew the basics about the power and anatomy of presence in regard to the nervous system, trauma and retriggering the trauma of sexual abuse. I presumed I'd become a master bodywork healer through the use of intuition—until I came across the somatic power of consent and learned the **real deal**.

> *True empowerment comes through making choices*
> *based on safety and connection.*

The first time I was asked how I wanted to be touched during a session was while lying on the table at an erotic massage training. I expected the practitioner to know, to read my mind, to feel intuitively into me and just do what my body needed and wanted. Instead, I was asked how I wanted to be touched. At that point I realised how much shame, guilt and fear was connected to making clear requests based on my own verbal expression of pleasure. I began to ask for the touch I wanted to receive and to readjust whenever I felt the need to. It was the best massage I'd ever had—smoking hot.

This is when I realised how little I really knew about the desires of my clients during a session and how my actions were based on my own assumptions—of what I *thought* they needed. That I'd only been guessing by reading body cues. I went on to study, practise and embody the true meaning of consent and how it relates to the somatic nervous system.

These days, the most important thing in the work I offer is creating crystal clear agreements with my clients, empowering them to make choices and requests, and showing them how to differentiate between *receiving* and *giving*. I leave it to the client to tell me which part of their body wants to be touched and how. This allows their body and nervous system to realign. If the client doesn't know what they want, we stay there until they do. This approach has resulted in clients becoming empowered in the most profound way, down to a cellular level.

The key to empowerment is to be able to make choices, which is really only possible when there's a sense of safety within the nervous system. This is especially true and important when working with women's sexual healing and de-armouring.

GIVING AND RECEIVING FOR HANDS-ON PRACTITIONERS

"As a therapist, you are a giver who is truly appreciated by your clients. In this way, there is nothing more nourishing than knowing your work makes a positive difference in the world."
- David Lauterstein

Touching a client/patient vs touching your lover

If your work as a practitioner means you come into tactile contact with your clients or patients, it can often be difficult to separate the kind of touch you do at work—and the kind of touch you experience with your lover. When with your lover, ask yourself whether *your action towards your own pleasure is evasive.*

Tuning into the inflow of your own pleasure when in action can be hard to master. And it can be especially challenging for those of us working in the fields of medicine, physiotherapy, massage therapy, sexual therapy and other professions who regularly utilise touch in our work. If your profession fits into these categories, I'm sure you can guess why. We're so used to healing others, to being the one in the *giving dynamic*—we're often closed off to receiving *for ourselves.* We're the ones with the expertise and answers. We're the healers. We're the strong supportive ones, right? When we get stuck in this mindset, it's difficult to admit that we need love and support too, and to be open to *receiving* it.

When touching a client or patient, two things happen in your brain:

- Your *noticing brain* is present to the inflow of sensations via the Direct Route as you palpate, are aware of subtle differences in muscle tone, temperature, form and so on.

- The *meaning making mechanism* in your working brain classifies this kind of touch in a professional setting as something *for the other*. Although your sensory inflow may be activated, it's clear to your brain that this is your job and not your personal life. Your actions are therefore, never *for you* and always *for them*.

While the above is optimal in a professional setting, it means that when we go home we tend to touch our lovers as we do our clients/patients—using the methods we've learned in the role of 'helper 'or 'healer'. This default setting is also often labelled by your brain's *meaning making mechanism* as 'the right kind of touch'. I'm sure you can see that if this is perceived as 'the right way', anything else would fall into the category of 'wrong'. This brings a whole new layer of possible shame and guilt into the equation when going into action to *receive pleasure for ourselves*.

Being in work-mode with your lover

When you're with your lover, do you tend to think or feel you have to be *doing something for them*? And would your lover prefer to be *worked on*, or be *with you* in shared experience?

If any of this resonates with you, be assured that it's totally possible to change this default 'work mode 'setting. First comes awareness. The more we reflect on how and why we do a certain thing or feel a certain way, bringing unconscious habits to the surface—the more easily we can fine-tune our ability to change our programming and evolve. Then, like any habit, it's just a matter of teaching your brain's neurons to fire together in a new way. And we do this through practice.

Once you've taught your brain to *receive while you're in action*, you'll soon begin to notice increased depth, richness and intimacy in your personal relationship. By utilising the SCES with your lover, what becomes clear in a deeply embodied way, is that you don't always need *to give* in order to create intimate connection. And that's what the *'your action for your pleasure dynamic'* is all about. In contrast to working with a client as a professional *for them*, you tune into your action while receiving pleasure *for you*, in *shared experience* with your lover. While experimenting with your lover, I suggest starting by touching their hand slowly until you clearly find the inflow of sensations *for you*. And after the Direct Route is firmly embodied, only then moving on to other parts of their body. Remember, this is a process of neuroplasticity, the rewiring of neurons within the noticing part of your brain, so it will take practice and time.

A couple of little adjustments will make an enormous difference to the outcome. To avoid feeling like you're working, instead of sitting opposite your partner—as you may with a client/patient—sit beside them while holding their hand in your hand. Then, just as you did when practising the Direct Route with an object, lean back to create ease rather than effort within your body to avoid your nervous system automatically being triggered into alert, working mode.

Start out by feeling the shape of your partner's hand, making micro movements as you tune into the pleasure being relayed via your hand to your brain—while simultaneously acknowledging that the action is *for you*. If you have difficulties in tuning in, go back to feeling an object for five minutes before feeling your partner's hand again. Notice the differences as you touch for *your pleasure*.

Your action for you - asking your lover for permission

When with your lover, try to avoid phrases and questions you'd use with a client/patient. These may include; "I'll give you/would you like... (a hand massage)", which are likely to close off the ability to tune into your own pleasure due to their association with work. Instead, ask for permission with the words; "Can I... (feel your hand)". The words, "Can I", make it clear that your action is *for you* and make it easier to focus on your pleasure.

I encourage you to keep practising because when this new habit is formed, you'll access tremendous amounts of pleasure, that to some degree or other, may have evaded you before (having been categorised unconsciously by your mind as 'wrong action 'and linked to emotional shame). I'm sure you'll be amazed by the difference between *receiving* for your pleasure and *giving* in work mode.

When you can truly **go into action to receive** for your own pleasure, you'll land into a *state of being* that never happens with a client. With this new embodied ability comes the realisation that **giving while doing** isn't always necessary in your private life. You'll be able to let go of *working on* your lover and *be with them instead*—in an uplifting, shared, intimate experience.

And, when embodiment of receiving happens, touch in a professional setting also improves. While you're certainly not working on a client to follow your own desires, your hands will be more relaxed, present and sensitive to subtle differences and therefore intuitively know more. This results in a win-win situation for you, your relationship and your clients.

THE 3 COMPONENTS OF PLEASURE FOR PRACTITIONERS

"Between stimulus and response, there is a space. In that space is our power to choose our response. In our response lies our growth and our freedom."
- Viktor E. Frankl

Specifically, when working on sexual trauma healing, there is always the risk of an emotional attachment forming between the client and the practitioner. This is due to the *meaning making mechanism* in the client's mind. It can occur when a story is attached to the stimuli and sensations experienced during the session. It can also happen when a client's only previous experience and prior understanding of touch and sensation connects to the meaning; "Now we are in a relationship, we have to marry, have children and stay together until death do us part". It is the practitioner's responsibility to make sure that no attachment pattern occurs.

Of course, you cannot prevent this kind of thought from developing in a client's mind, though if it happens, I deal with it in a compassionate way, from a place of love and care at the Apex. This means confirming that whatever the client is feeling, is fine—to accept and not reject. At first glance, this approach may sound counter-productive but is actually a portal to deep healing.

During a workshop many years ago, and long before I was ready to be a practitioner, I met Bert Hellinger, the father of *Family Constellations*.[73] Here I learned about one of the core wounds many female clients carry, which directly influences a projection of attachment to male practitioners. Hellinger shared that most women carry a deep, core wound of 'avoided abuse' that is difficult to deal with. From an early age, a girl's father is most often the first person she projects sexual energy upon. Usually, confused about how to deal with it, the father retreats from this kind of attention, withdrawing closeness and connection. And so, the young girl often concludes that her sexual energy is wrong and not welcome.

Hellinger spoke of three levels associated with this core wound.

1. Sexual misuse and abuse creates a deep wound with lifelong scars.

2. Sexual misuse and abuse creates the same wound but without obvious scars. The client can't remember that actual misuse or abuse took place but feels a wound within.

3. An unconscious urge to heal the wound of avoided abuse, to feel welcomed and acknowledged instead of rejected or misused.

Many women unconsciously look to heal the wound of avoided abuse, seeking acknowledgment of their sexual energy.

When a practitioner takes advantage of this aspect of the core wound by having sex with a client, it can be devastating. It takes the power away from the client to heal by reinforcing the father/lover projection. It creates sexual followers instead of providing paths to empowerment. This deep core wounding is another reason why a male practitioner can inhibit the healing of a 'love and sex projecting 'client if they have a sexual encounter *as a lover* with them.

With this theory in mind, Hellinger developed a method called 'Sentences that heal 'that I utilise whenever a female client projects this kind of attachment onto me as her practitioner. As a male practitioner, the healing dynamic of this early wound is a father figure who steps into their power and clearly expresses, "Your feelings are welcome. You are beautiful. I see you—and I am not available."

Beyond limitations of a false belief

Especially within the tantra and sexual bodywork scene, it's common for (especially heterosexual male) practitioners to approach women with the offer, "I'm a yoni massage practitioner, I can sense your yoni needs healing. I can provide this".

This not only implies that something is broken in the person they're talking to and that they need fixing, but that the practitioner possibly hasn't fully understood their own intentions. By offering their service in this way, they may come from the shadow of **giving to get**; pretending to be, or deluded about being at the Apex and offering their service in order to get something in return. This may be wanting to touch others intimately, whether for emotional, sensual or financial reasons. It could also be something more sinister, such as taking advantage of other people's sexual needs or addictions by using a position of power for personal gratification, satisfaction or status. We can see shadows emerge through action when the Direct Route is not embodied.

I fell into a similar trap in the past. I used to think that, as a sexual bodyworker and de-armouring practitioner, I could heal my clients. Some came for pleasure coaching and others to deepen their sex life with their partner. My go-to method was to provide pleasure and orgasm. People referred friends to me and I soon found myself in the position of an 'entertaining pleaser 'by fulfilling their expectations. I noticed they would come back for a top up experience, becoming both dependent on me and even more disappointed with their partner. I felt an urge to share my observations, making this dynamic transparent and to find a solution. To provide them with an empowered experience by guiding how to find their sensual access point, so they could discover their pleasure for themselves. To break through into independent and autonomous action towards the pleasurable experience they wanted to have.

Professional sessions between practitioners and clients always take place within the brother-sister realm

When the level of brother-sister innocence crosses into the lover dynamic, it's not possible to go back. We can't undo what we've done, we can't 'un-sex' once we've gone there. When you enter someone, you can't un-enter them. When you penetrate you can't un-penetrate. There are, as already mentioned, very practical reasons why male practitioners cannot heal women through intercourse. Apart from the obvious complications that can occur when not keeping a session professional, having intercourse introduces a completely different energetic component and connection which nullifies integrity as a professional.

Even more concerning is the fact that, once a woman's dorsal vagal parasympathetic state of immobilisation and surrender is active, the working brain switches off. This means that choices through permission and agreements cannot be given or made. Therefore, there is very little value in asking a woman in high sexual arousal if they want to have intercourse or not. For this reason there is a huge risk of re-traumatising rather than healing. This is why discussions about desires and limits are best made before any action begins, when both are fully aware and operating within their Social Engagement System.

According to the principles of the SCES, the main reason that a male practitioner cannot heal a client through intercourse, is that he would lose his erection if he wasn't experiencing pleasure for himself. When a male body wants to penetrate, it has to be led by desire—and if you are working as a practitioner while following your own desire—who is the session for? The action would not necessarily only be *for his client*, but for himself too.

As a practitioner, it's important to be aware that, due to past trauma, a high percentage of women project their sexual energy onto men in order to feel valued, recognised and connected. If this occurs and is taken advantage of, re-traumatisation can occur—and it cannot be reversed. If a female client asks for or tries to initiate intercourse during a session, instead of simply withdrawing (which can aid in heightening any connected trauma of sexual rejection), the male practitioner can acknowledge and voice their appreciation, while pointing out that they have a professional code of conduct with clear boundaries.

It is essential that practitioners embody their own power and come from a place of love and care at the Apex by remaining within the brother-sister role of engagement. For this to be possible, the practitioner must have a solid Base and be in full integrity with it. Then, a healing dynamic is possible by empowering the client to develop her own Base and awareness of sensory inflow—so that she has a fully informed neurological understanding of her bodily experience.

Before any interaction on a professional level, intentional agreements are made to clearly define the brother-sister role of pure play. No matter how emotional, informational or intensive, even when there is contact to genitals, whether during massage, pleasure edging or a de-armouring session, both choose and agree to encounter whatever is desired or is appropriate in the session being offered—except for intercourse and exchange of body fluids.

THE ZONE IN THE ZONE

The Direct And Indirect Routes For Practitioners

"We don't see things as they are, we see them as we are."
- Anaïs Nin

The Zone within the Zone Map is a practitioner map—for those specifically working hands-on with clients on a sexual level, but not limited to this field.

It shows the Engagement Zones with the Apex above and includes an extra Engagement Zone model within the ***for them*** side of the pyramid. This 'zone in the zone' illustrates the potential as a practitioner to embody both the **giving and receiving dynamic *simultaneously*** during bodywork and other professional sessions involving touch—when *the outcome of action* is always **for the client.**

This aspect of Somatic Consent for practitioners can seem a little complicated at times. If it gets confusing, I invite you to stop reading and come back to feeling an object and staying with the inflow of sensations. This helps to avoid making too much of a rational concept with the mind and rather be aware of creating the embodiment by self-practicing the inflow and developing the dynamics from within.

The practitioner's role is to enable the client to have an embodied experience of all four Engagement Zones. This includes the client learning how it feels to 'give'.

Giving happens when the client is in action (for you) or you are in action (for you). In both cases, the action is 'for 'the practitioner. Though, even when the action is 'for' the practitioner, in the bigger picture, everything is for the client, in service of their learning.

As a practitioner you have power—and with that power tremendous responsibility to operate from the interpersonal space at the Apex. You give yourself and your skills as a gift from a place of love and care, and never from a shadow dynamic, where you use your power for your own benefit.

When working with people on themes of intimacy, sexual relating, relationship and issues of abuse, you need to have all four zones embodied, in order to support people to embody their zones.

As a practitioner you go into action as a service—which provides a space to help clients understand what their desire is. You give your gift of power by being in service to the greater good and by making the ability to surrender easy for the other person. In this way, they are able to experience the deepest level of *receiving* for themself.

ZONE IN THE ZONE MAP

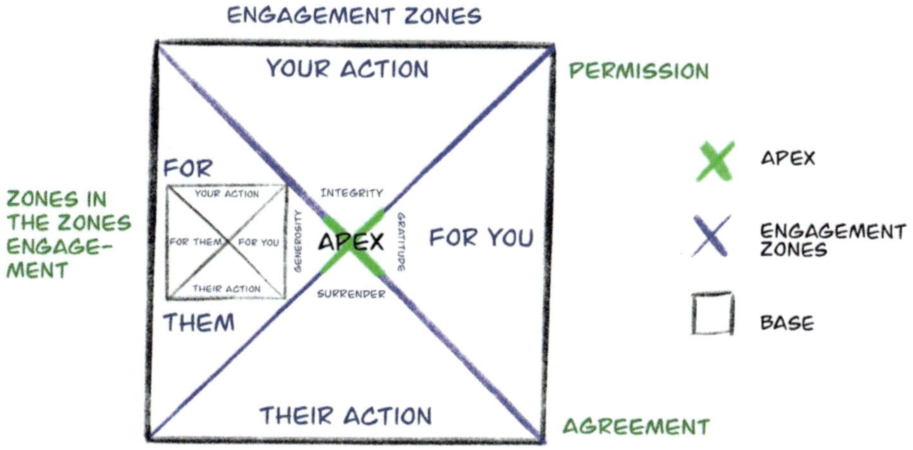

ENGAGEMENT ZONES

- YOUR ACTION — PERMISSION
- FOR YOU
- THEIR ACTION — AGREEMENT
- FOR THEM

ZONES IN THE ZONES ENGAGEMENT

Inner square: YOUR ACTION / FOR THEM / FOR YOU / THEIR ACTION — INTEGRITY, GRATITUDE, SURRENDER, GENEROSITY — APEX

Legend:
- ✗ APEX (green)
- ✗ ENGAGEMENT ZONES (blue)
- ☐ BASE

WITH EMBODIMENT COMES MORE KNOWLEDGE
WITH MORE KNOWLEDGE COMES MORE POWER
WITH MORE POWER COMES MORE RESPONSIBILITY

SPIRITUAL AND PERSONAL GROWTH HAPPENS IN CO-EXISTENCE BETWEEN THE BASE — BY EMBODYING OUR OWN ZONES — AND IN THE INTERPERSONAL APEX SPACE BY GUIDING OTHERS TO EMBODY THEIR OWN ZONES FOR THEIR OWN GROWTH.

DIVINE ART IS BEING AN INVITATION FOR 'ZONE IN THE ZONE' ENGAGEMENT.

EMBODIMENT COMES THROUGH PRACTICE NOT THROUGH KNOWLEDGE.

ENGAGEMENT SYSTEM

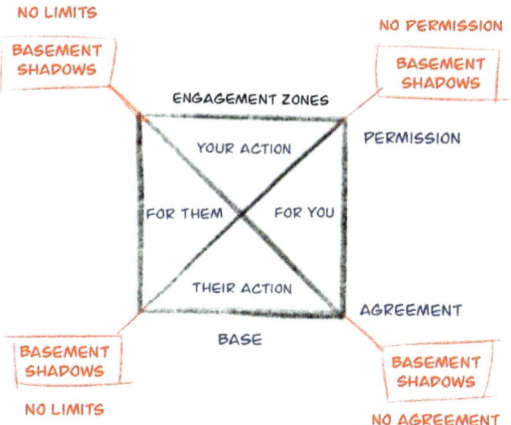

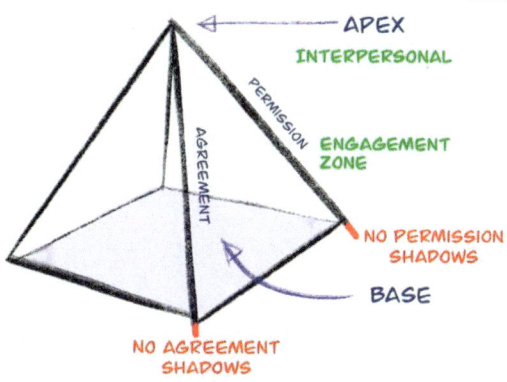

- NO LIMITS → BASEMENT SHADOWS
- NO PERMISSION → BASEMENT SHADOWS
- NO LIMITS → BASEMENT SHADOWS
- NO AGREEMENT → BASEMENT SHADOWS

ENGAGEMENT ZONES:
- YOUR ACTION — PERMISSION
- FOR THEM / FOR YOU
- THEIR ACTION — AGREEMENT
- BASE

TRANSPERSONAL

Pyramid:
- APEX — INTERPERSONAL
- PERMISSION / AGREEMENT — ENGAGEMENT ZONE
- BASE
- NO PERMISSION SHADOWS
- NO AGREEMENT SHADOWS

FOR ANYONE TEACHING SEXUAL EMPOWERMENT, TOUCH AND PLAY IN PROFESSIONAL SETTINGS (IN A POSITION OF POWER), EMPOWERMENT COMES FROM THE APEX (LOVE AND CARE) BY EMBODYING THE ZONES FIRST (INTEGRITY).
NOT FROM THE SHADOWS, IGNORING THE BASE FROM POWER OVER OTHERS FOR OWN BENEFITS

WWW.SOMATICCONSENT.COM

Initiating professional agreements

As a practitioner you have to be conscious that your actions are always *for the client*—even though it is agreed at the moment that you choose certain actions *for you* as part of the client's learning process. This is somewhat paradoxical but essential to providing support with maximum integrity.

> *This is **metacognitive** (knowing and understanding your own thought process). You know you are doing something for you in the moment—but in the bigger picture you clearly know what you're doing is ultimately for them.*

This multitasking requires focus on two things simultaneously. In my experience, women tend to more easily grasp the ability of both focusing on their feelings while simultaneously knowing that the action is *for the client*. This could possibly be due to their capacity for, or experience in caring for others, though I have no research to back up this claim. It isn't, however, more difficult for men to excel at this simultaneous tasking. German psychologists concluded in their research on performing simultaneous tasks, "Findings strongly suggest that there are no substantial gender differences in multitasking performance across task-switching and dual- task paradigms."[74]

Guiding a client to tune into the Direct Route of pleasure with another person

If a client wants to find their sensory inflow and experience receiving, you, as the practitioner, have to give them permission to touch you *for themself*, so they can have the experience of doing something that is pleasurable *for them*.

Guiding a client in the experience of integrity, gratitude, generosity and surrender

> *For the client to experience the **receiving-while-in action** role, the dynamic is their action for them. This means that the client needs to go into action to feel themself within your limits. This will guide the client into the value of **integrity**.*

> *For the client to experience the **giving-while-in-action** role, the dynamic is their action for you. As a practitioner, providing a session for the client, you have to take care not to make it too much about yourself. The client needs to go into action for you within their limits. The experience will guide the client into the value of **generosity**.*
>
> *For the client to experience surrender to their own experience in the **receiving-while-not-in-action** role, the dynamic is your action for them (and their desired request). You as the practitioner do what the client desires (within your limits). This will guide the client into the value of **gratitude**.*
>
> *For the client to experience the **giving-while-not-in-action** role, the dynamic is your action for you. This means that you, as the practitioner, need to go into action for you—and be capable of feeling your sensory inflow as you touch the client—while ultimately knowing that each action is paradoxically, for them. This will guide the client into the value of **surrender**.*

Before any action takes place, the client voices any limits they have regarding specific parts of their body or parts of the practitioner's body which will touch them. During the exercise the client voices any new limits as they arise. These limits are discussed, broken down and understood. In this way, awareness is also brought to any potential issues of past trauma and worked through.

Often women come to sessions having never experienced true surrender to someone else's action (their action for them). They present with the desire to experience their full sexual expression while not being taken advantage of.

This need is, neurologically and emotionally, a strong desire of wanting to be wanted—and to be touched while feeling protected and cared for so that boundaries and limits are respected.

Regardless of gender, surrendering to someone else's action is the most exquisite experience in the realm of the Apex.

The one not in action has no need to tense up to protect themself in any way. Because they know there is no hidden agenda (that the other may do something to get something in return) and so, their mind and body can fully relax.

They feel completely safe and cared for.

The one in action has full integrity and is in alignment with themself and the other. They can fully feel themself and also fully feel the other person. This means they are consistently, finely tuned into any change in the other's muscle tone, breathing rate, gestures and expression.

When this is the case, the practitioner goes into action for themself and simultaneously gives their gift of power to the other. This gift supports the other person in such a complete way, that they are able to fully let go and experience the exquisite state of surrender.

Surrender is an artform—and what, I think, this book is all about

How can you, as the practitioner, provide this experience if your clients desire it?

When someone comes with the desire to have that experience, it's important to make it clear that this type of surrender happens only in the lover's realm when both are at the Apex—when both want the same thing as much as each other.

As a practitioner, the possibilities to explore are limited because you are not the client's lover and it would violate the code of ethics.

I once had a client who couldn't articulate the kind of touch she wanted. When I guided her through the steps of feeling the inflow for herself (so that she could become aware of what she wanted) she became frustrated saying, "I know how it feels when I do it, I can feel the inflow, but I've never felt the same way when I'm being touched by somebody else". We discussed the concept of surrender. She'd been able to *receive* when touching for herself, but not to *surrender* while being touched by another person.

As part of the agreement we came to, she asked me not to stop (my action for me), despite what may come up. After just a few moments she broke down in tears, sobbing in deep grief at all the unfulfilled longing she felt. Of never having found anyone to touch her the way she wanted—in order to be able to surrender. It was a very profound healing session during which she realised that it was both possible to experience the touch she wanted—and that her body was capable of receiving pleasure from it.

To provide your client with the experience of surrender;

> *The conversation with the client must remain completely transparent. It must be clear that you, as the practitioner, are able to touch them to show them how they are able to surrender and how that feels—but that you, by no means, are available as a lover, and that this fact won't change.*
>
> *There is never any misuse of power or pretence that a lover's dynamic could develop.*
>
> *The practitioner has to be sure the client's Direct Route is open, otherwise a plethora of expectations could come up.*
>
> *Because you are going into action for yourself, you have to know exactly what their limits are and their history of trauma.*
>
> *You as the practitioner have to be very clear about your own limits and stick to them. While you are in action for you, you are actually in action for them. You must make sure they are consistently cared for.*
>
> *Encourage the client to practice with their partner so that learnings can be made by both, the relationship strengthened and no dependence on the practitioner (to provide this experience) develops.*

Certified SCES Practitioners

As a SCES practitioner, by staying somatically open and in tune with your own sensory inflow, you're able to experientially know the difference between going into an action *for you* and going into an action *for them*. Within a session, when you go into an action, it is always for the client (*for them*).

You shift between the Direct and Indirect Route of pleasure so that both dynamics can work in parallel as you read cues and co-regulate.

If you want to enable a client to find their ability to receive pleasure on a sensual level, it cannot be understood through explanation—as we cannot cognitively understand sensory inflow—it has to be felt with the skin.

Over the last years, I noticed many practitioners getting confused when learning consent dynamics with limited awareness and embodiment of sensory inflow. Many started to think they were functioning from a shadow when experiencing pleasure during their work—as they felt and enjoyed feeling when touching a client.

This confusion arose due to the presumption that *pleasure* was the indicator for who the session was for. Many stopped enjoying what they were doing because they were afraid of not being fully professional. I've seen many faces light up when practitioners realise it's totally fine to enjoy what they do. The indicator of *who your session is for* isn't to do with whether you feel pleasure and enjoy what you do, it's to do with the **agreement** you created before the session started.

Have you ever been in a session as a client and received exactly what you wanted from the practitioner—while the practitioner was in full enjoyment of their skill to give? What is essential as a practitioner is *not to get lost* in the joy of your skills, which may result in your pleasure becoming more important than the client's experience.

TREATMENT AND CO-CREATION

Healing And Co-Regulation - Offering The Best For Your Clients

"Life is in color, but black and white is more realistic."
- Samuel Fuller

Everyone has skills. Practitioners have many. As an expert, your job is to provide the experience that your client wants to have. The practitioner creates what is wanted and provides what's needed.

The thing is, if we are only doing what others want us to do during our sessions, if we avoid doing what we can clearly see they need—and are afraid to act in case we are accused of coming from a shadow dynamic—isn't that a waste of these skills?

It is impossible to get exact consent from a client regarding *treatment* that only the practitioner has expertise in. The client of an osteopath or a dentist for example usually has no idea which technique will help their ailment. Usually, the client trusts the professional to assess and do their best on their behalf.

If we experience the Zone in the Zone Map and what it means to come from the Apex as a practitioner—we feel that the Direct Route is embodied and the Indirect Route is utilised. If the client isn't able to ask for what they want, the practitioner can suggest doing something *for them* (and make a clear agreement before going into action).

The practitioner could ask; "How would it feel if we do this, would you like to try?"

This could appear to be a shadow when viewed from the outside—that you as the practitioner are doing it *for you* or are manipulating the client in some way. However, if the practitioner's intention is coming from a place of love and care at the Apex, fully offering themselves in service to the client—it is always *for the client (for them)*.

Treatment or co-creation?

A **Treatment Model** is based on a change of state. A treatment equals 'my skill set - for your benefit', 'my action - for your experience'. As a practitioner you fulfil this by moving your client from state A - to B - to C. This is a very clear, one-way encounter. The practitioner goes into action (doing) and the client is the *receiver* of the action. An example could be a pleasure massage. The practitioner asks where the client would like to and not like to be massaged on their body and agreements are made.

A **Coaching and Co-Creation Model** has the framework where both are experts and decide what will happen *together*. The practitioner is the expert of what they can do and the client is the expert of their body, their experience, where they are and where they wish to go. The client doesn't come for a simple A - B - C treatment. They come because they want to learn something.

An example could be someone who asks; "I really don't like it when my partner gives me oral sex. How can I learn to like it?" When they ask for this they are actually asking, "How can I ignore my limits more and go along with something I don't like?".

It would be more empowering to initiate them into the experience of the Direct Route of pleasure, guiding them in how to say "no" when a boundary is noticed—and how to ask for exactly what they want and how they want it. Then encouraging them to practise this approach at home with their partner.

TREATMENT AND CO-CREATION MAP

TREATMENT

- PRACTITIONER IS THE EXPERT
- TO FIX A PROBLEM
- FOR THE CLIENT
- TO HAVE AN EXPERIENCE
- CHANGE OF STATE
- BASED ON TECHNIQUE AND SKILLS
- ONE-WAY PRACTICIONER TO CLIENT

CO-CREATION / COACHING

- PRACTITIONER IS EXPERT AND CLIENT IS EXPERT
- CLIENT IS THERE TO LEARN
- CREATIVE, RESOURCEFUL, WHOLE
- CHANGE IN BEHAVIOUR
- LOSS, TRANSFORMATION, NOTICING, ADAPTIVE / CO-CREATIVE
- CAN BE A TWO-WAY CONNECTION

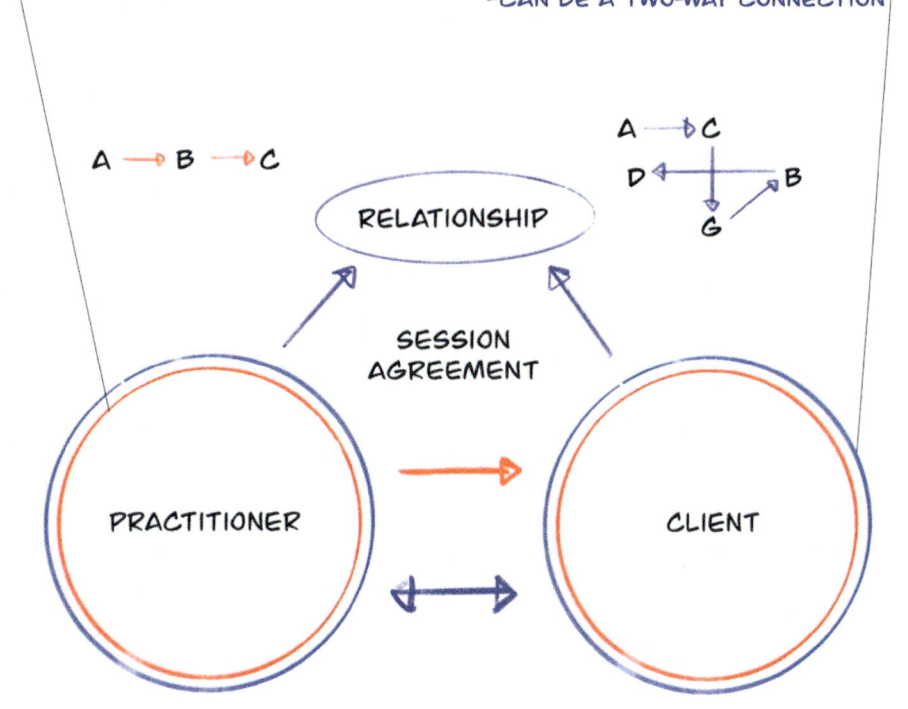

A → B → C

A → C
D ←
↓ ↘ B
G

RELATIONSHIP

SESSION AGREEMENT

PRACTITIONER ⇄ CLIENT

WWW.SOMATICCONSENT.COM

Co-creating isn't about fixing, it's a journey of discovery

When a client comes to my sessions, I know that they are already creative, resourceful and whole. There is nothing to fix or repair. Some come with the idea that I can 'touch a button' to make them whole, believing that I know where to push on their body to make them complete. Most often however, they only need a little shift in behaviour to understand certain things that have been blocking their capacity in one way or another.

This sometimes comes by releasing existing structures which aren't healthy and which may be painful to let go of. As a practitioner, it's important to be fully present with awareness of the client's feelings when they are going through transformation and deeper layers of themselves such as releasing or experiencing loss. This kind of session has a co-creative dynamic, a two-way engagement, unlike a *treatment* which is only ever one-way—from the practitioner to the client.

During a co-creation session, if, for example, the client wants to learn how to receive for themselves, you might give them permission to touch you—so that they can have a learning experience about themself by experiencing the Direct Route of pleasure *for themself*. There is no linear A - B - C in a co-creative session although a *treatment* can be included.

Some practitioners are insecure at times about what they offer their clients, because many people aren't able to ask for what they want, or don't express a specific desire—although expectations of results are often present.

One can never pre-determine where you will start or end. The most important thing is that the relationship created between the client and the practitioner is done during preliminary agreements (when the two Bases meet). These agreements form the *principle keystone* that determines what will happen—or not. They ensure that the client can feel safe during their experiences within the session. When it comes to the "Hell YES" and "Fierce NO" of the Limits Map, there is, of course, territory between the two which can offer a variety of options during a co-creative session.

The questions to ask yourself as a practitioner are;

"Have I really asked them what they want?"
"Are they able to ask for what they want?"
"Are they here for a *treatment* or have they come to learn something?"
"Do I have an urge to heal them in the form of a *treatment*?"

What has your client come for?

It is of utmost importance as a practitioner to ask the right kind of questions. To find out exactly why each individual client is here and therefore be able to provide the right kind of session *for them*. For practitioners working in the area of hands-on professional sessions, it is important to be guided by these questions throughout the entire session;

"Why are you here?"
"What can I do for you?"
"How would you like to feel afterwards?"
"What would you like to get out of it?"

It is paramount that the practitioner understands what the client has come for during the making of agreements. This way, it is absolutely clear whether the client has come for a *treatment* (according to what the particular practitioner has to offer) or a *co-creative coaching* session (which, as already mentioned, can also include a treatment). When handled in this way, the pressure to know all the answers for each and every individual client is removed. When we clearly establish what is wanted, we can admit when we can't provide what the client needs, and either refer them to a colleague, or offer an alternative.

One day a woman came for a session before I recognised the distinction between a *treatment* and *co-creative coaching*.

I asked her what she would like. She replied, "I just want to have a massage".
I asked, "What kind of massage do you want?"
"A nice massage", she answered.
"Are you looking for pleasure?" I asked.
"Yes, I'm looking for pleasure," she said.
"Can you tell me what pleasure means for you?"
"No, not really," she replied.
And so I asked her to take an object in her hand and to feel it, so that she could become more aware of what was pleasurable and therefore be able to ask me specifically for that. She started to get frustrated and annoyed. I didn't understand why. Then she told me, "Look, all I want is a massage".
It clicked.

What I'd done was begun an entire process of *co-creative coaching*, when all she'd come for was a pleasure *treatment*.

EMPOWERMENT MASSAGE

Co-Creation Coaching

*"It took me quite a long time to develop a voice, and now that I have it,
I am not going to be silent."*
- Madeleine Albright

An empowerment massage is just that. It's a perfect way for a practitioner to guide their clients into embodied self-empowerment. It illustrates how being able to **choose** is more important than the action itself—which may feel incredibly delicious, though is just a bonus. When the client knows they have a choice, they are able to trust themself to communicate their desires authentically. An empowerment massage is always a co-creation where the practitioner guides the client to communicate their desires and limits via permission and agreements. The client gets to practice the language of consent using the Engagement Zones and have an embodied experience of this kind of communication.

This highlights any difficulties the client has in communicating requests. It highlights any shadow strategies that may emerge and provides a safe container to explore these parts of themself in a fun way.

The client as the receiver; it's about the client *noticing* what their body **wants** (their/the practitioner's action for you/the client) and to *trust, value* and *communicate* desires—then to relax into the role of fully *receiving.*

The practitioner as the giver; the practitioner does exactly what the client wants (your action for them). It's about *noticing* what you are **willing to** do and to *trust, value* and *communicate* your limits.

An empowerment massage reveals how it feels, somatically and emotionally, to be in one's own power

The client practises voicing their desires through requests and gets these requests met their way. They simultaneously receive pleasure while respecting the giver's limits. It also brings awareness to how it feels to be in the vulnerable role of asking for what they want (facing the fear of rejection, when the practitioner expresses their own limits). For the practitioner it's the end of knowing everything better than the client, of 'good guessing 'and being the expert that fixes, heals and provides 'magic'.

The client becomes empowered by healing themself

It is valuable to acknowledge that all shadows that come up are strategies, motivated by the need to be accepted, mostly through avoiding vulnerability and rejection.

Here's how shadows might show up in an empowerment massage, for the practitioner and the client:

1. Permission line shadow: your action for you. OPPRESSING (perpetrator)
2. Permission line shadow: their action for them. PASSIVITY (victim)
3. Agreement line shadow: your action for them. PLEASING (rescuer)
4. Agreement line shadow: their action for you. EXPLOITING (entitled)

The oppressing/perpetrator shadow - this means any action by you for yourself without permission.

An empowerment massage gives the client the opportunity to explore the 'their action for you' dynamic, as it is the practitioner in action, for the client. This shadow can show up when the practitioner feels uncomfortable about not being in charge of the action. For example, when they give more than is asked for (to get a response), when they guess what's right *for the other person*, predict what the other wants next, feel impatient or unworthy when not in action—or when they push or force an offer to avoid their own discomfort.

The passivity/victim shadow - difficulties the client may have stopping and changing their mind or saying no, as well as going along with touch that is uncomfortable or uninspiring. This shadow is directly related to the fact we were all touched against our will before we could speak. The empowerment massage breaks this pattern.

The pleasing/rescuing shadow - when the client avoids asking for what they really want, pleasing or being 'nice 'so as not to appear difficult or demanding, asking for what they think they 'should 'want or what they think is ok for the giver instead.

The exploiting/entitled shadow - instead of the client asking for what they want; "Can you ...", saying instead, "You can ..." which either 1) gives permission rather than asks a question (to avoid vulnerability) or 2) is an order. It can also stem from a place of suppressed anger in not having received what they feel they deserved in the past.

There is a very high chance that the person coming away from this kind of session feels fully embodied, grounded, refreshed and empowered.

Due to its simplicity, the possibilities of finding transformative material are tremendous. The empowerment massage allows the client to find what they really want and to express desire. Some elements of the massage will be easier for the client than others and the process reveals with clarity which elements they're struggling with.

One main purpose of the empowerment massage is that the client moves away from enduring and going along with things they don't like. Changing this habitual shadow behaviour taps directly to the core of empowerment. Instead of enduring, the client changes what is happening by consciously choosing only what they really want.

There are other methods we can utilise to work through shadows. An example is a personal experience I had with Biodynamic Therapy.[74] With this method, the practitioner sets impulses, externally activating a neurological area by touching a place on the client's body such as the back of the knees, the sacrum, or back of the skull where nerve bundles are concentrated—then moves away. During the time the practitioner moved away, my body began craving more touch. The practitioner, however, came back in their own time and then set another impulse. I experienced deep relaxation in receiving this technique and it made me very aware of the kinds of touch I longed for and not.

During an *empowerment massage* we go even deeper as the impulses and craving for more touch is directed by the client through making and articulating choices (according to where and how they want the touch to happen). If there is no impulse to be touched, it is not articulated and so, there is no chance for the body to go along with anything unwanted. Due to this, deep relaxation and healing can occur in moments when nothing is done at all.

The empowerment massage is part of the Practitioner's Certification Course which anyone can learn with Somatic Consent. Scan the code to find out more details about the **Year Training**!

Asking A Regular Therapist For An Empowering Massage

If you go for a massage, do you fully enjoy it when the therapist goes through the motions of their learned routine? From A to B to C, treating your body just like all the others that land on their table? How does your body feel when the therapist isn't present, or doesn't do what you asked for at the beginning? Do you ever wish they'd concentrate on a specific part of your body for longer? How much better would you feel if you communicated what you wanted?

What would stop you from asking something such as, "Please start with firm pressure on my shoulders and continue until I ask you to stop". How about suggesting at the reception that they add an empowerment massage to the menu, where the client decides in-the-moment what they'd like the therapist to do?

A friend of mine related an experience she'd had: "I've been having regular massages for about three months now. I found a male therapist who listens and does whatever I ask. There's a specific technique he does when he massages my inner thighs, but he never does it for more than a few seconds. It feels soooo good. For weeks I've been afraid of asking him to do it for longer. It felt too 'edgy' because it's quite an intimate place and he's not a lover. This week I finally plucked up the courage and asked. I was feeling disempowered about my inability to risk feeling vulnerable—instead of just stepping out of my Window of Tolerance into possible growth, by asking for what I wanted. To do that I know I have to feel safe. So I had this conversation with myself; "Do I feel safe?" - "Yes". "Do I trust him?" - "Yes". "Then ask you big baby!" I did. It felt both empowering and delicious!"

DE-ARMOURING

Trauma Release And Re-Traumatisation

"What is armor after all but a cage that moves with you?"
- Rebecca Solnit

In the early 1900s, Wilheim Reich, an Austrian psychoanalyst and Doctor of Medicine, worked with the 'armour '(physical protection shields) that people's systems build within their bodies for survival. When the ventral vagus and social engagement switches off due to a sense of threat or danger, it triggers the nervous system to function on the unsafe side in 'survival mode '(fight or flight). Due to fight and flight responses during traumatic experience, tension or 'armour 'is created in various parts of the body. This can lead to dysfunction of the nervous system and inability to relax.

The side effect of living in constant fear and self-protection can then trigger parasympathetic dorsal vagal shutdown. People can feel numb, lethargic and fatigued. In such situations, the noticing and feeling part of the brain (which is aware of impulses within the body, as well as the working mind's thought process) is switched off. This means that conscious decisions can't be made. The person may feel stuck or 'frozen 'in some way. This can affect selected areas of the body where muscular holding patterns occur as physical defence mechanisms—due to the nervous system's need to shut off and protect from feeling chronic physical or emotional pain.

This can manifest differently in different people. When under psychological stress, the Psoas muscle, as a core muscle, informs other muscles to be in constant readiness for fight or flight. Tension can result in different areas of the body. Examples are the pelvic area, in the jaw due to clenching, pain around the diaphragm due to contraction from holding the breath, stiff trapezius muscles in the neck and shoulders, around the eyes causing tension headaches and contraction in the throat known as cricopharyngeal spasm.

De-armouring transforms the contraction and holding patterns we carry within us. The 'armour' is a result of blockages created over time by stress, thought-patterns, social programming, repressed emotion and trauma. Although this armour can desensitise our experience of life, it is there for a reason. It developed to protect us. By bringing awareness to the 'armour', we can take away the physical 'shield' and consciously choose to release it if it isn't necessary. This *releasing* is the de-armouring process. With the release of these blockages, we have a deeper capacity to feel pleasure and joy. De-armouring can be both external and internal, both physical, psychological and emotional.

When people come to a session, I usually recommend Waking Up The Hands as the first step so as to bring awareness to their sensory inflow. However, some people's nervous systems are so dysregulated and numb that they find it difficult to feel much at all. In cases like this, I sometimes offer the Psoas release mechanism first (also known as TRE). As mentioned in the Window of Tolerance section, this is done through gentle shaking and prompts the nervous system to discharge long-held tension or unconscious muscle contraction in the Psoas and other muscles in the body.

I recommend Bessel van der Kolk's book, *The Body Keeps the Score* for anybody interested in getting a detailed understanding about how trauma is created within the physical body. This book is a medical and psychological must for anyone working with people, especially hands-on practitioners.[75]

De-armouring physical protection shields

"Fear is excitement without the breath."
- Fritz Perls

We're unable to de-armour ourselves for the same reason we can't tickle ourselves. Research at University College London shows this is because a part of the brain called the cerebellum predicts sensations when your own movement causes them—but not when someone else does. This prediction cancels the brain's response to the stimulus.[76] Responses to actions that could cause us pain are also inhibited. This is the reason we usually need someone else to work with us during de-armouring.

Osho communities began to work with this phenomena in the 70s, using often intrusive massage techniques that were meant to push through these mechanisms. Later these techniques were largely reassessed through a deeper understanding of trauma and the nervous system. It was acknowledged that de-armouring cannot occur as a 'treatment '(which could lead to re-traumatisation). Instead, co-creation, a collaboration between the client and practitioner is necessary—as well as rapport, connection and a safe container to practice within.[78]

In around 2010, de-armouring became popular within the tantra scene. This unfortunately occurred with many practitioners not fully understanding nervous system dysfunction caused by trauma or creating the required need of safety. These early tantra de-armouring practitioners often believed they could heal by causing and 'pushing through 'pain.

De-armouring is *bodywork-art*—a combination of the art of facilitation and bodywork. The gift of power here is a two-edged sword that can either transform and liberate or the opposite—trigger core wounds and trauma. Of utmost importance in this practice is;

1) The practitioner never pushes.
2) The practitioner is aware when the client pushes.

It is the art of inviting the client to find the *pull* towards the edges of their Window of Tolerance so that they can follow the flow of their body's intelligence. At the same time, the practitioner is consistently aware that any action of theirs is for the client's benefit.

The De-armouring Map for practitioners is a very important map when it comes to bodywork, especially in regard to spiritual transformation.

A de-armouring practitioner must maintain a highly evolved state of being, where the noticing brain is constantly activated. This enables the practitioner to hold space for another person for up to three hours, during which any engagement is consistently for the client (*for them*).

DE-ARMOURING MAP

THE SOMATIC NERVOUS SYSTEM & DIFFERENCE BETWEEN THE DIRECT AND INDIRECT ROUTE IN SERVICE

ACTION FOR THEM
- NOT DEPENDENT ON RESULT
- NO ATTACHMENT TO THE OUTCOME
- NO NEED TO RECEIVE ANYTHING OUT OF THE SESSION IN RETURN
- CHECKING IN WITH RESPONSES AND REACTIONS
- NO PLEASING AND BEING NICE
- WITHIN THEIR LIMITS AND DESIRE
- RELEASING TENSION

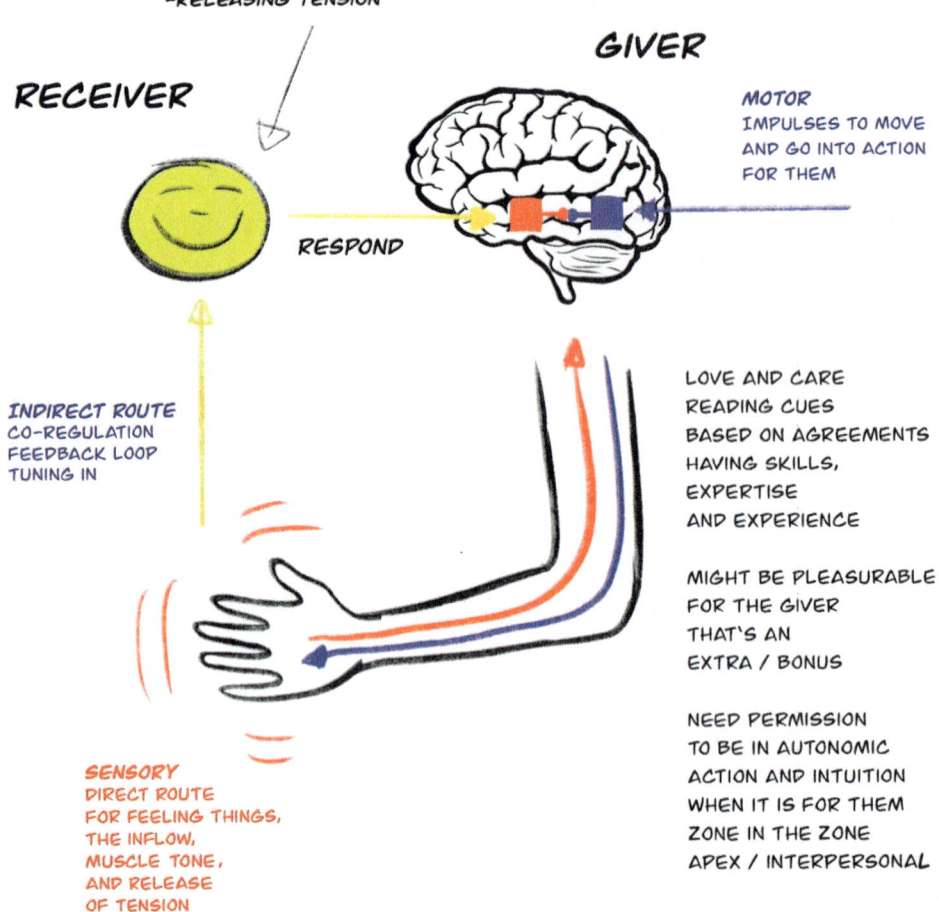

RECEIVER

GIVER

MOTOR
IMPULSES TO MOVE AND GO INTO ACTION FOR THEM

RESPOND

INDIRECT ROUTE
CO-REGULATION
FEEDBACK LOOP
TUNING IN

LOVE AND CARE
READING CUES
BASED ON AGREEMENTS
HAVING SKILLS,
EXPERTISE
AND EXPERIENCE

MIGHT BE PLEASURABLE
FOR THE GIVER
THAT'S AN
EXTRA / BONUS

NEED PERMISSION
TO BE IN AUTONOMIC
ACTION AND INTUITION
WHEN IT IS FOR THEM
ZONE IN THE ZONE
APEX / INTERPERSONAL

SENSORY
DIRECT ROUTE
FOR FEELING THINGS,
THE INFLOW,
MUSCLE TONE,
AND RELEASE
OF TENSION

WWW.SOMATICCONSENT.COM

The client comes to a de-armouring session because they have the desire to release tension out of their body—and therefore to release patterns of thought and behaviour that don't serve them any longer. These can be based on shame, embarrassment, frustration, pain, fear, anger and so on.

In 2010, I met a midwife called Silja Rehfeld, who worked with pregnant women, de-armouring cervical tissue to create expansion and enable ecstatic births. She had exceptional results. We then worked together offering the release of inner genital tension and points of pain, so that women could have orgasmic expansion in the uterus without giving birth.

This theory goes hand in hand with the Procreation Map—and the understanding that women, specifically when it comes to sexual encounter, have learned to clench their muscles to 'feel more'. As any good sexual therapist knows, when this happens there is no possibility of relaxation, softening, expansion and surrender. Sex is purely goal oriented towards climax.

Orgasmic expansion with your entire body is only possible if holding patterns and muscle contraction is released, otherwise the body can't conduct sexual energy. De-armouring the cervix helps to release old patterns, whether physical, psychological or emotional, so that feeling on a deeper level is possible. Sexual energy can then lead to a high level of transformation which occurs due to the release of melatonin, serotonin, oxytocin, dopamine and endorphins, which cross the blood-brain barrier in the state of immobilisation and surrender. This cocktail (as explained in detail in the section on cerebrospinal fluid and the Being on the Edge Map) prompts the release of DMT.

De-armouring essentials for practitioners

Each practitioner working with de-armouring the genitals must have a high level of integrity, assessment protocols, somatic embodiment and fully understand the nature of consent.

A professional practitioner educates others to see how far they want to—and can—dig into themselves.

Embodiment of the Direct Route

When it comes to touch and connection, before we can tune into someone else's story and understand their body's physical expression (their nervous system response and muscle tone), we have to know our own. It is *crucial* that a professional bodyworker or practitioner—especially one working on a sexual level—is fully embodied in the Direct Route. This is the foundation and default for a practitioner. It enables us to gift our power in full integrity in order for our clients to empower themselves.

Why is it so crucial? Because by being highly aware of our own somatic experience, we can be one hundred percent clear—in every given moment—that the action is *for the client*. When we are this clear about our own needs and desires, we don't get them confused with those of our clients and end up unconsciously engaging with our shadows by going into action for ourselves at the somatic level.

If body awareness of our own sensory inflow isn't activated, despite our good intentions, we more than likely go into action to get a response. This compromises our level of expertise and can cause harm. There can also be a risk that the practitioner isn't able to 'feel 'whether the client is pretending, performing or unable to access their deepest capacity.

With awareness of sensory inflow, we are easily able to put our own needs and desires aside—integrating our embodied learning with other professional skills.

Embodiment of the Base

A practitioner can only guide another person as deeply as they've gone themselves, having understood and integrated their own personal shadows, suppressed feelings and emotions. With this level of embodied expertise, we can use the Indirect Route with the skill and capability required to read neurological and energetic cues in the client's nervous system response.

Only when the practitioner has somatic embodiment of the Direct Route can they have complete clarity on the Indirect Route and its associated shadow dynamics (doing something to get a response). When the two separate routes are known, they can be ***utilised in unison*** to guide a client to the place they desire to be. This is where intuition, empathy and compassion come into play.

Embodiment of the Engagement Zones

De-armouring can only work if there is a connection between the practitioner and client and a clear container is upheld where the client feels safe. Connection and safety is established through *permission and agreements*. Agreements occur when the practitioner has fully embodied the Engagement Zones, communication is transparent and they are in full service to the client.

It is not only necessary to know what the client wants; it is essential that the practitioner knows the client's limits.

- What the client is *willing to* experience during the session, based on their intentional desire to release suppressed emotions, body tension and/or false beliefs.
- Where the client is *not willing* to go, i.e., beyond the edges of the learning zone outside their personal Window of Tolerance.

In other words, it's crucial to know what the client longs for and which boundaries they do not want crossing. Just like going to the dentist when you have a toothache, it may not exactly be a pleasant experience—however—are you willing to allow some discomfort to occur? Yes? How much? While the dentist is drilling in your mouth, does it feel like you're going along with something that you don't actually want? Yes? Do you feel the signs of shutdown? Yes? In the bigger picture the dentist is doing their best to do what you want—to relieve your toothache. And only the person sitting in the dentist's chair knows what they are willing to go through in order to heal.

De-armouring isn't always an uncomfortable experience. Some de-armouring methods include the use of pleasure. In these cases, whenever shame comes up, the practitioner helps to remove the fear of being 'wrong', so that instead, joy can be felt in the experience of its release.

The practitioner, as the giver, must also have exceptional clarity on their own boundaries and be well trained, with expertise gained both from working with clients and from their own personal experience.

Practice from the interpersonal space at the Apex

The practitioner's action is not dependent on a result. There is no goal, no attachment or need to push or force the client into a specific state. The work comes from a pure and unconditional offering where there is absolutely no need to receive anything in return (except of course payment for your time and skills). During a session, you are in full service with your action as a gift.

Discomfort can be caused by deep emotional tension and isn't always necessarily related to pain. When it comes to de-armouring, the client often doesn't know exactly what it is they want. Naturally, what we don't know, we can't ask for. As practitioners at the Apex, we can use our gifts of power and attunement to aid transformation. In these cases, your action may not be based on the client asking you to do each little step. Your action instead comes from a place of integrity based on the permission you got to touch them (clarified at the beginning of the session).

It is extremely important that the client understands and gives permission for you *to be in your own impulses of action*. When you are given permission to do this at the start of the session, check in often during the session to see if it's still what your client wants. "Would you like me to touch you here to see how that feels?" "Would you like me to continue?" "Would you like to have more or less pressure?" and so on.

The difference between the direct/indirect pleasure map and the de-armouring map for practitioners

The idea for the De-armouring Map came to me while teaching assessment tools and consent protocols for practitioners at a de-armouring training. I was watching a demonstration being given by the main teacher. Suddenly, I realised that he was utilising his Direct Route to feel the tension in the person's body he was demonstrating with, while simultaneously using the Indirect Route to fully tune into any physical and neurological cues. He was doing both while being one hundred percent in service for this person's benefit.

If we look at the Direct/Indirect Pleasure Map, the arm image represents 'the doer'. The purple arrow shows that the person is going into action (doing something). The green arrow represents the inflow of the Direct Route which is the awareness of sensed stimuli transmitted to the brain from this action. When the Direct Route is embodied, the other person's response (the smiling face of the Indirect Route) is *just a bonus* from the action. When we are tuned into the inflow of sensations, we don't need or become dependent on the other person's response.

If we look at the De-armouring Map, we see a similar image to the Direct/Indirect Route Map—with an important difference. The person in action is the *giver*, and the person they are *doing it to* is the **receiver**. The purple arrow in this case represents who it is for.

The Indirect Route isn't wrong or bad. When we touch a lover, the Indirect Route is secondary, a bonus on top of the direct experience.

In terms of service and bodywork, the Indirect Route is utilised to check that we're on the right track with the action we perform *for them*. It helps us to ensure that our action is always for the benefit of the client. It helps the practitioner to know that they are providing what the other person wants. As practitioners, we use the Indirect Route to read cues and responses as well as to be aware of neurological changes and energy shifts. Utilising the Indirect Route is a vital practitioner skill. Just like having an antenna, it helps us to finely tune into someone else's response—to be attuned to someone else's neurophysiology, mindset, gestures, expression, speech, emotions and defence mechanisms.

The Direct Route of inflow is equally necessary. A good practitioner is so in tune with their sense of touch that they can soften tissue and release tension—enabling relaxation without causing pain or shut down. They can also enjoy what they offer, which results in the client feeling a deep sense of safety and trust.

De-armouring is therefore based on a combination of deep understanding and awareness of both the Direct and Indirect Route. In essence, both routes are a moment-to-moment feedback loop of responses and reactions—of neurological expressions of the nervous system, muscle tone and gesture—which enable the practitioner to physically and intuitively feel where the client is at, and to consistently ensure that any action whatsoever is in attunement with them, *for them*.

A note for practitioners on anger in relation to dorsal vagal shutdown

Anger is a feeling we tend not to allow ourselves to have. We judge it as bad, though, as you know, anger is really just an indicator—showing us as clearly as a bell ringing—that one of our boundaries has been crossed. When we get angry it gives us the energy to deal with the situation that's triggered us. It allows us to clearly know where our boundaries lie. I'm sure you'll agree that it's important to normalise anger with clients, so that any associated guilt can be resolved.

Very often however, our clients come to us having had a confusing nervous system response to a traumatic event in their past. They may not have responded in anger at the time (which could happen in sympathetic fight or flight).
Instead they may have gone into shutdown (parasympathetic dorsal vagal response) where anger isn't accessible. Because of this automatic nervous system reaction, many believe that their body betrayed them. In these cases, it is essential to normalise their body's response. Their body knew how to keep them safe in the best possible way at the time.

It's possible for a client to reconnect their body and emotions by identifying their anger. Due to the fact that freezing indicates shutdown, by reactivating the body through movement (while working through the trauma with the focus on anger) they can bring their system back into fight or flight. We could ask, for example, how they would have wanted to move at that moment, then ask them to do this.

It's important to ask them to move slowly while focusing on the sensation of the movement—slowly punching, kicking, turning, hitting out or running on the spot. These movements trigger the nervous system from shutdown into fight or flight. From here they can be guided to the safe, thrive side of sympathetic activity (mobilisation) and from there, back to the social engagement state.

Because a memory forms via chemical communications across brain cell synapses (junctions), each time a memory is recalled, the connection is reactivated and strengthened. As a dissociative memory is explored, finding anger can allow a person to change this communication (neuroplasticity), therefore rewiring its influence on them.

The Window of Tolerance for practitioners

In a safe environment clients can extend their Window of Tolerance utilising therapies that give the opportunity to step out of their comfort zone while keeping one foot inside it. This way they can check out the edges of their Window of Tolerance and feel safe in knowing they can step back inside at any time.

One example of this is NLP's phobia cure which utilises hypnotic suggestion and altered, visualised sensory details to anchor alternative perception. This breaks the link between the object and the fear response, positively changing how the usual trigger is experienced.

In therapeutic two-way touch (co-creative) sessions, clients get to ask whether they can *feel themself* by touching the practitioner. By doing so, they're confronted by and can work through the obstacles of the Direct Route as they feel and express the findings during the session. They can, in this way, work on expanding their Window of Tolerance.

THE SESSION TREE

Clarifying Your Unique Offerings

"An epic world of infinite possibilities lies within our reach. All mankind has to do, is align itself; with its rules of being."
- Enrique Vega

The Session Tree defines what you *give* in service to your clients within your sessions, which take place in an unwavering brother-sister dynamic that never crosses the boundary into the lover dynamic realm.

The Session Tree Map helps you to clearly define and offer transparency when describing and offering sessions to clients. It encourages you to consider and acknowledge your own limits as a practitioner—what you are willing to and not willing to do—so that solid agreements can be made and boundaries aren't crossed.

THE SESSION TREE

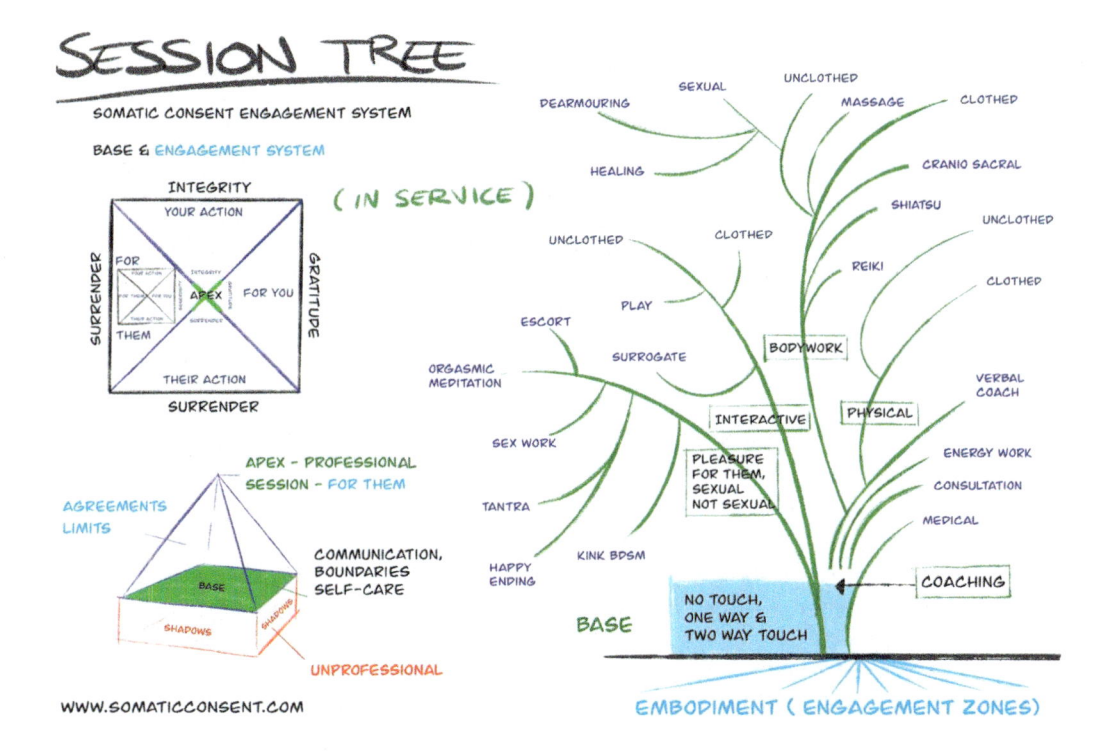

A session is always *for* the client, enabling them to experience the receiving role. What does your client want and how can you guide them into their desire?

If you look at this map, different branches of the Session Tree lead in different directions. Branches diverge to include or exclude aspects of your practice.

What do you offer?
What don't you offer?

- Is your practice a one-way engagement from practitioner to client (a treatment) or two-way engagement where both are involved in exploration or play (co-creation)?

- Are your sessions purely verbal or do they include physical activity such as training, ecstatic dance, heated yoga, physical adjustments or similar where the client may be unclothed?

- Do you offer healing bodywork such as sexual genital touch or de-armouring—and if so, with or without clothes?

- Do your sessions include pleasure for the client? Is the pleasure non-sexual or sexual?

- What do you include if you provide tantric or sexual transformation?

As a practitioner, embodiment of the Direct Route grows strong roots—enabling you to function optimally. Your Base will then be intact and your Engagement Zones stable, ensuring that you stay within the Radical Responsibility and integrity of your role at the Apex.

Becoming a professional with unique skills is accomplished through finding your own truth within. I know of no book that can tell you what kind of practitioner you 'should' be. I imagine there are as many different practitioners as there are humans—and in order to find their own truth, each and every individual client will be drawn to the practitioner that resonates with them.

One value that has guided me through these years as a professional is that in order to treat different people in a similar way, I need to recognise each person as an individual.

We are all unique. My intention therefore, is for each reader to clearly find their own personal and embodied way to freedom.

CONCLUSION

*When you reach the end of what you should know, you
will be at the beginning of what you should sense."
- Kahlil Gibrán*

The Direct Route of pleasure is your birthright. Many thousands of people have already been trained to tune into their sensory somatic inflow—the process that inherently sets you free.

Although the concept is quite simple when experienced physically and neurologically, it's too complex for the rational mind to understand alone. I therefore invite you to practise, to notice and to become and remain aware of your truth. I invite you to share that truth in relationship with others, so as to create safety, personal empowerment and the depth of connection and intimacy vital to well-being.

Ultimately the essence of Somatic Consent is about fostering interconnected relationships, a WE space, through loving connection to each of our selves, others and the world we live in.

I sincerely wish we will all meet in this essence.

ACKNOWLEDGEMENTS

I owe my unending gratitude to all my partners and lovers for our hands-on explorations of life into the unknown. To my many tutors and mentors, especially Harry Faddis for his inspiring coaching sessions. To Clinton Callahan for his expert mentorship, to the Somatic Consent family for all their ideas and creative input. To all my clients, friends, colleagues and those who have supported me emotionally, creatively and financially in completing and sharing this epic work.

The Somatic Consent MapBook Pro, has an overview of the SCES and includes all the maps. It was inspired by a little booklet of drawings I made for a couple during private sessions. I'm very grateful to graphic designer Ziska Rieman for converting my handmade drawings into the beautiful maps you find in this book. To James Redenbaugh, for branding and web design, Kaela Atleework, for copywriting, Nataliya Pidluzhna for graphic design and Sara Aznan for cover design and formatting. My thanks also goes out to Sebastian Layqa Morgensen for designing and developing The 3 Minute Game App and the upcoming Somatic Consent Dating App, 'APEX'.

As English isn't my native language, I owe my thanks to Karis McLaughlin, Rebeca Ofek, and Nina Edmondson for writing the Somatic Consent Student Handbook, free online for your learning and enjoyment. For online course concept design and writing, my thanks to Alice Whitehead and Nina Edmondson.

As the old saying goes, a picture is worth a thousand words. I realised however that to give a big picture overview, many more words were needed to create the best possible dialogue to bring the SCES maps alive.

Special thanks to Nina Edmondson for ghost-writing this book. For her dedication, creative ideas, honest feedback and for expertly weaving my words. I thank Karis McLaughlin, Heather Broussard and Bas van der Tang for the book's preliminary readings, their expert overview of the SCES and their keen eyes and suggestions. Lastly, my thanks to Sara Aznan for her beautiful layout design and cover illustration.

RESOURCES

When you become aware of the inflow of pleasure, you may feel inspired to investigate deeper into your potential for personal and spiritual growth. You are very welcome to attend the online Receiver Level classes; 'Reset 'and 'Self-Love 'to practice with yourself and others.

The 6 levels of development and education

1 Receiver Level - it's all about you
2 Explorer Level - starting the journey
3 Initiator Level - sharing your gifts
4 Educator level - professional upgrade
5 Leadership level - become a creator as a certified Somatic Consent practitioner/facilitator
6 Ambassador Level - Exclusive licence of Somatic Consent in your language in your country

SOMATIC CONSENT EDUCATION

Access embodied presence and pleasure

1 Receiver Level - it's all about you
2 Explorer Level - starting the journey
3 Initiator Level - sharing your gifts

Reset - free course

Self-Love

Pleasure and Play

Foundations of Somatic Consent. FoSC

4 Pillars of Relating 4PR

FOR PRACTITIONERS TO INTEGRATE SCES TEACHINGS INTO THEIR PROFESSIONAL PRACTICE

4 Educator level - professional upgrade

Practitioner Intensive PI

To Become A Certified Somatic Consent Trainer

5 Leadership level - become a creator as a certified Somatic Consent practitioner/facilitator

Leadership and Facilitation LaF

Become an Investor or Ambassador of the SCES and share the gifts of Somatic Consent around the world

6 Ambassador Level - Exclusive licence of Somatic Consent in your language in your country

WHAT IS THE CONSENTLAB?

An Example for Somatic Consent Community Building

The ConsentLab was created for people to practise the dynamics of consent in a safe container.

It's an experiential space for learning and play, where participants practise making requests based on the Somatic Consent Engagement System and The 3 Minute Game. We explore a series of exercises and encounters that create safety and connection. Participants practise feeling into their authentic yes and no, make requests and define boundaries in a fun and empowering way.

We practise real-life requests which anchor learning in relation to the power of desire—as well as the value of boundaries, limits and agreements. It's a playful opportunity to fluently explore and learn self-responsible consent and communication dynamics with others in a safe space.

All participation during the Lab is optional. Some people come solely with the intention of practicing their "no". This means that their level of participation within the group is to say "no" to every request during the entire event.

ConsentLab Online

REFERENCE LIST

1. Vagal activity, early growth and emotional development, Tiffany Field, Miguel Diego, 2008:
https://pubmed.ncbi.nlm.nih.gov/18295898/

2. The impact of institutionalization on child development, Kim Maclean, 2003: https://www.researchgate.net/publication/6358200_The_impact_of_institutionalization_on_child_development

3. The importance of touch in development, Evan L Ardiel, Catharine H Rankin, 2010: https://www.ncbi.nlm.nih.gov/pmc/articles/PMC2865952/

4. David J Linden - Touch: The Science of Hand, Heart and Mind, 2016

5. Preterm Infants Show Reduced Stress Behaviors and Activity after 5 days of Massage Therapy, Maria Hernandez-Reif, Miguel Diego, Tiffany Field, 2008: https://www.ncbi.nlm.nih.gov/pmc/articles/PMC2254497/

6. John B. Watson's Advice on Child Rearing: Some Historical Context, Kathryn M. Bigelow, Edward K. Morris, 2001:
https://psycnet.apa.org/fulltext/2014-55587-006.html

7. Tactile Communication, Cooperation, and Performance, Michael W Kraus, Cassey Huang, Dacher Keltner, 2010:
https://www.researchgate.net/publication/47642304_Tactile_Communication_Cooperation_and_Performance_An_Ethological_Study_of_the_NBA

8. The Touch Test, an online questionnaire developed by Goldsmiths 'Professor Michael Banissy in collaboration with Professor Alice Gregory, and UCL's Professor Aikaterini Fotopoulou, commissioned by Wellcome Collection, 2020.

9. Relational and Health Correlates of Affection Deprivation, Kory Floyd, 2014:
https://www.researchgate.net/

publication/271931280_Relational_and_Health_Correlates_of_Affection_Deprivation

10. Keep in touch: The importance of touch in infant development, Lynn Barnett, 2005: https://www.researchgate.net/publication/238318436_Keep_in_touch_The_importance_of_touch_in_infant_development

11. Innerbody Research, Nervous System, Tim Taylor, 2020: https://www.innerbody.com/image/nervov.html

12. Brain Facts, A Primer on the brain and nervous system, Society for Neuroscience, 2012: https://mpfi.org/wp-content/uploads/2019/04/Brain_Facts_BookHighRes1.pdf

13. Tactile C fibers and their contributions to pleasant sensations and to tactile allodynia, Jaquette Liljencrant, Håkan Olausson, 2014: https://www.ncbi.nlm.nih.gov/pmc/articles/PMC3944476/

14. Merkel cells and neurons keep in touch, Seung-Hyun Woo, Ellen A. Lumpkin, Ardem Patapoutian, 2015:
https://www.ncbi.nlm.nih.gov/pmc/articles/PMC4312710/

15. Touch sense. Functional organization and molecular determinants of mechanosensitive receptors, Yann Roudaut, Aurélie Lonigro, Bertrand Coste, Jizhe Hao, Patrick Delmas, and Marcel Crest, 2012:
https://www.ncbi.nlm.nih.gov/pmc/articles/PMC3508902/

16. Social Influence and the Collective Dynamics of Opinion Formation, Mehdi Moussaïd, Juliane E. Kämmer, Pantelis P. Analytis, Hansjörg Neth, 2013: https://journals.plos.org/plosone/article?id=10.1371/journal.pone.0078433

17. Memory distortion: an adaptive perspective, Daniel L. Schacter, Scott A. Guerin, Peggy L. St. Jacques, 2011:
https://www.ncbi.nlm.nih.gov/pmc/articles/PMC3183109/

18. Memory integration: neural mechanisms and implications for behavior, Margaret L Schlichting, Alison R Preston, 2016:
https://www.ncbi.nlm.nih.gov/pmc/articles/PMC4346341/

19. Roles of the Cerebellum in Motor Control—The Diversity of Ideas on Cerebellar Involvement in Movement, Mario Manto, James M. Bower, Adriana Bastos Conforto, José M. Delgado-García, Suzete Nascimento Farias da

Guarda, Marcus Gerwig, Christophe Habas, Nobuhiro Hagura, Richard B. Ivry, Peter Mariën, Marco Molinari, Eiichi Naito, Dennis A. Nowak, Nordeyn Oulad Ben Taib, Denis Pelisson, Claudia D. Tesche, Caroline Tilikete, Dagmar Timmann, 2012:
 https://www.ncbi.nlm.nih.gov/pmc/articles/PMC4347949/

20. I Feel, Therefore, I am: The Insula and Its Role in Human Emotion, Cognition and the Sensory-Motor System, Mani N Pavuluri, Amber May, 2015:
https://www.researchgate.net/publication/272362245_I_Feel_Therefore_I_am_The_Insula_and_Its_Role_in_Human_Emotion_Cognition_and_the_Sensory-Motor_System

21. Mindfulness practice leads to increases in regional brain gray matter density, Britta K. Hölzel, James Carmody, Mark Vangel, Christina Congleton, Sita M. Yerramsetti, Tim Gard, Sara W. Lazara, 2011:
https://www.ncbi.nlm.nih.gov/pmc/articles/PMC3004979/

22. Supplementary motor area provides an efferent signal for sensory suppression, Patrick Haggard, Ben Whitford, 2004:
https://www.researchgate.net/publication/8689368_Supplementary_motor_area_provides_an_efferent_signal_for_sensory_suppression

23. Vicarious Responses to Social Touch in Posterior Insular Cortex Are Tuned to Pleasant Caressing Speeds, India Morrison, Malin Björnsdotter and Håkan Olausson, 2011: https://www.jneurosci.org/content/31/26/9554

24. Afferent and Efferent Impulses, Akash Gautam, 2017: https://www.researchgate.net/publication/318259459_Afferent_and_Efferent_Impulses

25. Brain Plasticity Mechanisms and Memory: A Party of Four, Elodie Bruel-Jungerman, Sabrina Davis, Serge Laroche, 2007:
https://www.researchgate.net/publication/5944020_Brain_Plasticity_Mechanisms_and_Memory_A_Party_of_Four

26. Self-soothing behaviors with particular reference to oxytocin release induced by non-noxious sensory stimulation, Kerstin Uvnäs-Moberg, Linda Handlin, Maria Petersson, 2015: https://www.ncbi.nlm.nih.gov/pmc/articles/PMC4290532/

27. A Wandering Mind Is an Unhappy Mind, Matthew A. Kill-

ingsworth, Daniel T. Gilbert, 2010: https://science.sciencemag.org/content/330/6006/932.full

28. The Science Behind Holosync® and Other Neurotechnologies, A Revolution in Neuroscience: Tuning the Brain - by Bill Harris, Director of Centerpointe Research Institute, 2003

29. Neurobiological mechanisms of anhedonia, Philip Gorwood, 2008: https://www.ncbi.nlm.nih.gov/pmc/articles/PMC3181880/

30. David Aaron, Endless Light: The Ancient Path of Kabbalah, 1998

31. The Map of Mixed Emotions, The Numbness Bar, Low and High Drama and the Radical Responsibility Map stem from Clinton Callahan's work on Possibility Management, Expanding the Box.

32. Interoceptive Awareness Skills for Emotion Regulation: Theory and Approach of Mindful Awareness in Body-Oriented Therapy (MABT): Cynthia J. Price and Carole Hooven, 2018
https://www.ncbi.nlm.nih.gov/pmc/articles/PMC5985305/

33. The polyvagal theory: New insights into adaptive reactions of the autonomic nervous system: Stephen Porges, 2009
https://www.ncbi.nlm.nih.gov/pmc/articles/PMC3108032/

34. Oxytocin and Stress-related Disorders: Neurobiological Mechanisms and Treatment Opportunities, Lauren M. Sippel, Casey E. Allington, Robert H. Pietrzak, Ilan Harpaz-Rotem, Linda C. Mayes, Miranda Olff, 2017:
https://www.ncbi.nlm.nih.gov/pmc/articles/PMC5482285/

35. Yoga Therapy and Polyvagal Theory: The Convergence of Traditional Wisdom and Contemporary Neuroscience for Self-Regulation and Resilience, Marlysa B. Sullivan, Matt Erb, Laura Schmalzl, Steffany Moonaz, Jessica Noggle Taylor, Stephen W. Porges, 2018:
https://www.frontiersin.org/articles/10.3389/fnhum.2018.00067/full

36. Interview with Stephen Porges on co-regulation. 2016, Relational Implicit, relationalimplicit.com,
https://relationalimplicit.com/zug/transcripts/Porges-2016-09.pdf

37. The Oxytocin–Vasopressin Pathway in the Context of Love and Fear, C. Sue Carter, 2017: https://www.frontiersin.org/articles/10.3389/fendo.2017.00356/full

38. Neural and Mental Hierarchies, Gerald Wiest, 2012:

https://www.ncbi.nlm.nih.gov/pmc/articles/PMC3505872/

39. The Body Keeps the Score, Brain, Mind and Body in the Healing of Trauma - Bessel van der Kolk, 2015

40. The Chimp Paradox - Professor Steve Peters, 2012

41. Second time used - use same numbering - Brain Plasticity Mechanisms and Memory: A Party of Four, Elodie Bruel-Jungerman, Sabrina Davis, Serge Laroche, 2007:
https://www.researchgate.net/publication/5944020_Brain_Plasticity_Mechanisms_and_Memory_A_Party_of_Four

42. David Lynden, Touch: The Science of Hand, Heart and Mind, 2015

43. Mario C. Salvador - THE-WISDOM-OF-THE-SUBCORTICAL-BRAIN.pdf International Journal of Integrative Psychotherapy, Vol. 4, No. 2, 2013

44. Affective immunology: where emotions and the immune response converge, Fulvio D'Acquisto, 2017: https://www.ncbi.nlm.nih.gov/pmc/articles/PMC5442367/

45. Oxytocin and Stress-related Disorders: Neurobiological Mechanisms and Treatment Opportunities: https://www.ncbi.nlm.nih.gov/pmc/articles/PMC5482285/

46. Stop Doing Kegels: Real Pelvic Floor Advice For Women (And Men): https://breakingmuscle.com/fitness/stop-doing-kegels-real-pelvic-floor-advice-for-women-and-men

47. Gary Chapman, The Five Love Languages: How to Express Heartfelt Commitment to Your Mate, 1992

48. Marina Kronkvist, Ritual Play: https://www.ritual-play.com/

49. Possibility Management: https://www.clintoncallahan.org/

50. Global Ecovillage Network: https://gen-europe.org/about-gen-europe/who-we-are/

51. Interview with Stephen Porges on listening: https://www.youtube.com/watch?v=2fkOTd0mz68

52. Maya Yonika, No Mud No Lotus, 2013

53. Circumcision of Infants and Children: Short-Term Trauma and Long-

Term Psychosexual Harm, Gregory J. Boyle, 2015: https://www.researchgate.net/publication/275029542_Circumcision_of_Infants_and_Children_Short-Term_Trauma_and_Long-Term_Psychosexual_Harm

54. Dopamine and serotonin: Influences on male sexual behavior, Elaine M Hull, John W Muschamp, Satoru M Sato, 2004:
https://www.researchgate.net/publication/8227393_Dopamine_and_serotonin_Influences_on_male_sexual_behavior

55. Orgasm-induced prolactin secretion: Feedback control of sexual drive? Tillmann H.C. Kruger, Philip Haake, Uwe Hartmann, Manfred Schedlowski, 2002:
https://www.researchgate.net/publication/11524855_Orgasm-induced_prolactin_secretion_Feedback_control_of_sexual_drive

56. Mania Robinson & Gary Wilson, Your Brain on Porn and Your Brain on Orgasm:
https://www.yourbrainonporn.com/relevant-research-and-articles-about-the-studies/deltafosb-neuroplasticity-and-addiction/deltafosb-addiction-conditioning/

57. Functional MRI of the Brain During Orgasm In Women, Barry Komisaruk, Beverly Whipple, 2005:

https://www.researchgate.net/publication/6874948_Functional_MRI_of_the_Brain_During_Orgasm_In_Women

58. Is Internet Pornography Causing Sexual Dysfunctions? A Review with Clinical Reports, Brian Y. Park, Gary Wilson, Jonathan Berger, Matthew Christman, Bryn Reina, Frank Bishop, Warren P. Klam, Andrew P. Doan, 2016:
https://www.ncbi.nlm.nih.gov/pmc/articles/PMC5039517/

59. Gary Wilson, Your Brain On Porn Internet Pornography and the Emerging Science of Addiction, 2020

60. Sexuality Development and Developmental Psychology, 2017 by SAGE Publications, Inc.

61. Classical Conditioning of Female Sexual Arousal, Elizabeth J. Letourneau, William O'Donohue, 1997:

https://link.springer.com/article/10.1023/A:1024573420228

62. Barry Long, Making Love: Sexual Love the Divine Way, 2014

63. Sri Nisargadatta Maharaj, I Am That I Am, 1973

64. Mauro Zappaterra, Director of Regenerative Medicine and Clinical Research. Cerebrospinal fluid, 2019: https://www.youtube.com/watch?v=8p7_OaIF3LU

65. Pineal gland: A structural and functional enigma, Ashok Sahai, Raj Kumari Sahai, 2020:
https://www.researchgate.net/publication/338570541_Pineal_gland_A_structural_and_functional_enigma

66. Human Cerebrospinal Fluid Regulates Proliferation and Migration of Stem Cells Through Insulin-Like Growth Factor-1, Mingxin Zhu, Yun Feng, Sean Dangelmajer, Hugo Guerrero-Cázares, Kaisorn L. Chaichana, Christopher L. Smith, Andre Levchenko, Ting Lei, Alfredo Quiñones-Hinojosa, 2014:
https://www.ncbi.nlm.nih.gov/pmc/articles/PMC4291213/#:~:text=Human%20Cerebrospinal%20Fluid%20Regulates%20Proliferation,Insulin%2DLike%20Growth%20Factor%2D1&text=Stem%20Cells%20Dev.

67. Reissner's Fiber, Quanta & Consciousness, Lawrence Wile, Chaikin-Wile Foundation, 2012: https://www.researchgate.net/publication/277210437_Reissner's_Fiber_Quanta_Consciousness

68. Theos Bernard, *Heaven Lies Within Us, 1939*

69. Theory and Science of the Ajna Light, Guy Harriman, 2015:
https://www.researchgate.net/publication/316090457_Theory_and_Science_of_the_Ajna_Light

70. Rix Strassman's, DMT the Spiritual Molecule, 2001

71. Stephen Porges, The Polyvagal Theory, 2011

72. Bert Hellinger, Family Constellations:
https://www.hellinger.com/en/family-constellation/

73. Putting a stereotype to the test: The case of gender differences in multitasking costs in task-switching and dual-task situations: Patricia Hirsch, Iring Koch, Julia Karbach, 2019

https://journals.plos.org/plosone/article/authors?id=10.1371/journal.pone.0220150

74. Biodynamic Therapy, first developed by Norwegian Psychotherapist, Clinical Psychologist and Physiotherapist, Gerda Boyesen in the 1950s.

75. Bessel van der Kolk, The Body Keeps the Score: Brain, Mind, and Body in the Healing of Trauma, 2015

76. Why can't you tickle yourself? Sarah-Jayne Blakemore, Daniel M Wolpert, Chris D Frith, 2000:
https://www.researchgate.net/publication/247590119_Why_can%27t_you_tickle_yourself

77. Witnessing the Body's Response to Trauma: Resistance, Ritual, and Nervous System Activation
Philip Browning Helsel, 2014
https://www.ictg.org/uploads/1/2/9/5/12954435/phil_helsel_dec_2014_article.pdf

ALL MAPS

Free To Download Here For Your Personal Use:

JOIN OUR GROWING COMMUNITY

Somatic Consent On Mighty Networks

Somatic Consent is a transformative community of game changers and activists bringing a new form of relational engagement to the world.

The teachings guide towards interpersonal connection within teams, families and peers as well as deeper intimacy between couples and lovers.

Based on the natural function and needs of our human experience—and through a more embodied relationship with self, we explore below the surface of cultural demands and expectations.

Via open communication and playful games we learn to nourish and be nourished through self-care, self-responsibility and ownership of feelings and action.

Our leaders and ambassadors work with businesses, schools and individuals through facilitation, leadership training and private sessions—to support others to empower and transform themselves and their own environment. Reach out if you want to join our growing community or would like to explore our services and training courses.

Conversations, events and courses all under one roof!

SOMATIC CONSENT WEBSITE

Printed in Great Britain
by Amazon